SLAVERY FROM
ROMAN TIMES
TO THE EARLY
TRANSATLANTIC TRADE

The publication of this book was assisted by
a bequest from Josiah H. Chase to honor his parents,
Ellen Rankin Chase and Josiah Hook Chase,
Minnesota territorial pioneers.

SLAVERY FROM ROMAN TIMES TO THE EARLY TRANSATLANTIC TRADE

WILLIAM D. PHILLIPS, JR.

UNIVERSITY OF MINNESOTA PRESS • MINNEAPOLIS

Published by the University of Minnesota Press,
2037 University Avenue Southeast, Minneapolis MN 55414

Printed in the United States of America

Library of Congress Cataloging in Publication Data

Phillips, William D.

Slavery from Roman times to the early transatlantic trade.

Bibliography: p.
Includes index.
1. Slavery—History. I. Title.
HT861.P46   1984   306'.362'09   84-10470
ISBN 0-8166-1325-7
ISBN 0-8166-1328-1 (pbk.)

For Carla

CONTENTS

Preface   ix

Part I. The Background

   1 The Problem of Slavery   3
   2 The Rise and Decline of the Roman Slave System   16

Part II. Slavery in Medieval Europe, the World of Islam, and Africa

   3 Slavery in Early Medieval Europe   43
   4 Slavery in the World of Islam   66
   5 Slavery in Late Medieval Europe   88
   6 Slavery in Sub-Saharan Africa to 1650   114

Part III. The Atlantic Slave System to 1650

   7 Africa and the Atlantic Islands   131
   8 African Slaves in Europe   154
   9 The Early Transatlantic Slave Trade   171
  10 Slavery in Early Colonial Latin America   195

Notes   221

Selected Bibliography   257

Index   279

Maps

   1 The Slave Trade: Eighth to Eleventh Centuries   44
   2 Mediterranean and Adjacent Regions: Late Middle Ages   89
   3 Africa: Trade Routes and Trade Centers,
      ca. 1100-1600   115
   4 The Americas: Principal Spanish and Portuguese
      Settlements in the Sixteenth and Seventeenth Centuries   172

PREFACE

I first had the idea of writing this history because I was struck by several misconceptions held by students and by the general public, stemming from the rather cursory treatment afforded slavery in general textbooks. Although slavery, in historical terms, has affected most of the peoples of the world, students who complete survey courses in history could come to the conclusion that slavery was a temporary feature of the ancient world of Greece and Rome and thereafter died out in Europe. Every student certainly would know about black slavery in the United States before the Civil War, but most would have no idea about the preconditions for American slavery. Some would even believe that only African blacks had ever been slaves.

To correct some of these distortions, I first envisioned a short book to trace the history of slavery in the Mediterranean basin from Roman times to the end of the Middle Ages. It would have shown how slavery persisted in Europe throughout the medieval period and helped provide a background for the resurgence of slavery in the New World. That rather modest aspiration I thought I could complete in two or three years by relying on easily available secondary works. I seriously underestimated what I was getting into. Crosscultural comparisons proved to be essential, and connections had to be traced to different geographical areas and periods if the overall story of slavery were to be comprehensible. What emerged at last was a book substantially broader in its coverage than the one I first conceived. The interests of students and scholars guided my selection of the material covered in the book, and the detailed notes and bibliography that resulted can guide those who wish to know more about particular topics.

My graduate training as a medievalist gave me a comprehensive knowledge of European development and a general understanding of the history of Islam. I found, though, that the sources for slavery in Europe and the Islamic world were neither as abundant nor as easily accessible as I had imagined, certainly not in English. To fully treat European topics, I needed to add Italian to the other European languages I could read. My work in Spanish history gave me a fair acquaintance with colonial Latin America, but Latin American slavery has its own bibliography, large and growing larger. African history, a rapidly changing field, was relatively new to me when I began this project. Many of the best studies of African slavery were appearing as I wrote, forcing three major revisions in the African chapters over a four-year period, as new publications appeared with new discoveries and altered interpretations. In other fields as well, new studies of slavery are appearing rapidly. Of the bibliographical citations in this book, fully one-third have been published since 1974 and many of those since 1979. This outpouring of recent interpretations is a boon for scholarship and meant for me the necessity to master the new material and to incorporate it as quickly as it became available. So, what began as a book on slavery in the medieval Mediterranean has grown to a history of slavery from Roman times to about 1650, when the Atlantic slave trade was well under way.

In preparing this work I accumulated many debts to scholars who aided me in a variety of ways. Stuart Schwartz, Allan Isaacman, Paul Lovejoy, and Stanley Engerman read and reread the typescript for the University of Minnesota Press and at each stage were generous with their perceptive suggestions. Professor Lovejoy also forwarded a copy of the page proofs of his important work *Transformations in Slavery*. Joseph C. Miller read and commented fully on two of the drafts and also sent me copies of the updated entries for his slavery bibliography before they appeared in print. My colleague Ross Dunn read the African chapters and offered valuable suggestions. My sister Lyda Phillips, a scholar of the Middle East, critiqued the chapter on Islam. Students in my graduate seminar in 1981 read an early version of Chapter 2 and commented with the enthusiasm and thoroughness of budding professional historians. I am most grateful for the help of all those who took the time to comment and offer suggestions, but I did not always follow their advice to the letter and so absolve them of any responsibility for the errors and infelicities that may remain.

I owe special thanks to my dean, Robert C. Detweiler, himself an historian of slavery, who awarded me a Summer Faculty Stipend for this project in 1981 and underwrote the preparation of the maps, which were rendered by Barbara Aguado of the cartographical laboratory at San Diego State University.

Professional librarians at San Diego State University; the University of California, San Diego; the University of Minnesota; and the Casa de Velázquez in Madrid eased my task greatly. I would like to thank them for their help, especially the skilled and patient members of the interlibrary loan staff at San Diego State.

Thanks are also due to Lindsay Waters, who as an editor at the University of Minnesota Press cheerfully guided the development of this book. Virginia Hans did an excellent job of copy editing.

Finally, I thank Carla Rahn Phillips, historian and wife, who gave this book the benefit of her considerable historical and editorial skills, and who has given me much more. This book is dedicated to her.

San Diego   W. D. P.

PART I
THE BACKGROUND

1

THE PROBLEM OF SLAVERY

Slavery has been a constant feature of human history, appearing in nearly every part of the world. We can trace it back to the earliest civilizations of Mesopotamia and Egypt, and we can discover it in more recent societies at various levels of development.[1] Slavery proper still exists today.[2] Yet, if asked, many students and scholars would state that slavery was an important feature of ancient Rome, disappeared during the Middle Ages, and reappeared in the period of European expansion when labor needs for New World plantations could be satisfied by trade in human chattels from the West African coast. That they would have such an impression is understandable. Most scholarly research has focused on slavery in two historical periods and two geographic areas: the ancient Mediterranean and the modern Americas. Between the two came the Middle Ages in Europe, and concerning that period the common impressions are that serfdom and not slavery was the characteristic pattern of medieval rural society and that manufacturing and other urban pursuits were conducted by free or semifree labor. Although correct in general terms, these assumptions are misleading. They suggest that *all* rural workers in the Middle Ages were serfs or free peasants and that *all* urban workers were free. The majority were indeed serf or free, but a minority, small in most areas and larger in others, were true slaves.

Throughout the Middle Ages slavery persisted in the lands around the Mediterranean and in the regions linked with it, even though it occupied a far less important position than it had in Roman times. During the thousand years from the end of the Roman Empire to the beginning of European expansion in the Atlantic, slavery was a social and physical reality in the Christian world, and it was reinforced by contact with the highly developed slavery of the Muslims. In addition to the actual presence of slaves, the persistent and growing influence of Roman law, which contained a sophisticated set of regulations for slavery, helped shape the legal systems of the European West and provided a ready-made

3

set of rules that could be put into force easily when slavery again became economically significant. Slavery's resurgence was due to the creation of the New World plantation system, which initially produced sugar, and of an expanding market economy to absorb the production of the plantations. Sugar growing and refining required intensive labor, and, in the absence of the necessary numbers of Amerindian or European workers, the Spaniards and the Portuguese turned to black slaves, acquired by Portuguese traders who tapped preexisting trading networks along the West African coast and transported their human cargoes across the Atlantic.

This book, then, is an examination of the persistence of slavery from Roman times to its establishment in the Americas, tracing the Old World roots of New World slavery. Attention is given to surveying the continuities and assessing the changes in patterns of slavery; in methods of acquiring slaves; in uses to which they were put; and in the significance slavery had for the societies of Rome, medieval Europe, Islam, Africa, and the Americas up to the mid-seventeenth century. The book is also an examination of the practice of slavery in each area and an investigation of the degree to which slavery was based on past practice, the ways in which it conformed to and differed from practices in other times and places, the influences it had on the societies themselves, and the impact it had on neighboring groups.

The primary aim of the book is to follow the continuities in one thread of the history of slavery, a thread that led from Rome to the New World. Roman slavery and slave laws and the attitudes of early Christianity shaped the European experience with slavery, despite major changes in the basic economies and social structures of the countries of the European West. The slave systems of medieval and early modern Europe, both at home and in the colonies, could not have failed to owe something to the Roman experience. Islamic slavery, too, although it had its beginning in the history of the Arabs before the rise of Islam, was also affected directly by the Roman and indirectly by the Christian experience. Slavery in Africa, while it may have had indigenous roots, was heavily influenced by the Muslims, long before the Europeans reconnoitered the West African coast. Of course, the Spaniards and the Portuguese in the Americas made use of their inheritances from Rome and current practice at home and in the Atlantic islands as they established slavery in the Americas. Thus slavery in the New World was an outgrowth of Old World slavery.

Because of the book's focus, a process of selection was necessary, and many components of the vast history of slavery were excluded as peripheral to our major concerns. We do not deal with pre-Roman slavery in the ancient Near East and the Mediterranean, except for a few remarks about Greek slavery and its relations to Roman slavery. The path to American slavery began in Rome, not Athens. We do not deal with slavery in medieval Scandinavian societies except as it related to the Mediterranean. The story of slavery in Russia in the late medieval and early modern periods, fascinating as it is, does not relate to the main thread and is not covered here. Asian slavery is beyond the book's scope, and we have chosen to omit discussion of Amerindian slavery before the coming of the Europeans. Slavery in British North America was at several removes from the main thread we are following in this book.

Before we can begin, we must provide a working definition of slavery. At first glance, this seems to be quite a simple task; everyone has a definition of slavery readily at hand. But what does the term really mean? Here our perceptions are skewed by our familiarity with the history of slavery in the antebellum American South, a topic that occupies an important place in the popular historical imagination. In that system, slaves were acquired from a distant continent; they were different in their skin color; and, at least initially, their languages and cultures were distinct from those of the slaveholders. Slaves were totally the property of their owners, who could sell them and punish them, and who could force them to labor in plantation agriculture and other income-producing pursuits. They had few if any legal rights, not even the right to form families, although some indulgent masters did allow slave marriages. Lenient or harsh treatment could be afforded to the slaves, but always at the discretion of the master. American slavery was, nonetheless, only one case and atypical in several of its aspects, particularly the barriers to manumission.

For a general definition of slavery, the role of the master in regard to his slaves offers a key to the understanding of the position of slaves as property, the characteristic that Moses I. Finley considered to be the great division between slavery and other forms of coerced labor. Because slaves were property, a master could do with them as he wished, undeterred by the exhortations to kind treatment put forward by philosophers, theologians, or legislators. There were good masters and bad, kind masters and cruel, but there was never an effective way of ensuring that they would treat their slaves well. As Finley put it,

> The failure of any individual to exercise all his rights over his slave-property was always a unilateral act on his part, never binding, always revocable. That is a crucial fact, so is its reverse, the equally unilateral, always revocable grant by a slaveowner of a special privilege or benevolence.[3]

The stark reality of the slave's powerlessness has been emphasized by Pierre Dockès and Orlando Patterson, who described the dramatic parallel between slavery and death. For Dockès, the slave, at least if he or she had been captured in war or kidnapped,

> is one who should have been killed and who survives by the grace of the master; he is one of the "living dead" (*mort-vivant*). . . . To be reprieved, to be living dead is the fate of the prisoner of war, who would traditionally have been killed by his captor. If the captor allows his prisoner to live, the latter recognizes the former as his master, and in fact cannot but so recognize him.[4]

Orlando Patterson took up the same theme.

> Perhaps the most distinctive attribute of the slave's powerlessness was that it always originated (or was conceived of as having originated) as a substitute for death, usually violent death. . . . Because the slave had no socially recognized existence outside of his master, he became a social nonperson. [T]he slave, however recruited, [was] a socially dead person. Alienated from all "rights" or claims of birth, he ceased to belong to any legitimate social order. All slaves experienced, at the very least, a secular excommunication.[5]

Consequently, even long after capture, the slave remained socially dead. "Reprieved from death, set apart, isolated from every community, hence dead, alien to citizenship, a stranger to himself, the slave is no longer a man, but a member of a subhuman species. . . . "[6]

The slave's position as property and the unlimited rights the master had over him or her are two of the three necessary conditions that distinguish a slave from other sorts of dependent laborers. The third condition is that, barring a few exceptions that we will mention in their appropriate places, the slave was an outsider. The slave, as long as he or she remained a slave, was most often outside the kinship structure of the dominant society, thereby deprived of family ties and the ability to form them,[7] and deprived of any links with the host society except through the master. In the Roman world, in the Christian and Islamic societies of the Middle Ages, in many African societies, and in the European colonies, slaves were mainly brought into the dominant society from outside, either by long-distance trade or by more local exchanges. In world history this was not the only pattern that could and did exist; internal slavery was a common feature in Asia and in pre-Hispanic America. For the societies treated in this book, however, slavery was exogenous rather than endogenous.

Because the majority of slaves in the societies we will cover were acquired from outside, most societies had mechanisms for their acculturation, most provided means for them to become free, and most allowed a lesser or greater degree of assimilation into the dominant group. To return for a moment to the example of the American South, the freed slaves, because of easily perceived racial differences, faced barriers to full assimilation even after they had been freed. This is one more aspect that distinguishes the North American experience from the more usual pattern of slavery. Racial distinctions in North America led to continued discrimination against the freed slaves and their descendants and these distinctions have influenced modern perceptions of the essential features of slavery. It is not unusual for many people today to believe that slavery was something that involved only African blacks and that only blacks were ever slaves. That was certainly not the case, as subsequent chapters will reveal. At one time or another slavery has touched practically every society, and in numerous instances the physical differences separating slaves and free people were not so great as to hinder the eventual assimilation of the freed.[8]

In the face of common misunderstanding, we must take care as we define slavery to point out its essential characteristics in a manner that clarifies rather than obscures its main features as an historical phenomenon. The basic aspects of the general definition must be firmly established; slaves were property; slaves were subject to the total control of their masters; and slaves were outsiders with no ties of kinship to the dominant society and no legal rights. David Brion Davis stressed an additional criterion: that masters could, at their pleasure, move slaves physically from one place to another as the work required, unlike medieval lords, whose serfs had security of tenure in a defined location.[9]

Orlando Patterson, in his important comparative analysis of slavery, disagreed with the common emphasis on slaves as property and on slavery as a relation of production. He argued that the most significant definition of slavery is as a relation of domination. In slavery, the slave's relations with the master's society were controlled totally by the master, and the slave—alienated and socially dead—existed at the margin of that society. A parasitic relationship existed between the slave and the master, who gained greater honor from his domination of the slave. Patterson also suggested that the domination inherent in slavery gave rise to the concept of freedom. "Before slavery people simply could not have conceived of the thing we call freedom." Slaves had "a need that no other human beings have felt so acutely: the need for disenslavement, for disalienation, for negation of social death, for recognition of . . . inherent dignity."[10] Masters played on this complex and passionate need as they held out the possibility of manumission, and when they manumitted a slave they lost nothing on the ideological level, because manumission enhanced the honor of the master. By offering dominance as the key to an understanding of the master-slave relationship, Patterson has expanded the ways in which slavery must be analyzed. Nevertheless, the property relationship cannot be discarded, for it was a necessary component of the master's dominance.

For a thorough understanding of slavery, once the elements of its definition are established, it is necessary to consider the variety of positions that slaves held and the material conditions of their existence. Because of the many ways they could be and were employed, slaves cannot be fitted neatly into a single category, nor do they form a distinct social class or caste. Most were on the bottom of the heap, but others occupied roles with greater responsibility. Even though all slaves have suffered the same or similar legal, emotional, and ideological disabilities, there were gradations in their material circumstances. One way of approaching the matter is to describe the occupations to which they were assigned.

Scholars often divide slavery into two distinct types: agricultural or rural, and domestic or urban. This division is useful only to a certain point, because wide variations can be observed in both categories and because the categories themselves often overlapped. Romans used slaves on rural estates, most notably on the great latifundia of the late republic and of the empire at its height. We can find an example from the Muslim world in the vast slave labor force of the Zanj at work in lower Mesopotamia in the early years of Islamic expansion. Slave-run sugar estates in the Spanish Indies set the mold for plantation slavery in numerous places in the Americas. In many societies, slaves were often used as additional agrarian workers on small farms, where they toiled along with their smallholder owners and free workers. Rural slavery, nevertheless, did not always imply agricultural labor. Roman jurists understood these complexities very well. In the *Digest*, compiled in the sixth century A.D. from earlier Roman legislation, this precise point appears.

> When "urban slaves" have been specified in a legacy, some authorities distinguish property in urban slaves not by place, but by the type of work done, so that even if they are on a rural estate, they are considered to be urban slaves if they do not do agricultural work.[11]

Rural slaves also worked in manufacturing on the estates of the early Middle Ages in western Europe, and in the processing and refining of sugar on the American plantations.

There were gradations among domestic slaves as well. Household service performed by slaves continued from the beginning of our period to its end. It is not surprising that slaves were found in the large households of the Roman elite, but they were also present in more modest Roman homes. Slaves also served as domestic servants for Muslims who could afford to purchase and maintain them. In medieval Europe, where the use of slaves in agriculture virtually ceased, there were always some domestic slaves, particularly in those places close to the main routes of long-distance commerce. Domestic slaves were present in sub-Saharan Africa, and they were found in the households of Spaniards and Portuguese both in Europe and the Americas. Much of the employment of domestic slaves must be described as unproductive labor, for slaves were usually assigned to noneconomic tasks; their employment was often totally independent of the normal mode of labor in the society. As servants, guards, and sexual partners, their primary function in many cases was to demonstrate the wealth and luxury enjoyed by their owners. Even with domestic slavery, however, there were exceptions and variations. In the preindustrial world, much, if not most, of the ordinary manufacturing of goods for common consumption was artisan production, taking place in workshops within the homes of the artisans. In these workshops a few domestic slaves could aid their artisan owners, and collectively their activity made a significant impact on production. In other words, domestic slaves, employed in this way, must be judged to have been productive. The material standards of living for such slaves was usually higher than that of other slaves, and they had better chances of attaining freedom.

Other variations produce further complexities. The Roman Republic owned slaves and used them in public works projects and other governmental activities. The practice continued during the Roman Empire, when the emperor owned and directed a vast force of bureaucrats and public workers who staffed and maintained a number of essential services within the empire. In the Islamic world, the Mamluks (and later the Janissaries among the Ottoman Turks) were slave recruits who made up whole armies and were used to support the state; on occasion they took it over. In Rome and in the Islamic world, some masters employed their slaves as business agents who acted with wide latitude and often traveled long distances to carry out assignments on behalf of their owners. Such slaves had easier access to freedom and enjoyed relatively better conditions while they remained slaves.

These widely scattered examples show that slavery was far more complex an institution than is often presented in textbooks or perceived by their readers. The employment of slaves varied greatly, and their circumstances in a given society could be harsh or mild depending on the uses their owners made of them. The ways the masters chose to use their slaves, choices limited only by the cultural and economic constraints of the societies in which they lived, bring us to another major consideration in the history of slavery: the significance of slave use in the society and economy as a whole. We can observe societies in which slavery was essential to the functioning of the total economy and others in which slavery was merely an adjunct to a system of free or semifree labor. Stated differently, there is a distinction between a slave society and a society that uses slaves. Finley expressed it in this way: "if the economic and political elites depended primarily on slave labor for basic production, then one may speak of a slave society."[12] Marxist scholars use the phrase "the slave mode of production" to describe the same situation, in which slavery was dominant in and necessary for the working of the economy.[13] In the words of Pierre Dockès:

> If there is to be a slave system, then, slavery must constitute a relation of production. The collective slave must be a productive worker, a source of income for the master. . . . In order to speak of a slave system, however, a second condition must also be met: slavery must be the dominant relation of production.[14]

Another useful way of distinguishing between the two varieties of slave society is to consider large-scale, gang slavery as one manifestation of slavery, and the more common practice of introducing supplemental workers and domestics into societies that mainly used free labor as another.

A good deal of scholarly effort over a long period has been devoted to the questions of why slavery developed and of why some groups made intensive use of slaves when others did not. One of the classic interpretations was put forth in 1900 by H. J. Nieboer, who suggested that slavery would only become important in agricultural societies in which a high land-to-labor ratio existed, that is, in societies that had both available land and a low population. With an abundance of land and few potential laborers, those laborers had to be coerced (by being enslaved or enserfed) to work for others; if they were left free, they would drift away, find unsettled land, and work on their own.[15] Evsey D. Domar, in considering Nieboer's theory, postulated that something more than the land-labor ratio must have been necessary, and he found it in the political and military authority of the state. As Domar put it: "of the three elements of an agricultural structure relevant here—free land, free peasants, and non-working land-owners—any two elements but *never all three can exist simultaneously*. The combination to be found in reality will depend on the behavior of political factors. . . ."[16] Domar was specifically addressing the establishment of serf-dom in fifteenth-century Russia, in which the government tied the peasants to the land in order to enable the landowners to extract wealth from the peasants to support the landowners' military service to the state. Even though he dealt with a specific case, Domar believed that his model would be valid for all examples of agricultural serfdom and slavery, and he stated that he "would . . . expect to find a positive correlation between free land and serf-dom (or slavery)."[17]

In an elegant demolition of the Nieboer-Domar line of argument, Orlando Patterson criticized their failure to differentiate between slavery and serfdom and, using sophisticated statistical analysis, revealed the futility of any attempt to reduce the complex reasons for why slavery arose in any given society to simple ratios of available land and available labor. He proceeded to offer a wide range of other variables, including the social and psychological framework of the masters, the nature and aims of warfare, and the structures of agriculture and commerce. "It is the interaction of these factors both with each other and with the changing man-land ratio . . . that accounts for the development of servile labor. . . ."[18]

Jack Goody, in his large-scale survey of the various manifestations of slavery in the world, also disagreed that variations in the available land and labor were significant and proposed another explanation for the genesis of slaveholding. He believed that inequality was the key: the inequality within a society of classes, castes, or other social rankings; and the inequality between societies based on economic distinctions backed by military force. The latter "takes a number of forms, but it has been especially common where states existed side by side with zones inhabited by 'uncontrolled,' stateless or tribal peoples, whom they could raid for human booty without fear of reprisals, or when pastoralists lived near sedentary farmers who were unable to escape their depredations nor match their military force."[19]

Moses I. Finley, specifically dealing with the ancient world, approached the question of the origins of slavery from a different angle. He probably would have agreed with Goody about the importance of war and other forms of military activity, but he placed emphasis on the demand for slaves, rather than their supply. In Finley's view,

> the demand for slaves precedes the supply. . . . Existence of a sufficient demand requires at least three necessary conditions. First, in a world which was overwhelmingly agrarian, is private ownership of land, with sufficient concentration in some hands to need extra-familial labour for the permanent work force. The second is a sufficient development of commodity production and markets. . . . Hypothetically helots and other forms of dependent labour can be employed in non-commodity-producing societies, but not slaves, who must be imported regularly, in quantity, and therefore paid for. The third is a negative condition, the unavailability of internal labour supply, compelling the employers of labour to turn to outsiders. All three conditions must exist at the same time. . . . [20]

The earliest slave society we will deal with in this book and the latest that Finley fully treated is Rome in the periods of the republic and the empire.[21] Chapter 2 will show that Roman slavery was complex and displayed virtually every characteristic associated with the institution, but what made Rome a slave society, rather than one more society that used slaves, was the significance of slave production in agriculture. Roman cities, particularly those in the western portion of the empire, could not maintain their populations without the production of food by slave labor on the latifundia and smaller farms, which in turn depended on the great urban markets to absorb their output. To use Finley's words, Rome had "a sufficient development of commodity production and markets."[22] As the western empire declined and fell, the urban markets collapsed, and with their collapse came the end of the ability of the estates to sell their produce. A slow but fundamental change began to take place in the western European economy in the third century A.D.: a long-term transformation of agrarian organization that saw slavery replaced in the countryside by a system of serfdom by about the eleventh century, when western Europe had ceased to be a slave society. Chapter 3 will trace that transformation.

Seven centuries later, other fully developed slave systems could be found in Brazil, the Caribbean, and the American South. Chapters 9 and 10 will examine their origins in the Spanish and Portuguese colonial possessions, whose economies for a time were heavily dependent on a single commodity, sugar, whose use and methods of production the Europeans had learned from the Muslims during the Crusades. We will see that sugar's fifteenth- and sixteenth-century development rested on the creation of a plantation economy. Sugar production required large tracts of land in warm regions with sufficient rainfall or where irrigation could be provided. It also needed, at least before the advent of mechanization, a large labor force to plant, cultivate, and harvest the cane; to cut wood to fuel the boilers; to transport the cane to the mills; and to process and refine the sugar. We will examine the initial attempts to use the labor of Amerindians and their subsequent replacement by imported slaves.

The slave systems of Rome and the Iberian colonies were similar in numerous ways. They both employed a great number of slaves, and the prosperity of the elite was supported by the labor of the large slave population. They both relied on urban markets for profitable sale of the commodities produced. Both had sufficient, suitable land available as a result of conquest. Yet, along with the similarities, there were also major differences between the systems. The Roman slave system was based on food production in the heartland of the empire. The Iberian slave system rested on a foundation of luxury production, not the production of prime necessities, and it was located in the newly acquired colonial territories, linked to but not part of the European heartland, where freeholding, wage labor, and rental arrangements were in use.[23]

Separating these two slave systems were the centuries of the Middle Ages, during which the laboring classes were serf or free. Both the Islamic world and medieval Europe were able to solve the problems of food supply for the cities without having to resort to the use of slave labor in large agrarian establishments, and the market in pre-Renaissance Europe (if not in Islam) was not adequately developed to absorb a large output of luxuries. Aside from some rural employment, slaves were normally used in a specifically domestic context among the medieval Christians and Muslims, and they were used both as household servants and as artisans. In Africa south of the Sahara were to be found slaves used in a variety of ways: as transporters of goods, as domestics and artisans, as miners of metals and salts, and even as potential family members. Certain African societies were so dependent on slavery that the slave mode of production could be said to be present, but by no means did all African groups make intensive use of slavery. Thus, for the Middle East, the Christian and Muslim Mediterranean, and sub-Saharan Africa, the centuries preceding the discovery of America witnessed a persistence of slavery, albeit with geographical distinctions and variations in time.

The continuity of slavery, especially in its main features, is readily apparent. Detailed variations were present in different cultures, times, and places (all of which we will examine in their proper contexts); but slavery as an institution and the conditions of slaves within it remained remarkably constant. The recruitment of slaves, the uses to which they were put, the restrictions on their activities, their legal and social positions, their chances for manumission, and the status of their children were all more similar than not.

Most of the peoples with whom we will deal felt a strong reluctance to enslave members of what they considered their own group, and, as a result, they looked outside the group for slaves whenever possible. The definitions for exclusion—religion, language, level of culture, or race—may have differed, but the impulse remained the same. For this reason slavery was most widely practiced when two conditions were present. The first we have already described:

the economic organization of a given society that created a demand for slaves. The second relates to recruitment: given availability of sufficient numbers of individuals for easy enslavement, captives were brought into the dominant society by conquest in war or by purchase from slave dealers. Purchasing slaves rather than capturing them seems superficially to be less blameworthy, but the human merchandise of the slave trade almost always became slaves in the first place through some act of violence: war, raiding, or kidnapping. Such an act may have seemed remote to the eventual purchaser, yet for the slave it was a real and traumatic event of his or her personal history.[24]

We will examine other ways by which people became slaves. Birth to slave parents automatically conferred slave status on the child. This meant that in slave-owning societies the slave population was replenished by births to slave women. Whether this by itself was sufficient to maintain the slave population is often debated. The possibility of complete replacement or growth of a slave population by birth alone depended on the existence of a roughly equal balance between men and women slaves, and on their receiving relatively mild treatment and living under relatively favorable conditions. It also required a very low attrition, or none, through manumission. These qualifications were seldom met, and Eugene Genovese asserted that only in the American South did a slave population grow by its own biological efforts,[25] probably because there were so few opportunities for manumission. In every one of the societies we will survey, slavery by birth was present, and, in some, slave women were offered incentives for procreation. Even if total replacement of slave population was seldom attained by births, some slaves were constantly being born. Another, less frequent, means of creating slaves was by the sale or abandonment of children by destitute parents. Still another means, self-sale, was fairly common among the Romans, but because the term of sale was usually limited to a specified number of years, some scholars have denied that self-sale was equivalent to real slavery.[26]

Once individuals were enslaved, there were, as we will see, many different uses to which they could be put. The conditions they lived under also varied considerably, depending upon the legal strictures, the philosophical or religious system, and the humanitarian impulses of the dominant society. In general terms, however, it is apparent that few if any spokesmen before the sixteenth century advocated the abolition of slavery.[27] Slavery was considered to a normal part of the social organism, and the voices that were raised against it were almost always concerned with the amelioration of conditions within the system, not with ending the system. As we mentioned earlier in this chapter and as we will see in detail as we proceed, masters were allowed wide latitude in the treatment they could accord their slaves. Elements of coercion, harsh or mild, were essential for control of slaves by the masters, as they sought to derive benefits from their human property, and the masters' societies supported their prerogatives. Slaveholders controlled both the productive labor and the reproductive potential of their slaves. The sex lives of the slaves were not their own. Concubinage was a continual feature of slavery. Masters had sexual access to their slaves, and the extent to which they made use of that access depended on the society. Slaves could not marry without permission of the master. With some exceptions, the child of a slave mother was always a slave. In some societies, masters could castrate their male slaves.

All commentators agree that slaves detested their enslavement and in one way or another practiced resistance and sought their freedom. The most fearful specter for the masters was the prospect of slave revolts, but few ever occurred. We will deal with slave revolts in Rome and with communities of fugitives in colonial Latin America, but such overt resistance was unusual. Slaves more often resisted covertly, using a variety of tactics. Systematic work resistance could include the breaking of tools and mistreatment of draft animals and livestock. Theft and pilferage were common, and some slaves opted for harsher measures: self-mutilation or suicide; refusal to bear children, abortion, or infanticide.[28] References to fugitive slaves appear in the records of almost every slaveholding society, but in most of them the slaves could never hope to return to the land of their birth. Many fugitives were recaptured, and many others probably ended up in the hands of another master.

If successful flight was achieved by few slaves, many others reached freedom through manumission. There were wide variations in the ease and availability of manumission, as well as in the status of the freed person and his or her descendants. We will examine some systems in which manumission was exceedingly difficult to attain and in which assimilation of the newly freed slave was slow and incomplete. In others the trajectory was easier and more rapid. This distinction has been expressed as the difference between closed and open systems of slavery.[29] In some groups, such as the imperial slaves of the Roman Empire and the Mamluks, manumission was virtually automatic with promotion through the ranks. Some African societies allowed the slave into the kinship network of the dominant society. Because most freed slaves were never able to return to their homelands, they were forced to merge with the dominant group in some degree or another; their success in assimilation depended in large part on the attitudes of the dominant group.

This discussion of the common features of slavery will provide the foundation for the discussion of specific areas and periods to follow. As we proceed, we should be aware of the variations in scholarly treatment of the different slave-owning societies. Studies of slavery have appeared with regularity in the last few decades, increasingly so in the last few years. Making up the largest group of contributors have been historians and other social scientists who have studied slavery in the Americas, particularly those dealing with the United States in the last half-century before emancipation. They have been able to rely on a fund of diverse materials: law codes and court records, abolitionist literature and apologies for slavery, plantation account books, travelers' stories, the records of sales and manumissions, demographic information, and the narratives of former slaves. The findings of these scholars have been illuminating, provocative, and at times controversial. They have served to create new interest in slavery as an institution and have inspired specialists in other fields.

Slavery in Latin America has attracted a number of able scholars who have subjected the institution to a detailed scrutiny using sophisticated tools of analysis. Equally impressive have been the efforts of Africanists to assess the place that slavery occupied in indigenous African societies. The task facing the Africanists has been made more difficult by the necessity of disproving or discounting a massive backlog of misinterpretation and by the need to surmount obstacles in the historical record. Their work is not yet complete, and a general consensus in the study of African slavery has not yet emerged. Recently Roman historians have begun new approaches and offered new interpretations, some of them inspired by the new methodologies employed by scholars of slavery working in different fields. They have also relied on the groundwork of earlier studies, some of them now quite old but still crucial, of slavery in the ancient world.

The study of slavery in other societies has not drawn armies of researchers, armed with the newest weapons for conquering the historical record. The types of slavery practiced in Christian Europe and the Islamic Near East and North Africa have attracted smaller groups of hardy and successful researchers over the last five decades. Nonetheless, the number of studies remains small, in part due to the relatively limited importance that slavery had for the societies of the Middle Ages, both Christian and Islamic. Consequently, we must be aware that the fund of available studies is more extensive in certain areas than in others, but it is complete enough to allow us to analyze the continuities and changes in the history of slavery and to trace the long historical path that led to slavery in the Americas.

2

THE RISE AND DECLINE
OF THE ROMAN SLAVE SYSTEM

In contrast to their humane and praiseworthy gifts to posterity, the Romans left slavery as a major legacy, whose distant legatees were the slaves and slave-owners of the Americas. The Roman system of law, codified in the sixth century A.D. by the emperor Justinian and rediscovered and integrated into their own legal codes by the medieval Europeans, was the instrument of transmission. Thus Roman laws provided a strand linking the beginning and the end of the period covered in this book. The Roman experience clearly influenced the later practice of slavery in the Mediterranean, offering a concrete example and intellectual basis for the medieval societies. Consequently, we must consider Roman slavery fully. Thanks to the work of generations of scholars we know a great deal about it, even though some details remain obscure, and through an examination of its practice we can trace its elaborate framework. The system of Roman slavery will serve as a model to test other slave systems, not for the purpose of judging them on the basis of how closely they may have corresponded to Roman practice, but to lay out features common to any system of slavery.

We could begin earlier and elsewhere, at almost any place and time in the ancient world. Slavery was a common historical phenomenon among the societies that occupied the ancient Middle East and of the Mediterranean. It was present in the earliest civilizations in Mesopotamia for which we have records. Yet even though slavery was practiced widely in the ancient world, the only slave society that emerged before Rome was that of Greece—of Athens and other Greek city-states, to be precise—in the fifth and sixth centuries B.C. Among the politically precocious Greeks, with their heritage of qualified democracy in many city-states, slavery was an entrenched institution. Greeks preferred to enslave non-Greeks, barbarians as they called them, but they were not above enslaving other Greeks. The less sophisticated Romans learned much from the philosophical heritage of Hellenic civilization, but in that philosophy too slavery was accepted and justified. Although Plato raised no fundamental objections to slavery, he did favor enslaving non-Greeks. Aristotle considered slaves as possessions with souls, as property devoid of political rights, and he described the institution as a necessary support for the privileged citizen group. For Aristotle, slavery had arisen from the primitive family; it was part of natural law. Because of the lasting influence of his ideas, Aristotle's views were to have a bearing on all subsequent analyses of slavery. However, except for the prominent position of Greek ideas in Western and Islamic thought, Greek slavery[1] did not form a crucial part of the tradition that led to American slavery. Roman slavery did, and knowledge of the Roman experience will make our examination of later examples easier to comprehend.

From their earliest beginnings, the Romans practiced slavery on a small scale, using a few slaves as farmhands and household servants. After the Romans subdued Italy and began their overseas expansion, an increase in slavery kept pace with the rise of Rome as a great power. In the third, second, and first centuries B.C., Roman generals sent back thousands of slaves drawn from the ranks of defeated armies and from the citizens of conquered towns and cities. The very words the Romans used to describe slaves and their definition of slavery reflected the fact that many of their slaves were originally prisoners of war. It is well to quote in full the definitions relating to slavery that the Roman jurist Florentius provided.

> (1) Slavery is an institution of the common law of peoples (*ius gentium*) by which a person is put into the ownership (*dominium*) of somebody else, contrary to the natural order. (2) Slaves (*servi*) are so called because commanders generally sell the people they capture and therefore save (*servare*) them instead of killing them. (3) The word for property in slaves (*mancipia*) is derived from the fact that they are captured from the enemy by force of arms (*manu capiantur*).[2]

Coinciding with the wars of imperialism were social and economic alterations that made possible a vastly more intensive and extensive use of slaves; together they accounted for the evolution of Rome from a slaveholding society to a true slave society in the sense discussed in the first chapter. The elements of that transformation were increased wealth and landholding by the Roman elite; the dispossession of the Italian peasants from their lands and their flight to the cities, particularly Rome; and vast numbers of captives who were enslaved and took the place of the departed citizens in the countryside.[3]

The process of transformation included a series of interlocking components that, taken together, fulfilled the three conditions that Moses I. Finley proposed as necessary for the creation of a slave society: private ownership of land with a concentration requiring a work force larger than a family unit, a sufficient development of commodity production and markets, and the unavailability of an internal labor supply.[4] These three factors, when the availability of a sufficient number of slaves is added to them, explain why Rome became a slave society.

First, there was the increased wealth of the elite, which permitted its members to invest more heavily in land, a socially acceptable investment for the senators, who were forbidden by law to engage in trade and manufacturing. Part of the land they acquired was in the provinces, but part was also in Italy, where they received grants of public land, the *ager publicus*, and where they purchased the lands of distressed peasants. They either amalgamated their new acquisitions into large-scale latifundia (similar to plantations) or continued to operate the farms they collected as individual units.[5] The elite confronted a problem of providing labor for their estates, because their agrarian holdings were too large to be worked by a single tenant family and because the traditional workers were leaving the land in great numbers. Many of these workers entered the armies, and, of those who left to fight, few returned. Many fell in battle; others received new lands granted to them in the provinces and never returned to Italy. Of those who came home, few were able to hold their farms: some had their mortgages foreclosed, and those who tried to resume production succumbed to competition from the elite with their larger, and presumably more efficient, agricultural enterprises. The cities exerted a powerful attraction for the dispossessed peasants, particularly Rome itself, where subsidized and later free distribution of food allowed the poor to subsist despite limited opportunities of employment. All told, it has been estimated that over a million of the peasant population of Italy left their native hearths, and that by the end of the republic there were some two million slaves in Italy, with the free population numbering about four million.[6] Thus the proportion of slaves in the Roman population was very close to that at the heyday of American slavery, some 30 percent.

The Roman elite benefited from their large landholdings. As the city's population grew, the market for agricultural produce expanded accordingly, and Rome's subsidized distribution of food indirectly underwrote the profits of the landowners. In the absence of an internal supply of labor, the elite turned to slaves to work their estates. Slaves were certainly available. As they embarked on the wars of expansion, the directors of Roman policy may not have been motivated in the first place by a desire to secure slaves as booty, but acquiring slaves was an inevitable consequence of the policies they endorsed. Rome's inexorable spread over the Mediterranean basin and its hinterland provided an almost inexhaustible supply of captives.

Roman writers delighted in noting the number of captives that the victories produced. Livy's indications of captives taken by Rome before 149 B.C. add up to at least a third of a million, and he also made references to other victories for which he did not provide specific figures. Julius Caesar reportedly made as many as one million captives during his Gallic wars from 58 to 51 B.C. Of those captives, some were brought back to Italy by the state and sold there; some came as the personal property of returning Roman soldiers; some were sold to slave dealers who followed the victorious armies. Pirates in the eastern Mediterranean

also provided many slaves before Pompey mounted a successful campaign to
crush them in 67 B.C., not primarily because of their enslaving activities, but
rather because they threatened the grain trade of the Adriatic, and possibly because of their abortive connections with the revolt of Spartacus.[7]

Slave use in Roman agriculture was nothing new; during the early republic,
the small farmers of the Italian peninsula generally worked the land themselves
with the assistance of a few slaves who formed part of the owner's household.
The situation changed drastically during the period of expansion, for the reasons
we have already mentioned, and slave-worked estates on a much larger scale
than before became common in many parts of the Roman world. The large holdings were characteristic of Italy and Sicily, as well as the new territories secured
in North Africa and in Spain. Elsewhere, particularly in many of the eastern
provinces, traditional peasant economies were let alone, and agricultural slavery
was not introduced.[8] In Italy and the western provinces, the Roman elite exploited their lands so as to derive the maximum benefit from them. In the initial
phases of the expansion, with vast lands and huge numbers of slaves available
to Rome's elite, a common use of slaves was as herdsmen in the pasture lands
of Sicily and southern Italy.

Even if the slaveowners profited greatly from their ownership of rural slaves,
they were not exempt from periodic problems. Discipline for the slave herdsmen—often working without much supervision—was difficult to maintain,
despite the varied and brutal means of control the Romans kept at their disposal.
At the height of expansion, just when the greatest number of slaves were being
brought back to the heartland, a series of three major slave revolts broke out
precisely in the herding areas of the Italian south. These rebellions were terrify-
ing to Roman society, both because of their immediate threat and also because
of their dire implications for a society whose slaves made up a quarter to a third
of the population. Concentrated in a seventy-year period, the revolts began with
the first Sicilian slave war (139 or 135 to 132 B.C.), continued with the second
slave war in Sicily (104 to 100 B.C.), and ended with the massive insurrection
of 73–71 B.C. organized by Spartacus and his fellow gladiators in southern
Italy.

The first slave rebellion broke out in two places in Sicily, initially led by
Eunous, a Syrian household slave owned by Antigenes, a wealthy landowner of
the town of Enna. Angered by their master's haughty and brutal treatment, the
slaves of another citizen of Enna, Damphilous, revolted and chose Eunous as
their leader. He set himself up as a king, following Near Eastern models of king-
ship, and attracted several thousand followers from the slaves on the island.
Eunous was joined by a second band of rebels, slave herdsmen who had fled
their owners previously and were operating as brigands in the southwestern sec-
tor of Sicily around the city of Agrigentum. The herdsmen's leader, Cleon, took
his men and linked up with Eunous, who was by that time calling himself Antiochus. Quelling the rebellion of Antiochus, whose effective strength may have

numbered as many as ten thousand, was a difficult and costly task that took the Romans until 132 B.C.[9]

The second rebellion in Sicily was the result of slave resentment coupled with miscalculations on the part of the Roman authorities. In 104 B.C. Marius the consul was launching a campaign to prevent two Germanic tribes, the Cimbri and the Teutones, from entering Gaul, and he asked allied states to supply him with troops. The king of Bythnia demurred, stating that he had no young men to send because of the depredations of Roman tax collectors who had seized many of his people and sold them as slaves. The Senate decreed that each provincial governor should identify and free all citizens of allied states held as slaves. In Sicily, the governor Publius Licinius Nerva announced the decree and ordered the slaves to assemble in Syracuse to be processed and repatriated. When the news reached the ears of the Sicilian landowners, they were furious and persuaded Nerva to defy Marius and rescind the decree of emancipation. The slaves, justifiably angered by the governor's instructions to return to their masters, fled and sought religious sanctuary. The first outbreak of violence was in western Sicily, where slaves murdered their masters. Nerva crushed the initial uprising with ease, but he then blundered by moving his troops to eastern Sicily. Two more uprisings then broke out, one in southwestern Sicily, led by Salvius, and one in the west under Athenion. Both rebel leaders set themselves up as kings and secured widespread support from the slaves and, more ominously from the Roman point of view, from many free people, whose participation gave the second Sicilian slave war the coloration of a social rebellion or civil war. The two rebel kings combined forces, and Salvius, with the larger contingent, made Athenion his subordinate and took the name Tryphon. They were able to hold out against the Romans until 100 B.C.[10]

The third slave rebellion is the most familiar, thanks to Hollywood. Its leader was Spartacus, a Thracian who roused his fellow gladiators in Capua to flee from their camp. They first armed themselves with gladiatorial weapons and then defeated the Roman garrison at Capua and seized military weapons. At the word of Spartacus's success, many slaves in southern Sicily rose and joined him. He probably knew that his men could not hope to reach their homelands, and he chose to lead them to Sicily, where an insurrection might be kindled. His arrangements with Cilician pirates to transport his men to the island fell through, and his band was forced to face Roman troops led by Crassus, who eventually defeated them and lined the Appian Way with the crucified bodies of those who escaped death in battle.[11]

The three rebellions were similar in aims and outcome. They reflected the desire on the part of the recent captives to secure their own personal freedom rather than any desire to end slavery as a system, and they indicated that the means of social control at the disposal of the Romans were still not sufficiently well developed to deal with the large influx of new slaves. The slave revolts were not the only upheavals occasioned by the transformation of Rome into a slave society. An indirect consequence was the political movement of Tiberius Gracchus, who supported the Italian poor then being displaced by the great alterations in patterns of landholding. Gracchus was assassinated, but the underlying social unrest, exacerbated by the growth of large-scale slavery and vast estates and by the influx of the dispossessed into the cities, was not to be solved until Augustus created the empire.

Although he billed it as a return to the good traditions of the republic, Augustus (31 B.C.–A.D. 14) created a political settlement that changed the face of the Roman world; the empire replaced the republic. The ensuing Pax Romana was a period of relative peace within the imperial frontiers. The end of the wars of expansion and the suppression of piracy by the imperial navy meant a greatly reduced pool of potential slaves. Subjects of the empire could not be enslaved legally, and slave dealers had to make do with existing slaves and their offspring or go beyond the Roman borders to purchase slaves and bring them back, causing increasing prices for scarce merchandise. Although a decline of Roman slavery began, almost imperceptibly, in the first two centuries of the empire and accelerated thereafter, slavery in imperial Rome maintained its characteristic features.

By the time of Augustus, however, fundamental changes in the system of rural exploitation were taking place. With increasing specialization, less land and fewer slaves were devoted to herding, and large-scale agriculture developed to produce commodities for sale in the urban markets: grain above all, but also wine and olive oil. Villas proliferated in the lands of latifundia, with houses and warehouses for the managers and dormitories for the slaves. The villas spread over much of the western portion of the empire, and recent scholarship has revealed that the villas covered much larger areas than was previously believed.[12]

The usual pattern for the estates was absentee ownership, at least until late in the empire, with the local management delegated to overseers, often slaves, who organized the work of slave gangs, usually divided into groups of fewer than ten slaves for efficiency. Columella, who was born in the first century A.D. in Gades (modern Cádiz) and later moved to central Italy where he owned a series of farms, addressed the point of relatively small slave gangs in his manual, *On Agriculture*.

> This arrangement not only stimulated rivalry (and consequently output), but it also disclosed the slothful; for when a task is enlivened by competition, punishment inflicted on the laggards appears free from censure.[13]

In his agricultural writings, Varro (first century B.C.) provided the famous definition of slaves as articulate implements (*instrumenti vocale*). He nonetheless proposed mild treatment for rural slaves, so long as efficiency could be maintained.

> The foreman must not only give orders but also take part in the work, so that his subordinates may follow his example, and also understand that

there is good reason for his being over them—the fact that he is superior to them in knowledge. They are not to be allowed to control men with whips rather than words, if only you can achieve the same result.[14]

Not all masters administered their estates in such a manner. There is evidence that many rural slaves worked in chains, although it seems doubtful whether all the tasks on the farms could be performed by chained slaves. Cato the Elder, writing on agricultural management in the second century B.C., proposed a harsh regimen for rural slaves. He suggested that they be worked at will and punished by whipping. They should be given only the necessary clothing, and when old or disabled they should be sold as an economy measure along with worn-out implements. Cato was considered harsh by his contemporaries, and no doubt by his slaves as well. In writing of Cato, Plutarch said, "I myself regard someone who uses slaves like pack animals and drives them away and sells them when they get old as unbalanced."[15] Cato also said that food was to be given to the slaves according to their activities. Field workers at all times were to receive larger rations than slaves doing less demanding work, and during summer, when they expended greater physical effort, their rations were to be increased.[16]

As he gave advice on slave treatment, Columella revealed himself to be a strict but generally kind master, even if patronizing. He reported that he talked

rather familiarly with the country slaves, provided only that they have not conducted themselves unbecomingly . . . , and when I perceived that their unending toil was lightened by such friendliness on the part of the master, I would even jest with them at times and allow them also to jest more freely. Nowadays I make it a practice to call them into consultation on any new work, as if they were more experienced, and to discover by this means what sort of ability is possessed by each of them and how intelligent he is.[17]

Not all masters or overseers were as kind as Columella. In addition to beating and branding their slaves, other masters shackled them in dormitories at night. The most horrifying feature of rural slave conditions was the *ergastulum*, a special prison for recalcitant slaves.[18]

Both Varro and Columella endorsed positive inducements and rewards for overseers and slaves. Varro suggested the following:

They are made to take more interest in their work by being treated more liberally in respect either of food, or of more clothing, or of exemption from work, or permission to graze some cattle of their own on the farm, or other things of this kind; so that, if some unusually heavy task is imposed, or punishment inflicted on them in some way, their loyalty and kindly feeling to the master may be restored by the consolation derived from such measures.[19]

In a passage that provides one of the strongest pieces of evidence that Roman masters allowed even their slaves on the rural estates opportunities to reproduce themselves, Columella described one other method of reward for slave women.

> To women, too, who are unusually prolific, and who ought to be rewarded for the bearing of a certain number of offspring, I have granted exemption from work and sometimes even freedom after they have reared many children. For a mother of three sons exemption from work was granted; to a mother of more her freedom as well.[20]

More general attitudes appear in Columella. In his advice on choosing a slave overseer, the age-old urban-rural dichotomy appears.

> So my advice at the start is not to appoint an overseer from that sort of slaves who are physically attractive, and certainly not from that class which has busied itself with the voluptuous occupations of the city. This lazy and sleepy-headed class of servants, accustomed to idling, to the Campus, the Circus, and the theatres, to gambling, to cookshops, to bawdy-houses, never ceases to dream of these follies; and when they carry themselves into their farming, the master suffers not so much the loss in the slave himself as in his whole estate. A man should be chosen who has been hardened by farm work from his infancy, one who has been tested by experience.[21]

Slaves remained expensive, even at the peak of Roman expansion when thousands of captives swelled the market, but Roman landowners continued to purchase them to staff their estates. Was the use of slaves efficient and profitable? We lack the necessary documentary evidence to make a statistical analysis, but it is clear, nonetheless, that we should reject the long line of argument, from Adam Smith to Max Weber and beyond, that slave labor was inefficient and ultimately unprofitable. Such an argument is based on the assumption that an immoral institution can be neither efficient nor profitable. In his usual incisive manner, Moses I. Finley warned us not to give much credence to the moral argument, for such a "suggestion would have astonished Greek and Roman slave-owners, who not only went on for many centuries fondly believing that they were making substantial profits out of their estates but also spending those profits lavishly."[22]

Who were the slaves? Not all were captives; there were also indigenous slaves. Children born to slave parents, or specifically to a slave mother, were for that reason slaves. Children born free could be enslaved. Destitute parents often resorted to one of two methods for disposing of children they could not support: sale and exposure. Although Romans frowned on the practice and legislated against it, parents at times pledged their children against debts or sold them outright. A harsher, more direct measure was exposure of unwanted babies,

Sources of slaves

more often female than male. This was not an automatic death sentence; rescuers took advantage of the right to claim the child and raise it as a slave (or as a free person, if they wished). Helpless children could also fall victim to kidnapping by slave dealers.[23] Not only did freeborn children face the threat of slavery; adults too could lose their freedom for a variety of reasons. One was by legal sentence, often for nonpayment of taxes, and this implied loss of citizenship. The destitute could pledge themselves as the price of continued existence. Debt bondage (*servitus poenae*) was a temporary condition and should not be considered true slavery, especially because the condition did not pass to the convicted person's heirs. Adults could fall into the hands of kidnappers and be sold as slaves, but proof of Roman citizenship was sufficient to free them again.[24]

So far we have been concerned mainly with large-scale rural slavery, of which gang slavery was an important part, but we must not forget that Roman slavery was far more complex and encompassed a wide range of other uses for slaves. All slaves of the Romans may have occupied the same legal category, but in practice there was a wide variation in the social and economic roles they played.[25] Aside from rural slaves, domestic slaves were probably the most common.

The use of slaves as household servants was constant throughout the period covered in this book because it did not correspond closely to the economic structure. The comfortable, the well-off, and the wealthy, whatever the sources of their income and however those sources might change, all employed slaves as domestic servants. At the height of the empire, slaveowners came from a broad spectrum on the social scale, from aristocrats down through the middle classes to the artisans. The richest households maintained large numbers of slaves, and even the more modest had one or more slaves. Complaints of poverty often came from those who owned several slaves. A. H. M. Jones related one famous fourth-century example.

> Libanius, urging the council of Antioch to augment the stipends of his four assistant lecturers, represents them as poverty-stricken on their present scales; they do not marry if they are prudent, they have to live in lodgings like cobblers, they owe money to their bakers. . . . As a climax, Libanius declares that they can afford two or three slaves only, who, not belonging to a proper establishment, are insolent to their masters.[26]

Owners assigned slaves to all types of household duties, as maids, guards, repairmen, cooks. Elaborate households had eunuchs as servants. Because few survived castration, eunuchs were expensive and doubly scarce because the operation was forbidden in Roman territory, forcing importation from outside the empire.[27] Romans had sexual access to their household slaves, both male and female. Some Romans, according to their sexual preferences, bought boys or girls to serve as partners in sex. Others bought slaves and employed them as prostitutes, and prostitution was the eventual lot of many female infants exposed by their parents and raised by those who found them.[28]

Roman slaves often were found in industrial and commercial pursuits. Applying the term *industrial* to Roman building and manufacturing may seem anachronistic. There were no factories in the modern sense, because most Roman manufacturing took place in small workshops where artisans produced pottery, glassware, jewelry, bricks and dressed stone, metalwork and baked goods. In these pursuits, slave and free were employed, but slaves and convicts were often used in mining, since few free men would accept the harsh conditions in the mines. Slaves worked on the docks and in warehouses and occupied higher positions. They were agents for their owners, acting as shopkeepers, managers, secretaries, and accountants. A fortunate slave might even receive the bequest of the master's business.[29]

It often has been suggested that slavery retarded technological progress, a Roman weak point, by rendering labor-saving devices and techniques unnecessary, and that slave labor could not compete efficiently with free labor. These are old and persistent ideas, but recent scholarship tends to suggest the opposite conclusions. There was apparently no real distinction between free labor and slave in regard to working conditions, efficiency, and profitability. Manumission blurred the distinctions in status among workers—free, freed, or slave. Craftsmanship did not suffer when tasks such as ceramic making were assigned to slaves. The well-known relief pottery of Arretium (modern Arezzo) was made by slave artisans and artists. In Finley's opinion, "No one can distinguish, in the ruins of the Erechtheum, which mouldings were carved by Simias, which by his five slaves."[30] To address satisfactorily the question of Roman industrial backwardness and technological stagnation requires a different perspective, one that takes into account the beneficiaries of the profits of artisanry, who were the owners, not the workers themselves. Owners generally lacked the specialized knowledge of the processes involved, and workers who might have devised labor-saving techniques or tools had no incentive or means for putting them to use. The presence of slavery was a "social block" to "the use of a good many technological opportunities theoretically within the grasp of the ancients."[31] Equally influential was the perennial distinction between the empire's more advanced eastern portion, where commerce and industry were better developed, and its more rural and agrarian west, where technological backwardness was particularly acute.[32]

Within the ambit of domestic slavery, several occupations of Roman slaves gave their practitioners more responsible roles, to give the modern designations—child care, education, and medicine. It is be expected that in a society making heavy use of slaves, nurses and governesses would be household slaves. More surprising is that education and medicine were pursuits associated with the unfree. Trusted older domestic slaves commonly taught the younger children comportment and accompanied them to and from school when their charges reached a suitable age. In the schools, organized by the municipalities and financed by subscriptions paid by the pupils' parents, the teachers were often slaves. Scientific medical practices came to Rome with transported slaves from Greece or elsewhere in the eastern Mediterranean, who often started out as slaves of wealthy householders and later set up their own practices when freed. The explanation for this lies in the attitudes of the Roman elite, who typically channeled their creative activities into military and political efforts. Therefore they needed and certainly used the education and training in the arts and the liberal professions that many eastern slaves possessed.[33]

A special group of slaves and freedmen in Rome was the *familia Caesaris*, literally translated as "the family of the emperor." Not to be confused with those slaves brought by the state to Rome and auctioned there, the *familia Caesaris* occupied two major categories: the imperial household staff and those who handled the administration of the empire. The duties of the imperial household slaves require little explanation, but the administrative group performed a variety of functions. They staffed the bureaucracy, handling record keeping and correspondence, collecting taxes and disbursing money. They ran the libraries and the postal system. The water supply of Rome was administered by imperial slaves—indeed, municipally owned slaves had built it in the first place. Imperial slaves ran the aqueducts, the mines and quarries, and the mint. State factories such as the linen and woolen mills were in their hands.

The situation of the imperial slaves was unlike that of other slaves. Members of this group could generally look forward to emancipation and often continued their careers as imperial freedmen. At times they acted as investors on their own account, lending money they had accumulated and investing in urban and rural enterprises. Why did the empire make such use of these special slaves, who came to compose a distinct social category in Roman society? The Roman state needed skilled technicians, managers, and bureaucrats, but the elite shunned all public service occupations except for military and political duties. For the other necessary tasks of running an empire, recruitment had to be conducted among those who had neither traditional prejudices against such tasks nor conflicting loyalties, those who could be acquired cheaply and quickly, and who could be compelled to work by force. Hence the imperial slaves and freedmen.[34]

Military service was closed to slaves. Except during isolated periods of dire emergency, as when Pompey armed eight hundred of his slaves and herdsmen to join his armies in the struggle against Octavian, slaves could not serve in the ranks. In fact, a slave risked the death sentence by posing as free to enter the army. The same prohibition applied in the fleet (galley slaves are the product of a much later period). While imperial slaves could command ships, this was unusual and an additional indication of the special status of the *familia Caesaris*. Even though they could not bear arms and enter combat, slaves did contribute to the functioning of the military machine. They were used in quartermastering and nonmilitary support, and all officers and even ordinary soldiers took slave servants along on the march.[35]

Conditions slaves endured were theoretically harsh in the Roman world. The slave had no legal personality; he or she was considered a *res*, a thing, the chattel of his owner. He was under the sole authority of the master, who could mete out punishment at will, including death in certain circumstances. To prevent slaves from readily recognizing their fellow slaves and thereby gaining an appreciation of their numbers and potential power, the Roman state declined to assign them distinctive clothing.[36]

The head of a Roman household, the *pater familias*, exercised wide powers over his dependents, including his wife, children, servants, and slaves. These powers never disappeared totally, but in the imperial period legal practice increasingly limited them. In A.D. 319 Constantine specified what a master could and could not do to his slaves.

If an owner has chastised a slave by beating him with sticks or whipping or has put him into chains in order to keep him under guard, he should not stand in fear of any criminal accusation if the slave dies; and all statutes of limitations and legal interpretations are hereby set aside.

But he should not make excessive use of his rights; he will indeed be accused of homicide if he willingly

—kills him with a stroke of a cane or a stone;
—inflicts a lethal wound by using something which is definitely a weapon;
—orders him to be hung from a noose;
—gives the shocking command that he should be thrown down from a height;
—pours poison into him;
—mangles his body with the punishments reserved to the State, viz. by having his sides torn apart by the claws of wild beasts; or applying fire to burn his body;
—or by forcing the man's weakened limbs, running with blood and gore, to give up their life spirit as the result of torture—a form of brutality appropriate to savage barbarians.[37]

Under normal circumstances, Roman slaves could not be witnesses in court; but, when their testimony was deemed absolutely essential, it was only admissible after they had been tortured.[38] An especially inhumane requirement, one that was actually carried out at times, was that if a master were murdered, all the slaves in earshot when he was killed were to be tortured and executed.[39] An oft-repeated story concerns Vedius Pollio, who, while entertaining the emperor Augustus at a dinner party, threatened to throw a slave into his fishpond to be eaten by lampreys for having broken a crystal cup. Augustus was genuinely shocked at the suggestion and sharply rebuked Vedius Pollio for his cruelty.[40]

Examples of harsh treatment by the legal system and by individual masters could be multiplied; but, except for the usual treatment of large slave gangs on the latifundia or in the mines and among the gladiators, there often were mitigating factors in the system that allowed the slave the chance of a life, if not satisfying, then at least comfortable and secure. First, slaves formed a recognized category within the master's family. While they were absolutely subject to his discipline, they also enjoyed his protection and a degree of fellowship in his household, as well as the security of food, shelter, and clothing. They could participate in the religious life in the pagan cults and later in Christianity. They could join benevolent societies that provided fellowship for the living, and funeral rites and burial for the dead. Slave marriages were sometimes recognized, especially after the empire became Christian. The possibility of manumission was strong, and manumission implied citizenship, at least for the slave's children or grandchildren.[41]

A special feature of some slaves' condition was the *peculium*, a fund of money under their control. Legally it belonged to the master; in practice it formed the slave's working capital, derived from gifts, a portion of the wages a slave might receive for work outside the home, tips from guests, or from savings from the slave's allowance. The slave could use the *peculium* for investments and ultimately accumulate enough to purchase freedom. Slaves could use the *peculium* to purchase other slaves to stand in for them (*vicarius, vicaria*). The *peculium* gave certain slaves a small measure of independence and was a humanizing feature of the inhuman system to which they were subjected. Of course, the *peculium* was usually reserved for urban, skilled slaves, not for rural workers. The institution of the *peculium* was a necessary recognition that if Roman slaveowners were to use some of their slaves as managers and business agents, they had to allow them an expense account and some control over capital.[42]

Considering the security—even if it was a forced security—that the slaves possessed and the special status enjoyed by the *familia Caesaris*, Ramsey MacMullen has argued that the free poor were far more insecure and that they, not the slaves, occupied the lowest rungs of the Roman social ladder. The slaves were assured that their masters were obliged to provide for their needs; the free poor were alone in facing a hostile world. As one distinction between the two groups, exposure or sale of children because they could not be supported was done by the free, not by the slaves.[43]

From early in their history, the Romans considered slavery to be part of the *ius gentium*, meaning that it was sanctioned by human regulations in all the societies they encountered.[44] The Romans regarded slavery as degrading for those subjected to it, especially for those born free. Beyond this the Romans considered manual occupations, especially when carried out by slaves, as degrading in themselves. Whole categories of human endeavor came to be considered unworthy—medicine and the arts, as well as trade and manual labor.[45] This was another of the Romans' unfortunate legacies to posterity.

If the highest in Roman society considered slavery degrading, the slaves certainly shared this attitude and went to great lengths to escape from servile status. They had at their disposal the expedient of flight, but this offered only limited possibilities. Many of the newly enslaved had come from long distances, rendering their hope for return to their homelands almost futile. No doubt some fugitives did escape entirely; some were even elected to public office before their status was discovered.[46] But most fugitives were probably recaptured. Escape to the cities might have offered some hope, but even among the urban throngs they could have had little chance of attaining a safe position, especially since the system of registration worked against them, their language would identify them as non-Roman, and rewards to informants and other legal mechanisms reinforced the efforts of the state to return runaways to their masters. From the second century A.D., metal collars inscribed with the name of the owner began to be used instead of branding for ordinary slaves. Some of the collars have survived. One carried these words: "I have run away. You will get a gold *solidus* if you return me to my master Zoninus." Another stated: "I am called Januarius. I am the slave of Dexter, Recorder of the Senate, who lives in the Fifth Region, at the field of Macarius." The collars became so common in time that the legend "T. M. Q. F." (*tene me quia fugio*, "arrest me since I am a fugitive") by itself would suffice. Until the fourth century A.D., apprehended fugitives were commonly branded on the face, but, bowing to Christian pressure, Constantine in 315 or 316 restricted branding to the hands and legs. Because of the numerous obstacles, simple flight was an ineffective means of reaching freedom.[47] Far more attractive and secure was the possibility of manumission.

Manumission was, in the vast majority of cases, the prerogative of the master. He could decide to emancipate for a variety of reasons: in gratitude for long service, for the money a slave had saved to purchase freedom, to free a woman slave to marry him, to grant a dying slave a last request. Cynical reasons cropped up at times. A master realized that slaves were expensive to maintain, and even if he freed them, they still owed him certain obligations.

> On the lowest material plane an enfranchised slave in the city of Rome . . . became a literal breadwinner for his master's household since, now registered as an independent Roman citizen domiciled in Rome, he qualified to be put on the list of those entitled to receive the monthly grain allowance which from 58 B.C. onwards was given free.[48]

The depths were reached when masters manumitted aged or disabled slaves, in effect granting them the freedom to starve in the streets or be maintained by the state.[49]

The master could choose to manumit during his lifetime or by testament after his death; in either case the state collected a tax of 5 percent. Manumissions during the master's life required the master and the slave to present themselves before a public official who declared the slave to be legally freed. Manumission by testament could be a pious act or it could be calculated to keep the prospective freed persons in a state of anxious anticipation. The failure of the deceased's heirs or agents to fulfill the stipulations of the will were apparently common enough for the legal system to provide means of redress. While the law held the slaves to be legally incompetent and barred them from the courts except as witnesses, they could seek legal action in cases regarding manumission.[50] Early in the imperial period, if a slave could get a free person to represent him or her in court, he or she could obtain a legal ruling concerning his or her status. Later regulations allowed slaves to go to court on their own if the master had provided manumission by testament and the master's agent had not fulfilled the specified terms. Complications also could arise when a slave was owned jointly by a group of masters. In such a case, all masters had to agree to the manumission or it was invalid.

In many instances, citizenship did not follow automatically from the act of manumission. If the master were less than twenty years of age and the slave less than thirty, the new freedman became a Junian Latin, not a Roman citizen, with limitations on his legal status. In the special circumstance that the under-thirty freedman could prove that he had married a citizen or freed wife and fathered a child that lived at least a year, he could legally secure full citizenship. Under new laws enacted in A.D. 24 the Junian Latin could acquire full citizenship through military service or through service in the Roman fire brigade. Later, participation in economic activities deemed useful to the empire—grain shipping, construction in Rome, or wholesale baking—could bring a Junian Latin full citizenship.[51]

Even with the new status, the free person still suffered under legal disabilities and social discrimination. He could not hold public office nor officer rank in the army. He owed some duties, usually symbolic, to the former master and his family, and often labor or money. Children born after their parents were manumitted were free, but those born before their parents' freeing were still the slaves of the master.

Aside from voluntary acts by the masters, slaves could gain their freedom through the direct intervention of the state. Two broad categories are apparent: as a reward for a slave's meretorious service to the state, and as a consequence of a master's punishment for crimes. The first generally came to the slave who revealed a crime, by denouncing deserters, illegal coiners, libelous writers, rapists of virgins or widows. If a slave could prove that another slave was illegally cohabiting with a free woman, the accuser could win freedom. The cases in which freedom was gained as a result of the slaveowner's having been convicted of a crime reveal the limitations the state set upon a master's ability to inflict harm on his slaves. Castration in Roman territory was illegal, as we have seen. The perpetrator was punished, and, after the fifth century, the victim was freed. Masters could not expose sick slaves or make prostitutes of their chattels; in both these cases the state could prosecute the owner and free the slave.[52]

Manumission was popular in imperial Rome, both with the slaves and with their owners, and cases of manumission increased with time. While the state on occasion attempted to restrict the right of masters to manumit and to permit the freed to be reenslaved, such measures were seldom enacted. Augustus placed limits on certain categories of manumissions. In 2 B.C. the number of slaves who could be freed by testament were specified according to the number of slaves held. Those masters who owned between two and ten slaves could free only one-half; between ten and thirty, one-third; between thirty and one hundred, one-quarter; between one hundred and five hundred, one-fifth; and, finally, no one could free more than one hundred slaves under the terms of a will. In A.D. 4 another law provided that criminals and runaways, if later freed, could never acquire full rights of citizenship.[53] Manumission continued and grew over the centuries of the Roman Empire, along with the practice of providing gifts or bequests to the newly freed for their support.[54]

From a variety of sources, scholars have provided biographical details about many individual slaves and ex-slaves of the Roman period, but no actual life is more fascinating, and repellent at times, than that fictional creation of the satirist Petronius, whose freedman Trimalchio enlivens the pages of *The Satyricon*. The career Petronius imagined for his creation provides a vivid portrayal of common features of the lives of Roman slaves, and many of the details of that career can be corroborated in the lives of real slaves and freedmen from the documentary sources.[55]

The narrator of *The Satyricon*, Encolpius, first encountered Trimalchio, "a bald old man in a reddish shirt,"[56] playing ball with some boys and accompanied by two slaves, one with a bag of balls to give the players so they would not have to stoop when they dropped one. Later, as he entered Trimalchio's house for dinner, Encolpius passed a sign stating "any slave leaving the house without his master's permission will receive one hundred lashes" and then came upon an elaborate mural detailing Trimalchio's rise from slavery to freedom and wealth. Before they entered the dining room, Encolpius and the other guests had to settle a dispute between a house slave and the steward, thereby permitting the slave to avoid a beating. Throughout the house they encountered ostentatious reminders of the host's wealth: in the dining room were pieces of silver plate with their weight and Trimalchio's name inscribed on them. In the course of the inordinately elaborate meal, slaves trooped in to serve the courses, singing as they did. At one point, Trimalchio ordered in the chef to instruct him about serving a pig.

> He then said to the man in a loud voice:
> "Which division are you from?"
> When he replied that he was from number forty, Trimalchio asked:
> "Were you bought or were you born here?"
> "Neither," said the chef, "I was left to you in Pansa's will."
> "Well, then," said Trimalchio, "see you serve it up carefully—otherwise I'll have you thrown into the messenger's division."

So the chef, duly reminded of his master's magnificence, went back to the kitchen, the next course leading the way.[57]

After the pig was served theatrically, "the chef of course was rewarded with a drink and a silver crown, and also given a drinking cup on a tray of Corinthian bronze."[58]

Later, Trimalchio's desire to interrupt the meal to dance was diverted by the entrance of his accountant, who proceeded to read from the estate books:

"26 July: Births on the estate at Cumae: male 30, female 40. Wheat threshed and stored: 500,000 pecks. Oxen broken in: 500.

"On the same date: the slave Mithradates crucified for insulting the holy spirit that watches over our dear Gaius [Pompeius Trimalchio].

"On the same date: Deposits to the strong-room (no further investment possible): 10,000,000 sesterces.

"On the same date: A fire broke out on the estate at Pompeii beginning at the house of Nasta the bailiff."

"What!" said Trimalchio. "When was an estate bought for me at Pompeii?"

"Last year," said the accountant, "so it hasn't yet come on the books."

Trimalchio flared up:

"If any land is bought for me and I don't hear of it within six months, I refuse to have it entered on the books."

The official edicts were read out and the wills of certain game-keepers. In very flattering terms they said they were leaving Trimalchio nothing. Then the names of some bailiffs; the divorce of a freedwoman, the wife of a watchman, on the grounds of adultery with a bath-attendant; the demotion of a hall-porter to a job at Baiae; the prosecution of a steward; and the result of an action between some attendants.

Finally the acrobats arrived.[59]

In describing Trimalchio's banquet, Petronius provided many other glimpses of the details of the lives of slaves and freedmen; for instance, Trimalchio threatened his slaves several times during the course of the meal, some jokingly, others seriously. One freedman guest became fed up with the host's ostentation and attacked him verbally.

"You're a Roman knight, are you? Well, my father was a king.

" '*Why are you only a freedman?*' did you say? Because I went into service voluntarily. I wanted to be a Roman citizen, not a subject with taxes to pay. And today, I hope no one can laugh at the way I live. . . .

"I've bought a bit of land and some tiny pieces of plate. I've twenty bodies to feed, as well as a dog. I bought my old woman's freedom so nobody could wipe his dirty hands on *her* hair. Four thousand I paid for myself. I was elected to the Augustan College and it cost me nothing. I hope when I die I won't have to blush in my coffin."[60]

Trimalchio told his own story later that night, including the favor he won from his master and mistress by means of his sexual activities.

"I came from Asia as big as this candlestick. In fact, every day I used to measure myself against it, and to get some whiskers round my beak quicker, I used to oil my lips from the lamp. Still, for fourteen years I was the old boy's fancy. And there's nothing wrong if the boss wants it. But I did all right by the old girl too. You know what I mean—I don't say anything because I'm not the boasting sort.

"Well, as heaven will have it, I became boss in the house, and the old boy, you see, couldn't think of anything but me. That's about it—he made me . . . his heir and I got a senator's fortune. But nobody gets enough, never. I wanted to go into business."[61]

And through shipping, Trimalchio became even richer.

At the time of his banquet, he was making plans for a princely tomb, "a hundred feet facing the road and two hundred back into the field."[62] Elaborate tombs were popular, if unproductive, investments for moderately successful Roman freedmen, especially those who had not acquired landed property. One inscription stated as much:

Caius Hostius Pamphilus, freedman of Caius, physician, bought this for himself and for Nelphia Hymnis, freedwoman of Marcus, and for their freedmen and freedwomen and their descendants.
This is our eternal home, this is our farm.
These are our orchards, this is our tomb.
13 feet across, 24 feet deep.[63]

Perhaps the most fascinating tombstone discovered from the classical world, and one doubly appropriate for our purposes, was that of Aulus Kapreilius Timotheus, an ex-slave and later slave dealer who died in Greece in the first century A.D. Of marble, seven feet tall, the memorial stone of Timotheus depicted three scenes: a funeral banquet, a work scene, and one showing a man leading two women and two children and eight chained slaves. The stone is inscribed with the words: "Aulus Kapreilius Timotheus, freedman of Aulus, slave trader."[64] In describing the funeral stone, Moses I. Finley remarked that the unusual feature was not that Timotheus commemorated his manumission but that he would express pride in his occupation, because slave dealers often were scorned for their activities. Timotheus's monument lends additional credence to aspects of Petronius's description of Trimalchio and his possessions, particularly the "mural of a slave market, price tags and all."[65]

In the course of the fourth century A.D., the Roman empire underwent a complete religious transformation, as Christianity passed from being a proscribed religion, to a tolerated one, and finally to the sole legal religion. Because this momentous departure from the classical pattern of religious multiplicity coincided roughly with the decline of slavery in the Roman world, many earlier scholars postulated a causal relationship between the two phenomena. They argued that Christianity, and to a lesser extent the philosophy of the Stoics, with their emphasis on the universal brotherhood of humankind, worked a change in the mental attitudes of the slaveholders, rendering them so morally uncomfortable that they gradually divested themselves of their human chattels and altered slavery's institutional rules. More recent scholars almost universally have rejected this argument.[66] Jewish law recognized slavery, and the practice was prevalent during the lifetime of Jesus. Neither Jesus nor the early Christians challenged the theory and only minimally altered the practice. Joseph Vogt has shown that references to slaves and slaveholding abound in the New Testament, even though they are obscured by modern translators who consistently represent the Greek word for slave with such terms as *servant* or *bondsman*.[67]

The early church from the time of St. Paul was able to reconcile slavery with Christianity. All God's human creations were originally equal, but wars and other manmade inequities had irreparably disrupted egalitarianism and made slavery an integral part of the human experience. Church fathers saw a direct connection between sin and slavery. For St. Augustine, as one example, the external, sinful world drew distinctions between slave and free and between rich and poor, and he believed that only through Christian faith could all attain freedom, which he defined as internal and spiritual, independent from and opposed to the sinful structure of society.[68]

Augustine further muddied the distinctions between slave and free by describing Christian obedience to God as a sort of benevolent slavery.

> All slavery is filled with bitterness: all who are tied to slave status complain at having to serve. But you must not be afraid of the service of this Master: there will be no groaning, no grumbling, no dissatisfaction here. No one wishes to be sold away from this household, since it is so wonderful that we should all have been brought back ('redeemed'). It is a great joy, my brothers, to be a slave in this great household, even a slave with chains on his feet. . . .
>
> You [as a Christian] are both a slave and a free man; you are a slave because that is what you were made; but from that status you have become free, because you love Him who made you. Do not complain at having to serve; your complaints will not bring it about that you cease serving, but that you serve as a bad slave. You are the Master's slave, and the Master's freedman; you shouldn't want to be set free with the result that you leave the household of Him who set you free.[69]

The church itself held slaves, especially on the lands of the monasteries, and threatened with anathema those who encouraged slaves to resist their masters. Only reluctantly did it allow entry of slaves into the religious life as priests, monks, and nuns, since the church considered that those subject to the authority of another were unable to give full allegiance to God and church discipline. At a minimum, the church required the master's permission for a slave's entry into holy orders and preferred that the slave first be freed.[70]

Christianity and the established church had some effect on manumissions, but the effect was not great. Manumission was a pious act, and the lives of the saints sometimes mention the freeing of large numbers of slaves. St. Melania reportedly freed 8,000 slaves out of 24,000 she is said to have owned with her husband. Hers seems to have been the largest mass liberation recorded, but a former prefect of Rome, Chromatius, supposedly freed 1,400. We should not put too much reliance upon such figures. Ancient statistics are notoriously unreliable, and hagiographers exaggerated the acts of the saints in order to magnify the image of their piety. The emperor Constantine, who legalized Christianity and moved the imperial capital to Constantinople, granted clerical authorities the right to manumit in church. For William L. Westermann, this indicated more the church's acceptance of the continuation of slavery than any desire to end it. The church in North Africa, even though in close contact with Rome, did not exercise this right to manumit for some seventy-five years.[71]

Why did the Romans free so many slaves? This perennial question was considered once again by Keith Hopkins, who has been able to provide some new explanations. In contrast to Roman writers and modern scholars who see manumission as an ameliorating feature of the Roman slave system, Hopkins views it "not as a solvent of the slave system, but as a major reinforcement . . . , because Roman slaves frequently, even customarily in my view, paid substantial sums for their freedom."[72] Slaves who strove to accumulate enough to buy their freedom were undoubtedly more docile and productive. The master who received his slave's market value as the price of freedom could use the proceeds to purchase a younger slave to replace the freedman. Manumission contracts, in addition to exacting semifilial obedience from the ex-slave, at times provided clauses requiring him to work for his former master on special terms.[73]

Neither Christianity nor Stoicism had any impact on the institution of slavery beyond fostering some recognition among the masters that they should adopt more humane methods as they dealt with their slaves, as Cicero advised his son:

> Let us remember that we must behave justly even towards the lowest kinds of people. The most inferior status and fate is that of slaves. Those who tell us to use them in the same way as if they were hired workmen don't give us bad advice—we must insist that they do their work, but grant them what is just.[74]

Heightened moral or religious attitudes were not sufficient by themselves to end slavery. Nonetheless, the last two centuries of the western empire's existence did witness a slow decline in the numbers of slaves and in their significance in society and the economy.[75]

Some of the reasons for this are simple—the end of large-scale war and the constant and increasing numbers of manumission—others are more complex. It used to be suggested that Germanic society had no slaves, and Germans, consequently, did not make good slaves when captured. But now we know that slavery and slave trading were entrenched in the tribal areas north of the imperial frontiers. The assumed inefficiency of slave labor and the supposed inability of slave populations to replenish themselves biologically seem on the basis of modern research to be inaccurate appraisals. More important as explanations for the decline in the number of slaves are the economic and demographic changes the western empire experienced.

Owing to a variety of causes, including a series of epidemics in the second and third centuries, the Roman population in Italy, and in the western portion generally, began to decline. The cities no longer held their former numbers, and industry—always less developed in the west—fell off drastically. As a result, fewer slaves could be employed profitably. Even greater changes took place in the countryside, where slavery ceased to be as important as it had been at the empire's inception, not because of an improvement in the status of slaves, but because of the increasingly depressed status of the free peasants. The owners of the villas gradually disbanded their slave gangs and divided their lands into small plots granted to free peasants, freed slaves, and the so-called hutted slaves (*servi casati*).[76] The tenant farm workers, as early as the third century, lost their freedom of movement when a decree of the emperor Diocletian tied them to their holdings. "[W]hile the rule was introduced in the interest of the state, to facilitate [tax collections] . . . , it proved very convenient to landowners, who were short of agricultural labour and welcomed a rule which prevented their tenants from abandoning their farms."[77] In time the tied tenants, the *coloni*, now legally existing under a system, the colonate, very like serfdom, lost other rights. In the early fifth century, they were debarred (as were slaves) from military service, and they lost many of their privileges before the law. By the end of the empire, there was little to distinguish the varieties of rural workers; in practice all were tied to their plots.

Finley convincingly argued that the relative decline of slavery in the later Roman empire "was a reversal of the process by which slavery took hold." Private ownership of land was still concentrated in the hands of a small group, but commodity production declined along with the urban markets.[78] The key element in the decline of slavery was that *coloni* were now available for labor, and owners no longer had to rely as heavily on slaves. In the retreat to the countryside, owners took slaves with them and established workshops for small-scale production for local consumption.[79]

For all these reasons, in the fifth and sixth centuries when the Roman Empire in the west disintegrated into a series of successor states ruled by Germanic conquerors, slavery retained less significance than it had under the Roman Republic and the first phases of the empire, but it had not disappeared, nor would it. On a theoretical plane, Roman law took little note of the structural changes. In practice, too, slavery continued as a social reality, although by then the numbers of slaves were greatly reduced.

While the Roman Empire was disintegrating in the west, its eastern portion remained cohesive and was able to last for a thousand years, although it lost Syria, Palestine, Egypt, and much of North Africa to the Muslims in the seventh and eighth centuries. The Byzantine Empire, as the eastern portion came to be called, maintained control of its Balkan heartland and part of Anatolia until the fifteenth century, when Ottoman Turks took Constantinople. In the fifth, sixth, and seventh centuries, Byzantine slavery preserved most of the features of Roman slavery.

The sources of slaves in the Byzantine Empire were much the same as before. Children were sold to pay the debts of their parents, although Byzantine laws tried in vain to prevent such sales. The practice of exposure continued, too, and until the sixth century those who found exposed infants could raise them as slaves. Children born to a slave woman were slaves themselves; they belonged to the woman's master, even if the master himself were the father. Such children remained slaves even if the mother were later freed, but any subsequent children she bore as a freedwoman were free. There was an exception to this rule: a slave concubine who lived with her owner until his death was thereafter freed, together with any children she had borne him.[80]

War, the great generator of slaves in the period of Rome's expansion, continued to provide slaves for the Byzantine world. Major wars of conquest were long past, but frequent frontier skirmishes provided prisoners, who often became slaves. Allowing captured enemies to be ransomed was an uncommon practice, because selling prisoners of war as slaves was a great source of Byzantine income. On the other hand, it was considered a sacred duty to ransom Byzantine prisoners, a duty incumbent on all levels of society, from the emperor down to the families of the captives. If a Byzantine ransomed his fellow citizens, they were obliged to repay their redemptor, and those who could not do so were required to work for the rescuer for five years, often as virtual slaves. Still other slaves were the product of a slave trade that was mainly directed toward the northern frontiers and the shores of the Black Sea. Many Byzantine towns and cities had slave markets; the one in Constantinople, appropriately enough, was located in the Valley of Lamentations.[81]

From the late fourth century onward, the Byzantine church occupied an influential place in the Byzantine state. The relationship between church and state in Byzantium was far more intimate than in the medieval West, due in large measure to the Byzantine emperor's unquestioned position as head of the church. As we have seen, Christianity did not advocate abolition, but church leaders did suggest some ameliorations for the lives and conditions of slaves. The Byzantine church, tied as it was to the state, at times adopted ambivalent or contradictory positions. Church officials did, for example, allow slaves to flee to church property to seek sanctuary from oppressive masters, but they examined each fugitive carefully to determine the merits of the individual case and did what they could to reconcile slaves with their masters. Marriage was considered to be almost the duty of the Christian laity—or at the very least a privilege—but if slaves married they would be entering into a legal contract, and that would violate the principle that a slave had no legal personality. Not until 1095 did a Byzantine emperor permit slaves to be married before a priest, an innovation that took some time to become fully accepted.[82]

One special feature of slavery in the Byzantine Empire was the extensive use of eunuchs in positions of public trust and authority. Eunuchs had been used in the Roman Empire, but their presence was much more forceful among the Byzantines, where they formed a special corps of administrators for the emperors.[83]

Byzantine slavery did decline over the course of the Middle Ages, and the conditions that slaves lived under gradually improved. The decline in numbers of slaves, however, was due to structural changes in the economy, rather than to enlightened legislation by the emperors or moral pronouncements by the church officials. In the sixth century, when slavery was still at its height, the emperor Justinian (527–65) embarked on a course designed to restore the empire to its former glory. Many of his initiatives, such as the effort to reconquer the lands of the western empire, failed, but he did have some solid accomplishments. For the history of slavery, the most important was his codification of Roman law.

Roman law before Justinian was a confusing mixture of senatorial legislation, imperial decrees, and the opinions of jurists. It lacked order and cohesion. Justinian created a panel of legal scholars to bring order to the system; the product of their work was the *Corpus iuris civilis,* the body of the civil law, commonly called the Code of Justinian. Composed of four sections, the code provided a compendium of legal doctrine by which Byzantium was governed until its demise. First was the *Codex*, a compilation of Roman legislation. The *Institutes* made up a manual and guide to jurisprudence. The *Digest* contained the laws that were commonly in use in the sixth century and provided references to the time and circumstances of their enactments. The *Novels* were the new laws created by Justinian, and this section was expanded by his successors.[84]

Justinian's law code provided a finely worked instrument for Byzantine administration throughout the Middle Ages. In addition to its value to modern scholars as an historical source, it had a crucial impact on the continuity of slavery in the Western world. Rediscovered in western Europe in the eleventh century, it formed the basis of the legal codes of many European kingdoms, most notably for our purposes, Spain and Portugal. Even before the great expansion of slavery in the fifteenth and sixteenth centuries, while slavery still lived but was of relatively small importance in the economies of the states of Mediterranean Europe, the rediscovery of the *Corpus iuris civilis* provided Western lawyers and legislators with an easily available manual for the administration of a slave system.

Justinian's code was one component of the dual legacy of the Romans. They bequeathed to the medieval West an ongoing, if diminished, slave system and a sophisticated legal code with elaborate rules for operating such a system.

PART II
SLAVERY IN
MEDIEVAL EUROPE,
THE WORLD OF ISLAM,
AND AFRICA

3

SLAVERY IN
EARLY MEDIEVAL EUROPE

In the seven hundred years between the fifth century and the twelfth, the history of slavery in western Europe shows a continuing transformation of rural slavery and the replacement of rural slaves by a dependent peasantry. In short, it is the story of how serfdom gradually supplanted slavery.[1] The transformation was never total, and we will see that Europeans held slaves long after 1100, but the vast majority of slaves who remained were not agricultural workers. Rather, they were domestics or artisans or the assistants of artisans. Consequently, the medieval West was not a slave society. The elite, it is true, still derived much of its wealth from the land, but the land was worked by peasants, who, while not totally free, nonetheless had certain guaranteed rights and therefore a different legal position from that of slaves. Even though rural slavery practically ceased to exist in Europe, slavery persisted, both in a legal sense and in actual practice. When the economic circumstances changed again in the fifteenth and sixteenth centuries, as large-scale plantation agriculture reemerged, the West had to invent no new institutional rules for the use of slaves.

FROM SLAVERY TO SERFDOM

This evolution cannot be understood without considering the general political, social, and economic changes that western Europe experienced, changes whose complexity must not be underestimated. There were two major time divisions in the early Middle Ages. First was the period of the Germanic successor kingdoms to the Roman Empire, from the fifth to the eighth century, and the attempt by Charlemagne (786–814) to reunify western Europe. His reign can be seen as a transition between the first period and the second, which ran from the ninth to the late eleventh century, during which serfdom gradually developed and Europe began its rise as a mature, expanding, and developing region.

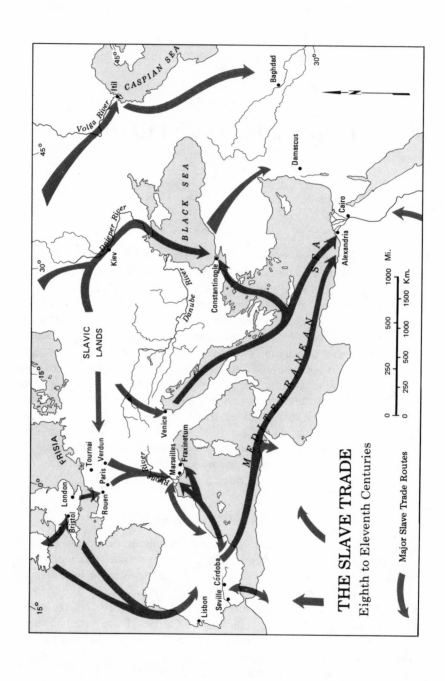

THE SLAVE TRADE
Eighth to Eleventh Centuries

Major Slave Trade Routes

CASPIAN SEA

Volga River

Itil

Baghdad

45°

30°

Damascus

BLACK SEA

Dnieper River

Kiev

Danube River

Constantinople

Cairo

Alexandria

MEDITERRANEAN SEA

SLAVIC
LANDS

FRISIA

London

Bristol

Rouen

Paris

Tournai

Verdun

Rhône River

Marseilles

Fraxinetum

Venice

Lisbon

Seville

Córdoba

0   250   500   1000 Mi.
0   250   500   1000   1500 Km.

In the first period, while the Byzantines were preserving the Roman Empire in the east and developing a distinctive civilization there, Germanic tribal leaders were carving the empire's western portion into kingdoms. Despite considerable scholarship over the years, a lack of sources concerning the Germans before they entered the empire has limited what can be known about them, but we do know that in the first four centuries A.D. they developed a more complex agricultural and pastoral economy, and undertook a certain amount of trade with the empire. During the third and fourth centuries they began to display an increasing desire to enter imperial territory. The reasons for the vast Germanic migrations are open to speculation, but a number of likely motivations are apparent. Their newly develped agriculture had contributed to something of a population explosion among the Germans, and they quite reasonably looked to the warmer lands of the south, with their more easily worked soils, for better farming conditions. Agricultural technology and practice were several millennia old by then and were based on the scratch plow, a device originally invented in the Middle East and successfully adopted by Mediterranean peoples. Such a plow was well suited to the semiarid regions with light soils characteristic of both the Middle East and the lands around the Mediterranean. The scratch plow and the ancient harnessing techniques were totally unsuited for most of the land of continental Europe north of the Alps and the Pyrenees, where rainfall was abundant, vegetation was dense, and soil was compact and clinging. Until heavier plows and improved harnesses were invented and their use became general, agriculture could not spread widely and rapidly in continental Europe.

Additionally, in the fourth century, the nomadic Huns from central Asia began to push upon the most easterly of the Germanic tribes, triggering a chain reaction of pressure impelling the Germans west and south. With their empire already weakened internally, the Romans could not resist this pressure completely, and later emperors allowed small groups of Germans into the empire as federates, granting them land for settlement in return for their assistance in frontier defense. By the beginning of the fifth century, the Germans' insistence on entry increased, and, starting with the Visigoths, entire nations of Germans forced the borders open and took imperial territory by force and by threats. That the eastern empire could defend itself sufficiently to turn the Germans westward is one additional indication of the superior resources and cohesion of Byzantium. The Visigoths breached the Roman dam, and thereafter waves of German tribes overflowed the West: Ostrogoths, Vandals, Lombards, Franks, and many others, including the Angles and Saxons, who combined to create the English kingdoms.

For slavery as a legal and social institution, the creation of the Germanic kingdoms meant little change. In one degree or another, the tribes before the invasions had known slavery and permitted slave trading.[2] Nevertheless, there were some alterations in legal practice and slight variations in the sorts of people enslaved and the uses to which they were put. Even before the Germans reached southern Gaul, there had been a series of slave revolts against the Roman masters there, and Romans at times had been enslaved by their former Gallic slaves.[3] The Germans entered imperial territory as agriculturists, and two groups in the first wave, the Visigoths and the Vandals, had as their goal the rich grainlands of Roman North Africa, the imperial breadbasket. Only the Vandals reached Africa; the other Germans remained in Europe. Once they took Roman lands, the new Germanic settlers often practiced "thirding," taking one-third of the slaves and two-thirds of the land for themselves, and leaving the Roman proprietors the remainder. Slaves of the Romans at times won their freedom by fleeing their masters to join the armies of the invaders.[4]

In theory, too, slavery persisted. Finding their orally preserved customary law inferior to the written Roman code, the Germanic kings employed Roman jurists to convert their legal traditions into written form. As they wrote down the Germanic customs, the Roman scholars almost unconsciously allowed part of their own legal heritage to slip into the Germanic laws. For a time, the Germans allowed the subject Romans and Roman provincials to live under their own laws, but later true amalgamations of the two legal systems were produced. Despite the many obvious differences that separated the Romans and the Germans, common features were to be found among both, as Georges Duby pointed out.

> Neither Roman nor Germanic society was composed of equals. Both alike acknowledged the pre-eminence of a nobility, constituting the senatorial class in the Empire and comprising kinsmen and companions of war-leaders in the barbarian clans. . . . Both societies practiced slavery, and perennial warfare kept up the numbers of a servile class, replenished each summer by forays into the territories of neighboring peoples. The migrations . . . hardened these inequalities by ruralizing the Roman aristocracy and blending with it the barbarian nobility, as well as extending the field of military aggression and thereby revitalizing slavery, which found renewed vigor on all frontiers where different ethnic groups were coming face to face on the turbulent confines of the Christian world.[5]

Since slavery was present in Germanic law and prominent in Roman, it is not surprising that, with few exceptions, the rules governing slaves survived intact.

Sources of slaves were much the same as they had been in the Roman Empire: birth, capture in war, the merchandise of the slave trade, and the rearing of exposed children. In addition, many barbarians entered Roman territory singly or in small groups, and many of them became slaves whose descendants remained in that situation for centuries. In the Germanic kingdoms, enslavement of the freely born as the consequence of criminal convictions was more far-reaching than it had been among the Romans, as was the practice of the poverty-stricken selling themselves as the only alternative to starvation. In the Anglo-Saxon kingdom, penal slavery often was imposed for refusal to comply with judicial decisions. In Visigothic Spain, the same applied, as well as slavery as a mandatory penalty for certain offenses. Public crimes carried the possibility of enslavement to the royal treasury or to a person the king designated.[6]

Germans did not enslave the conquered Romans and provincials in a wholesale fashion, and domestic warfare did not usually produce slaves. The Germans seem to have felt considerable compunction about enslaving those defined as part of their own group, although by allowing slavery for debt, criminal sentence, and self-sale, they exhibited a more relaxed attitude than the Romans had. However, there was always an uneasiness attached to the slavery of one's own. So the Germans were forced to look beyond the immediate group for slaves. Their search was simplified by the ethnic and religious divisions present in the regions they conquered. The Anglo-Saxons enslaved some of the conquered Celts in Britain. Because each considered the other to be heretics, Arian Christians used Catholics as slaves, and vice versa. When the Catholic Franks conquered southern Gaul from the Arian Visigoths, huge numbers of captives entered the slave markets. Pagans and Jews could be made slaves by Christians of every persuasion, and slave traders always brought slaves from distant lands. Captured Slavs, who gave their name to slavery in every Western language, were brought through western Europe to be sold in the Mediterranean lands, and pagan slaves from North Africa reached France and Spain in the mid-sixth century.[7]

Drawing harsh distinctions between slave and free, the legal codes of the Germanic kingdoms were quite explicit in their pronouncements concerning slaves. A slave was deprived of most legal rights. He could not bear arms; he could not initiate legal actions; his testimony in most cases was invalid without his master's corroboration; and unlike free men he could be tortured. The Germanic law codes usually called for compensation to be paid to the victims of crimes or to their kinsmen. Each free person had a price, a *wergeld*, which a murderer or his family would have to pay to the victim's family. A slave had a smaller price, and his master collected it. Whereas slaves usually were punished by their masters for their crimes, the sovereign was responsible ultimately for the punishment of free transgressors.[8]

Distinctions of status were quite apparent in the penalties imposed for criminal acts. As illustrated by the Burgundian Code, the compensation for a Burgundian's knocking out a person's tooth depended on the victim's status: for upper-class Burgundians and Romans, fifteen *solidi*; for the middle ranks, ten; and for the lowest order, five. If a slave of the Burgundians did such a deed intentionally, he lost his hand; if unintentionally, he or his master could pay according to a scale based on the victim's status. If someone knocked out a slave's tooth, the master, not the slave, received compensation. For many offenses a free perpetrator could get off with a payment of money, but a slave was beaten. For aggravated assault on a maidservant, a native freeman was to pay twelve *solidi*; a slave was to receive 150 blows. A slave could be condemned to death for stealing a horse or a cow, and receive 300 blows for stealing lesser livestock.[9] If a slave seduced a slave woman in the Merovingian Frankish kingdom, he could be castrated as punishment.[10]

With wide powers over his chattel, a German master could sell, trade, or dispose of his slaves with little limitation. While a slave of the Germans often possessed a *peculium*, the master retained legal ownership of it.[11] German slave-owners generally had the right to judge and punish their slaves, a right at times extended to all their tenants, whether slave or free.[12] Among the Visigoths, a master had the right to judge and punish his slaves if no outsider were involved.[13] Gregory of Tours, writing in the Merovingian Frankish kingdom during the sixth century, preserved a horrifying story of the punishment one master meted out. Two slaves fled to a bishop to be married. Their master, named Rauching, pursued them, and the bishop, after receiving Rauching's pledge not to punish them, forced them to return. Rauching promised that

> they never shall be parted by me but I will rather cause them to continue in this union permanently, because, although it is annoying to me that this was done without my consent, still I welcome this feature of it, that he has not married a maid belonging to another nor she another's slave.[14]

Rauching's idea of fostering a permanent union was to bury the slaves alive together. The gullible bishop got word of the deed and hurried to the scene in time to save the man but not the woman. Merovingian times were harsh and brutal, but this story was undoubtedly not typical. Gregory was not a dispassionate observer, but a moralist, and even if he did not invent or exaggerate, the story must have been sufficiently unusual for him to bother recording it.

At the very least, Gregory's tale illustrates that masters still had much to say about the marriages of their slaves. In the Visigothic kingdom, too, slave marriages were not allowed without the master's permission, and children born to a slave couple belonging to two different masters were divided equally between the masters, with a monetary payment compensating for an odd number of offspring.[15] On the other hand, there were some improvements, especially for couples of different status. In Merovingian France, there were possibilities of slave and free marrying without necessarily condemning their children to slavery, and the children of unfree mothers could be free if they were dedicated to the church. In Spain, a master's permission was required for matches between the free and the nonfree.[16]

Mitigating rules sometimes surface. King Alfred, the Anglo-Saxon ruler of England from 871 to 899, decreed that

> the four Wednesdays in the Ember weeks are to be given to all slaves [as holidays], to sell to whomsoever they choose anything of what anyone has

given them, in God's name, or which they can earn in their leisure moments.[17]

Even if we can point out some marginal improvements in the status of slaves in the early Middle Ages, we should not conclude that slaves in the Germanic kingdoms did not hate their status and try to escape from it. Fugitive slaves were so common in the Visigothic kingdom that detailed regulations for dealing with them became embodied in the legal code. Rewards for those who returned fugitives were coupled with punishments for those who harbored them. Free people who disguised slaves by cutting their long hair, a mark of slavery, were treated as harshly as those who encouraged them to flee. Even if the slave's flight were successful, he could not legally attain freedom until a considerable period, usually thirty to fifty years, had passed.[18]

An innovation in the early German states was the military use of slaves. Perhaps because slaves of the Romans had joined the invaders and fought beside them, or perhaps because the Germans were a small minority wherever they established themselves and needed to augment their forces, on occasion the Germanic monarchs required all those who were to fight in the royal hosts to bring with them one-tenth of their slaves, under the threat of confiscations for those who did not comply. These slaves were not just nonmilitary support forces; they were armed infantry and fought side by side with the free.[19]

Neither church doctrine nor practice proposed the abolition of slavery, and Robert Latouche has argued that by preaching resignation in the face of temporal conditions the church in fact helped to preserve the institution.[20] The church did impose certain restraints on slaveowners and did secure some improved conditions for the slaves. However, although it encouraged manumission for the slaves of laymen, it kept a close hold on its own. In the Frankish monarchy, at least, masters could not kill their slaves without risking excommunication. Ordination of the nonfree was still difficult and unusual, and, although fugitives must have sought refuge often in the monasteries to escape their lords, the abbots would not receive them without their masters' permission. Through the accumulation of power and real estate, the church found itself in possession of large numbers of slaves. One eighth-century law code specified their duties.

> Slaves of the church shall render their tribute in accordance with the law: fifteen measures of barley beer, a pig worth one *tremissis*, two measures of bread . . . , five chickens and twenty eggs. Female slaves shall carry out their prescribed tasks conscientiously. Male slaves shall perform half the ploughing service on their own account, half on the demesne. . . .[21]

Slaves and freedmen of the church were subject to ecclesiastical courts. Church slaves were so common that one Visigothic church council even decreed that a parish church had to own one hundred slaves or it could not be assigned a priest. Lay persons were often patrons of monasteries and parish churches, and, at clerical insistence, the Frankish kings prohibited lay patrons from arbitrarily freeing slaves of the church. Although the church did prescribe better treatment for its slaves, they found it difficult to attain freedom because their institutional master was permanent; they could not benefit from manumission by testament.[22]

Of the paths to freedom, manumission was still the safest. There were a few instances of freedom granted as a result of a slaveowner's having been convicted of a crime, but most emancipations came from the voluntary action of the master. As in Roman times, manumissions could be done by means of testament or by actions taken during the master's lifetime. Unlike the Roman experience, most manumissions were performed by authorities of the church, not by the state. In Anglo-Saxon England, crossroads were usual, and quite fitting, places for the acts of manumission, symbolic of the ability of the freed to choose their own path. Often slaves exchanged one form of servitude for another lighter one, when they were freed on entrance into one of the manors as serfs. Also, again unlike Roman times, emancipation could be revoked for actions the masters deemed unacceptable, principally ingratitude. Finally, the freed slaves often were subject to certain legal disabilities, as the Roman freedmen had been.[23]

In the Germanic states a complex gradation existed among the nonfree, who made up a sizable percentage of the population. To the number of slaves were added the former *coloni* of Roman times and their descendants. The Roman *coloni* had been considered personally free but bound to their plot of land. *Coloni* still existed in early medieval Europe, and many lords seem to have ignored the fine distinctions and lumped together both slaves and *coloni* as unfree persons subject to the lords and tied to their plots of land.[24]

In the period of the successor states of the western Roman Empire there was a progressive ruralization of the economy and the society. This signaled a continuation of the conditions of the later Roman Empire in the West, and, although the towns and urban life never completely disappeared, the countryside and rural pursuits were far more important. The rural slaves varied considerably in their degrees of status. Among the slaves of the nobility, the *idonei* occupied the positions of trust in the lord's household, acting as house managers, estate managers, record keepers, and other specialists. They were the most privileged servile group, able to escape the most onerous rules of slavery. Certainly they were a small minority among the slaves, most of whom were domestic servants and agricultural workers (*vilis* or *vilissimi* and *rusticani*). Most slaves worked the lord's land and enjoyed land tenure of a sort (land could be part of the *peculium*). In this way their status approached that of later medieval serfs. Throughout Europe, the greater labor requirements as a consequence of the extension of agriculture into newly cleared lands and the introduction of specialization, such as vine growing, allowed some agricultural laborers to secure improved conditions of land tenure, and thereby better status.[25]

Similar to the Roman *familia Caesaris* were the crown slaves, called *pueri regales* or *pueri aulici* in the Merovingian kingdom, who filled royal offices and had a much higher status than ordinary slaves. They could be witnesses in court, unlike other slaves. They could own slaves of their own, but could free them only with the lord's permission. Crown slaves served the king in the royal administration and ran the crown estates. Many had begun their careers as *idonei* of other lords, and if the king were impressed with their competence he often took them into royal service, much to the annoyance of their former masters.[26]

In the early Middle Ages, the transition from slavery to serfdom in rural Europe moved almost imperceptibly. Its consequence was "one of the great landmarks in labour history and was undoubtedly a decisive factor in economic development"[27]—the creation of the great medieval landholding unit, the villa or the manor. Similar to the villas of late Roman times, the medieval villa was characterized by a two-part division of the arable (cultivable) land: one part, the demesne, was reserved by the lord (*dominus*) for his direct use; the remainder was granted to the peasant families in individual plots, called *manses* in French and *mansi* in Latin. Peasants worked on their own lands, for which they gave the lord part of their production as rent, and they were required to work part of the time on the lord's demesne.

This development was a fundamental change from the classic Roman villa, worked exclusively by gangs of slaves. Even before the end of the empire, the owners of villas were replacing slave gangs with *coloni* and *servi casati* (slaves given their own plots). This process was not complete by the time the empire ended, and slave gangs persisted on large estates into the Middle Ages. The slaves were designated in the early medieval documents as *servi* (sing. *servus*); female slaves were often called *ancillae* (sing. *ancilla*); a variant term was *mancipia* (sing. *mancipium*). The bishop of Le Mans, Domnole, in 572 granted several properties to the Abbey of Saint-Vincent in Le Mans. On one, the villa of Tresson, all the workers living on the lands of the villa were designated as *mancipia* and were living in the master's house and outbuildings. They were granted to the abbey along with the other property of the villa and included a man and his wife and child, four male and two female servants, and a stable boy. On another holding, the Villa Fraxnetum (La Frênaie in French), ten *mancipia* made up the labor force. Not all estates in the early Middle Ages were worked by slaves, but Duby reports that no large estate in the seventh century for which records remain did not have at least some slaves.[28]

Nonetheless, slavery was dying out in the countryside; everywhere in continental Europe a new system of agricultural management was replacing it. The lands of the estates gradually came to be divided into manses worked by *coloni*, a direct continuation of the process at work in the late empire. The reasons to account for it are several and simple. Rural workers with their own plots would require less supervision. Because they owed their lords part of what they produced, the workers would make the payments in kind that the lords wanted. Self-sufficiency for the estate was one of the major goals, with the sale of the excess production in local markets. No great urban markets yet existed in Europe. The workers may have worked more efficiently on their own plots, and, as a result, the lords may have enjoyed higher returns and the arable may well have been extended. The lords also could demand labor services on the demesne. The burdens of raising new workers from birth to their productive years now fell on the parents instead of the lords. As many former slaves were given permission to marry and the possession of a family farm, the birth rate and the survival rate of those born both increased. Slowly, intermarriage between the slaves and the *coloni* brought about a leveling of the social status of those at the lower end of the hierarchy.[29]

This process was characteristic of the large estates already in existence. There was a parallel development as other large estates came into being. In parts of France there were villages called *vici* (sing. *vicus*) composed of small farmers. Due to a need for protection, or perhaps because of coercion on the part of the local lords, the inhabitants of these *vici* gave up their independent status in exchange for the protection only a powerful lord could provide. Together with the granting of individual plots on the villas to the former slaves, the transformation of *vici* into villas marked a further step in the assimilation of the former slaves and the former free into an increasingly homogeneous group of dependent rural workers.[30] The process was not yet complete; in fact, it would never be completed during the Middle Ages, and the persistence of the slave trade meant that some slaves still entered western Europe.

In the late eighth and early ninth centuries, Charlemagne, the ruler of the Frankish kingdom, created an empire for himself and tried to revitalize the West. Through inheritance, conquest, diplomacy, and threats, Charlemagne extended his control over the greater part of western Europe, excluding only Scandinavia, the British Isles, the Iberian Peninsula, and southern Italy. He crowned his achievements by the assumption of the title of Roman emperor on Christmas Day in the year 800. Poorly educated himself, he drew scholars to his court in an effort to stimulate intellectual life, particularly literacy. Deeply concerned with efficient management of his kingdom and the royal properties under his control, he issued numerous proclamations about estate management and insisted on detailed record keeping. In this written evidence we can find firm indications that, although slavery persisted during the Carolingian period, the transition to serfdom on the rural estates continued.

After Charlemange's conquest of Saxony, during which many pagan Saxons were enslaved, he set up a network of parish churches. To provide for the maintenance of the priest and the church, those living in the parish were to donate a house and land as well as a male and female slave to the church for every 120 people in the parish.[31] That the state owned slaves is indicated by a provision that if royal agents were called in to mediate the settlement of an estate, the royal treasury would be compensated by receiving one-tenth of the land and the slaves of the estate.[32] Numerous past practices continued. Church regulations still insisted on the owner's permission for slaves to enter holy orders. Slaves of the crown, male and female, could enter the life of the church provided "that they should not receive the tonsure or the veil except in moderation, and only where there are enough of them and the estates will not be deserted."[33]

Our evidence from the private estates in the Carolingian period most clearly shows the evolution away from the use of slave gangs and toward dividing the estates into manses. These manses were of various sorts; the larger were held by the free, the smaller by slave families. Even if a slave were allotted a less desirable manse, he still found through his attachment to it a more secure life for himself and his descendants. No longer was he likely to be sold to a different master and forced to move; now if the estate changed hands he would retain his manse. The *servi*, still designated by the ancient word for slave, were attaining in practice and custom the situation of serfs, whose full definition would not be set until the late Middle Ages. *Servi* had different labor requirements from those of the free (*franci* or *coloni*): they usually had to work three days each week on the demesne, whereas the free had specified tasks that usually fell due at specified times during the year. Although their status was hereditary and their freedom limited, the *servi* were not yet subject to all the obligations of serfdom that would arise later. Only a few of them were subject to the tax of *chevage* in the Carolingian period. They were tied to their plot of land and its owner, who had the right to pursue fugitives and punish offenders. Marriage to a woman owned by another master created problems of ownership of the children, but already in the ninth century masters were agreeing to such marriages if the *servus* made a monetary payment. *Servi* were still excluded from taking holy orders and testifying in court.[34]

Household slaves, the lord's *familia*, still remained; their numbers were far smaller in continental Europe, although many were still present on Mediterranean estates. In most parts of the Carolingian empire, their status was improving. Some household slaves came to be entrusted with such specialized tasks as milling, brewing, baking, and management. A few former household slaves occupied even higher positions as agents of the greater nobles and the kings. As such they were known as *ministeriales* or *chevaliers-serfs*.[35]

Charlemagne's coordination of his empire was remarkably successful and restored a high degree of state authority in the regions under his control; but his consolidation, far from creating a centralized government, was personal and required a strong and farsighted ruler. Unfortunately, his successors lacked his vision, his ability, and his opportunities. Within two generations his empire was divided and royal authority was in a steep decline. For over two centuries after Charlemagne's death in 814, Europe disintegrated into a number of components. The western portion, which had felt the onslaught of the Muslim invasion in the eighth century, found itself in the ninth and tenth threatened by Viking raids from the north, while the eastern portion had to turn back the Magyar incursions. Weak monarchs and the need for local defense caused governmental authority to devolve into smaller units over much of Europe: counties in the western Frankish area (modern France), duchies in the German areas, and bishoprics and cities in Italy. Only the Anglo-Saxon monarchs were able to retain a fairly strong control, although they lost territory to the Danes and were forced to pay them protection money.

In the area that would become France, the disintegration proceeded most rapidly, and feudalism developed earliest there. In the system of feudal government, the petty rulers, counts for the most part, became de facto sovereigns in the areas under their control, with military, economic, and judicial powers over the regions' inhabitants. This was not an overnight change; rather it was the logical culmination of preexisting patterns. The counts under Charlemagne in theory had been the crown's representatives, but in fact they were free to do much as they liked, subject only to dismissal by the ruler. The localization of government was a consequence of the economic disintegration of an underdeveloped Europe, unable to produce and distribute goods over wide areas, unable to create a sufficient surplus to maintain a bureaucracy or a military machine capable of asserting control over large regions.

Intimately related to feudalism as a governmental system was the growth of seignorialism as its economic and social corollary. Subject to the same internal and external stresses, the economy paralleled the breakdown of government, influenced it, and in turn was influenced by it. For protection from invasion and from acquisitive neighbors, each feudal lord had a fortified stronghold. By means of his band of armed retainers and the judicial power he exercised, the lord could dominate and control the peasants living on his lands. Yet this is only part of the story. For the peasants, the lord represented oppression but also the only protection they could hope for in a threatened world. The peasants, with no other course open to them, willingly, if perhaps reluctantly, exchanged the vestiges of their freedom for the lord's protection and a guaranteed home on his estate. This was in essence the final consequence of the leveling process which, since the later Roman Empire, had found the free poor depressed into servile status and amalgamated with the slaves.

In this period, from the tenth to the twelfth century, the manor was the characteristic economic and social unit. Generally similar to the later Roman and early medieval villa (although the word *villa* in time came to be applied to a village of hamlet), the manor was divided into the lord's portion (demesne or *réserve*) and farms for the peasants. The demesne comprised the manor house (simple or elaborate according to time and place), barns and other buildings, a garden and the lands for various uses: arable, pastures for grazing, perhaps a vineyard, and certainly woods and wasteland. Each laborer's farm consisted of a house, a small gardenplot, and a share in the arable and grazing lands not part of the demesne. In addition, each worker had the right to collect some wood and to keep pigs in the woods and wasteland. Because of the constant need for protection that existed throughout the Middle Ages and beyond, the houses were grouped tightly together. The nuclear agricultural village thus became the typical pattern, and many such villages survive in Europe today. The increased security amply compensated for the inconvenience of walking from home to the fields and back each day.

The unitary manor, with all the farm owned by the lord and consigned to the peasants and with the manor house at its center, is the one most often diagrammed in the general textbooks, but it was probably not the most characteristic. Two other types predominated: one in which the farms were held by both free and subject tenants, and another in which the manor house was in one of several villages under the lord's control.[36]

The peasant could devote most of his time to working his personal holdings, in particular the arable, which was divided into a number of large plots that he often shared with the other peasants. Each individual had the right to grow grain on strips in several of the plots. He could graze cows on the pasture lands or harvested fields and grow vegetables and herbs on his garden plot. In return for hereditary control over his farm, the peasant owed the lord certain obligations. In the early period, these were mainly labor services: plowing, weeding, and harvesting the lord's portion of the arable; and repairs to the lord's buildings, bridges, and roads. By the eleventh century, obligations were becoming better defined, and they usually related to the type of manse the peasant held. There were two major types and a less usual third type. *Manses ingénuiles* were those granted originally to the free. They were larger than the manses of the other major type and their holders owed less burdensome dues: transporting the wood and the harvests, and seasonal duties at the time of plowing, haying, and harvest. By contrast, the *manses serviles* had been granted originally to slaves. They were smaller and the holder usually owed the lord three days' labor each week of the year.[37] The third type of manse, unusual everywhere but seen more often in Germany than France, was the *manse lidile*, whose origins and functions are more obscure than those of the other two. Guy Fourquin stated that such manses had been granted to the freed, as opposed to the slave or the free, but Robert Latouche believed the term had an older origin and was derived from plots granted to *laeti* or barbarian settlers.[38]

The proliferation of manses clearly revealed a further progression of the movement toward granting individual plots to the peasants. Why the change? Why didn't the lord simply maintain slave gangs to do the work? To answer, we have to review the economic and political changes under way from late Roman times through the early Middle Ages. Agricultural slavery only worked properly when the government was strong enough to prevent runaways and keep the workers on the land. It was only feasible in an economic sense when a flourishing market system allowed specialized commodities to be sold in the towns for money. As Rome declined and as medieval Europe developed, both features were lacking. The govenments were weak and the market economy was restricted. With the cities in decline, there were no great urban markets. From the lord's point of view, it was better to make the manor as self-sufficient as possible, although true self-sufficiency was never achieved. It was always necessary to purchase such trade items as salt and iron. In these circumstances, with both government and economy weak, the local lords no doubt thought it was better to dispense with the use of slaves and to secure a more dependable, contented, and cheaper labor force by granting improved conditions to the workers, giving them security of tenure and individual houses and plots. In return the workers would devote a portion of their time to work the demesne, so many days per week, with more time devoted during periods of plowing, planting, and harvesting. In this manner, the lords could obtain sufficient labor for the demesne without having to maintain slaves during the long periods of each year when there was nothing for them to do. The output of the demesne provided the lord with supplies of food to maintain his family and retinue, and generally a small surplus to sell in the admittedly restricted market. The money he received would in turn allow him to buy the needed items and goods he could not produce locally.[39]

The labor-saving devices invented or adopted in the early Middle Ages were truly impressive: better plows to cope with the dense soils of continental Europe, harnesses that permitted horses and oxen to pull heavier loads and to be harnessed in tandem, horseshoes for better traction, and water mills. Invented at various times and places in the early Middle Ages, the use of these devices became general by about the mid-eleventh century. Their increased use reduced human labor requirements, causing still another motivation for using fewer slaves to perform the necessary tasks, while the free, who needed less supervision, could be farm workers. Improved draft animals, the product of centuries of selective breeding, further eased the requirements for human labor.[40] As a consequence of all these changes, slavery ceased to be the normal pattern for rural labor in western Europe. We can see very easily that the social organization of the early Middle Ages (and of the late Roman colonate) was a transitional phase between productive agrarian slavery and the fully developed serfdom of the later medieval period.

There remained other slaves, those not engaged in farming. Domestic slavery certainly continued, although we do not know much about its specifics in the early Middle Ages. The remaining cities and towns, as well as the larger manors, provided places for the skilled slaves in technological activities, in the sort of pursuits practiced by the Roman industrial slaves. Manufactured goods of common use—glassware, pottery, metal work—were necessary items and were produced in the towns in small artisan shops owned by free people and worked at times by slaves. On the estates, too, slave artisans, especially textile workers, labored under the direction of the higher class of the lord's slaves. Specialized occupations on the manor—managers, record keepers, smiths, messengers, soldiers, beekeepers, experts in cattle raising—were filled by the lord's dependents, who had the same servile legal status as the agricultural laborers, but who through their skills attained a better and more highly regarded status than the others. For the skilled occupations, the children of the servile families on the manors formed a pool of potential trainees, which the lords could tap as needed.[41] The assimilation of the formerly free and slave into a more or less uniform class of serfs was a process that moved with glacial slowness, but it was substantially complete by the twelfth century. Free peasants became serfs by their own choice only rarely; far more often the peasant family went through several generations of small changes in their condition, while lord and peasant alike commonly came to regard their status as servile. The relatively infrequent manumissions of slaves had a considerable cumulative impact over the long term.

Language itself altered as the new social realities were recognized. The word for serf comes from the Latin word *servus*, slave, but the medieval serf was far different from the *servus* of the Romans. Administrators and legists of the Middle Ages, whose written language was Latin and whose training was in Roman law, simply applied the word the Romans had used to describe their lowest class to the lowest class of medieval society. The word *servus* (as well as the feminine variant, *ancilla*) was transformed so completely from its original meaning that it could no longer be used to describe true chattel servitude and ceased to be used in France around the early twelfth century. To describe the true slaves a new word was coined, derived from the most numerous ethnic group in the medieval slave trade, the Slavs. The word has cognates in all Western languages: *slave* in English, *esclave* in French, *esclavo* in Spanish, *escravo* in Portuguese, *schiavo* in Italian, and *Sklave* in German.[42] At the same time, the word *serf* came to be used to describe dependent peasants.

France, where the slave trade was least important, had the earliest and most complete development of serfdom. Marc Bloch reported that in the village of Thiais in the region of Paris, the heads of households changed from less than 20 percent servile in the early ninth century to almost 100 percent by the late twelfth.[43] We should note that neither were the manors of the Middle Ages ordinarily in the same spots the Roman villas had occupied, nor were the new serfs necessarily the biological descendants of the Roman *coloni* and slaves.

The medieval serf was not a slave. No longer was the dependent class absolutely subject to the whims of the owner. Master and serf were bound together in a web of mutual rights, obligations, and economic relations. Fundamentally, the lord was to provide land, protection, and justice to his dependents. In compensation, they turned over a portion of what they produced, both directly in a crop-sharing arrangement and indirectly in the numerous customary payments they owed. Among the direct charges was the *chevage*, which, while small, signified the obedience the lord demanded. The lord had a monopoly of justice, and the fines he levied in his court were a source of extra income and a powerful tool for economic exploitation. He had the ability to approve or disapprove marriage between persons of different statuses, and between one of his dependents and one belonging to a different lord. Permission for such a marriage (*formariage*) could be granted, but the lord exacted a monetary compensation. On the death of a serf, the lord could demand a tax on inheritance (*mainmorte*), consisting of the best animal, the best piece of furniture, or a monetary settlement. The lord maintained certain monopolies (*banalités*) to ensure a return on his capital investments. Only the lord's water mill could be used, only his bake ovens, only his wine or cider press, only his brew house. Hunting in the wasteland and woods was always a noble prerogative. *Taillage* was an irregular requisition placed on the peasant at specified times and paid in kind. By the later Middle Ages, *taillage* was usually compounded and regularized as a monetary payment.[44] Earlier on, dependent peasants had been required to devote part of their labor to the production of needed implements, furniture, and cloth in manorial workshops, when these were not run by slaves. With the growth of urban manufacturing centers, and with the lords having more cash at their disposal as the use of money expanded, needed goods could be purchased in the marketplace. Beginning in the twelfth century labor services slowly ceased to be imposed on the serfs, although monetary payments remained. In the late Middle Ages, most lords had higher incomes from their monopolies than from their lands.[45]

We can safely assume that by the twelfth century most rural workers in western Europe were serfs, but small numbers of free peasants and slaves were still to be found. Freeholders, those with allodial tenure, owned plots called allods. They were theoretically on their own, but they too owed certain obligations to the local lords and enjoyed their protection.[46] Slaves were spread over the continent, even though in small numbers. Some few trickled through in the slave trade; illegitimate children born on the manor came to be regarded as if they were slaves. However, by the thirteenth century the creation of a class of paid household servants and the near disappearance of slavery in continental Europe had taken place, and most peasants were treated uniformly as serfs.[47]

In our discussion of the shift from slavery to serfdom, we have been concerned with France, particularly non-Mediterranean France. Serfdom developed earliest and most completely there, in part because it was the region most shielded from alien peoples, always the most fertile source of slaves. The process was similar in other regions, although with local distinctions and different timetables.

The Scandinavians maintained slavery in their homelands until the late Middle Ages and also functioned as slave traders. Their slaves, of Scandinavian as well as foreign origin, occupied legal and social positions similar to those in other western European areas. They could marry and they could gain their freedom, but while slaves they did heavy labor and were despised by free men. As Scandinavian society and economy developed, slavery gradually faded away. In 1335 the king of Sweden decreed that all offspring of Christian slaves were to be free from birth.[48]

Slavery in England abruptly ended shortly after the Norman Conquest of 1066. The Anglo-Saxons had a well-developed slave system, and it has been estimated that slaves made up nearly 10 percent of the English population at the time of the conquest. Although, like other Scandinavian groups, the Normans had traded and held slaves during their period of raiding, after they received Normandy they gradually gave up slavery. As conquerors of England, they could impose their own system there, and they began at once to phase out slavery. Clerical influence was strong in the Norman state, and Norman clerics inveighed against the slave trade and praised manumussion. Nevertheless, the main reason the Normans enserfed former slaves was to avoid the necessity of close supervision and management of slaves. Within a generation or two after the conquest, slavery ceased to be an important institution in Norman England, replaced by widespread serfdom.[49]

In Germany, even though it was closer to the slave-hunting grounds among the Slavs, something similar to French serfdom developed. Domestic slavery in Germany, however, continued longer and on a larger scale than in France. Because of the need to attact settlers to the lands newly acquired along the Baltic shore in the German eastward movement, peasant settlers got generous terms, and, until the later Middle Ages, serfdom was absent in the German Baltic lands.

Conquered by the Muslims in the eighth century and, for the rest of the Middle Ages, the scene of an intermittent reconquest, the Iberian Peninsula offered Europe's most unusual prospect. The Christian kingdoms of the reconquest generally had strong enough monarchs to avoid feudal government, and they bordered Muslim lands, which were a fully integrated part of the wider world with its slave system and from which a steady supply of slaves could be drawn. As the kingdom of León and Castile pushed southward, peasants secured favorable charters that allowed them to avoid serfdom by settling in the initially insecure lands along the frontier. Serfdom proper only developed in the older lands of dense settlement in the north of the peninsula, particularly Catalonia in the northeast.[50]

Medieval Italy also exhibited an unusual development. Italian urban life and economic activity continued to be vital in the Middle Ages, and this kept the Italian manors from attaining the importance they had in France. Slaves and dependent peasants could easily flee the land, at least before the thirteenth century, and secure freedom in the cities and towns. Much of the industry in medieval Italy was urban, even though the most important industry, cloth manufacturing, was in the hands of slaves of the great monasteries. Yet in the twelfth century, urban workers were able to break that monopoly.[51]

THE EARLY MEDIEVAL SLAVE TRADE

With the weakened economy of early medieval Europe, with slavery giving way to other forms of dependent labor in the countryside, there was no great internal market for foreign slaves. Markets for slaves did flourish outside western Europe, however, primarily in the Muslim world from Spain to the Middle East, as we will see in the next chapter, and secondarily in the Byzantine Empire; and European slave merchants took advantage of these external markets. The geography of the slave trade was relatively simple. Its main recruiting grounds were located on the fringes of Europe, and its routes passed through the Frankish heartland and pointed to the more advanced regions of the Mediterranean.

Although members of the dominant group were enslaved occasionally in the Germanic kingdoms, they could not be exported. The most general prohibition was on the sale of Christian slaves to non-Christians. Among the Alamanni, slaves could not be sold outside the borders without the express permission of the duke. There were also religious distinctions. In the Visigothic kingdom Christians could not be sold legally to Jews; but Jews and other slave dealers did export slaves, possibly North Africans and possibly, too, enslaved Christians. From the Merovingian kingdom there was a constant slave trade. The church Council of Orleans in 627–30 prohibited the export of slaves, but apparently this did not stop the trade, because the decree had to be repeated during another council at Chalon in 639–54.[52]

While not much is known in detail about the slave trade in the very early Middle Ages, a few texts indicate something about its spread. First it should be noted that from the period of the late Roman Empire there had been a gold drain from the empire's western portion to the eastern. The more rural and less developed western provinces imported manufactured goods and luxury products from the East. This continued in the early Middle Ages, and slaves were one of the few commodities for which the West could find markets in the East and in the Muslim world. The routes the early Western slave traffic followed are not well known, but there may have been an overland route as well as sea routes from Italy and southern France. The traffic in slaves was one reason the gold drain eastward probably slackened about the year 500.

Marseilles was the best known nexus of the European slave trade in the early Middle Ages. One group of slaves on sale in Marseilles were Moors, the pagan inhabitants of North Africa, probably imported by sea from Spain. There was a north-to-south overland slave trade across Merovingian France passing through Arras and Tournai before crossing France to Marseilles. Some of the slaves were pagan Angles and Saxons from Britain. In the late sixth century, according to a probably apocryphal story, Pope Gregory the Great saw Angles sold as slaves in Rome and conceived the idea of buying them, training them as clerics, and returning them to Britain as missionaries. Gregory himself bought slaves in Marseilles, but the ethnic origin of his slaves is not known.[53]

One of the earliest groups of western European slave traders were the Frisians, who lived along the coast of the North Sea in what is now the Netherlands and West Germany. Flourishing in the seventh and eighth centuries, they traded into Scandinavia and the British Isles. They purchased prisoners of war in Anglo-Saxon London and took them, along with other commodities, into western Europe along the rivers as far south as Paris and as far east as the towns of Germany.[54]

A major route followed by the slave traders, Frankish in this case, started in the eastern European lands of the pagan Slavs, passed through Bavaria, and crossed the Alps to Venice, from which the Italians transported slaves by sea to the Byzantine and Muslim markets. A second route also began in the Slavic lands of eastern Europe, crossed Germany, and entered France. It followed the valleys of the Moselle and the Meuse to Verdun, a collection point and a castration center; thereafter the slaves were taken down the valleys of the Saône and the Rhône to Arles and Marseilles. From there they were shipped to Spain, either by sea or land routes. Another route went by sea from the British Isles to Islamic Spain. Once Spain was reached, many of the slaves were absorbed there, while others were sold in North Africa or beyond to Egypt.[55]

We can examine the trade in greater detail. The Frankish merchants, according to the sources, began their activities by opening the land routes into eastern Europe sometime early in the seventh century, and sending Slavic captives back to the Frankish kingdom. Verdun's role as a slave entrepôt and as a castration center for the production of eunuchs probably began about the same time. The Slavic trade continued until the tenth century. In the eighth century the Frankish wars against the Saxons put many of them on the slave market until they were finally conquered and Christianized. From Britain, too, Frankish dealers acquired slaves to be taken to Verdun and thence along the path to the Mediterranean.[56]

Once the Frankish kingdom reached its peak in the early ninth century, the slave trade through Frankish territory became mainly a transit trade, with slaves from outside passing through on their way to markets in non-Christian lands. The church tried to prohibit the trade, but the frequent repetitions of the prohibitions served to indicate that they were not very effective. Part of the reason was economic: the slave trade was one of the few generators of foreign exchange for western Europe in a period when the East produced goods that Westerners could not obtain elsewhere. As previously suggested, the sale of slaves was one of the few ways the West had for obtaining gold. Another part of the reason the trade continued was the non-Christian origin of many of the slaves. Finally, many sources state that Jewish slave dealers were involved in the traffic. As non-Christians they were not subject to the decrees of the church. In 743 the church Council of Estinnes forbade the selling of Christian slaves to the pagans. A century later in 845 the Council of Meaux discussed the slave traffic through France conducted by both Christian and Jewish merchants who were taking slaves to be sold to the Muslims. Probably recognizing that the trade itself could not be stopped, the clerics at Meaux suggested that the pagans be purchased by French Christians to keep them from falling into the hands of the Muslims. Accusations were also made that the Jews were capturing native Christians and selling them to the Muslims.[57]

For a time in the ninth century the Muslims established strongholds on France's Mediterranean coast, the longest lasting of which was Fraxinetum (La Garde-Freinet), and these spurred the slave trade. The raids of both sides produced captives who became slaves; Christians came into the hands of the Muslims, while Muslims fell under the control of Christians. In the tenth century, the wars of the German emperor Henry the Fowler against the Slavs placed many of them under the control of slave dealers. By the year 1000 the slave trade in the West was slackening, although Rouen still had a slave market where Irish and Flemish slaves were sold. By the twelfth century the Slavs converted to Christianity, and the slave trade from eastern Europe through France to Muslim Spain practically ceased.[58] The eleventh century, too, had been a period of turmoil among the Muslims of Spain, and the Spanish Christians had taken advantage of the disarray of their adversaries to reconquer Muslim lands. Both factors had the effect of seriously curtailing the slave trade to Muslim lands.

At the same time (ca. 700–1000) that France was a transfer point for slaves to the Muslim world, Italy was occupying much the same position. In the eighth century the Byzantines still maintained a degree of control over Italy, but they were unable to prevent the Venetians from selling slaves and timber across the Mediterranean. The slaves were usually Slavs brought across the Alps and transferred through Pavia.[59] The Venetians were the earliest successful Italian sea traders, and, because profits on trade with the Muslims were lucrative, they resisted efforts to stop them. In 748 they bought slaves in Rome itself for sale to the Muslims. The Byzantine emperor Leo V tried to stop the trans-Mediterranean trade, but he had little success.[60] Even Byzantine traders trafficked in slaves from Italy. Pope Hadrian I wrote to Charlemagne in 776 to deny that Romans were selling slaves to the Muslims.

> We find in your sweet letter a mention of the sale of slaves, to the effect that they were sold by our Roman people to the unspeakable race of Saracens [Muslims]. We have never sunk to such a disgraceful act, and God forbid that we should; nor was it done with our approval. The unspeakable Greeks [Byzantines] have always sailed along the coasts of Lombardy, and it was they who bought some families from the region and struck up friendships with the Lombards themselves and through their agency received the slaves in question. When this happened we sent straightway to Duke Allo, instructing him to prepare a large fleet, arrest these Greeks and destroy their ships by fire; but he would not obey our command, because we have neither the ships nor the sailors able to make the arrest. Nevertheless, we did out utmost, and call God to witness that we strove mightily in our desire to prevent this scandal; the ships belonging to the Greeks we had burned in the harbour of our city of Civitavecchia, and we kept the Greeks themselves in prison for some considerable time. But, as we have said, many families were sold by the Lombards at

a time when famine was pressing them hard; indeed, some of the Lombards went on board the Greek ships of their own accord, having no other hope of staying alive.[61]

By the ninth century the Venetians were prospering from the profits of their sea trade with the Muslims. In return for their exports of timber, iron, and slaves, they brought in oriental luxury products, mainly fine cloths, which allowed them to trade with other Italian cities and further enhance their income. The slave supplies before the early ninth century came from Italian sources, but in 840 Venice signed a pact with other Italian cities in which the Venetians undertook to return futigive slaves and not to seize Christians to be sold as slaves.[62] Thereafter they were forced to look farther afield for their slaves. These they found in nearby Dalmatia across the Adriatic, where they purchased slaves from the traders living at the mouth of the Narenta River and conducted their own raids to obtain Dalmatian slaves. They also purchased slaves, as well as metals, from the dealers in Prague. These slaves and goods were brought to Venice through the eastern passes of the Alps. Despite sporadic attempts by civil and clerical authorities to halt the slave traffic, the Venetians never gave it up.[63]

The most westerly component of the early medieval slave trade in Europe was the British Isles. In the eleventh century the Vikings were active slave traders in Ireland, and apparently the English in Bristol were selling slaves to Ireland. The English sold many of those they captured in the long wars against the Celts, and to these were added children sold by destitute parents. From Ireland the Vikings took slaves to be sold in Muslim Spain and Scandinavia, and even to be transported into Russia; some may have been taken as far as Constantinople and the Muslim Middle East. The English also sold some slaves across the Channel to Frankish slave dealers.[64]

In the vast lands of the eastern European steppes from the eighth to the twelfth century, there was a well-developed slaving network, the ultimate termini of which were in the Byzantine Empire and the Islamic world. The inhabitants of the steppes were seminomadic tribesmen of various ethnic groups. The Slavs occupied the more westerly regions, in the area of present-day Poland, Czechoslovakia, and northern Russia. In the Nordic forests to the east of the Baltic lived the Finnish tribes. In the area north of the Danube River and in southern Russia dwelt the Khazars, the Bulgars, and the Magyars. Beginning in the eighth century a group of Scandinavians (called Rus, Varegs, or Varangians) entered the region and, using their longboats on the rivers, established commerce throughout the entire area. Some of their strongholds, such as Kiev and Novgorod developed into principalities. They brought forest products, including amber and precious furs, and slaves to the Byzantines and Muslims to the south. From Kiev on the Dnieper, the Scandinavians had two major routes running southward; one went down to Constantinople, the other eastward to Itil at the north of the Caspian Sea. Muslim merchants of the trading community of Itil received the slaves there and took them to Persia and Iraq, either by water across the Caspian or by a land route paralleling the western shore of the sea. Many slaves passed through Armenia and were castrated there to fill the Muslim demand for eunuchs. On the upper Volga was the town of Bulghar, containing a Muslim community, from which Finnish slaves were transported into the Muslim world by a land route passing between the Caspian and the Aral Sea and entering Khwarzim, a state in which Bukhara and Samarkand were slave markets and castration centers. Slavs and Finns, called *saqaliba* indiscriminately by the Muslims, entered the Muslim world by these Caspian and Black Sea routes.[65]

THE EMERGENCE OF EUROPE

The slow but steady economic growth of western Europe in the early Middle Ages began to pay dividends in the second half of the eleventh century, which marked a substantive change in the relations of the Christian West toward the Islamic world. Until then the West had been on the defensive, fighting for its very existence against a series of invaders. In the eighth century it was the Muslims who came and conquered Spain and later Sicily. Despite the short-lived Carolingian empire, Europe lacked internal political cohesion, and its main energies were directed against external threats. In the ninth and tenth centuries, Europe had to defend itself against the Vikings from the north and the Magyars from the east. In the eleventh century, though, the tide began to turn. The Vikings had been Christianized and westernized, and the Magyars had been contained and driven back. The West was poised to make its first coherent attempt to take the offensive against the Muslims.

The aggressive new posture of what had been the weakest of the three successor civilizations of the Roman world was due to several circumstances. First was the full flowering of the medieval agricultural revolution. Improved agrarian techniques invented in the early Middle Ages—the heavy plow, improved harnessing for horses and oxen, and iron shoeing for horses—spread across western Europe. Selective breeding improved the size and strength of draft animals. The new three-field system increased the acreage under cultivation by one-sixth and improved the fertility of the arable, while new lands were cleared for farming. The spread of water mills allowed the increased produce to be processed with less expenditure of human energy. These improvements had been invented over many years in widely scattered regions, but by the mid-eleventh century their use was general in western Europe. One of only a handful of decisive leaps in the history of food production, the medieval agricultural revolution supported a larger population and provided Europe with the material prosperity it needed to begin to expand beyond its own frontiers.

In their initial struggle against the Muslims, the Westerners took advantage of the disarray in the Islamic world. From one end of their vast holdings to the other, the Muslims were torn by internal strife. In the east, at the center of the caliphate, the Seljuk Turks had seized a large degree of authority and had launched a series of raids into Byzantine territory in Anatolia. At the western extremity of Islam, Muslim Spain had experienced the fall of the Umayyad caliphate and the fragmentation of the land into a series of "party kingdoms" (*reinos de taifas*), which would soon be invaded by the Almoravides, a puritanical Moroccan sect. In these circumstances, the Spanish Christians extended their control as far south as Toledo and Valencia in one of the successful stages of the reconquest. Italy, too, shows the shift in the winds. The Muslims made one of their final attacks on the northern shore of the Mediterranean in 1015, and by 1035 a Christian fleet from Pisa raided North Africa for the first time with an attack on Bône.[66] In the very last years of the eleventh century, the West launched the First Crusade. The consequences of the Crusades for slavery and the slave trade were profound and in some cases surprising.

4

SLAVERY IN
THE WORLD OF ISLAM

Across the Mediterranean from Europe was the vastly different world of Islam, a world that was religiously and linguistically distinct. Larger in territorial extent than Europe, it was more advanced economically, more urbanized, and more cohesive. In the seventh and eighth centuries, the expansion of Islam brought about fundamental changes in the political and economic geography of the Mediterranean world. Starting from rather small beginnings in the Arabian Peninsula, in the course of little more than a century Islam came to encompass a vast swatch of territories eastward from the Atlantic Ocean to the Indus Valley. Most of Spain, all of North Africa, Arabia, Syria, Iraq, and Iran were all brought into the Dar-al-Islam, as the Muslims called the region under their control. Muslim armies were able to take over this great expanse due to their organization and, perhaps more important, because of internal unrest in the lands they conquered. By 800 their integration of the conquests was substantially complete. In the course of their victories the Muslims permitted cities that surrendered to them to maintain their religion and internal self-government, while in those where there was resistance, the men were killed and the women and boys sold into slavery.

The new world assembled from the conquests is often called the *Arab* world, but that term is inaccurate, because only at the beginning were Arabs a majority among the conquerors. New elements were integrated into the whole, and the population soon came to include Syrians, Egyptians, Persians, Berbers, Greeks, and Latins in addition to the original Arabs. The Arabic language offered unity at the intellectual and administrative levels, but local vernaculars often prevailed at the level of everyday life. The major common feature that transcended regional and local distinctions was the religion of Islam. For that reason the best terms to use for this new world are *Islamic* world or *Muslim* world.

Islam was above all an urban civilization. In some areas the Muslims encoun-

66

tered flourishing cities; these they preserved and encouraged. In others they found urban life in decay; there they rebuilt and refurbished older cities and in some cases created new ones. The outcome was a vast economic unit, based on the cities and their hinterlands. Throughout this great expanse, roughly the size of the empires of Alexander and Rome combined, there was a common religion, a common language, a set of similar currencies, and similar business practices. We cannot deny that local differences did persist and that political fragmentation did take place, but—to use the term popularized by Immanuel Wallerstein— Islam was a *world-economy*, an economic commonwealth with ties of trade connecting it with the surrounding regions. Among the most important trade links were the routes of the slave trade, which fed the constant demand for domestics and soldiers, artisans and assistants.

Among the Muslims, slavery was a persistent feature. Nevertheless, we must recognize that Islam was not a slave society. Although the Muslims traded and owned great numbers of slaves, they mainly assigned their slaves to nonproductive tasks. As Moses I. Finley put it: "No matter how many slave women a historian may tot up in the harems of the Caliphate of Baghdad, they count for nothing against the fact that agricultural and industrial production was largely carried out by free men."[1] Nonetheless, even if Islam was not a slave society, and even if Islamic slavery was not as significant in a productive sense as Roman slavery had been, it was still much more important than slavery in Christian Europe. This chapter begins with a survey of the main features of Islamic slavery and concludes with descriptions of two economic components of the Islamic world that were to influence the later development of slavery in the Americas. The first component was the growth of sugar cane planting, and the production and marketing of sugar. Slaves only occasionally were engaged in sugar production in Islamic territory, so we cannot trace a continual identification between slaves and sugar. On the other hand, western Europeans acquired their major knowledge of the use, cultivation, and manufacture of sugar as a result of their contacts with Syria and Palestine in the period of the Crusades. Without that knowledge it would be unlikely that they would have been able to develop sugar production as extensively as they did in the fifteenth and sixteenth centuries. The other component was the trans-Saharan caravan traffic, by which the Muslims developed a trade in gold and slaves, among other commodities, from black Africa. Desires to share in that trade were to be prime motivations in the initial phases of Iberian expansion.

Even before Islam attracted its first adherents, slavery and the slave trade were established institutions in the Arabian Peninsula.[2] As the Muslims expanded to cover the whole of the Middle East and North Africa in the century following Muhammad's death in 632, they conquered lands where slavery was present. We have already discussed slavery among the Byzantines, from whom the Muslims wrested Egypt and the eastern shores of the Mediterranean. The Islamic conquest of the Sassanid Persian empire gave them Mesopotamia, where for a century sugar cane had been grown on plantations manned by black slaves brought from East Africa, many of whom had reached Mesopotamia via the Arab caravan network along coasts of the Red Sea.[3]

The religion of Islam shows many similarities to both Judaism and Christianity. Indeed, it often has been suggested that one of Muhammad's purposes may have been to work out a religious amalgamation that would appeal to Christians and Jews as well as to the tribesmen and traders of Arabia, polytheists before the advent of the new religion. Whatever the Prophet's motives, Christianity and Judaism offered nothing to challenge slaveholding, because both religions countenanced the institution. Thus, three strands—past practice, traditions of conquered societies, and religion—intertwined to bind slavery into the fabric of Islamic society.

Muslim slavery was as fully developed as anything the Roman world had known, and it has ended only recently, having carried on into the twentieth century.[4] In the medieval period, the slaves of the Muslims were forced to be useful in a wide range of activities. They occasionally worked in gangs on plantations and often in the mines. They staffed the households of their masters. Male slaves at times received an education and positions as business agents. Female slaves could be trained as entertainers, or they could end up as sex objects in the harem system, whose guards were eunuch slaves. All these uses were not unlike the practices we have examined among European societies, but there was a significant departure in the Muslim world: the military use of slave troops, who at times even seized the reins of government.

Means of enslavement were similar to European practice: capture in war, purchase, or birth as slaves. In the early years when Muhammad and his followers were establishing control in Arabia, the prisoners of war they captured, other Arabs, were enslaved if they were not ransomed. When the Muslims carried Islam beyond Arabia, the situation changed, and the possibilities of enslavement through war declined sharply. The Koran set forth that members of the other major religions—Jews, Christians, and by implication Zoroastrians—should be considered "people of the book," fellow seekers after truth whose holy books governed their religious actions. As *dhimmi*, protected aliens, they could not be enslaved outright, although this prohibition was violated often in the wars of expansion. Free Muslims could not be enslaved, but slave converts remained unfree. There was no mass freeing of slaves in conquered areas, even if the slaves later embraced Islam.

As an example of how the practice of slavery unfolded with the wars of conquest, we can do no better than to choose the Iberian Peninsula. It is an interesting case because it is one of the very few places where Islamic and Christian societies faced one another across a common land frontier. It is also important because the proximity of Islam allowed the Spanish and Portuguese kingdoms to maintain slavery as a more fully developed institution than in most other medieval European states.

In the early eighth century, after their absorption of North Africa, the Muslims crossed the Strait of Gibraltar, defeated the last Visigothic rulers, and secured the Iberian Peninsula. After a series of rapid campaigns through Iberian territory, the Muslims made excursions beyond the Pyrenees until they were driven back by Charles Martel and the Frankish army in the famous battle fought between Poitiers and Tours in 732. Thereafter the Muslims devoted their attention to building in al-Andalus, as they called their new holding, a brilliant province of the Islamic world.

The impact of the Muslim conquest of Iberia on the practice of slavery was conservative in two senses. First, the Muslims brought with them their own servile law and traditions, and, second, they allowed the newly subject Christians to retain their ownership of slaves. At the same time, new features of slavery developed in Iberia. The Muslims enslaved many Christians—the inhabitants of cities who resisted the Muslim advance—and continued the normal importation of numbers of slaves from outside the Islamic world. If "people of the book" voluntarily accepted Muslim dominance in Iberia, they could retain their liberty, their lives, and their property, including their slaves. Thereafter they paid a head tax for their slaves. If they resisted and were defeated, the women and children were enslaved, and the men were killed or enslaved. Initially, the status of the Mozárabes (Christians living under Muslim rule) was sharply reduced: they could not acquire Muslim slaves; and any of their existing slaves who converted to Islam were sold to Muslim masters, since no non-Muslim could hold a Muslim as a slave. By the ninth and tenth centuries, though, Mozárabes could purchase slaves who reached the peninsula through the slave trade.[5]

Slavery within Spanish Islam shows all the features of traditional Muslim slavery in the Middle Ages, with certain features heightened because of the presence of Christian states across an ill-defined and constantly shifting frontier. Before the tenth century the Muslims generally bought Christian Europeans as slaves, adding them to the descendants of the slaves conquered in the eighth century. By the tenth century, Slavs became the most numerous imported group. Called *sakaliba* in Arabic—still another case of a newly coined word for slave derived from the name of this group—Slavs were purchased from slave traders. Some were brought to Spain as eunuchs, and the word *sakaliba* was also used to designate any eunuch. Byzantine Christians, captured by other Muslims in the eastern Mediterranean, were present as slaves of the Spanish Muslims by the eleventh century, along with North African Berbers enslaved following unsuccessful revolts. Blacks from Africa south of the Sahara arrived beginning in the eleventh century, a consequence of the increased Islamic penetration into sub-Saharan Africa. After the twelfth century, fewer African slaves reached the peninsula; and during the late Middle Ages, until the fall of Granada in the late fifteenth century, most slaves of the Spanish Muslims were Christians from the northern kingdoms of the peninsula.[6] Muslim raids—*razzias*—into Christian territory were designed for quick seizures of booty and prisoners, and the captives were held in underground prisons until they were ransomed. Because the captors wanted as large a profit as possible, they skimped on provisions; the normal diet for prisoners consisted of a daily loaf of a pound and a half of bread. The conditions the Christian captives endured were difficult. They were often chained, and one pathetic prisoner was forced to operate a grain mill in Ronda with a bit between his teeth to prevent him from eating. Numbers of captives are hard to come by and those we do have probably are exaggerated by chroniclers, but just after the Muslim conquest, the caliph in Damascus is said to have received 30,000 Christian slaves sent from Spain. As one-fifth of all booty was owed to the caliph, the total bag must have been reported as 150,000. Centuries later, in 1311, the Aragonese sought papal aid in an attempt to ransom 30,000 Christians they said were held in Granada.[7]

The Muslims held their Christian captives under tighter control than slaves of other origins. Because many tried to flee back across the frontier, they had to be guarded closely to prevent flight. If not ransomed, they were sold at auction. The majority ended up as farm workers, but others worked at urban tasks. One Christian slave became the property of three Muslims, one a carpenter, the second an olive oil merchant, and the third a shopkeeper. The slave's lot was to work for all three in rotation and in addition to grind grain daily for all three.[8] The greatest peril for the Christian captives was to be sold to North Africa or other more distant parts of the Islamic world. Then they would be farther from potential redemption, and because slave prices were higher in North Africa, the cost of their ransoms would be greater. Galley service for slaves was characteristic of the Turkish period beginning in the fifteenth century, but, even in the fourteenth and fifteenth centuries, there was the possibility that North Africans used slaves to row their galleys. Escape from North Africa was almost impossible and unsuccessful attempts were punished by mutilation of noses and ears. Catalan texts describe the slaves' lot as "atrocissima et ferocissima" (most atrocious and harsh).[9]

Once the bounds of the Islamic world were set, there were no more slaves to be obtained legally within the frontiers, except the children of slaves. In theory, Muslims could sell neither their children nor themselves into slavery, and they could not be enslaved for debt; but these provisions may well have been violated in practice.[10] An interesting story comes from the first century of Islam. A Muslim noble lost his fortune while gambling with another. He proposed to his opponent: "I will play you once more, and the one of us that loses shall be the slave of the other."[11] He lost again, and the winner took him as a slave, but not before the loser's tribe declined the chance to ransom him for ten camels. This story is strikingly reminiscent of one that Tacitus related in the late first century A.D. concerning the Germans outside the Roman frontiers. So fond they were of dicing, Tacitus asserted, "that, when everything else is gone, they stake their personal liberty on the last decisive throw. The loser goes into slavery without complaint. . . . "[12] As curiously parallel as these stories are, such sources of slaves must have been of miniscule importance in both societies.

In practice, two legitimate means of acquiring slaves were open to the Muslims: war and the slave trade. After the first two centuries of Islam, war produced few slaves, and consequently the slave trade gained great importance.

During the early centuries of its existence, the Islamic world experienced a golden age. Thanks to its great wealth and the advantages that it possessed over its neighbors, it could afford to import what it needed from outside. The necessities included timber for fuel and construction, metals (iron and gold above all), and slaves. Slaves formed an important component of the Islamic commercial system; even though they were seldom used in agriculture, they still were imported in large numbers for artisan labor and for domestic and military service. One indication of the volume of the slave trade comes from a single, albeit brilliant, city in the Muslim world: Córdoba in Spain under the caliph Abd ar-Rahman III (912–61), when the city may have had nearly 14,000 slaves.[13] One reason for the great demand for slaves was the equally great accumulation of riches the Islamic elite acquired during the period of the conquest, a wealth preserved through many generations by their descendants. To meet that demand the Muslims looked beyond their frontiers to four regions of slave supply in this period: Europe, the area of the Russian rivers, the East (particularly Turkestan but also India), and sub-Saharan Africa.[14] We discussed the northern trade in chapter 3, and we will deal with the trans-Saharan trade later in this chapter. The Turkish trade is somewhat remote from the main concerns of this book, but we should mention its main staging points: Samarkand and Bukhara in Khwarzim, from which captive Turks were taken first to Iran and Mesopotamia and then to other parts of the Islamic world, where the slaves were sold in each city's special market, known as the *suqi-er-raqiq*. The ninth-century slave market of Samarra is perhaps the best known. Its form was square and it was surrounded by the establishments of slave dealers. Most slaves were sold in such a market, but the merchants sold the most distinguished and expensive slaves privately.[15]

Whatever their origins, the slaves of the Muslims endured conditions that did not differ greatly from those in other societies, although the absence of large-scale agrarian slavery meant that some of the most onerous occupations were not present. The Koran treated slavery as an established institution, and it provided explicitly that slaves should be treated well.

Be kind to your parents, and the near kinsmen,
and to orphans, and to the needy,
and to the neighbor who is of kin,
and to the neighbor who is a stranger,
and to the companion at your side,
and to the traveler, and to that
your right hand owns.[16]

In a *hadith* (traditional saying) attributed to Muhammad, slaveowners are enjoined to treat their charges well: "Give them such food . . . as you eat your-selves, clothe them in such garments as you wear yourselves, and burden them not with labours too heavy for them. Those of them that you like, keep; those you dislike, sell; but do not torment God's creatures."[17]

Despite these injunctions, slaves had no legal rights in theory. Islam, as many observers have reported, was a community of believers, all held to be equal. Ex-cluded from true participation, however, were women, aliens, and slaves. Slaves, in consequence, were considered legally, as well as morally and physi-cally, inferior. Their evidence was seldom valid in court; they could neither own nor transmit property. Owners could sell and bequeath them; their labor could be hired out and they could be set to any task the master wished. A free Muslim who killed another's slave had to compensate only the slave's master at the pre-vailing market price. Masters could punish their own slaves or kill them without fear of retribution, even though such murders were theoretically illegal. A slave could not bring suit against a master who mistreated him, but the authorities could punish masters who denied their slaves the exercise of their religious rights. This was also the case for those masters who overworked slaves or denied them sufficient rest. For certain crimes—unlawful sexual intercourse and drunkenness, among others—a slave was not punished as harshly as a free man could be; this was an unusual provision for any slave system.[18] As is often the case, theory and law were abandoned or disregarded in practice. Although this could work to the slave's disadvantage, it also could be beneficial. Benevolent masters could allow their slaves to keep property and pass it to their children. The inclination of the master, to good or evil, was all-important, a characteristic of every slave system.

Uses to which the slaves of the Muslims were put ranged widely. As there was little use of slaves in industrial and agricultural pursuits, domestic or busi-ness uses were most common, but harsher and more demanding jobs could be forced on them. Mine labor was often the preserve of slaves. Smuggling into Old Cairo (Fustat) to avoid taxes was often in the hands of slaves.[19] Female slaves could be forced to act as prostitutes. On this point the Koran counseled the master to "constrain not your slavegirls to prostitution, if they desire to live in chastity. . . . "[20] As musicians and dancers, slaves were much in demand, and in Medina special schools developed for training slaves in these arts.[21]

Slaves were most commonly used as domestic servants, an occupation free people shunned. Domestics, especially females, were often well treated. At times they became real members of the family through adoption, and domestic slaves were generally sold only if they offended the family. Nursemaids occu-pied an honored position.[22]

Male slaves often served as business agents of their masters. Although the practice is reflected in Islamic law, our best evidence on this point comes from the records of the Cairo Geniza, a storage room in the synagogue of Old Cairo, where pious Jews placed outdated documents so that writings containing the name of God might not perish improperly. Although the Geniza records come from the Jewish minority of the Muslim world, their society no doubt reflected the practices of the Muslim majority. From these records evidence appears that bourgeois masters devoted great attention to the selection of new male slaves and great care to their training. In studying the Geniza papers, S. D. Goitein found many references showing friends and relatives congratulating the master on the purchase of a new male slave in terms similar to those used for the birth of a son. The normal Arabic word for slave (*abd*) was not used for a servile business agent; rather he was the "young man" (*ghulam*) of the master. While the male slaves could be the chief business agents of their masters and even engage in business on their own account, they also could be put to a variety of other uses, including menial tasks at times. The slaves had their own hierarchy, equivalent to and dependent on the status of their masters. One who was the *ghulam* of a leader of the community contributed to a charitable appeal at the same rate as rich merchants.[23]

Muslims seem to have shown considerable humanity toward their slaves, as numerous episodes attest. As one example, Goitein reports the case of a presumably Muslim master who in 1245 agreed to pay a Jewish physician to cure an eye problem of his slave. It was both illegal and unusual to separate mothers and daughters when slaves were sold. Slaves could join fraternal associations, and there was no bar to their participation in religious life. Still, runaways were frequently reported.[24]

Female slaves could enjoy a better situation than that of males, as their treatment in Islamic Spain shows. Most slave women in the peninsula were purchased from slave traders, since the preponderant number of Spanish captives were male warriors. In the special slave markets in each city, particular care was taken in the sale of women, and they were inspected by matrons in the employ of the *muntasib*, the president of the market. Divided into "distinguished" and "gross" categories, the latter went into domestic service, while the former were destined for service as concubines or entertainers, if they had been trained in Spain or other centers of the Islamic world. White women were more prized and more expensive than blacks, although a growing number of mulattoes in Andalusian society indicates that the black slaves did not fail to find buyers. The concubines were readily integrated into family life in Spain, as in the rest of the Islamic world.[25]

Marriage patterns and slavery were linked in an intricate pattern in Islam. A free Muslim male could have up to four legal wives and as many slave concubines as he could afford. The master could give any of his female slaves in marriage to anyone he wished without seeking their permission, but before he could marry one of his slaves himself, he was required to enfranchise her and seek her approval of the marriage. If a Muslim male bought a slave to be his mistress, any previous children she had were his slaves too; but if she bore her new master children and if he recognized them, the woman acquired certain rights. No longer could her master sell her, although he still could give her in marriage without her permission. On his death, if he had not freed her or married her to another, she and her children became free. Normally, the children of slave women were themselves slaves. Because concubinage was so widespread and because its consequences could bring forth legal complications, the law obliged the master to refrain from sexual intercourse with his new slave woman until she had experienced one menstruation. This provision was designed to allow the master to be sure that any child was his own. Such abstention was required if the woman's former master was a man, and it was recommended if she had been owned by a woman. A male slave had to seek his own master's permission to marry a free or a slave woman and that of his bride's master, if she were a slave owned by a different master. A prospective bridegroom had to offer a dowry he had earned himself, although the practice seems to contradict the idea that slaves could not hold property. The dowry became the property of the wife's master, and any children the couple produced were the slaves of the wife's master.[26]

Marriages between free Muslims and slave women were common, and the offspring of such unions enjoyed full freedom. In the Koran, in fact, marriage with a pious slave woman was regarded as much more suitable than with an unbeliever.[27] The most spectacular cases of free-slave marriages involved the Abbasid caliphs (eighth to eleventh centuries). Hoping to avoid family alliances and the particularism this might engender, the Abbasids adopted many aspects of the Near Eastern concept of the exalted god-king. As part of their attempt to create the largest possible distance between themselves and their subjects, they proclaimed that no one was equal to them. Because no marriage could possibly add luster to their station, the Abbasid caliphs married slave wives, with the result that "after 800 not a single caliph was born the son of a free mother."[28]

Muslim males kept their female dependents isolated from the world, segregated in a special portion of the house known as the harem. There the women could entertain their own guests, but they could only venture out for specific purposes.[29] Most free Muslims could afford no more than a single wife; only the wealthiest could carry the harem system to extremes. One such example was provided by the Fatimid viceroy al-Malik al-Afdal (1094–1121), who left eight hundred slave concubines in his harem when he died. To give an idea of his jealousy, he is reported to have beheaded one mistress on the spot for looking out a window of the harem while in his presence.[30]

As harem guards and servitors, eunuchs were especially appreciated throughout the Islamic world. Because strong traditional Muslim prohibitions limited the opportunities of castration and because many who were castrated did not survive the operation, these scarce and unfortunate individuals commanded high prices for their owners. Slave traders brought prospective eunuchs from the great slaving regions outside the frontiers and had them castrated in special centers along the trade routes: Verdun in France, Samarkand and Bukhara in the East, and Christian communities in southern Egypt. Egypt seems to have been the center of the use of and commerce in eunuchs. By the fourteenth century black African eunuchs were reaching Egypt mainly by way of Ethiopia, where they had been brought, already emasculated, from farther south. Ibn-Battuta, the fourteenth-century Moroccan world traveler, mentioned that eunuchs also came from Borno in sub-Saharan Africa.[31] A ninth-century Muslim, Jahiz, left behind an account in his *Book of Animals* that may well reflect the popular wisdom of the medieval Muslims concerning eunuchs and help to explain why they were in such demand as servants.

> Another change which overcomes the eunuch: of two slaves of Slavic race, who are . . . twins, one castrated and the other not, the eunuch becomes more disposed toward service, wiser, more able, and apt for the various problems of manual labor, and you find him more lively in intelligence and conversation. All these qualities result only in the castrated one. On the other hand, his brother continues to have the same native torpor, the same lack of natural talent, the same imbecility common to slaves, and incapacity for learning a foreign language.[32]

Jahiz's pronouncements on the abilities of slaves were echoed in many another slave society.

Manumission was a widespread custom in the Islamic lands, as an act of piety counseled by the Koran:

> Those your right hands own who seek emancipation, contract with them accordingly, if you know some good in them; and give them of the wealth of God that he has given you.[33]

A slave could be manumitted by testament or by specific act during the master's life. If the master agreed, a slave could purchase freedom and had to be granted the right to work to earn his purchase price. There were automatic freeings in certain circumstances. A slave mistress who bore children to the master gained privileges and could win freedom on his death. Slaves who came to be owned by a relative were on that basis freed, as for example, if a master's will left slave children to a previously freed father.[34]

After emancipation, the freed person was the client of his former master's family, who provided protection and patronage in return for certain services or payments. In effect, the client was a member of the former owner's family. Education of the patron's children was often the freedman's responsibility, and sometimes the resulting relationships were quite strong. Clients of the powerful became strong in their own right, securing administrative posts in the government.[35] "The freedmen of the House of Muhammad enjoyed in the Abbasid state the same financial prerogatives as the genuine members of the House."[36]

The majority of the slaves in the Muslim world were put to work as domestics and business assistants or used as sexual partners.[37] Agricultural and industrial labor was generally free. As the Muslims expanded, a two-fold process was at work: land granted to Muslim warriors was worked by free peasants, by hired labor, or according to sharecropping arrangements; at the same time much previously agricultural land reverted to pasture, with lower labor requirements. Reversion to pasture threw many agricultural workers temporarily out of work, but cities were growing and could absorb the surplus. The result was a sufficiency of indigenous workers, both urban and rural, so that there was no reason to import vast numbers of slave laborers. In certain Muslim countries, state factories made use of slaves, but this was exceptional.[38]

Free labor was the norm, but there were exceptions to this general rule. One was isolated and had little influence—the eleventh-century Karmatian state around Bahrain on the Persian Gulf. It was so wealthy that the state maintained a labor force of 30,000 black slaves. Mainly employed in agriculture, the state slaves could also be assigned to aid citizens who needed to repair their homes or mills. A second exception occurred in ninth-century Ifriqiya (modern Tunisia and part of Algeria), where there were huge agricultural holdings worked by a servile labor force.[39]

A third exception—much more important in its implications—was in southern Mesopotamia, where the Zanj (or Zindj) revolt took place in the ninth century. Aftershocks of the rebellion rocked the entire Muslim world and probably contributed to the Muslim disinclination to concentrate large numbers of slaves and create the potential for a similar revolt. The Zanj were black slaves and ex-slaves from East Africa; since before the Muslim conquest they had been used in the region to work on sugar cane plantations. The Muslims in the ninth century began to employ the Zanj as slaves to transform the ecology of the lower reaches of the river system, where the Tigris and the Euphrates flowed into a vast swamp of some ten thousand square miles just above the Tigris's outlet into the Persian Gulf. The land was exposed to tidal inundations, and in time the fertile soil had been overlaid with polluted soil, rich in salt and nitrates, but impossible to cultivate. Organized in gangs of fifty to five hundred, the Zanj swept the upper layer into huge piles, with the dual result of exposing the arable soil and allowing the nitrates and salt to be collected and processed for use elsewhere. Conditions of the Zanj slaves were seemingly hopeless. They were driven by harsh overseers; their food and housing was poor. Muslim missionaries began to filter into the region, gaining converts and preparing suitable ground for the emergence of a rebel leader, Ali b. Muhammad, who came into the region in 868 or 869 and began to rouse the slaves. He promised an improvement of their material lot, social justice, and freedom. Strangely enough, an end to slavery was not part of his message, for he told his followers that he would give them property and slaves of their own.

Not much is known of the origins of this leader, and most of his career was reported and transmitted by hostile witnesses. A native of Persia, he apparently claimed to be an ''Alid,'' a descendant of the caliph Ali, Muhammad's cousin and son-in-law and his successor from 656 to 661. Ali b. Muhammad made much of his desire to restore the purity of Islam, which he considered corrupted by the ruling Abbasid caliphs, and on the coins he minted he called himself the Mahdi, the promised redeemer of Islam. His followers gave him the title of Master of the Zanj (*Sahib az-Zanj*); his enemies called him the Rascal (*al-Khabith*). The Master of the Zanj won the support of the slaves, forged them into an army, and used them to raid nearby towns and villages for weapons and supplies. Within two years the new army had taken several towns in southern Iraq and set up a capital of their rebel state in a newly built town. In 871 they captured the large city of Basra. The following years were ones of success for the Zanj. They made incursions into central Iraq, raiding towns for booty and freeing slaves to join their forces.

In Baghdad the caliph was not oblivious of the threat of the Zanj rebels; but his armies were occupied on other fronts, with revolts elsewhere, and they could not devote their full attention to the Zanj. Even when they did, conditions favored the rebels. They knew the terrain, and consequently their infantry could harass the royal cavalry from ambush. Yet time and resources were on the side of the caliphal armies. As successful as the Zanj were, they alienated urban dwellers and peasants, and gained support only from some groups of unreliable Bedouins. The end came in 883. The caliph's brother finally defeated the Zanj armies and executed Ali b. Muhammad and his officers.[40]

The consequences of the revolt were far-reaching and affected the whole Muslim world. Weaknesses of the Abbasid caliphate had been laid bare, and secessionist tendencies brought forth new and independent states in the Persian area and in Egypt. Other contemporary revolts merged with the Zanj uprising into a widespread insurrection—the Qarmat movement—which altered the very structure of Islam.[41] For the Muslims, it seems likely that knowledge of the Zanj revolt, and fears of a similar situation arising elsewhere, confirmed their position that slave gangs were not a suitable organization of labor and that slaves were best employed in smaller concentrations.[42]

Nevertheless, some Muslim rulers did use concentrations of slaves, as slave soldiers. The widespread use of slave troops, the Mamluks, was the most unusual aspect of Islamic slavery. The origin of the Mamluks was in the ninth century, when the future caliph al-Mamun began to build a personal army of slaves. When he gained the caliphal office, he expanded their numbers greatly, mainly recruiting Turks, but also at times enrolling Slavs and Berbers. The original impetus for the use of slave troops was a fairly simple one: they were loyal. Completely cut off from their homelands and families, their only allegiances were to themselves and their master. Loyalty was a rare and precious commodity for those who held power in the Islamic world. Factionalism was endemic, exacerbated by a plethora of ethnic and linguistic distinctions along with political squabbles and family disputes. Thus it is quite understandable that the concept of buying loyal troops spread widely, from India to the caliphate of Córdoba in Spain.

An argument could be made that the Mamluks were not really slaves, that their status and conditions varied so greatly from those of ordinary slaves that they did not fit within the usual definition of the term. Nonetheless, they were slaves who were taken by slave traders from their places of origin and thus suffered total alienation from the society of their birth. Most were Turks, Circassians, or others from the Black Sea or Caspian regions; some were sub-Saharan Africans. They experienced the same legal disabilities as other Muslim slaves. Living under conditions virtually identical to traditional military discipline, the Mamluks went through a training program designed to reward loyalty. Young recruits were placed under a "tent commander" and trained in infantry tactics during their first year. In the second year, they were given horses; and in the third year, elaborate belts indicating their rank. In the fifth year, they gained better trappings for their mounts and better weapons for themselves. Ordinarily, in the seventh year a Mamluk was eligible for the office of tent commander. Thereafter, he could rise as far as his ability and skill at intrigue permitted. He could attain freedom, and many Mamluks rose to high office, some even becoming heads of state. The ninth-century Tulunid dynasty of Egypt was founded by a freed Turkish Mamluk, ibn-Tulun. The later Mamluk rulers of Egypt were corps commanders of Mamluk troops; succeeding Mamluk sultans were those who gained power by military support.[43]

Mamluks and state slaves were also an important element among the servile population of Islamic Spain. Mercenary soldiers first appeared under al-Hakam (796–822). Their numbers included Berbers, African blacks, and Christian Europeans; and, while we read of special guard units composed of blacks, the predominant element consisted of Slavs. In time, many Slavs came to occupy important posts in Islamic Spain, either as freedmen or as slaves. By the late tenth century the Spanish caliphate was in trouble, with three rival political forces vying for power: the urban population of Córdoba, the Berbers, and the Slavs. Conditions deteriorated to such a degree that in 1031 the caliphate was abolished, ushering in the period of the *reinos de taifas* or party kingdoms, some thirty independent city states controlled by members of the three groups. Those dominated by the Slavs were generally in the eastern portion of the peninsula.[44]

Far from being ordinary slaves, the Mamluks should be compared to the *familia Caesaris* of the Roman Empire. The members of both groups were legally slaves but also were part of a prestigious organization that gave them communal support and companionship and that offered them a path to freedom and power. The Mamluks were unique; no other slave system of the Middle Ages made such use of slave forces, even though Roman commanders and the leaders of the armies of the Germanic kingdoms at times had integrated slaves into infantry units. The practice continued among the Turks with their Janissaries into early modern times.

SUGAR CANE PRODUCTION

One special economic feature of the Islamic world, the expansion of sugar cane agriculture, was to be of lasting importance for the later history of slavery, although the Muslims ordinarily did not use slaves in sugar production. In ancient and early medieval times, the Mediterranean did not know sugar; sweetening came from honey and fruit juices. Honey, of course, remained a luxury because its supply was limited and could never be expanded much. Sugar cane was entirely different; its growth is limited only by the availability of suitable land and labor. With certain gaps, the early history of sugar is well known. Its cultivation originated either in the islands of the Pacific or in Southeast Asia. By 325 B.C., when the armies of Alexander the Great entered the Punjab, they encountered sugar cane. It was already being cultivated in China, and later, in A.D. 640, the emperor Tai Tsung sent Chinese skilled in sugar to study the more advanced techniques practiced in India's Ganges Valley.[45]

From India the Persian emperor Chosroes I Anushirwan introduced sugar cane into Mesopotamia, where the region of Khuzistan became the chief Middle Eastern center for its cultivation. When the Muslims conquered the region in the seventh and eighth centuries, they established a labor force of blacks imported from East Africa to work in the cane fields, a foreshadowing of the links between sugar cane cultivation and black slavery. This did not set an immutable precedent, because in the Islamic world and in the Christian Mediterranean, free labor predominated in sugar production. It was only in the Atlantic in the sixteenth century that black slaves came to be virtually the sole source of labor in the sugar plantations.[46]

The plain of Khuzistan was eminently suited for the cultivation of sugar cane. Located just to the north of the Persian Gulf, bounded on the north and east by mountains and on the west by the lower Tigris, numerous streams watered Khuzistan and allowed the irrigation of the cane fields. Production flourished, and the region paid taxes in kind to the caliph. In the eighth century those taxes amounted to thirty thousand pounds of sugar annually. It is possible that through academic studies carried out in the cities of Ahwaz and Kjondisapour the chemical processes for clarifying and crystallizing sugar were invented. Previously, the processing of sugar had been done by crushing the cane, extracting the juice, and boiling it down into a black paste. Sugar was used as a medicinal agent as well as a sweetener, and through the academic pharmaceutical research in Khuzistan, the method of adding potash (potassium carbonate) to clarify the sugar in the refining process was invented. From Khuzistan, sugar refining spread to Baghdad, which lasted as a refining center until the end of the Middle Ages.[47]

Egypt was the next step along sugar's westward march; the first sugar plantations were established there in the early eighth century. From Egypt, the Muslims spread sugar cane to the lands around the Mediterranean: Syria, Sicily, southern Morocco, and southern Spain. Byzantium and the West were to obtain their first taste of sugar from the Muslims. Venice's first recorded importation of sugar was in 996.[48]

By the tenth century, sugar production was thriving in several places in the Islamic world. Khuzistan was still the prime producer of finest quality sugar, but by then its production had spread to Yemen and to southern Iraq. Syria also began its cultivation. Cane was planted along the Mediterranean coast from Sidon to Palestine and in Galilee and the Jordan Valley; its center was around Tyre. Most of Egypt's production was in the eastern area of the Nile Delta. Cane growing spread in part because cane could be planted on lands too poor for grain and it helped improve the soil in the process. Because of the special requirements of sugar cane production—large tracts of land and mills and machinery—only the rich were able to pursue it. Large landholders were the main ones who could afford the investment necessary for successful production. E. Ashtor does not hesitate to characterize the sugar industry in Syria and Egypt in Fatimid times as a capitalist enterprise. The intensive nature of the industry has been a feature of cane sugar production ever since. Egyptian processes became famous throughout the world. The Egyptians probably invented the manufacture of cube sugar, called *misri* (Egyptian) sugar in the Far East. For centuries, the Egyptians had used two minerals, natron (sodium carbonate) and alum (aluminum potassium sulfate), for the refining of honey, and in about the eleventh century they began to refine cane sugar with the same minerals. These techniques were so successful that in the thirteenth century Kublai Khan imported Egyptian experts to revitalize the Chinese industry. Egyptian and Syrian sugar, particularly the extremely pure *al-kifti* sugar of upper Egypt, was traded widely in the Near East, even to places such as Iraq that already had a domestic sugar industry.[49]

Egyptian sugar production prospered in the thirteenth and fourteenth centuries. The areas under cane cultivation spread to new areas of Egypt—around Alexandria and in the Fayyum—and sugar mills became a favored investment for physicians and other rich Muslims. Despite the economic depression of the Islamic world in the fourteenth and fifteenth centuries, sugar held its own for part of that period. In the fourteenth century, large amounts of sugar were consumed by Muslims, and Egyptian sugar was exported to the commercial centers of Italy, France, and Spain. Yet at the same time, the sugar industry in the Near East began to fall victim to the same forces that were causing a decline in the economy of the Islamic world. Closures of sugar factories began to take place around the middle of the fourteenth century, and the process accelerated in the fifteenth. Cairo had sixty-six sugar mills in 1325; by the first years of the next century nearly half had been abandoned.[50]

Part of the decline in Egyptian sugar production was attributable to internal changes in the Islamic economy. Another factor was the increasing sugar production by Europeans, who from the time of the Crusades had begun to develop sugar plantations and refining centers. We will return to the story of sugar when we consider the Crusades, but at this point we must examine the other feature of Islamic slavery that, with sugar, was to have an equally important influence on the later development of the history of slavery: the trans-Saharan trade, a commerce that brought to North Africa and the Mediterranean two principal commodities, gold and slaves, that were to play crucial roles in later European expansion overseas.

THE TRANS-SAHARAN SLAVE TRADE

The Arabs had traded African slaves even before the advent of Islam, and blacks were present, free as well as slaves, in the Islamic world throughout its history. As slaves, the blacks were especially important as domestic servants, and, as free people, they often attained high positions. The historian Bernard Lewis aroused controversy by publishing *Race and Color in Islam*, in which he related many negative attitudes expressed by medieval Muslims toward the blacks.[51] Regardless of whether such attitudes were at all typical, Lewis's citations do reveal regular Islamic familiarity with Africans from south of the Sahara during the Middle Ages.

The Muslims developed a strong interest in Africa early in the period of their expansion. In the mid-seventh century, about the same time as the conquest of Egypt, Muslims raided Nubia. As an indication of the close connection between Islamic expansion and slavery, the Nubians were able to get the Muslims to desist from further raids by bribing them with an annual tribute of 365 slaves. By the early eighth century, after the Muslims had taken the whole of the southern shore of the Mediterranean and while they were engaged in the more famous invasion of Spain, a Muslim leader, Habib b. Ali Ubaida, crossed the western Sahara from Morocco via Mauretania and arrived in the Sudanic belt of grasslands in search of gold. The Muslims must certainly have appreciated the opportunities for trade with the gold suppliers of the Sudan, for in 757 they founded the city of Sijilmasa in southern Morocco to serve as an entrepôt and staging area for commerce with the Sudan.[52] Within the next two centuries the Sahara dwellers converted to Islam, a fact that facilitated commercial relations. South of the Sahara, Islam expanded among the ruling groups of the strong states.

It was along the trans-Saharan routes that trade developed. First established at an early date, perhaps as early as 1000 B.C., the Saharan routes began to be seriously exploited in the eighth century and flourished from the tenth. There was a series of them running north and south across the desert. The most westerly went from Morocco to the mouth of the Senegal River and paralleled the Atlantic coast from Awlil to Noul, a sure indication that the nearby sea route was impractical in the state of maritime technology of the central Middle Ages, a subject we will return to later. There were a number of other trans-Saharan routes. From the eighth to the fourteenth century, the most important western route went from Sijilmasa to Ghana through Tamadest, Idjil, Chinguetti,

Wadan, and Awadaghost. With the rise of Mali in the fourteenth century, the trajectory changed. It still left from Sijilmasa, but then it passed through the salt fields of Taghaza before reaching Walata and ending at Mali. With the rise of Timbuktu as a trading center in the same period, a branch passed directly from Taghaza to Timbuktu. There was another route from Sijilmasa to Kano via Tuat, Hoggar, and Takedda. This route was less important because gold could not be obtained at Kano. Farther to the east it was possible to go from Kairouan and Tripoli to Gao by way of Ghat, Hoggar, and Es-Souk, and from Tripoli to Borno through Zawila, Kawar, and Kanem. From Egypt there was a route to Kanem via Asiut and Darfur.[53]

The Saharan routes contained four varieties of stages. The northern termini—such as Mogador, Fez, Algiers, Tunis, and Tripoli—were located on or near the seacoast, facilitating the distribution of African goods to Middle Eastern and European markets. The North African merchants prepared their goods and traveled to rendezvous points located near the northern edge of the Sahara. In towns such as Sijilmasa, Ghadames, and Tenduf, the caravans were assembled, staffed, and outfitted. From these points the caravans began the desert trek, stopping on the way at refreshment stations in the desert to take on food and water, to repair damaged equipment, and to rest before the next part of the desert crossing was attempted. Stations in the desert were often local markets as well, and goods could be bought and sold there. Guides usually specialized in only one section of the route, and they were picked up and dropped off at the refreshment stations. After the desert was behind them, the caravan traders reached the commercial emporia of the Sudan. In Jenné, Timbuktu, Gao, Kano, and other cities that owed their prosperity to commerce, the northern traders unloaded and sold their goods, purchased Sudanese goods, and prepared their caravans for the return trip to the north. The desert caravan merchants were most often Arabs and Berbers, whose permanent homes were in North Africa. The goods they brought in from the north were acquired at wholesale by Sudanese merchants, who then distributed them to native retailers throughout the savanna and south to the forest regions, while collecting local goods to be sold to the caravan merchants.[54]

A recent economic historian has provided this assessment of the Saharan trade:

> by a feat of daring more impressive because it was repeated annually over many centuries, African and other merchants succeeded in creating an overland trade which, in size and organization, deserves to rank with the most famous achievements of merchant venturers in the era before industrialization removed the hardship from international commerce.[55]

The activities of the fourteenth-century North African firm of the five Maqqari brothers serve to illustrate the complex mechanism of the trans-Saharan trade. Along the Sijilmasa-Taghaza-Walata route, they dug and repaired wells and supplied guides for other caravans, as well as operating their own. Two brothers established themselves in Walata to manage the distribution of North African goods and the collection goods of the Sudan for shipment northward. Two brothers resided in Tlemcen to handle the northern end of the trade, while the remaining brother lived in Sijilmasa to regulate the firm's commerce according to the information he received from his brothers at both ends of the route.[56]

The elaborate management that the Maqqari brothers provided was necessary for the smooth functioning of their caravan trade. Such a business was complicated in planning, for it had to be done well in advance. Many merchants traveled with each caravan, with four camels per merchant, one for food and water and three to carry the merchandise. The caravan leader (usually called the *khabir*) was vested with full authority to direct the caravan and to handle the varied business dealings that were its reason for existence. Although the leader hired guides as the caravan traversed each section of the route, he still had to be a navigator in his own right. Skilled guides and leaders could tell the correct path not only by the sun and the stars, but also by the smell and touch of the sand and the local vegetation. Each caravan carried its own scribe to keep the business records and messengers to carry orders up and down the line of march. On the route, aside from the necessary chores of pasturing and watering the camels at night and getting them ready to move in the morning, there were human obstacles to be overcome. Each oasis charged a fee, and local chieftains would often charge transit duties or insist that local guides be hired (often thinly disguised bribery). There was an annual pattern to the movement of the caravans. They generally spent the winter in the Sudan, and this required them to leave North Africa in September or October and begin their return journey in April or May. By following this schedule they could hope to avoid the summer's heat and the equally hazardous winter cold of the desert. In the mid-fourteenth century, the Moroccan traveler ibn-Battuta encountered a heavy snowstorm on the last leg of his return journey from the Sudan to Morocco. Travelers might be caught at any time by sandstorms that destroyed the path, cruelly afflicted humans and animals, and scattered the caravan. If things went well, they could count on making the crossing in two or three months.[57]

Our best contemporary evidence of the Saharan caravans comes from ibn-Battuta, who recorded his epic journey throughout the world from the Atlantic to China, visiting Muslim communities along the way. After returning from Asia to Morocco, he undertook a tour of West Africa. From Marrakesh he traveled by way of Fez to Sijilmasa, one of the staging points for the Sahara crossing. Having purchased camels and a supply of food for four months, he left Sijilmasa in February 1352 in a caravan with a number of Sijilmasa merchants. Twenty-five days later he reached Taghaza, the center of a salt-producing region, which he called "an unattractive village, with the curious feature that its houses and mosques are built of blocks of salt, roofed with camel skins.'' Slaves mined the salt, bringing it out in large blocks that were loaded at the rate of two per camel. Blacks from the Sudan came north to Taghaza and took back salt, which was also carried by the North African caravans. Ibn-Battuta remained ten days at Taghaza while the caravan was reprovisioned. In the next stage the caravan reached Tasarahla after ten days. This stretch was harsh; water was usually unavailable, although it rained during ibn-Battuta's crossing. At Tasarahla they rested three days and hired an experienced guide, who, despite being blind in one eye and diseased in the other, led them safely through the remainder of the desert and into the Sahel at Walata. The journey through the desert from Sijilmasa to Walata had taken the caravan two months.[58]

The trans-Saharan trade was made possible by four factors: (1) the camel as a useful transport animal, (2) the Saharan peoples living along the route who could serve as intermediaries, (3) Islam as the common religion of the North Africans, the Berbers, and the Sudanese merchants and rulers, and (4) the existence of well-organized states in the Sudan. Yet these factors by themselves cannot account for the trade. Trading commodities were needed, and in this regard each side had something to offer the other. The North Africans provided the black states with dates, figs, sugar, and cowries (shells for use as currency). Manufactured goods were quite important: copper utensils, ironwork, paper goods, Arabic books, tools, weapons, and cloths of cotton and silk. The Sudanese had cotton cloth of their own, but imported dyed fabrics had an appeal for them. Jewelry, mirrors, and glass, especially Venetian glass, went south with the caravans. North African horses were easily sold, because the military strength of the Sudanese states depended on cavalry, and horses were in great demand below the Sahara. The North Africans provided another commodity that they purchased along the caravan route. This was salt, a necessity that could not be produced in the Sudan, but for which the region had a continuing demand. Although salt could be obtained by drying sea water, maritime salt was not well suited for wide distribution in the humid regions, especially in the forest belt. Far better were the bars of rock salt obtained—often by slave labor—from the mines of the Sahara. Caravans transporting Mediterranean goods would load salt bars as they passed through the producing regions and carry them to the commercial towns of the Sahel, where they would be distributed throughout Sudan. Beyond, in the forest belt, salt was in such great demand that Sudanese merchants could often exchange it very profitably for gold.[59]

Gold and slaves remained the significant exports from the Sudan to the Mediterranean, despite the presence of a long list of other items: ivory, ostrich feathers, skins and leather, kola nuts, ebony wood, and a variety of pepper. In his suggestion that for Africa the trade had ultimately a detrimental impact, Raymond Mauny pointed out that all the Mediterranean imports can be classified as luxuries, whereas the Sudanese goods—particularly gold and slaves—were valuable or productive.[60] This may be true in general terms, and the slave trade may have deprived Africa of potential workers, but we must not overlook, where slaves are concerned, that in the Muslim world they generally were not used as productive labor. Most of the slaves from Africa who ended up in Muslim lands were used as domestic servants, concubines, or soldiers, not as laborers. There was a marked bias in favor of women for trade, reflecting the household destinations of many of the slaves. Nevertheless, although we have no way of measuring accurately, each slave exported was a potential loss in labor and reproductive potential for the Sudanic states.

Gold was perhaps the most important export from sub-Saharan Africa to the Mediterranean world. Muslim gold coinage during the first centuries of Islam had depended mainly on the supplies of gold taken as booty in Syria and Egypt, and on the loot taken from Christian churches and monasteries in North Africa and Spain. In the second half of the ninth century, new sources were found in Egypt's eastern desert between Aswan and the Red Sea, in the region of Wadi Allaqi. After the Arabs conquered the region, groups of Muslim merchants operated the mines, using free Beja laborers and black slaves from the Sudan. Until the thirteenth century, when the veins of Wadi Allaqi became exhausted, the mines there supplied Egypt with the bulk of its gold. It is no coincidence that the caravan routes from Egypt to Lake Chad and beyond, which had been virtually unused for centuries, began to assume more importance in the fourteenth century, when Egypt began to look to West Africa for its gold.[61]

Even though from the tenth through the thirteenth centuries Egypt had its own gold supply near at hand, other Muslim states depended on West African gold from an early date. By the end of the eighth century Muslims already knew of the gold from the region. The tenth-century Arabian scholar al-Hamdani said that Ghana possessed the most productive gold mine in the world. The source for his information came from the master of the mint in San'a in Yemen. From the tenth century through the fifteenth, the Muslim world and Europe derived much of their gold from West African sources and received it by way of the trans-Saharan trade routes. The Muslims of the Maghrib, the Umayyad caliphs of Spain, and the Fatimids who later took over Egypt all used gold from the Sudan. The Sudanic states grew wealthy and powerful as a result of their ability to supply the metal and thus to pay for their imports from the Maghrib. From the thirteenth century, Europe, too, received African gold.[62]

It is important to note that the states of the Sudan could only supply the gold; they did not produce it themselves. They obtained it in the form of dust and nuggets from regions farther to the south, first from the goldfields of Bambuk in Wangara, a region between the Senegal and Falémé rivers, which was the chief source of gold at the time of Ghana. The Buré goldfields along the upper reaches of the Niger began to be exploited around the twelfth century and helped to finance the rise of Mali. New fields, even farther to the south in the Akan forest, became important around the fourteenth century.[63] The actual goldfields in all cases were outside the area of control of the rulers of the Sudanic states, who took great pains to shield the regions from interlopers.

Many historians offer a description of the strange system of barter called the "silent trade," although the existence of such a system has long been questioned. As the story goes, traders from the states of the Sudan brought merchandise to the vicinity of the gold producers, laid their goods in designated places, and withdrew. The forest people came with their gold, put down what they considered a suitable amount next to the merchandise, and withdrew in their turn. If the amount of gold satisfied the merchants, they took it and started back, while the forest people returned and collected the goods they had bought. The gold-producing regions kept their independence from the Sudanic states, despite periodic threats. Writing in the early sixteenth century, the Portuguese Valentim Fernandes said that he considered the "silent trade" to be a hoax designed by the gold traders to keep outsiders from learning the true source of the treasure.[64] Nevertheless, the notion keeps cropping up in modern histories.

The trade in slaves across the Sahara was probably next in importance to the gold trade for the western Sudan, but not for the central Sudan. There, because there was no gold, slaves were the mainstay of the export commerce. The Muslim world had a constant demand for black slaves that continued throughout our period and kept up long after 1500; it maintained its volume even during the period of the trans-Atlantic slave trade. The black slaves, if they survived the desert crossing, were spread out through the Maghrib, where many remained. Others were sent on to other Muslim lands. By the fourteenth and fifteenth centuries, some black slaves reached the Christian regions of the Mediterranean; we will examine them in a later chapter. Whatever their final destination, the sufferings of those who were forced to make the trek were horrifying. In addition to the heat and cold, the threat of storms, and a lack of water that they shared with the other members of the caravan, the slaves at times had to act as bearers of other goods; even when they did not carry loads, they had to load and unload the camels and help with the camp preparations.[65] The conditions they endured approach those faced by other Africans on the Middle Passage to the Americas.

Their numbers also compare closely to those of the Atlantic slave trade. In an elegant survey of the available evidence, Ralph A. Austen has provided a global estimate of the volume of the trans-Saharan slave trade, an estimate he carefully labeled as tentative because of the limited and fragmentary nature of the documents in the early period.[66] Table 4.1 reproduces Austen's estimates; they should be compared with those of the Atlantic slave trade given in chapter 9. Austen's figures provide an indirect index of the great demand for slaves in the Islamic world. Even though it was not a slave society in the strict definition of Finley and others, it still absorbed vast quantities of outsiders as servitors, soldiers, and sexual partners.

Table 4.1. Estimated Numbers of the
Trans-Saharan Slave Trade

Period	Annual Average	Total
650–800	1,000	150,000
800–900	3,000	300,000
900–1100	8,700	1,740,000
1100–1400	5,500	1,650,000
1400–1500	4,300	430,000
1500–1600	5,500	550,000
1600–1700	7,100	710,000
1700–1800	7,100	715,000
1800–1880	14,500	1,165,000
1880–1900	2,000	40,000
Total		7,450,000

Source: Ralph A. Austen, "The Trans-Saharan
Slave Trade: A Tentative Census," in *The Uncommon Market: Essays in the Economic History of the
Atlantic Slave Trade*, ed. Henry A. Gemery and
Jans S. Hogendorn, (New York, 1979), p. 66. To
the total Austen added 5 percent for slaves retained
at the desert's edge and 20 percent for deaths in
transit.

From this examination of slavery among the Muslims during the Middle
Ages, we can see that in many respects it corresponded closely to the European
tradition present in the Roman Empire and inherited by medieval Christendom.
While most slaves of the Muslims were domestics, there were special cases of
the use of slave gangs and the unexampled use of slave armies on a large scale.
Theoretically harsh but with many ameliorating factors in practice, Muslim slavery kept the institution alive and flourishing on the southern shores of the Mediterranean. From the Muslims, the western Europeans learned sugar cultivation
and refining, as well as a virtually unslakable hunger for sugar. The Muslim caravan traders of the Sahara extended the slave traffic into black Africa and
brought back the gold that helped spark the commercial rise of the medieval
Mediterranean. As a result, late medieval and Renaissance Europeans had at
hand both a commodity—sugar—and a potential labor force—black slaves—to
enable them to produce a lucrative commodity in greater commercial quantities
in their colonial territories. Islamic slavery and related economic features of the
Muslim world, therefore, provided an important background for the later development of American slavery.

5
SLAVERY IN
LATE MEDIEVAL EUROPE

In the later Middle Ages, from the twelfth century through the fifteenth, Europe's internal economy continued to develop and strengthen. Slavery was still present, although agriculture throughout most of Europe was the concern of serfs or free peasants. Domestic and artisan slavery persisted, particularly in Italy and the Iberian Peninsula. In this chapter we shall examine late medieval European slavery, both as an important segment of slavery's long history and as a prelude to the development of American slavery. Such an examination is especially important, because slavery in the New World would owe its origins to several late medieval traditions. First, the Crusades greatly expanded the activities of the Italian merchants, the most active European slave traders of the period, and, as an additional result of the Crusades, Europeans vastly expanded their knowledge of sugar, whose history in the Americas is impossible to disentangle from that of slavery. The Spanish and Portuguese reconquests kept slavery alive and flourishing in the Iberian Peninsula. The revival of Roman law and its influence on European legal development was also crucial, because the rules regulating slavery occupied such an important place in the Roman legal system. As a consequence of that revival, Spain and Portugal both had fully developed laws regulating servile status even before they began to expand overseas. We also shall consider the consequences of the Black Death in creating a heightened demand for slaves.

THE CRUSADES AND SUGAR

As we have seen, slavery was constantly present in the Mediterranean lands from ancient to modern times. In the society of Christian Europe, slavery persisted around the shores of the inland sea even as it was declining in continental Europe. When western Europeans embarked on the Crusades, the Middle Ages'

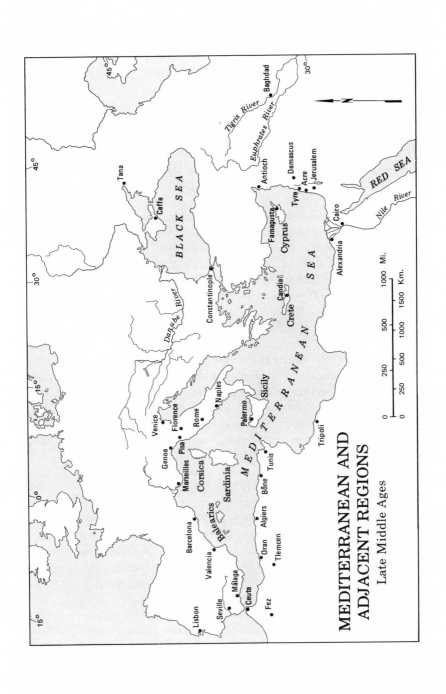

MEDITERRANEAN AND ADJACENT REGIONS

Late Middle Ages

energetic though abortive movement of territorial expansion, the participants of all ranks and callings knew slavery as an unquestioned aspect of their society, although the numbers of slaves were small everywhere in Europe. In the Muslim lands the crusaders found slaves and, more important, the opportunity for economic expansion.

In 1095 Pope Urban II, in a sermon preached in the southern French city of Clermont, called for Western knights to march to Jerusalem and free Christianity's most holy city from Muslim control. The Crusades, as the Western campaigns came to be called, owed their origins to a complex set of conditions present in several cultural regions. It is not sufficient to account for their origin solely on the basis of the appeal of papal propaganda for the knights and nobles of western Europe. One must go back several decades before 1095 and examine Near Eastern events in order to understand the background of the Crusades. In the middle of the eleventh century a group of nomads from central Asia, the Seljuk Turks, seized influence over the caliphate of Baghdad, the nominal center and directing force of Islam. Called in first as mercenaries, the Seljuks made themselves the most powerful group at the center of the Islamic world, able to dictate to the caliph. Thereafter a group of Seljuks began to move into Byzantine territory in Asia Minor. Once they had gained the land, the Seljuk conquerors sought to reestablish Byzantine agricultural practices. They "recolonized their devastated lands with Greek, Armenian and Syrian farmers, often kidnapping and enslaving entire villages and towns in Byzantine and Armenian lands."[1] Beyond the economic losses they suffered, the Byzantines clearly recognized the strategic threat of the Turks in their Anatolian possessions. Therefore the Byzantine emperor Alexius Comnenus called on the pope for a contingent of Western knights to cooperate with his own troops in driving the Turks from Anatolia.

Because the pope never recorded his reasons for calling the First Crusade, historians have speculated and suggested a number of possibilities, most of which have little to do with the Byzantine request for a limited number of knights to help regain Anatolia. The most startling departure from what the Byzantines wanted came when Urban II called for the crusaders to go on to Jerusalem and described their goal as a land of milk and honey. Why the change? There was one strong connection between aid to the Byzantines and military action beyond Anatolia: the pilgrimages by Western Christians to Jerusalem had been quite popular, and the Seljuk irruption threatened to cut the routes used by pilgrims. Perhaps the pope did not distinguish carefully among the several Muslim groups, only considering it improper and unfortunate for Muslims to control the most holy places of Christianity. Another papal desire may have been to use the crusaders as part of a campaign to heal the division between Rome and the Byzantine church, a split that had existed for centuries but had only been formalized since 1054.

Internal changes in Europe were probably additional motivations for the pope's actions. For some time the papal administration had cooperated with secular authorities in an attempt to reduce domestic warfare, establishing the Truce of God and the Peace of God to limit the periods of war and shield non-combatants. What better way to save Europe from unwanted and destructive combat than to direct the energies of the knights, whose whole life was devoted to war, toward acceptable goals outside their homelands? For the knights, as for the nobles who led them, the compensations were more than adequate. They could gain religious rewards for participation; the pope allowed a moratorium on their debts while they campaigned; and they could hope to gain lands for themselves. The latter was especially important in a Europe that was in the first phases of its great medieval population rise, with available land for seigneurial holdings increasingly difficult to secure.

In addition to the secular warriors and the church, one other European group had much to gain from the Crusades. This was made up of the merchants and seamen of the Italian towns, principally Venice and Pisa, who saw great economic opportunities in the carrying trade and possibilities of commercial privileges in the eastern Mediterranean. Their activities, too often neglected by historians of the Crusades, had a great impact on slavery.[2]

The response to the Byzantine appeal as relayed by the pope was overwhelming. By 1100 the crusading armies had established a line of enclaves along the shores of the eastern Mediterranean. The more familiar part of the story covers the kingdom of Jerusalem and the other principalities set up by the crusaders, but more significant for our study were the concessions the Italian merchants secured. For their support in conquering numerous towns, including Acre, Tripoli, and Beirut, Italians were given a portion of the urban land and the countryside. In Antioch in 1098 the Genoese, for example, received the "church of St. John and the square in front of it, a fonduk [a combination office building-residence-warehouse], a well, and permanent exemption from all taxes."[3] From their new possessions in the crusader states, the Italians engaged in agriculture, producing market commodities such as sugar and cotton, and, above all, they engaged in commerce.

The crusader states lasted fewer than two hundred years before the Muslims were able to reassert control over the territory. For those two centuries, although the crusaders imposed their own code of laws, they did little more than preserve the preexisting tenurial arrangements and labor dues of the Muslim peasants. As we know, agricultural slavery was atypical in the Muslim world. In Palestine before the Crusades, the peasants were subject to wealthy and powerful landlords: the state, rich nobles and townsmen, and religious foundations (*waqf*). The cultivators leased the lands they worked for a payment of one-third or one-half of the crops to the owners. Because the crusaders were few in number and did not import European peasants to work the land, they were content to displace the Muslim landowners and continue the traditional relations with the peasants. The Europeans had little direct contact with the peasants living on their lands, dealing with the communities through the *rayises* (village headmen). The lease payments were generally collected in kind, and, since there was no demesne land, corvée labor was required only for the upkeep of roads and bridges. One of the most recent historians of the Crusades quotes a contemporary Muslim as reporting that Christians treated the peasants more favorably than the previous Muslim masters had done.[4]

Even though most Muslim laborers in the crusader states were free, slaves were still present. H. E. Mayer described Castle Safed, which controlled Jacob's Ford, the most important crossing of the Jordan River, on the road from Acre to Damascus. After it was rebuilt in 1240, "the castle held a garrison of 50 Templar knights, 30 serving brothers, 50 Turcopole cavalrymen, 300 archers, and another 820 men and 400 slaves. . . . "[5] Muslims enslaved as a result of their capture in war and eastern European slaves brought in by the Italians were sold in urban slave markets, such as the one in Acre, and were mainly employed as domestics. No Christian could be enslaved, but Muslims who accepted Christianity were not guaranteed enfranchisement unless they had fled into Christian territory. Local converted Muslims generally remained in their servile condition. In fact, abuses were constantly reported. Landowners prevented Muslims from accepting baptism; some even prevented them from attending Christian sermons. Italian merchants fraudulently brought in numbers of eastern European Christians for sale as slaves, passing them off as Muslims.[6]

Since most of the rural labor force was free, slavery did not play a crucial role in the internal economy of the crusader states. Nevertheless, the Crusades, taken as a whole, did have an important impact on the European experience with slavery in several indirect, but important, ways. By providing commercial bases, the crusader states allowed the Italian traders to expand their trading contacts throughout the eastern Mediterranean, including their hold on the slave trade.

This expansion came at a propitious time for them, just when Europe's economy was beginning to grow. The Crusades were in part a consequence of this economic quickening in Europe, and in turn they stimulated it. Taking advantage of their position in the eastern Mediterranean, the Italians extended their commercial connections north into the Black Sea and south to Egypt, unconcernedly crossing religious frontiers in the process. One of the most profitable portions of the Italian trade was slaving, and it was one that outlasted the Crusades by two centuries and more.

In addition, Europeans learned a great deal from their exposure to the sophisticated ambience of the civilizations of the East. It was after the Crusades that rich Europeans, both noble and bourgeois, embraced a more elaborate style of life, with better clothes, a more varied diet, increased consumption, and richer houses. The example of the East stimulated these demands in the West: Italians in the East catered to the demands, providing spices, silks, sugar, and slaves. In urban houses servants were required, and the Italian merchants could easily supply slaves to fill the need. The fine Italian households of the late Middle Ages and the Renaissance were staffed with slaves, an aspect often forgotten when scholars wax eloquent about "Renaissance individualism."

One discovery that the Europeans made during the Crusades was sugar production. Sugar cane, as we saw in chapter 4, had been grown by the Muslims in the Middle East and the Mediterranean, and it continued to be grown by Europeans in the crusader states. It is not true, as it is sometimes said, that the first direct contact that Westerners had with sugar was in Syria and Palestine at the time of the First Crusade. Sicily and parts of Spain already produced sugar, and we have seen that Venice imported Egyptian sugar in the late tenth century. Some Europeans, and perhaps some crusaders, had already tasted sugar. Nevertheless, sugar cane plantations were new to the Frankish invaders and attracted the attention of the chroniclers. Fulcher of Chartres reported the hardships that limited food supplies caused for the army of the First Crusade and went on to say that

> in those cultivated fields through which we passed during our march there were certain ripe plants which the common folk called "honey-cane" and which were very much like reeds. The name is compounded from "cane" and "honey," whence the expression "wood honey" I think, because the latter is skillfully made from these canes. In our hunger we chewed them all day because of the taste of honey. However, this helped but little.[7]

William of Tyre, in his description of the irrigation projects around Tyre, also mentioned sugar.

> All the country round about derives immense benefits from these waters. Not only do they supply gardens and delightful orchards planted with fruit trees, but they irrigate the sugar cane also. From this latter crop sugar (*zachara*) is made, a most precious product, very necessary for the use and health of mankind, which is carried by merchants to the most remote countries of the world.[8]

Western sugar manufacturing and trade in sugar to the West dramatically increased as a result of the Crusades. After they reached Jerusalem, the crusaders maintained the cultivation of sugar cane in the states they established. This afforded them immediate revenues and, more important in the long run, created additional demand in the West, as returning crusaders and pilgrims took home samples of cane sugar and thus helped to spread the taste for it. Sugar plantations were controlled by the king of Jerusalem, by corporate groups such as the military orders and the Italian cities, and by individuals. As one example, the Knights of St. John, or the Hospitalers, received lands in the crusader states for their maintenance. Scholars have identified 858 pieces of property in the kingdom of Jerusalem; of these, the Hospitalers held 171 at various times. Like other wealthy landholders in the region, the Hospitalers generally allowed the native communities to continue their normal life without interference; they normally asked only that a rent be paid by each community. Exceptions to this rule were farms devoted to specialized crops: truck gardens, vineyards, olive groves, and sugar cane fields, proof of sugar's importance in the economy. The king of Jerusalem also received indirect income from sugar. Among his regalian rights was the ability to impose duties on manufacturing: dyeing, tanning, and the production of sugar.[9]

Sugar production, dependent as it was upon water for irrigation and for motive power to turn the mills that crushed the cane, was concentrated in those places where water was readily available. The main centers for sugar production were coastal: Sidon, Acre, and Tyre (the latter the most important), and inland in Galilee and the Jordan Valley. In these places sugar production predated the Crusades, and soon the Westerners expanded production. The king of Jerusalem possessed sugar plantations and mills near Acre, and in 1160 King Baldwin III farmed out the royal mills to Renaud Fauconnier and gave him the right to construct new mills.[10]

Disputes over water rights emerged among the Western landowners in the crusader states. One example of this was the long-term acrimony that developed between the Templars and the Hospitalers over the watercourse called the Flum d'Acre. In the 1230s the Templars built a dam on the river to increase the water flow to their mills at Doc and Recordane. Rising waters threatened the Hospitalers' lands upstream, and the two orders agreed to a compromise about the level that the river would be allowed to reach. By 1262 the dispute reemerged. The Templars were accused of obstructing the river with additional construction, while the Hospitalers—because of their intensive cultivation of sugar cane—had diverted so much water to irrigate their fields that the level of the river had fallen far enough to render the Templars' mill at Doc useless. Another dispute was between the monastery of La Quarantaine and the widow of the lord of Sidon, Eustace Garnier, who had controlled the water rights in the area and had restricted the monks' use of irrigation water to one day in each two-week period. Because of pressure exerted by the viscount of Sidon, Garnier's widow allowed the monks weekly use of the water.[11]

Italian cities, too, received land grants in the crusader states. The example of Tyre will serve to illustrate the general pattern. Even before the Crusades, merchants from Amalfi, Venice, and Pisa had traded in Tyre for silks and sugar. In the division following the European conquest, Venice gained control of Tyre. In 1240 the Venetian agent in Tyre reported on the twenty-four estates owned in the city's vicinity, devoted to market crops and including truck gardens, vineyards, orchards, and cane fields. The labor in these estates was Syrian and was employed under sharecropping arrangements. The reputation of Tyre as a sugar-producing region was widely known. It was from there that Frederick II secured experts to help revitalize the Sicilian industry in the mid-thirteenth century.[12]

Although their existence was precarious toward the last, the Christian states continued to produce sugar for their own use and for export. When the Muslims drove the last of the Westerners from the mainland in 1291, the Christian refugees moved to the Mediterranean islands and took sugar production with them.[13] Sugar thereafter underwent a westward progression, as its intensive cultivation and processing spread to the islands and mainland areas held by the Christians. In most of these regions, sugar had been grown by Muslims since the eighth or ninth centuries, but only in the later Middle Ages did it come to be exploited more fully.

Parenthetically, it must be noted that the fall of the crusader states in the East did not mark the end of commerce in sugar between Muslims and Christians. Even though sugar from the Christian-held Mediterranean islands soon began to be exported to Europe, Damascus and Tripoli in Syria and Alexandria and other Egyptian ports continued to provide Western merchants with sugar and other goods.[14]

Among the first islands to be exploited for sugar production was Cyprus. Sugar cane had probably been grown on the island since it was introduced by the Muslims in the seventh century, but it was only after the crusader states had fallen that it became important in the island's economy. Famagusta, the principal city, became a vital trading center when it inherited Acre's role as the nexus of Christian trade in the region. Its prosperity depended on shipbuilding and exports, of which the most valuable were sugar, salt, wine, and cloth. The first recorded export of sugar from Cyprus dates from 1301 when a Genoese merchant in Pisa purchased ten chests of the commodity. Sugar was produced in several parts of the island, and numerous producers were involved: the Lusignan dynasty itself, the Knights of St. John, Venetians such as the Corner (or Cornaro) family, and a Catalan family—the Ferrers. The most important plantations were those of the Corner family at Piskopi, in the southern part of the island along the river Kouris. Although some slaves were used in Cypriot sugar production, especially on the royal estates, the bulk of the labor was nonslave and included Greek and Syrian immigrants given special political status by the Venetians. The Syrians were often skilled sugar workers, brought in especially for their expertise. In 1494 an Italian visitor reported that some four hundred workers were engaged in sugar production at Piskopi. Sugar cane in Cyprus was grown in irrigated fields, and there, too, disputes over water rights involved rival producers.[15]

Other islands in the eastern Mediterranean also produced sugar. Crete was in Byzantine hands until the early thirteenth century, when the Catalan count of Monserrat conquered it in the aftermath of the Fourth Crusade. Shortly afterward the Venetians bought Crete and in the fifteenth century fostered sugar production there.[16]

Sicily was probably the most important Mediterranean center for sugar in the late Middle Ages. Sugar cane had been introduced shortly after the Muslims conquered the island in 878, and by the end of the ninth century Sicilian sugar was being sold in North Africa. Palermo was in the main region of sugar produc-

tion in Sicily, and ibn-Hauqal wrote that "the banks of the streams around Palermo, from their sources to their mouths, are bordered by low-lying fields, upon
which the Persian reed is grown."[17] In the eleventh century the Normans took
Sicily, and their conquest was motivated in part by sugar. The Christians of
Sicily had provided samples of sugar, among other products, to the Normans
in order to demonstrate the island's wealth and to encourage them to expel the
Muslims. The sugar industry persisted in Norman times. Both the king and the
cathedral of Montreale in Palermo owned sugar mills. One indication of the
novelty that sugar cane presented to the Norman knights when they first saw it
under cultivation is provided in a letter that Hugh Falcandus wrote to the trea-
surer of the diocese of Palermo. Falcandus described the

> great extension of wonderful reeds which are called by the inhabitants
> honey canes, from the sweetness of the juice they contain. The juice of
> these canes, when it has been boiled with care and to the right extent, con-
> verts itself into a kind of honey; if on the other hand it is subjected to a
> more complete and perfect boiling, it becomes condensed into the sub-
> stance of sugar.[18]

No doubt because of the destruction accompanying the Norman conquest of
Sicily and of the inexperience of the new estate and mill managers, the Sicilian
sugar industry underwent a decline during the Norman period. The reign of the
emperor Frederick II (king of Sicily from 1197 to 1250) marked a temporary
revival. Consistently sponsoring enlightened reforms for the economy of the
kingdom, Frederick was particularly interested in sugar production. He had the
fields hedged to prevent damage to the cane, and once, during an infestation of
caterpillars, he mobilized the population and assigned a daily quota for the hand
collection of the pests. In 1239 he had two experts in sugar refining sent from
Tyre to Sicily to examine the industry there and recommend improvements.[19]

After Frederick's death, Sicily underwent over a century and a half of disor-
dered political conditions, which rendered Frederick's reforms useless. Sugar's
decline was exacerbated by the expulsion of the Muslims from the island. Sugar
received favor from Sicily's rulers early in the fifteenth century, and stability
returned under the Aragonese king Alfonso V (1416–58). During his reign the
Sicilian sugar industry reached a peak, aided by studies of proper irrigation of
the fields undertaken by the University of Palermo.[20]

It has often been asserted that the famous three-roller sugar mill—so characteristic of the New World plantations—came into use in Sicily during Alfonso
V's reign. This is almost assuredly not the case, and the new mill did not appear
until after the discovery of America.[21]

Despite the lack of the three-roller mill, the support of the island's rulers did
help sugar reach new heights in Sicily in the fifteenth century. An indication of
its importance there was the designation of one of the entries into the city of
Syracuse as the *Porta degli Zuccheri*, or the gate of the sugars (or sugar

workers). Also, in 1446, one of Syracuse's streets was named *Cannamella*, honey cane.[22]

Because of its potential profitability, sugar production spread to the Italian mainland, although it never became important there. In the thirteenth century a small amount of sugar cane was grown in Lombardy. Some sugar was produced in the kingdom of Naples, and around 1550 Ferdinand de' Medici introduced it unsuccessfully near Florence.[23]

Most labor for the Mediterranean sugar industry—on both the Christian and Muslim sides of the sea—was free. Although here and there some slaves may have been used, they were unusual. The close identification of sugar cane and slave labor came later, in the lands of the Atlantic. At this point we must defer the continuation of sugar's history in order to examine the parallel paths of slavery and the slave trade in the later Middle Ages.

SLAVERY IN ITALY

From ancient times to the seventeenth century, Italy knew slavery. While slavery declined in Europe north of the Alps and serfdom rose, the trade in and the use of slaves persisted in Italy. One reason was the durability of urban life in the Italian peninsula, and urban life in preindustrial societies often included domestic slavery. More important was Italy's geographic location and the propensity of many Italians for long-distance trade. Located in the center of the Mediterranean, Italy had links with the entire basin of the inland sea and with what Fernand Braudel has called "the greater Mediterranean,"[24] those lands beyond the shores of the sea but linked to it. Through the passes of the Alps, Italians developed trading ties with the northern parts of western and central Europe. Italian traders journeyed to the Byzantine cities, to the markets of the eastern Mediterranean from Anatolia to Egypt, to the North African ports (where trans-Saharan products could be obtained), and to the cities of the Iberian Peninsula (which gave them an opening on the Atlantic). They even ventured beyond Constantinople to reach the markets of the Black Sea. At one time or another, all these areas served the Italian traders as markets for the sale or purchase of slaves. Early on the Venetians exported slaves to the eastern Mediterranean; around the late eleventh or early twelfth centuries they were joined by merchants of other Italian cities. Our task now is to examine slavery in Italy proper from the eleventh century to the end of the fifteenth.

The Italian use of slaves was widespread, and most were recruited by the slave trade. In the late eleventh century, when the Normans conquered southern Italy, they often enslaved members of the defeated population, but this was an atypical situation.[25] Wars in the Italian peninsula only rarely ended with the enslavement of the defeated. The Norman aberration was likely due to the position of the Normans as invaders from outside who did not identify with those they vanquished.

Italians mainly imported their slaves from outside. Already by the twelfth century, Venice had a slave population that was recruited from a wide area, though it was a small percentage of the total Venetian population.[26] By the mid-twelfth century Genoa possessed Muslim slaves, and there is documentary evidence that one of the wealthy Genoese merchants of the time, Guglielmo Burone, was a slaveowner.[27] In 1300 the will of a Genoese resident in Famagusta on Cyprus indicated that he owned five female slaves and one male slave.[28] Iris Origo wrote that

> by the end of the fourteenth century there was hardly a well-to-do household in Tuscany without at least one slave: brides brought them as part of their dowries, doctors accepted them in lieu of fees—and it was not unusual to find them even in the service of a priest.[29]

In the fourteenth and fifteenth centuries, slaves in Italy came from a number of areas and ethnic groups. There were Muslims, Tatars, Circassians, Russians, Bulgarians, Armenians, Albanians, a few from the islands of the Mediterranean, and fewer still from black Africa and the Canaries. Most were women, and most were used as domestics and concubines. They and their children could attain freedom in a variety of ways.[30] One story illustrates several aspects of the common pattern. In 1427 Cosimo de' Medici of Florence had an illegitimate son by a Circassian slave girl. The child later was legitimized and ended his life as the archpriest of Prato.[31]

In the Italian states probably the greatest number of slaves were used as domestic servants, and a percentage of these acted as concubines for their masters. Small numbers of others were used in artisan and craft workshops. There is little evidence of slave use in agriculture. Small market farmers may have employed a few slaves as laborers, but plantation agriculture was not important in the peninsula. Italians did make use of a limited number of slaves in agricultural pursuits on the islands they controlled in the Mediterranean, but the practice was not translated often to the mainland. There were other slaves in Italy, additional victims of the slave trade, acquired elsewhere and present in Italy only until they could be transshipped for sale elsewhere.[32]

Because most slaves were young women living in the household, it is not surprising that sexual liaisons developed between them and their masters. Scholars have uncovered a plethora of Italian documentary evidence concerning concubinage and the complications it produced. Sexual use and abuse of slaves were features of most slave systems, but for medieval Italy we have our first relatively complete records of such activities. Iris Origo has pointed out the psychological turmoil that the presence of young, defenseless female slaves created in the slaveholding families. Not without justification, free women came to hate slaves, and often the slaves reciprocated.[33] Giovanna Balbi found that in twelfth-century Genoa

> domestic concubinage between masters and female slaves [was] certainly

widespread and frequent. . . . The affectionate relations between slaves and free citizens was not limited only to the family ambience, but also [included] those outside the family: in that case they led not only to procreation but sometimes to matrimony as well. . . . [34]

Several paths were open to the master who impregnated his own slave. He could arrange a marriage for the slave; he could raise the child as a slave; he could sell the mother while she was still pregnant; or he could free the mother and marry her. The last option has not left many traces in the records. Origo quoted two letters written by an agent of a merchant who owned a female slave.

The slave you sent is sick, or rather full of boils, so that we find none who would have her. We will sell or barter her as best we can, and send you the account. Furthermore, I hear she is with child, two months gone or more, and therefore she will not be worth selling. [35]

The agent wrote again some time later about the same slave. ''No man will have her. She says she is with child by you, and assuredly seems to be. The pother she makes is so great, she might be the Queen of France.''[36] A letter describing a different situation tells the same story of the helplessness of the slave and the indifference of the master.

We spoke to the chaplain to whom your slave belonged and he says you may throw her in the sea, with what she has in her belly, for it is no creature of his. And we deem he speaks the truth, for had she been pregnant by him, he would not have sent her. . . . Methinks you had better send the creature to the hospital. [37]

Not all slaveowners were this harsh and uncaring. Many treated their slave mistresses and their illegitimate children with great kindness and bequeathed them generous amounts in their wills. [38]

In cases in which an outsider rendered a slave pregnant, the law in the Italian cities was clear: the master, not the slave, was to be compensated, because her economic value had been diminished as a result of her pregnancy. ''Laws which provided financial compensation to the master of an impregnated slave were motivated by a desire to avoid economic loss to the master and to take into account the possibility of death in childbirth.''[39] The offspring produced by such liaisons could be dealt with in a variety of ways. The master could rear the child or could turn the newborn infant over to its father. The child could be exposed. The mother could be rented out as a wet nurse for a high price.[40] Infants lucky enough to be taken in by orphanages were free, and the hospital itself was listed as the father, thus conveying legitimate status on the orphans.[41] The compensation owed to the master varied in different Italian cities. In Genoa it was one-half of the slave's value. In Siena and Florence it was one-third of the value in addition to the full costs of the birth if the woman lived. If she died, the master would be entitled to her full value, though such laws were not always enforceable.[42]

In 1462 a statute came into force in Florence carrying a fine of one thousand florins if two eyewitnesses or four people with secondhand knowledge of the event swore that a man came into another's house "to visit a slave or to lie with her."[43] Given the penalties that could be imposed, it is not surprising that insurance contracts could be purchased in Genoa by the fathers of the unborn children of slaves to idemnify the master in the case of his slave's death.[44]

The antinatalist policies of the Italian slaveowners is additional evidence of the domestic use they made of their slaves. The owners of rural slaves often encouraged procreation as a long-term measure to gain new workers, whereas those who employed domestics did not want to lose the short-term advantages.

Aside from domestic service, there were other jobs for slaves, but they were not especially numerous. Artisans bought a few slaves as helpers in manufacturing, since the artisan workshops were small and required few workers. Michel Balard believed that one or two slaves in artisan and merchants' families were typical in thirteenth-century Genoa. The will of Guglielmo Caffaraino, a cloth maker of that city, provided for the freeing of his six slaves upon his death. Five were male and probably were employed in their master's workshop, while the woman probably worked as a domestic in the household.[45] In the fifteenth century there were some black slaves who were gondoliers in Venice, but they were a quite small minority. Most of the gondoliers, one to two thousand in number, were self-employed. Origo portrayed oarsmen in the Italian galleys as slaves, but this has been effectively refuted by F. C. Lane, who reported that while there may have been some few slave oarsmen used on private vessels, the Venetian laws prohibited slaves on board the municipally controlled vessels.[46]

Some other uses for slaves were possible. They could be pledged as security for loans. They could be rented to craftsmen, and they would later return to their masters with enhanced values once they had learned their crafts. After acquiring a craft, slaves could usually be sold only to masters in the same craft. Certain occupations were closed to them. In Venice, slaves could not be taught certain specialized procedures in the manufacturing of fine cloth. Genoese pharmacists were prohibited from teaching slaves of Turkish or Tatar origin the secrets of their profession.[47] The services of slaves could be rented out. "In 1281, for example, Bartolino de Asture sold to Opossino de Aldono the services of his slave Martino *dragumannus* from Slavonia, for a period of fifteen years. . . . The said slave, used as an interpreter, swore on the Bible to observe the contract."[48]

The methods of acquisition of slaves in the Italian cities were recorded in deeds of sale, which specified the details of the transactions, such as the price and origin of the slave, as well as the slave's complete physical description. The seller guaranteed that the slave was free of physical defects or pregnancy. If a purchaser later discovered that his slave had been pregnant at the time of sale, he could have his purchase price refunded. The new owner got full control over the new slave, including the right to discipline his new slave by beating or whipping. He had the same rights over his own family, a legacy from Roman family law. As a result, slaves were not in too different a position from that of other family members. The master could treat his slaves harshly, but definite limits existed. No master could kill his slave with impunity, and the state dealt strictly with violations.[49]

The new slaves entered quickly into a process of integration with the family. If they had not been baptized at an earlier point on their journey to Italy, they were baptized and given Christian names. It was important that the baptism came after the enslavement, because Christians were not permitted to be enslaved. Violations of this rule occurred with some regularity, as impious slave dealers passed off Greek Orthodox and even foreign Catholic slaves as non-Christians.[50] Once baptism took place, the new slave was on the way to becoming a member of the new household both legally and physically. Because slavery in Italy was above all an urban phenomenon, and space in the cities was at a premium, with no possibility of separate slave quarters, slaves shared their masters' houses. In the more elaborate households, they lived in the attics, in small rooms between the main floors, or in Venice on the sea floor (the ground floor).[51]

Many slaves resented their status and made efforts to run away, but there was not much hope for successful flight. The church provided only temporary sanctuary and in most cases turned the runaways over to their masters. An illustration of a failed attempt appeared in a merchant's letter.

We hear from Ibiza that Ser Antonio Dello has arrived there with many Moorish captives on his ship, and twelve of them ran away with his rowing boat. . . . But because of the weather, the said Moors came here [to Majorca] and for the present have been imprisoned, which is a great piece of good fortune.[52]

Pursuit could be far-reaching. A slaveowner in Barcelona wrote to an Italian living in Avignon asking him to be on guard for two runaways.

One is named Dmitri, a big man and very handsome. His flesh is good, fresh and rosy. [The other] lacks a tooth in front and has a rather greenish skin. . . . I pray you . . . to have them caught, let them be strongly fettered, and send them back by boat to me.[53]

Iris Origo found an insurance policy dating from 1401 for the shipment of a Tatar slave, Margherita, from Porto Pisano to Barcelona. The value of the slave was set at fifty gold florins, and the owner would receive reimbursement if the slave met misadventure at sea. But the policy specifically excluded the illness or death of the slave and "any attempt at flight or suicide—'if she throws herself into the sea of her own accord'—a risk which would hardly have been specified, had not such incidents occurred fairly often."[54] This illustrates the desperate lengths to which some slaves would go to escape their bonds.

There were other avenues to freedom, and among them manumission was the most common. The slave population in the Italian cities was constantly changing as manumissions freed existing slaves, who then were replaced by newly imported people. The major reason for this regular turnover is that the majority of the slaves were young females destined for domestic work. Their proximity to the family and their racial background, generally white, meant relatively easy assimilation. We have discussed the sexual ties that developed between slave and free. They were only part of a wider array of often affectionate attachments that in some cases linked the slaves and the families they served.[55]

Women slaves could attain freedom by matrimony. If a master married his own slave, she was considered to be free, and this was also true in the case of a female slave who married a free man with her master's permission. A master who wished to make his own child by a slave mother legitimate could do so on his accord only if he were living openly with the child's mother. If he were not, if he had a legal wife, he needed permission of the authorities.[56] Francesco Datini, the famous merchant of Prato, had a daughter by one of his slaves. He later gave his mistress her freedom and arranged a marriage for her. He also adopted his daughter and left her two hundred lire in his will.[57]

As we noted, most slaves were baptized at or shortly after their sale, and thereafter they were expected to conform to Christian practice. But adherence to Christianity was not by itself a path to freedom. Manumission always required the volition of the master, who often would specify some conditions for the newly freed person to fulfill. In Genoa in 1186 records indicate that a female slave of Muslim origin was freed on condition that she remain in her master's service for ten years. In 1190 Otto Guercio and his wife Anna freed Elena, a Sardinian slave woman, contingent upon her resisting the sexual advances of one Armanino until he married her.[58] Monetary payments were often required before manumission was permitted, and this fact indicates that some slaves had the opportunity to acquire their own money. One Genoese slave was freed when she was able to pay ten lire for her freedom, while another bought her manumission for eight lire and the promise to pay her former master one lira for each of the next six years. Genoa may have had small groups of freedmen from various ethnic groups who aided their countrymen in purchasing their freedom.[59]

Manumissions by testament were common, usually by the will of the master, but occasionally by the will of his widow. The newly freed were often required to serve the masters' heirs at low pay. As one example, a Genoese resident in Cyprus left instructions in his will to free three female slaves. Two obtained freedom immediately, as well as living quarters and money. The third was to serve the widow for four years, after which she would receive a small house, some furnishings, and ten barrels of wheat. After freedom, the newly manumitted could rise in the social hierarchy, sometimes very quickly and far.[60] The mobility can be explained by the ethnic origin of the majority of the slaves in Italy. They were mostly white and not easily distinguishable from the native born, once they had learned the language and the customs of their host society.

We can account for their ethnic origins by an examination of the recruitment of slaves for the late medieval and Renaissance Italian cities.

The slave trade to Italy was almost exclusively in the hands of long-distance traders who purchased people in distant markets. True, the Normans had enslaved some women and children as they conquered areas in the Italian south and in Sicily in the late eleventh century, and in later centuries prisoners captured in the wars among the Italian states were held for ransom at times and threatened with slavery, but these were the exceptions that proved the rule. Italian merchants were among Europe's most energetic and successful traders in distant regions. An important part of their trade was devoted to slaves, and while the bulk of their slave trade was concerned with supplying third parties, especially the Muslims of Egypt, with slaves purchased in other regions (the Balkans and the northern ports of the Black Sea especially), they also brought slaves home to Italy to be sold.

In the early Middle Ages the Italians, particularly the Venetians, had supplied the markets of the eastern Mediterranean with wood and central European slaves in return for luxury goods purchased there. This began to change in the twelfth and thirteenth centuries. Wood gave way to manufactured goods, especially woolen cloth, and the Italian merchants shifted from central and eastern Europe to the Black Sea in their search for slaves. This important Christian-Muslim trade was vigorous, despite papal attempts to limit it by forbidding exports of arms, war materiel, and slaves to the Muslims. R.-H. Bautier, however, believed that "the blockade does not seem to have been very effective since in 1154 Pisa undertook to deliver precisely those forbidden commodities to the sultan."[61]

In Genoa the slave market seems to have come into full flowering around 1190. Before that there had been only sporadic sales of slaves, including some probably Muslim black slaves who had been brought in by non-Genoese sellers. In the 1190s a regular series of slave sales began. Balbi studied the sales in Genoa in the period 1186–1226 and found recorded sales or manumissions of fifty-eight slaves. The accompanying tabulation summarizes Balbi's findings.[62]

	Males	Females
Muslims	17 (3 black)	13 (1 black)
Sards	3	10
Corsicans	1	—
Greeks	—	1
Unspecified	2	11
	23	35

These figures, although they record a relatively small number of cases, are consistent with scholars' views of slavery in Italy. Women outnumbered men, no doubt because domestic slavery was more important than industrial or agricultural. Italians bought slaves to act as servants and preferred women for domestic work. In these years we see a recruitment pattern based solidly on the western Mediterranean; the Black Sea became important for Genoa only later. Muslims from North Africa or Spain, and non-Muslims from the islands predominated. Only one Greek appeared in the records. The relatively low numbers of slaves are interesting, too. They reflect the strictly occasional demand for slaves as domestic laborers in the thirteenth century, when the general European population was on the rise and when Italian cities could fill most of their labor needs with the native free. Only in the fourteenth century, when an escalating series of disasters caused a severe decline in population, was there a substantial rise in demand for slaves.[63]

   In the thirteenth century, the Genoese were especially active in the slave trade. They had participated in the First Crusade, and thereafter they maintained a steady commerce with Muslim Egypt. Until the second half of the thirteenth century, they played a secondary role to Venice, whose doge persuaded the leaders of the Fourth Crusade to divert their armies to the conquest of Constantinople from the Byzantines. As a consequence, the Venetians received favored trading rights in the Byzantine Empire and easier access to the Black Sea. When Michael Paleologus drove the Westerners from the Byzantine Empire in 1261, the Genoese, thanks to a previous treaty with the new Byzantine ruler, replaced the Venetians in the eastern imperial trade and received a near monopoly on trade to the Black Sea. In Pera, a suburb of Constantinople, and in Tana and Caffa on the north side of the Black Sea, the Genoese merchants maintained commercial posts, from which they obtained slaves among other goods, until the fifteenth century. During the second half of the thirteenth century, Genoa regularly supplied Mamluk Egypt with slave recruits for its army, due in large part to the fact that the normal overland caravan routes from the Black Sea across Anatolia to Egypt were cut.[64]

   The shift had repercussions back to Italy. Thirteenth-century slave recruitment in Genoa illustrates the common Italian pattern. In the first three-quarters of the century, Muslims made up around 75 percent of the slave population, reflecting the well-established trading links with Iberia and North Africa. The Aragonese conquest of the Islamic kindgom of Valencia in the 1230s placed numerous Muslims on the market, and many of these found their way to Italy. Most of these Muslims were sold in Italy before they had been baptized and given Christian names. In the final quarter of the thirteenth century, the situation began to change dramatically, as the primary area of recruitment shifted to the Black Sea. In 1275 the first recorded Russian slave, a man named Balada, appeared in Genoa. He was the first of many slaves brought from the still-pagan areas of the Black Sea. Their numbers grew rapidly when the Genoese set up trading stations in Pera beginning in 1281 and in Caffa around 1289. Most of the slaves brought in from the Black Sea reached Genoa after having been baptized.[65]

This set the pattern for the fourteenth and fifteenth centuries. Until the Turks cut the straits connecting the Black Sea and the Mediterranean in the mid-fifteenth century, the bulk of the slaves came from the region of the Black Sea. This is borne out by Origo's analysis of the official list of slaves sold in Florence between 1366 and 1397. The ethnic distribution of the 357 slaves listed is shown in the accompanying tabulation.

Tatars	274
Greeks	30
Russians	13
Turks	8
Circassians	4
Bosnians or Slavs	5
Cretans	1
Muslims	22

Origo reported that 329 of the slaves were female, either women or young girls, while only 28 were males, and only 4 of them were over the age of sixteen.[66] Michael E. Mallett also found that most of the slaves in Florence were from the region of the Black Sea. Many came overland to Florence from Ancona on the Adriatic, where several Florentine merchants had set themselves up as slave traders. With Florence's conquest of Pisa and its port, the city's merchants had maritime access to the Black Sea. Thereafter they could purchase their chattels directly in the Black Sea slave markets and were no longer dependent upon the Venetian or Genoese traders. After the mid-fifteenth century, when the Black Sea markets could no longer be reached, Florentine galley masters began to import more blacks from markets in Catalonia and Portugal.[67]

The Black Death changed the situation drastically in the middle of the fourteenth century and created a heightened demand for slaves. The plague probably originated in central Asia and was brought to the Crimea across the Asian steppes with the caravan trade. It reached the Black Sea in 1346; two years later it entered Italy and spread to most of the rest of western Europe. Probably one-quarter to one-third of the European population died in a three-year period.[68] The consequences were catastrophic, and one was an increase in slavery. Because of the high death rate, the workers who survived easily found good jobs in the countryside or in the cities. They could not be induced to become household servants. Death had not spared the elite, but the rich who remained had a larger supply of money available, as fortunes were consolidated through inheritance. It is not surprising that slavery grew as a result and supplied supplemental workers and domestics. In 1363 the Florentine government allowed the unrestricted importation of slaves from outside Italy, stipulating only that they be of non-Christian origin.[69] Venice took a different course, probably because of the large influx of slaves over the preceding two decades, and prohibited slave auctions in 1366, no doubt to reduce sales. Venetians could still import slaves, but sales had to be by private contract.[70]

Tatars, Russians, and Circassians continued to enter Genoa in this period, but their numbers declined in the second half of the fifteenth century, as access to the Black Sea diminished. In response, the Genoese turned back to the western Mediterranean. Muslim slaves in increasing numbers came to be purchased in North Africa, Spain, and Portugal. Because of the varied ethnic structure of Islam, the Genoese divided their captives into several categories: white, black, *indaco* (indigo), *lauro* (mulatto), and *olivegno* (olive). Whereas black slaves were fairly common in southern Italy and Sicily, relatively few of them reached Genoa or other northern cities. Domenico Gioffrè found them mentioned in only ten of the 1,600 notarial acts referring to slaves in fifteenth-century Genoa. A few Guanche slaves from the Canary Islands also found their way to Genoa.[71]

With the recruiting grounds for non-Christian slaves reduced by the political changes in the greater Mediterranean region, but with demand for domestic servants still high, the Italians turned to indentured servants. The Venetians were in the vanguard in fostering this temporary servitude. Euphemistically called "souls" (*anime*), indentured servants were predominantly young, purchased by Venetian shipmasters from their parents in Dalmatia, Albania, Istria, and Corfu. Their legal situation distinguished them from ordinary slaves. Bound only for a defined period of service, after that they could buy back their freedom, if they had the money. Theoretically they could not be exchanged or sold to another master, but the Venetian government had to take steps to ensure that they were not taken to other Italian cities where they ran the risk of falling into perpetual slavery. The Venetians were not totally disinterested in keeping them from being taken elsewhere, for the prohibition was enacted partly "in view of the shortage of male and female slaves for serving our own gentlemen and citizens."[72]

The existence of slavery in Renaissance Italy was pervasive. The account books and notarial records have preserved evidence of the presence of numerous slaves of various ethnic origins in the peninsula, and their existence also intrigued the portrait painters of the Renaissance. Yet as dramatic and well documented as their presence was, it was not important in a statistical sense. The Venetian census of 1563 listed only 7 to 8 percent of the population as servants, and this included free as well as slave.[73] Within Europe in the late Middle Ages and the Renaissance, slavery was never crucial for social or economic development, and it was not practiced on any great scale in Europe proper. Rather it was Europe's colonial areas—first the Atlantic islands and then the Americas— that would witness the rise of slavery to heights it had not reached since the end of the Roman empire. The motor behind that rise was plantation agriculture, of which sugar cane growing and sugar processing were the most important components. Because of their early acquisition of new lands, it was the Spaniards and the Portuguese who created the great expansion in sugar plantation agriculture.

SLAVERY IN SPAIN AND PORTUGAL

Christian Spain and Portugal were part of the European world where slavery gradually declined as serfdom and free labor grew. For most of the early Middle Ages the Christian states of Iberia were too poor to purchase slaves in large numbers. Their economies were weak, far closer to the subsistence level than those of the Muslim states. As a result, the possibility of slave use in large-scale ventures producing goods and commodities for urban markets was restricted. Yet, unlike the rest of western Europe, the Iberian kingdoms were frontier states, sharing borders with non-Christian states whose inhabitants could be raided and enslaved with complete legality. This meant that slavery persisted there longer and more vigorously than elsewhere in Christian Europe. When the Iberians began their overseas expansion in the fifteenth century, slavery was a living institution that could be transplanted with ease to the Atlantic and Caribbean islands and the American mainland.

In the early phases of the Christian reconquest, from the eighth to the twelfth century, there had been two distinct slave systems at work in the Christian states. One was a continuation of traditional Roman and Visigothic slavery. Its victims were primarily Christians, whose conditions were virtually identical to those of the Visigothic slaves. But Christian slaveholding, except in the isolated Asturias in the northwest, gradually underwent decline. Slowly but resolutely the slaves and their descendants blended into the "free" class of rural peasants. Since the reconquest and repopulation of newly acquired territories created a need for rural labor, peasants could almost always secure favorable legal and tenurial conditions in return for their participation in the resettlements. By the twelfth century the use of Christian slaves had almost ended, but slavery as a system persisted. Even during the early period, numbers of Muslim slaves had been present in the Christian states, but after the twelfth century most of the slaves were Muslim prisoners of war, captured in the fall of conquered cities and in the course of Christian raids into Muslim territory. In fact, many raids had the capture of slaves as their principal goal. As one example, after the eleventh-century reconquest of Avila, some two hundred Muslim slaves were put to work in chains to build the town's famous walls.[74]

During Portugal's reconquest in the twelfth and thirteenth centuries, the Portuguese crown and nobles conformed to general Iberian practice and employed Muslim prisoners of war as slaves. But after the Algarve (southern Portugal) was absorbed early in the thirteenth century, Portugal no longer bordered on Muslim territory. Although at times the Portuguese crossed into Castilian territory to participate in raids on Granada and gained slaves there, the most fruitful source of slaves was Africa. There the Portuguese purchased slaves or raided to secure them. Even before they began their maritime expansion down the African coast in the fifteenth century (which we will examine in detail later), African slaves came to be used in Portugal. In 1317 King Diniz of Portugal gave command of the kingdom's fleet to a Genoese, Manuel Pesagno, who was licensed for privateering in Moroccan waters and could retain one-fifth of all the slaves captured.[75]

In the central kingdom of Castile during the twelfth, thirteenth, and fourteenth centuries, slaves were almost exclusively Muslim in origin. Positive and negative factors account for this. Muslim lands lay on Castile's southern boundaries, and border raids and larger military engagements provided numerous captives. As one example, after the significant Christian victory over the Muslims at Las Navas de Tolosa in 1212, several thousand defeated Muslim warriors entered the market as slaves. The normal procedure was to offer the prisoners of war the possibility of repatriation if ransoms were paid; if they were not redeemed they could be sold as slaves. Before the fifteenth century, Castile was not an important Mediterranean power; therefore the wide range of ethnic groups sold as slaves in the Mediterranean reached Castile only infrequently.[76]

After the thirteenth-century conquest of the cities of the south, far more Muslims remained in Christian territory than could be profitably used as slaves, and large populations of free Muslims came to be governed by Christian rulers. As a result, free Muslims were more numerous than Muslim slaves, who tended to be concentrated in the frontier regions where raids ensured a steady supply. They were less numerous, though not nonexistent, in the parts of Castile more distant from the frontier.[77]

The Christians themselves were not immune from Muslim raids and could be enslaved in Muslim territory. There they were offered for ransom, and Christian rulers and subjects sought to raise and deliver the ransoms. In the twelfth century Alfonso VIII of Castile entrusted redemptionist efforts to the military religious orders. By the thirteenth century, the Trinitarians and the Mercedarians had ransoming as their main activity, and they coordinated fund raising for that purpose. Cities such as Cuenca regularly taxed their citizens to raise funds for ransoms, and the monastery of Santo Domingo de Silos sent agents to ransom captives in the Muslim cities of the kingdom of Granada and in North African centers such as Tangier and Ceuta.[78]

If Castile was cut off from the Mediterranean until late in our period, the lands of the Crown of Aragon—Aragon proper, Catalonia, and later Valencia—were open and receptive to the influences of the inland sea. Benjamin of Tudela, a Spanish Jew who made a fabulous journey around much of the known world and described it in prosaic terms, found the port of Barcelona in the mid-twelfth century packed with ships from around the Mediterranean, with cargoes—according to Jaime Vicens Vives—consisting mainly of gold and slaves. The trade in gold and slaves predated the cloth trade, the late Middle Ages' great generator of commerce. For Vicens this traffic in humans and precious metals

> explains why in 1062, for example, the merchants of Barcelona owned slaves, why in 1104 Ramón Berenguer III collected a tithe on the profits from the capture and sale of slaves, and why in 1148, when Ramón

Berenguer IV was planning the conquest of Tortosa, he found support among . . . the bourgeoisie of Barcelona. . . . All this justifies our thesis that between the ninth and the eleventh century Barcelona was one of the great points of contact in the western Mediterranean between the Christian world on the one hand and the Muslim world on the other.[79]

All the customary ways of enslaving were prevalent in the Crown of Aragon: by birth, marriage, judicial sentence, and debt. Until the end of the thirteenth century, conquest and raids supplied many slaves; thereafter Aragon had completed its mainland expansion, and the chief sources of slaves were piracy and trade.[80]

The great period of Aragonese expansion was the thirteenth century, when James I and Peter of Aragon took over the kingdom of Valencia and cooperated with Castile in the conquest of Murcia. Prisoners of war were regularly sold into slavery, and James I was particularly well supplied with slaves. He sent some two thousand as gifts to kings, emperors, the pope, the cardinals, and nobles.[81] The capture of large numbers of slaves was a continuing tradition. In 1280, after Peter took Montesa, "slavers continued for at least a year and a half their purchases among the multiple prisoners of war. . . . "[82] Slavery in the newly conquered kingdom of Valencia conformed to the normal Mediterranean pattern— urban rather than rural, domestic rather than agricultural, even though a minority of the slaves certainly lived and worked in the countryside. There was a wide spectrum of slave owners; Robert I. Burns has identified slaveholders ranging from artisans to bishops to the king.[83]

Strong legal limitations bounded the existence of the slaves in the thirteenth-century kingdom of Aragon. Their legal status was almost nil, though they could appear in court as plaintiffs or defendants in special circumstances. Muslim slaves could be ransomed or purchase their freedom, but if they remained as slaves they were subject to the domestic jurisdiction of their owner, except that those accused of serious crimes were judged in the royal courts, as were cases of disputed servile status. A century later localities had promulgated harsh regulations for slaves, based on the assumption that slaves were rebels and prisoners. Prohibitions on their drinking in taverns and public places kept them segregated from the general population.[84]

So far we have been concerned with Christian slaveholders, but slave owning by non-Christians continued in a restricted fashion. After the conquest of Valencia neither Jews nor Muslims could hold Christian slaves, but it is quite likely that Muslims continued to own Muslim slaves. There was a constant attrition as Muslim slaves fled their Muslim masters to accept baptism (which did not mean automatic manumission), and this loss to local Muslim slaveowners could not be made up. Muslims were, after the conquest, cut off from the Muslim slave trade, and their worsening economic situation meant that they could not easily purchase slaves from Christian suppliers. Free Muslims, too, often ran the risk of being enslaved. Merchants from the Crown of Aragon took slaves to southern France, and Muslim envoys who visited Barcelona often bought Muslim slaves there. The economic benefits Christians could derive from the slave trade meant that they used legal and extralegal means to increase the supply of Muslims to put on the market.[85]

Because of the exposed Aragonese coastline, Christians were in danger of being carried off by Muslim pirates and being held for ransom. The numbers of captives grew so large that the crown and the church began to organize means of ransoming the hostages. A crown official, the *exea*, was charged with coordinating these activities, but what the government could do was limited. As a result, the church assumed a major portion of the burden. The military orders in the Crown of Aragon were active in the effort, as in twelfth-century Castile, but the new redemptionist orders were more important. The most prominent was the Mercedarian order (the Order of Our lady of Mercy), founded in the 1230s by St. Peter Nolasco, who himself was credited with the redemption of some fourteen hundred captives. From their motherhouse in Barcelona, the Mercedarians spread out along the Christian frontier and into Castile, as we have seen. They were present at the capture of the city of Valencia, and, once the conquest was completed, they expanded their activities to the Castilian frontier with Granada and to North Africa, aided in their efforts by pious donations.[86]

By the end of the thirteenth century, the Iberian Peninsula no longer occupied the unique position regarding slavery that it had held during most of the middle Ages. Portugal had completed its reconquest and was still a century away from beginning its African conquests. Castile still had Muslims across its southern frontier, but outside the border regions slavery was on the decline. For both Portugal and Castile, slavery would only experience an upsurge when Africa and the Atlantic became important theaters of action in the fifteenth century, a topic we will treat in later chapters. For the Crown of Aragon, the conquest of Valencia, together with the joint Aragonese-Castilian conquest of Murcia, precluded further expansion within the peninsula and deprived them of a Muslim presence across their frontier. Thereafter, the traders and seamen of Catalonia and Valencia turned their complete attention to the Mediterranean, where their forebears had been active for centuries.

One of the most important preconditions for the emergence of New World slavery was the recovery and assimilation of Roman law into the legal systems of the medieval kingdoms. The elaborate slave laws contained in the Code of Justinian could easily be applied when new conditions called for them. In the eleventh century the Italian legal scholar Irnerius had begun the academic study of the Roman code, and in the next two centuries knowledge and application of Roman law spread widely in western Europe. In Iberia the Castilian king Alfonso X in the mid-thirteenth century produced a new code for his kingdom, known as the *Siete Partidas*, with heavy influences derived from Roman law. Although it never fully became law in Castile, the *Siete Partidas* still had a significant influence on late medieval and early modern legislation in Spain, both for the home country and for the American colonies, and thereby ensured that many Roman rules for slavery entered Spanish law.[87] By the end of the Middle Ages, Iberia had ample historical experience with slavery and a legal code for operating a slave system. The third element necessary for a great expansion of slavery was sugar cane agriculture, also well known to the Iberians.

The peninsula had long been a sugar-producing region. From the time of Abd ar-Rahman I, who ruled Islamic Spain from 755 to 788, sugar cane was grown in the southeast. Abd ar-Rahman was a member of the recently overturned Umayyad dynasty and had escaped Damascus following the Abbasid revolution. After fleeing across North Africa to Morocco, he was able to unite sufficient political and military support to set himself up as the head of an independent emirate in Spain. In an attempt to build Spain's economy, he sent for seeds and cuttings from the Levant and introduced a number of new crops into Spain, including sugar cane. Like many other plants, sugar cane was first grown in Spanish soil under carefully controlled conditions in royal gardens, initially in Córdoba and later in Toledo and Almería, where the water requirements were carefully monitored to ensure that the best growing conditions could be determined. By the tenth century, cane prospered in southern Spain, and, at the beginning of the fourteenth century, sugar from the Muslim city of Málaga was sold as far away as Flanders. Sugar from Morocco at the same time was exported to England.[88]

Sugar could be produced readily in southern Spain, but attempts to spread its cultivation northward were relatively limited until the late Middle Ages. King James II of Aragon (1291–1327) undertook to grow sugar in Valencia, the kingdom on Spain's eastern Mediterranean coast. To do so he secured plantings from Sicily together with a Muslim slave skilled in sugar techniques. It is interesting to note that the second wife of James II was Mary of the Cypriot ruling house of Lusignan; part of her dowry was paid in sugar and sold by Barcelona merchants at the behest of the king. After James II's initiative, sugar took quite a time to prosper. The first production mentioned was in the 1380s. In 1433 the cathedral chapter of Valencia attempted to secure the right to collect a tithe on sugar production, and in the process they provided an important account of the growth of production in Valencia. The canons reported that since the 1380s and 1390s both Christian and Muslim farmers had planted sugar cane as a secondary crop and sold their cane in its raw state as a delicacy for children and adults. In the second decade of the fifteenth century, planting increased as grain gave way before cane in many places. In 1407 the Valencian government gave financial aid to Nicolau Santafé, a sugar expert, to set himself up in Valencia. The first evidence of a mill in Valencia comes from 1417, when the master potter Thahir Aburrazach contracted to move to Burriana and make ceramic forms and vessels needed for the mill (*trapig de les canyes mels* in the Valencian dialect) owned by the merchant Francisco Siurrana. Nobles, too, constructed mills. The knight Don Galceran de Vich built one at Jeresa and later another at Gandía, and the soldier-poet *mosén* (Sir) Ausias March owned a sugar plantation and later built a mill on his property. By the 1430s numerous mills were in full operation. This expansion in Valencia took place just at the time when eastern Mediterranean sugar production was faltering and commerce there was being threatened.

In these circumstances it is obvious why Valencian sugar should draw the attention of a large German merchant house, the Ravensburger Handelsgesellschaft. After its foundation in the 1380s the company—which, unlike other German houses such as the Fuggers and the Welsers, concentrated on commerce and avoided banking—expanded rapidly and established branches in various parts of Europe. By 1420 they had agents and warehouses in Valencia and exported Valencian products, including sugar. The production and export of Valencian sugar generally increased in the first half of the fifteenth century, and by 1460 the company's profits were great enough to encourage them to enter the production side. They acquired land from Hugo de Cardona along the river Alcoy near Gandía and built a mill and refinery managed by *maestre* Santafé, probably the son of Nicolau de Santafé. The manufacturing complex prospered at first, and the quality of sugar produced there was extremely high. But in the 1470s difficulties intervened. A lawsuit involving Hugo de Cardona slowed production, and this coincided with the company's loss of some of its markets, difficulties in transportation, and competition from Madeiran sugar. The company's directors sold the facility in 1477 and a few years later rejected a proposal to reopen it.[89]

Portugal also played a vital role in the spread of sugar production. In the later Middle Ages, sugar was being produced with some profitability in the Algarve (southern Portugal), and the desire to tap the wealth of Morocco's sugar plantations may have entered into the motivations for Portuguese expansion in Africa.[90] Beyond this, the major importance of Portugal and Spain in the expansion of sugar production came as a result of their discovery and exploitation of the islands of the eastern Atlantic. The Azores and the Cape Verdes, to a lesser extent, and Madeira and the Spanish-held Canaries, to a much greater extent, were to be staging areas on the eve of the discovery of America.

Before concluding, we should examine the methods of growing sugar cane and of obtaining marketable sugar from it. The cultivation of sugar cane remained more or less constant in the Mediterranean and Atlantic growing regions. Cane was planted from cuttings of mature stock, not from seed. The "setts," as these roughly foot-long cuttings were called, needed a slightly acid soil, and cane did best with a rainfall of some sixty to seventy inches per year. Few, if any, Mediterranean lands had that much rain; therefore irrigation projects were used to increase the water supply to the setts, which were planted at the bottom of the furrows of the plowed fields to receive the maximal amount of water. When the plants reached maturity, the long stalks were cut back near the ground, leaving the bottom (or ratoon) in the ground to produce the next crop.

The next stage was the transportation of the cane from the field to the mill, carried on the back of draft animals, in carts, or by humans. At the mill it was cut into appropriate lengths and crushed, with the juice dropped from the crushed cane collected for refining. The fresh juice contained a small percentage of foreign matter that had to be removed if the sugar were to attain its pure form. Boiling the juice with an additive made the separation of the pure sugar easier. In the late Middle Ages natron and potash were commonly used as clarifying additives, as the juice was boiled in successive stages to drive off the water, until it was ready to be dried in loaf-shaped molds of pyramidal or cone shape.[91] In the fourteenth century the Italian Pegolotti, in his famous manual of commerce *La Practica della Mercatura*, described the varieties of sugar on the market. The best was *mecchera*, in pyramidal shape, white and dense. Next in order came *caffetino*, shaped like a cone with a rounded top; then *bambillonia, musciatto,* and *domaschino*, the least preferred. Powdered sugar was pressed into the form of a loaf, but it usually turned to dust during transport. Perfectly transparent candy sugar was also produced and sold.[92]

Sugar found a ready market as European demand constantly expanded. The Mediterranean producers could not keep up with that demand, and they had to face the competition of sugar coming from the Atlantic islands and from America in the fifteenth and sixteenth centuries. These two new regions were where the complete identification of sugar with slavery would take place, a development we shall examine in later chapters.

6

SLAVERY IN
SUB-SAHARAN AFRICA TO 1650

For centuries before the discovery of America and the opening of the Atlantic slave trade, there was a well-developed trade in slaves, as well as in other commodities, across the Sahara from black Africa to the Islamic world. In addition to their exportation of slaves, several African states south of the Sahara made use of slaves in a variety of ways: as domestics and concubines, as soldiers and agricultural workers. In this chapter we will discuss the involvement of the states of black Africa with slavery and the slave trade in the period when their major outside influences and links with the rest of the world were Islamic and not European.

A preliminary word about sources is necessary. In the last two decades, as the study of the African past has reached a high degree of maturity and sophistication, one of the principal concerns of the large group of Africanists—anthropologists, sociologists, and economists, as well as historians—has been the study of slavery in the African context. Their very able work most often has focused on the later manifestations of slavery, in the eighteenth and nineteenth centuries, a period for which it is possible to make use of a large quantity and a wide range of indigenous sources in addition to those provided by contemporary European observers.[1] For the period from the eleventh century to the sixteenth, the material for historical reconstruction is less abundant, most of it provided by Islamic writers, such as ibn-Battuta and Leo Africanus, who actually visited the region, or others, such as al-Bakri, who never traveled across the desert but relied on the writings and oral testimony of those who had.[2] For the study of slavery, the Arabic sources have certain limitations. The Muslim writers provided ample descriptions of trade and the power and glory of the rulers of the Sudan, but they devoted less attention to the social structures that underlay and supported those rulers. Medieval Muslims, as we know from chapter 4, accepted slavery without question as a normal part of life, and therefore they did not consider it worthy

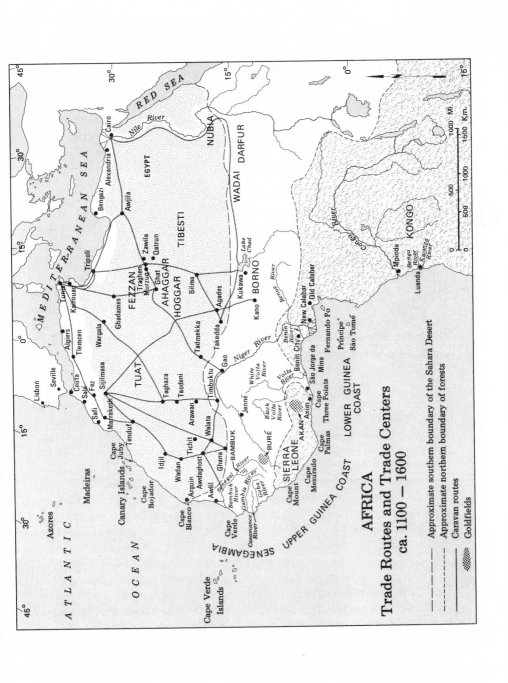

AFRICA
Trade Routes and Trade Centers
ca. 1100 – 1600

----- Approximate southern boundary of the Sahara Desert

----- Approximate northern boundary of forests

——— Caravan routes

░░░ Goldfields

RED SEA

MEDITERRANEAN SEA

ATLANTIC OCEAN

Azores

Madeiras

Canary Islands

Cape Verde Islands

Lisbon
Seville
Ceuta
Safi
Fez
Marrakesh
Safi
Tenduf
Sijilmasa
Tlemcen
Algiers
Wargala
Tunis
Karfouad
Tripoli
Bengazi
Alexandria
Cairo

Nile River

NUBIA

EGYPT

Awlila

Ghadanes

FEZZAN
Traghen
Murzuq
Zawila
Qatrun
Ghat

AHAGGAR

HOGGAR

TIBESTI

WADAI

DARFUR

Tadmekka
Takedda
Agades
Bilma

Lake Chad

BORNO
Kukawa
Kano

Benue River

Cape Bojador

Cape Blanco

Cape Verde

Arguin
Awili
Wadan
Idjil
Awdaghost
Tichit
Ghana
BAMBUK
Tenduf

Taghaza
Taodeni
Arawan
Walata
Timbuktu
Gao

Niger River

Jenné

BURÉ

White Volta River
Black Volta River
Volta River
Benin River

SENEGAMBIA
Senegal River
Bambuk River
Gambia River
Casamance River
Geba River

SIERRA LEONE
Cape Mesurado
Cape Mount

UPPER GUINEA COAST

Cape Palmas

AKAN
Axim
Cape Three Points

São Jorge da Mina
Benin City

LOWER GUINEA COAST

New Calabar
Old Calabar
Fernando Po
Príncipe
São Tomé

TUAT

Congo River

Kwanza River
Bengo River
Luanda
Mpinda

KONGO

0   500   1000   1500 Km.
0   500   1000 Mi.

45° 30° 15° 0°
45° 30° 15° 0° 15°

of a great deal of attention or comment. That explains why there is an abundance of sources for this period dealing with trade, but few descriptions of slavery in the Sudanic region, despite the careful investigations and interpretations of modern scholars. We have already dealt with the trans-Saharan trade in chapter 4. As we proceed in this chapter, we will first consider indigenous slavery in the Sudanic states, although still taking into account the pervasive influence of long-distance trade.

Africa is a large continent, and, although many people still refer to it as an entity, it is now and was then a diverse collection of geographical and climatological regions, as well as a mosaic of ethnic and linguistic groups. For the purposes of this chapter, we will consider Africa north of the equator and concentrate on the Islamic-influenced areas and the nearby regions with which they traded. A series of ecological zones runs from east to west across the continent. Along the southern shore of the Mediterranean, North Africa in the Middle Ages was divided in its turn into three major parts: Egypt in the east, the eastern Maghrib (modern Libya, Tunisia, and part of Algeria), and the western Maghrib (the rest of Algeria and Morocco). By the eighth century North Africa was solidly in the Islamic world and an important part of it. South of the Maghrib was the Sahara, the harsh desert dividing the Mediterranean coastal region from black Africa, crossed by several long-established trading routes, as we saw in chapter 4. Along the southern reaches of the Sahara was the region called the Sahel, an Arabic word meaning shore. For centuries it has been commonplace to describe the Sahara as a sea of sand and the Sahel, where desert and grassland meet, as its shore. Farther south still the Sahel gave way to the Sudan, the bilad al-Sudan (in Arabic, the land of the blacks), a savanna region of open or wooded grasslands stretching eastward from the Atlantic to Ethiopia and encompassing most of the important black states of our period. South again from the Sudanic belt was the region of tropical forests, where states were mostly small and less developed and where Sudanese merchants and warriors ventured in search of gold and slaves. Eastward from the Sudan were Nubia and Ethiopia, which were more firmly tied to the culture and economy of Egypt and the Middle East than to the Sudan. Finally there was the East African coast, peripheral to our interests in this chapter, but the scene of Muslim coastal trade. Subequatorial Africa and the lower West African coast remain, but they will not attract our attention just yet.

One tends to think of the Sahara as a barrier, a totally arid expanse of desert forming an impassable region isolating Sudanic Africa from North Africa and the Mediterranean. Yet, even though the desert did create obstacles to trade, the numerous oases allowed several important nomadic groups in the desert to support themselves. The Tubu, the Tuareg, the Zaghawa, the Sanhaja, and others had a life centered on the oases. Through careful husbanding of the available water, they were able to plant irrigated fields and obtain food from the palm groves. Nonetheless, agriculture was only supplementary; they obtained their main food supply by nomadic and pastoral skills used for maintaining animal herds. Even this was not enough for prosperity; what allowed the desert peoples to rise above the subsistence level was the trans-Saharan trade, which allowed them to exchange livestock products for grain. The existence of scattered oases permitted a series of routes to cross the desert, and where natural oases were not available, the desert peoples dug wells and created new ones.[3] From ancient times, traders crossed the desert using horses and oxen, sometimes as pack animals, sometimes pulling carts. It was the introduction of the camel from the Near East, sometime between the second and fourth centuries A.D., that allowed greater mobility and increased trade. The nomads of the desert at times participated directly in the trade, but more often they benefited from the North African caravans coming through. They could charge tolls; they could hire out guides to the merchants; they could buy and sell; and they could even extort and plunder the caravans. Often the caravan trade, and the share the Saharan peoples gained from it, meant the difference between prosperity and subsistence. At the same time, the trade allowed them to supplement their small population with slaves from the Sudan.[4]

The Sahel connected the desert with the grasslands of the Sudan. For the most part lacking sufficient rainfall for cultivation, the Sahel contained grazing lands that alternated with sand. It was in this transitional region that the great commercial entrepôts developed, established by the Sudanese having close contacts with the desert dwellers, and from these towns came the wealth of the large states of the Sudan. It is hard to define the limits of the Sahel with any precision, for from north to south the desert gave way almost imperceptibly to milder lands. In the Sahel Muslims from the north met pagans from the south, and camel herding gave way to cattle raising.[5]

Below the Sahel, the Sudanic belt stretched east and west across the continent from the Ethiopian highlands to the Atlantic, between the Sahara and the forest lands. Currently some twelve to forty inches of rain falls annually, with the smallest amount of rain in the north, steadily increasing as the land reaches southward. This permits grazing in the northern ranges; in an intermediate zone agriculture and grazing combine; in the south richer agricultural lands meet the forest. The inhabitants of the savanna region made good use of the relatively benign climate, which was probably wetter before 1600 than it is today, to provide themselves with a varied diet. They grew millet in the north, cereals in the center, and sorghum in the south. Agriculture was the economic key in the region, but the peoples of the Sudan were also accustomed to engage in artisanry and trade during the dry season each year. This gave them a more complex and varied degree of specialization than they might have enjoyed otherwise.[6]

On this strong agricultural base, aided greatly by the widespread availability of iron and the early knowledge of working it, the strong states of the northern Sudan arose, created by black rulers. The earliest of the states in the western Sudan of which we have reliable knowledge was Ghana, which had its origin in the eighth or ninth century and flourished from the tenth through the twelfth century. It took its name from one of the titles of its ruler, who, like those of later states, controlled a collection of tributary regions. With its capital at Awkar, the land of Ghana owed much of its prosperity to its position as an intermediary between the Saharan trade routes and the lands farther south. Mali, which succeeded Ghana and reached a peak in the fourteenth century, encompassed the regions of the Senegal and Gambia rivers, in addition to the upper reaches of the Niger River, and stretched northward to the desert. It was replaced by Songhay, which lasted until the late sixteenth century when it fell before a Moroccan invasion. Songhay stretched north to the Taghaza salt fields and east into the Hausa lands between the Niger and Lake Chad. Around Lake Chad in our period there were two states, Kanem and Borno (the latter previously spelled Bornu). These large Sudanese kingdoms were headed by rulers who depended for control and tribute collecting on strong military forces that in turn depended on cavalry for their effectiveness.[7]

Scholars have long engaged in a debate about the origins of slavery in Africa. The main opinions are, on the one hand, that slavery and slave trading were characteristic of indigenous African society, and, on the other, that slavery was introduced into Africa by outsiders, either by Muslims in the medieval period or by Europeans in the fifteenth and sixteenth centuries. There are very heavy emotional overtones connected with any attempt to resolve the question. Philip D. Curtin has provided one of the best descriptions of the issues involved.

> The abolitionists of the last century made their point very well—the slave trade was evil, and it had to be ended. Perhaps they made it too well, at least for the sake of retrospective understanding: their intense publicity for slavery and the slave trade alike left historians with a false sense of confidence in their understanding of both. . . .
>
> As it turned out, the abolitionists had made a number of subsidiary points that were still accepted [in the 1950s] as articles of faith. For one, Africa was supposed to be a savage continent, made that way largely by the slave traders. As "savages," the Africans had been seen only as victims, never as men in command of their own destiny, having a serious role to play in their own history. To new historians of Africa it was obvious, on reexamining the evidence, that African societies had been slandered during the nineteenth-century heights of racism and cultural arrogance. Yet, if [the new historians] said African savagery was largely mythic, some of those who still held the old view would think they were trying to minimize the evil of the trade. If they said that African states had real and legitimate interests, which they pursued through diplomacy and wars—that they were not mere puppets in the hands of the slave traders—the new Africanists could be accused of trying to shift the burden of guilt for the horrors of the trade from European to African heads.[8]

The states into which Islam first penetrated exerted an influence on slavery in several crucial ways. Most important, of course, was the trans-Saharan slave trade, which continually extracted large numbers of Africans. The supply of those slaves was intimately related to the development of the states whose rulers and merchants supplied the goods for the caravans. By the year 1000 the Sudanese elite was becoming Islamized, and in the process they absorbed traditional Islamic attitudes toward slavery. This consequently may have hastened the development of indigenous slavery and have altered prior practices of slavery as well. It is certainly true that the regions where Islam was most influential—the Sahel and the northern savanna—were also the regions where indigenous slavery, slave raiding, and slave exports were most highly evolved. As Paul E. Lovejoy has said: "Islam . . . became the religion of slaveholders in large parts of Africa, so that the Islamic dimension became an indigenous factor at the same time that it remained an external influence."[9] A similar duality can be seen in regard to the slaves themselves: they were both commodities for export and labor for production within the African states.[10]

In addition to the outside influence of Islam, the growth of the states of the Sudan was also played out against a background of environmental and technological constraints, all of which affected the process of state development and the various manifestations of slavery and the slave trade. First, because sub-Saharan Africa lacked the plow, agriculture was extensive rather than intensive, and the hoe was the main farming implement. Second, there always was, and to a degree there still remains, a rather low population in relation to the available land. This meant that acquisition of control over land was relatively easy, whereas acquisition of control over people was rather more difficult. Growth of political power, therefore, was closely linked to control over people, not over land as in western Europe or the Islamic world. To gain control over people and to extend their power, the successful Sudanic rulers made use of their cavalry units to protect towns, villages, and trade routes and to raid neighboring societies for slaves.[11]

Cavalry warfare naturally implies a supply of horses, but the peoples of the area faced two problems as they sought to build their herds. First, the horses native to the region by the year 1000 were relatively small and needed to be supplemented by the importation of larger breeds from North Africa. Second, horses only flourished in the northern part of the region, and their health and their owners' success in breeding them deteriorated farther to the south. Below a line paralleling the forest belt but some several hundred miles north of it, horses could not survive long and could only be bred with difficulty. The primary reason was that they fell victim to parasites and diseases carried by insects. One scourge was African horse sickness, carried by one species of midge. More threatening were several varieties of a fly-borne disease known as trypanosomiasis, called sleeping sickness when it attacks humans. Horses are most affected by trypanosomiasis brucei, spread by the fly *Glossina morsitans*. Both to maintain the size of the herds and to bring in larger breeds, a regular horse trade across the Sahara developed, concerning which we have the first evidence in the thirteenth century; and by the late fourteenth and early fifteenth centuries, horses were being systematically bred for trading purposes in suitable areas in the northern reaches of the savanna.[12]

In the fifteenth and sixteenth centuries, Sudanic kingdoms regularly purchased North African horses. In the western Sudan they came from Morocco, and in the east, in Borno close to Lake Chad, they came from Egypt and Tunisia. By the sixteenth century, however, it seems that the volume of the horse trade across the Sahara diminished, probably due in large part to successful breeding efforts, by then producing large horses in the Sudan. By the fifteenth century, horses were being traded from the northern Sudan into regions to the south; and this trade continued, both because of the rapid demise of horses sent south and because of what may have been a deliberate northern policy not to sell mares, thereby preventing local breeding of horses in the southern areas.[13]

The connection of the horse trade with the slave trade is a close one. Horses were paid for most often with slaves. Because the plow had not yet been developed in sub-Saharan Africa, the horse was useless in agriculture, and it was almost never used for transport. Most horses were used for military purposes, with ceremonial uses in a distant second place, and their acquisition was directed and controlled by the political authorities. They, in turn, often used the horses to conduct wars and raids whose main object was to acquire more slaves. As Robin Law remarked:

> The exchange of horses for slaves . . . tended to become . . . a "circular process": horses were purchased with slaves, and then could be used in military operations which yielded further slaves, and financed further purchases of horses. Trade and war thus fed upon each other in a self-sustaining process. . . . [14]

An analogous circular process, and one that is far better known, would develop in the seventeenth and eighteenth centuries along the Atlantic coast, when African kings and chiefs traded slaves for guns and then used the guns to capture more slaves.

Slave raiding, although it was only one method among many ways of acquiring slaves, probably produced the greatest number of them. Capture of slaves in war or raids was a phenomenon common to many societies. We have already pointed out many such examples in previous chapters. It was no different in Africa, where the practice was widespread. Larger and stronger states, those better provided with horses and weapons, were naturally those most heavily involved in war and raiding. They had better resources to conduct the campaigns, and their greater wealth created a greater demand for human capital. In the late eleventh century, al-Zuhri reported that

The people of Ghana make raids on the land of Barbara and An-ima. . . . Sometimes they conquer them and sometimes they are con-quered. These people have no iron and fight only with clubs of ivory. For this reason the people of Ghana overcome them, for they fight with swords and spears. Any slave of them can run on his own legs faster than a thor-oughbred horse.[15]

Another such raiding practice was described by al-Idrisi, who in the mid-twelfth century wrote that the people of the town of Gharbil

make raids into the land of Lamlam, capture them, bring them back and sell them to the merchants of Ghana. . . . [They] ride thorough-bred camels. Taking with them provisions of water, they travel by night, and reach the land of Lamlam in the day-time. [As soon as] they succeed in capturing their booty, they return to their country with the captives they have succeeded in taking from the people of Lamlam.[16]

According to Leo Africanus, writing in the early sixteenth century, the ruler of Borno derived his wealth exclusively from selling prisoners his men had cap-tured to North African merchants. This ruler had three thousand mounted troops for slave raids, their horses obtained from the North Africans in exchange for slaves.[17] In later sixteenth-century Borno, its ruler Alooma raided for slaves even in the Islamic holy month of Ramadan.[18] Muslim Africans, following Is-lamic doctrine, usually confined their slaving activities to non-Muslims captured in war. Non-Muslim groups tried to make treaties with the Muslim states to save themselves from the slave raiders, or, if that failed, they tried to elude capture. Although the Koran firmly forbade it, there were also instances of Muslims en-slaving other Muslims.[19]

The history of Kanem in the Lake Chad region from the eleventh to the thir-teenth century serves as an example and a case study of several of the previously discussed themes: the North African demand for slaves, the coming of Islam, and the influence of cavalry. From an early date in the eighth or ninth century, the pagan rulers of Kanem provided slaves from among their own subjects to the caravan traders who took them north to Ifriqiya. But Ifriqiya itself was unsettled by the invasion of the Banu Hilal, Berber nomads, in the mid-eleventh century. One consequence was a disruption of the economic life of Ifriqiya, which in turn depressed the demand for slaves from the Sudan. This affected Kanem, which just at this time experienced a widespread movement of conversion to Islam among the lower ranks of its society, those who had long been subject to en-slavement and exportation from their homeland. By 1075 a Muslim, probably of Berber stock, built up sufficient power to seize command in Kanem; this was Hummay (ca. 1075–86), who founded the long-lasting Sefawa dynasty, which remained in power until the early nineteenth century. Hummay had probably been helped in his successful bid by the slave merchants, and certainly his suc-cessors rebuilt and expanded the slave trade. One of those successors in the twelfth century, Dunama Dibalami, created a strong cavalry force and dominated the Zaghawa and Fezzan trading regions to the north and east, while initiating massive slave raids into pagan territory to the south and west. Kanem, under its Muslim Sefawa dynasty, continued to export slaves for centuries as the major component of its foreign trade.[20]

Other ways of enslaving people were undoubtedly present, but for the period before 1650 we know very little about them from direct evidence. Scholars studying later periods have identified a variety of ways that groups acquired outsiders as slaves. The following discussion indicates the ways that African groups have exchanged people and should serve as a set of suggestions as to how these processes probably worked in the earlier centuries.

As we have seen, Africa's Sudanic belt and the forest belt below it have been homes for numerous societies possessing a relative abundance of land while containing a relatively small population in relation to that land. To balance population with available resources, it often was necessary to exchange people between groups. Groups with growing power sought outsiders to augment their own populations; and those groups that were in trouble, through ecological difficulties or military defeat, had to relinquish surplus members whom they could no longer support. The rights of individuals were subordinated to the control of families or the state, and the transfer of those rights were the prerogatives of the leaders of the groups, either the heads of families or the rulers of societies. The transfer could be of a temporary nature through the institution of "pawning," a process by which an individual was exchanged for a loan of food or money. The person pawned would be at the disposal of the host society for a period equivalent to the value of the loan in question. "Bridewealth" relates to a similar institution, in which the group a bride left would be compensated for the loss of her economic and childbearing potential; but, unlike pawning, the arrangement was permanent. An individual could also leave the group he was born in and seek membership in a stronger or wealthier group, but such individual arrangements were unusual. The norm was for the exchanges to be conducted between the heads of the groups involved. Finally, criminals could be punished by being sold. Thus there was a spectrum of ways for transferring people and their rights in African societies, running from the acquisition of wives and other family members to purchase, or other forms of acquisition, of those whose status could be considered that of slaves. All along the spectrum, purchase and sale was one of the normal means of transfer, and the transfer of slaves was not a separate category, but merely one part of the wider spectrum.[21] These patterns were present in earlier centuries, scholars believe, and indicate that there were many ways of acquisition in addition to slave raiding. What is clear from the documents of the eleventh through the sixteenth centuries is that not all of those who ended up as slaves were sold outside the Sudan; many remained in black Africa.

African societies used slaves in as wide a range of activities as any of the societies we have studied. Here it should be emphasized once again that the limited picture many people have of slavery is conditioned by impressions of North American and Latin American slavery in the nineteenth century. Although recent scholarship is showing that slavery in the Americas was more complex than previously recognized, the usual impression in this regard is generally correct: slaves in the Americas were acquired for their use and value as labor. Their legal status, living conditions, and social mobility all stemmed from that central fact. It was different in Africa, as it was in the Islamic world and Europe, where slavery was more complex and comprised a wider range of uses for slaves than there was in the Americas.

Of the people obtained as slaves in Africa by whatever means, their acquisitors no doubt made an initial sorting: those who would be retained and those who would be sold out of the region, either to the caravan traders or to a different Sudanic state. The selection depended in part upon the possibility of their assimilation. Adult men from nearby places ordinarily would be sold, for they would be difficult to integrate into the new society and they would be more likely to attempt to escape. Women and children would be retained more often: women because they might well end up in the harem of the chief or another member of the elite, and children because they would easily be taught the ways of the group and absorbed into it. A complicating factor was the North African demand for large numbers of slave women, the result of their widespread use in the Islamic world as domestics and concubines. Thus the trans-Saharan trade carried more women than men, just the opposite of what would develop in the transatlantic slave trade.

Concubinage was also an important way of using women in the Sudan, particularly useful for masters, who could purchase a slave woman rather than pay a bride-price of a free wife. If the slave produced children, she had fulfilled an important part of her functions and was awarded status. If she did not, she could be sold.[22] The Spanish Muslim writer al-Sharishi in the early thirteenth century praised the qualities of the slave women of Ghana.

> God has endowed the slave girls there with laudable characteristics, both physical and moral, more than can be desired: their bodies are smooth, their black skins are lustrous, their eyes are beautiful, their noses well shaped, their teeth white, and they smell fragrant.[23]

Domestic labor was the task for many slaves, both men and women, although the Arabic sources do not tell us much about it because it was such an accepted institution among the Muslims. Ibn-Battuta made several references to domestic slaves in his fourteenth-century travel account, but in each case he mentioned them only incidentally as he made other points. In one reference he described the bowls made from the large gourds grown in the Sudan and tells us that when a prosperous African traveled, ''he is followed by his male and female slaves.''[24] On another occasion, he found himself presented by his African host with a slave boy, "a youth five spans high. . . . "[25] When ibn-Battuta wrote reprovingly of nudity in African households he visited, he offered another glimpse of domestic slavery.

> their female servants and slave girls . . . and little girls appear before men naked, with their privy parts uncovered. During Ramadan I saw many of them in this state, for it is the custom of the *faraiyya* to break their fast in the house of the sultan, and each one brings his food carried by twenty or more of his slave girls, they all being naked.[26]

Other scattered references suggest widespread slaveowning. In eleventh-century Awdaghost, as well as in the Songhay empire in the sixteenth century, it was reported that as many as a thousand individuals could be held by a single slaveholder.[27]

While south of the desert, ibn-Battuta twice tried to purchase a rare commodity, an educated slave woman. The education of female slaves, he reported, was practiced in several places in the Sudan, although the numbers of such women always were small. In both his attempts, the masters initially agreed but later had changes of heart and rescinded the sales.[28]

Agriculture was an important area in which slaves were used in the Sudanic region. In fifteenth century Kano, for example, the king secured large numbers of slaves from farther south and put them to work as agricultural laborers (as well as using them for other tasks). In the sixteenth century Leo Africanus reported the agricultural prosperity of the region.[29] One key feature of agriculture in the Sudan was the practice of establishing slaves in special villages to work the land and to turn over the excess they produced to the ruler. Slaves were also used as herdsmen and fishermen. The income thus produced provided an important source of revenue for the ruler and his court. In Songhay, major towns were reported to have been ringed with villages of servile laborers, supervised by overseers. Each year they were responsible for receiving seed grain from the king's storehouses, making sure that the crop was produced by the slaves in the village and turning over the villages' quotas after the harvest. Whether the servile agricultural establishments of fifteenth- and sixteenth-century Songhay should be considered as similar to plantations or feudal estates is debatable, but their existence is not. They provided a basis of prosperity for Songhay, spreading along the valley of the Niger and growing in size, to reach a peak in the sixteenth century. With irrigation, they produced grains, vegetables, cotton, indigo, and other goods that were traded with the dwellers of the Sahel and the desert.[30]

In a region such as the Sudanic belt, where horses were scarce and expensive but where internal commerce was highly developed, it is not surprising that we find references to slaves used as porters for caravans. Some were also used as guards for the caravans.[31] Slaves often participated in artisanry, although for this period the direct references to that practice are scant. The Moroccan Judar

Pasha, who conquered Timbuktu in 1592, used local slaves to build a fortress there. In this period, too, slaves worked in construction and cloth manufacture and in the mining and processing of gold, copper, and salt.[32] Taghara, in the southern part of the western Maghrib, was a city in the salt-mining region, constructed of salt blocks from the mines worked by slaves.[33] Mining was a dangerous and exhausting occupation in Africa, as it was in other regions we have studied. Men had to be coerced into working in the mines, and, if slaves were available, they were the ones to be coerced.

We have noted the existence in Muslim society of slave soldiers, of which the Mamluks were the most memorable, and Sudanic states also made military use of slaves. The best example is that of Songhay, whose ruler the *askiya* (king) Muhammad took power in 1493 and began building a professional army by recruiting from the populations he had conquered. His soldiers had the status of slaves.[34]

Slaves were used extensively in other ways by Sudanese rulers to build state power. Some uses were symbolic: al-Umari in the fourteenth century described the audiences conducted by the ruler of Mali, who could be seen sitting ''in his palace on a big dais. . . . About 30 slaves (mamluk) stand behind him, Turks and others who are bought for him in Egypt.''[35] Slaves could sometimes enter higher positions in the state. In Mali, there was a body of royal slaves who served the king as bureaucrats, administrators, and advisers. As Mali conquered other states, its kings appointed royal governors, agents of central authority selected from either the royal family or the royal slaves. In Mali the royal slaves were at the heart of government and had a great deal of responsibility in the running of the state. Because they had no competing loyalties, they were immune from pressure from the king's rivals among the powerful families. For these same reasons, many African states used slaves in a like manner long after 1650. Another logical, but often unstated reason for the use of slaves in such positions of responsibility, rather than members of the kingdom's powerful families, was that slaves could be removed from office without starting feuds. When the kings of Mali were strong men, the slaves carried out their orders; when weak kings came to the throne, the slaves became de facto rulers.[36] In Kano, slaves were used in similar ways,[37] and in the states along the Atlantic coast, slave officials were responsible for other slaves in the society.[38]

Rulers of the Sudanic states often used slaves as gifts to ensure support or to demonstrate piety. ''The power of Mali depended upon its military strength and this enhanced the importance of the army commanders in the king's court. The king cultivated their good will by grants of slaves'' and other luxuries.[39] Itinerant Muslim scholars enjoyed high regard in the Sudan. To show their piety, the rulers often showered lavish gifts on the scholars. In the eleventh century, when the first Muslim missionary reached Kanem, the ruler give him ''100 slaves, 100 camels, 100 gold coins and 100 silver coins, in gratitude for instruction in the

Koran.''[40] The *askiya* Dawud, ruler of Songhay in the mid-sixteenth century, favored Islam, contributed to the building of the mosque in Timbuktu, and gave land and slaves and other gifts to Muslim scholars.[41]

As the elite of the Sudan were Muslims, it was natural that some of them would make the pilgrimage to Mecca. Although there are reports of pilgrimages as early as the end of the eleventh century, the first significant pilgrimage recorded in the Islamic sources was that of Mansa Musa, ruler of Mali, who crossed to Egypt and visited Cairo on his way to Mecca in 1324. As al-Maqrizi recorded it, Mansa Musa, who supposedly brought 14,000 slave girls with him, reached Cairo

> proposing to make the Pilgrimage. He stayed there three days beneath the Pyramids as an official guest. . . . He crossed to the Cairo bank . . . and went up to the citadel [to pay his respects to the sultan]. He declined to kiss the ground and was not forced to do so though he was not enabled to sit in the royal presence. The sultan commanded that he be equipped for the Pilgrimage. Then he came down. He paid out so much gold in buying what he desired in the way of slave girls, garments, and other things, that the rate of the dinar fell by six dirhams.[42]

Mansa Musa's pilgrimage made the greatest impression, but over the next century several other pilgrimages from West Africa were recorded: in 1344, 1351, 1416, and 1436. In all but that of 1344, the Sudanese brought slaves with them, and in 1436, at least, most of the slaves were sold in Egypt. These pilgrimages greatly impressed the Egyptians and may have helped to encourage the reopening of the direct east-west caravan route from Egypt to Lake Chad.[43]

The pilgrimage traffic also brought forth a surprising turn: the slave trade with the Islamic heartland became two-way. Al-Maqrizi reported that members of Mansa Musa's entourage brought Turkish and Ethiopian slave girls back with them.[44] Some three decades later ibn-Battuta visited a village on the Niger River whose emir, the traveler reported, owned ''an Arab girl from Damascus who spoke to me in Arabic.''[45] Sixteenth-century Borno acquired Turkish musketeers to strengthen the army and train native troops in the use of firearms, and a century later Borno received Europeans sent from Tripoli.[46]

The rules of Islam at times conflicted with traditional pagan practice in the Sudanic kingdoms, and the French scholar Jean-Pierre Olivier de Sardan has identified some of these conflicts. Islam recognized only one category of slaves, who could be subjected to that status either by birth or by capture in war. The rulers of Songhay followed Islam to the letter on this point, but in the pagan, peasant villages of the kingdom, two categories existed: trade captives, taken as prisoners of war, and house slaves, born in servitude. Differences also existed in treatment. Regarding marriage, the Songhay royal rules, following Islamic practice, considered that the marriage of a free man and a slave woman, or a slave man with a free woman, were equally possible, although not recommended. In the peasant society of Songhay, on the other hand, a free man could marry a slave woman without restriction, but it was impossible for a free woman to marry a slave man.[47]

Because of the ways slaves were selected and brought into the new societies and the ways they were used, slave revolts did not develop in this period. We do not know too much about manumission. Flight, though, was an option for dissatisfied slaves. It was hard for the political authorities to police vast areas, and a runaway often could find asylum with a nearby group, even if he did not succeed in reaching his home. If he did not reach his home, he may haved ended up the slave of new masters. Fearful their slaves would flee, purchasers were selective, buying slaves from distant regions and rejecting those from nearby. Buyers preferred children, as we have seen, because they were more easily assimilated. Prisoners of war and those captured in slave raids were sold to merchants to be taken to distant areas or exported from the Sudan.

Although many questions about slavery in the Sudanic belt of Africa in this period still remain, some may never be answered because of the lack of sources. The available evidence, nonetheless, reveals in broad terms the flourishing of slavery and slave trading in the Sudan from an early date, and we do know that, long before the Atlantic slave trade began, millions of Africans had been taken across the Sahara. If we turn to the West African coast to examine slavery there before the coming of the Europeans, our knowledge is less secure, and our most complete sources come from the records the Europeans kept as they explored the coast and established trading contacts. We will examine that evidence in our next chapter.

PART III
THE ATLANTIC SLAVE SYSTEM
TO 1650

7

AFRICA AND
THE ATLANTIC ISLANDS

The slave trading component of the Atlantic system, which came to link Europe, Africa, and America in a huge web of economic relations, lasted from the decade of the discovery of the Americas well into the nineteenth century and accounted for what became the largest forced migration in world history, whose numbers were rivaled only by the trans-Saharan slave trade. In this chapter we will examine the origins of that system in the fifteenth century, before anyone had the slightest idea that the Americas would be discovered, ending our account in 1650 when the Atlantic slave trade was about to reach its mature development.

It is important for us to be aware that when Europeans began to explore the West African coast in the fifteenth century they were not seeking a route to India, although that did come to be one of their motivations by the end of the century. Obviously, they had no knowledge that the New World would be discovered or that slavery would become important there, and, not quite so obviously, the search for slaves was a rather low item on their list of priorities for maritime expansion. Gold and grain were what they most eagerly sought in the beginning. Yet, with time and with the discovery of America, the slave trade increasingly became more significant in the economic calculations of the Europeans who sponsored and carried out the voyages and in those of the African merchants and rulers with whom they traded. The European need for labor is a constant theme in these two and a half centuries, not so much for Europe itself, but for the European colonies in the Atlantic islands, in the Caribbean islands, and on the American mainland, as they came to be settled. In this period, slavery came to be identified with African blacks, and African blacks with slavery, for the simple reason that they were most frequently, and soon almost exclusively, the slaves whom the Europeans used.

In previous chapters we have traced the persistence of slavery in the Mediterranean world, and we have had many occasions to discuss numerous ethnic groups whose members were forced into slavery. By the fifteenth century and certainly by the sixteenth, fewer and fewer areas for slaving were available to the Europeans, just when a demand for labor was growing. The overland trade in slaves from eastern Europe had stopped centuries before, as stronger states had developed there and as its inhabitants had become Christian. Access to the Black Sea ports, a favorite slaving ground that Italians had tapped successfully for slaves for themselves and for the Egyptians, was steadily becoming more difficult, and by the mid-fifteenth century Italians were effectively barred from the area. Another source of slavery was removed as a result of the reconquest of Muslim lands by Iberian Christians. All that remained in Muslim hands in Europe was the kingdom of Granada across Castile's southern border. Neither the Crown of Aragon nor Portugal had a land frontier facing the Muslims. Other sources of slaves did remain, but they could not supply a great number. Black Africans were available in the slave markets of the Muslim ports of North Africa, but they were brought there by the caravan traders who crossed the Sahara. These merchants were Muslims, and their main purpose was to fill the needs of the Islamic world. Christian corsairs in the Mediterranean would raid Muslim shipping and enslave the seamen and travelers they captured, but such captives regularly were exchanged for Christian captives of Muslim corsairs, thus allowing few captives to remain available for slave labor. That left West Africa as the greatest potential reservoir of chattel slaves, especially for the Portuguese, indirectly for the Spanish, and illicitly for the English, French, and Dutch interlopers.

As we proceed in this chapter, we will look closely at the European, mainly Portuguese, expansion down the West African coast and place the emerging slave trade in several contexts: the European development of African trade, in which slavery only slowly became a crucial component; the African responses to the demands the Europeans made and the opportunities their trade offered; and the spread of sugar plantations to the Atlantic islands and thereafter to the New World, which substantially heightened the need for labor and consequently the slave trade.

THE WEST AFRICAN COAST TO CA. 1650

The lure of West Africa was already powerful when the Portuguese began to expand in the early fifteenth century. Since the twelfth century, Europeans, mainly Italians and Spaniards, had been trading in the North African ports for goods coming from south of the Sahara. The Genoese began the European exploration of the Moroccan Atlantic coast in the same century, reaching Salé in 1162, but they apparently had little reason to press farther. It was not until nearly a century later, in 1253, that the Genoese reached Safi, only about 225 miles south of Salé. In 1291 the Vivaldis, a pair of Genoese brothers, outfitted an expedition to go farther to the south and sailed off into the unknown. They never returned. Except for Morocco, Africa never assumed much importance for the Genoese, who were among Europe's most successful Mediterranean traders in the late Middle Ages.[1] They were generally content to devote their energies to North Africa and the Iberian Peninsula, where profits were easily made. Castilian seamen were interested in the Atlantic waters off the coast of Africa for fishing and trade, but the Castilian government, until the end of the fifteenth century, was too concerned with internal problems and the task of dealing with the Muslim kingdom of Granada—the last Islamic possession in western Europe—to devote much attention to or to offer much support for African exploration. In the fourteenth century, several groups of Europeans made voyages to the Canaries, off the southern coast of Morocco, and from 1402 the continuous occupation of the Canaries began under the auspices of the crown of Castile. Nevertheless, Portugal was to become the leader in Atlantic Africa.

Neither Portugal nor Castile had participated greatly in the medieval slave trade in the Mediterranean. For slaves, both relied mainly on Muslim captives, and, after the Portuguese conquered the Algarve in the late thirteenth century, they began to exploit the Atlantic waters off the Moroccan coast. In 1317 a Genoese, Manuel Pesagno, received command of the Portuguese fleet with a license for privateering off Morocco and an agreement to turn one-fifth of all captives over to the Portuguese king. Another Genoese in Portuguese service, Lanzarotto Malocello, raided the Canaries and captured Guanche slaves there.[2] After nearly a century of activity in Morocco, the Portuguese were well aware of the economic importance of North Africa, and in 1415 they captured Ceuta, motivated in part by a desire to make it a base for gaining access to North African markets. In the next two decades they began to settle two island groups in the Atlantic: the Azores and the Madeiras. In 1434 a Portuguese expedition headed by Gil Eannes sailed beyond Cape Bojador, the long-standing limit of African commerce. That marked the true beginning of West African expansion.

Why the new European interest in Africa? And why did the Portuguese become the most successful Europeans in West Africa in the fifteenth and sixteenth centuries? Part of the answer lies in the lack of interest exhibited by the other maritime powers of southern Europe. With profits flowing from Mediterranean ventures, they simply lacked the urge to investigate the Atlantic coastal regions. More important was a technological barrier that Europeans had overcome only recently. Ship design in the Middle Ages concentrated on two types of vessel. The galley was a long and narrow vessel usually provided with one square sail. It could run before a following wind, but for maneuverability and for periods of contrary winds, it was propelled by ranks of oars operated by human rowers. The galley was better suited for the Mediterranean and was mainly used there. In the Atlantic waters of Europe, the round ship performed better. This ship, also used in the Mediterranean, with its square sails and high sides, could surmount the rough seas in Atlantic waters. Neither type was suited for African exploration. The round ship, dependent on the wind for mobility, could only travel when a following wind blew. The prevailing wind patterns along the African coast south of Cape Bojador were from the north, so it was a simple task to sail to the south in a round ship, but virtually impossible to return to the north. A galley, independent of the wind, also suffered from inherent drawbacks. It was narrow to reduce resistance in the water, and that narrowness cut into the available cargo capacity, as did the large number of oarsmen necessary to propel the vessel. In fact, the crew was so large in relation to the galley's size that supplies of food and water could be carried only for relatively short distances. In Africa, once southern Morocco had been passed, some six hundred miles of desert cut off the milder lands of the coast farther south, and reprovisioning stations were not available. Given these circumstances, the technological limitations of both types of vessel meant that West Africa throughout the Middle Ages was effectively beyond the reach of seaborne trade.

Two episodes illustrate particularly well the inability of medieval vessels to make their way back up the West African coast. The first we have already mentioned: the ill-fated voyage of the Vivaldi brothers in the 1290s. The second took place in the first half of the fourteenth century. Muslims from Almería in Spain set sail and passed the Strait of Gibraltar making for a Moroccan port.

> But winds played with us and the waves crashed together so that we went beyond the place we were making for. This state of affairs continued so long that we were no longer able to anchor and so continued to penetrate the ocean wastes to the south. . . . [Finally,] the wind died down. . . . At last we reached land and anchored and left the ship to seek deliverance. We saw signs indicating the proximity of a city, so we made for it and found it inhabited by a population of Sudan. . . .
>
> We remained with them until some of them set out for a neighboring country on some business or other and we went with them. And so we moved from place to place until we reached Morocco.[3]

We do not know what happened to the Vivaldis, but the fact that the Spanish Muslims abandoned an apparently sound ship without even attempting to sail back north supports the contention that medieval vessels were incapable of making that trajectory.

The major shortcoming was remedied in the fifteenth century with the development of the caravel and similar types of ship. Rather than a startling new discovery, the caravel was the outcome of the gradual introduction of detailed improvements in ship design by the pragmatic shipwrights of Portugal and Spain, who based their innovations on Islamic, Mediterranean, and North Atlantic precedents. The caravel with lateen rigging—triangular sails for sailing close to the wind—was a Portuguese invention, and the Spaniards developed the *carabela redonda*, a full-rigged vessel with a combination of lateen and square sails. Larger ships, called *naos* in Castilian and *naus* in Portuguese, began to incorporate features pioneered in the caravels; consequently, by the late fifteenth century, Europeans had vessels with a fairly large carrying capacity and much improved maneuverability. This, of course, did not mean that they were totally reliable; the paths of European expansion are liberally strewn with lost and wrecked ships. Nevertheless, the caravels and *naos* could sail to almost any point on the world's oceans and return with a degree of reliability.[4]

That they were able to find their way was due to the progress made in navigational instruments and charts in the late Middle Ages. The Iberian vessels that explored Africa carried compasses, probably a Chinese invention passed to Europe by the Muslims, to set direction, and after midcentury they had astrolabes and quadrants for determining location, another adaptation of Muslim precedents. They had means of estimating their speed, and they had charts, called portolanos, that noted the location of geographical features and the compass directions between them. The charts were useless in sailing into unknown regions, of course, but once a point had been reached, its location was determined and the chart expanded to include it. This use of charts vastly simplified the return voyage and all subsequent trips.[5]

With the new types of ships and improved navigational aids, by the second quarter of the fifteenth century, the Portuguese had the means of exploring the African coast. When they reached the region of northerly winds south of Cape Bojador, they could now sail back, using the small daily changes in wind direction. It was a laborous task, to be sure, but for the for the first time it was possible, and the Portuguese were quick to exploit their advantages.

The Portuguese royal house was a driving force behind the country's African expansion. In the thirteenth and fourteenth centuries, a close relationship had developed between the crown and commercial interests. The crown was concerned with fostering trade, licensing commerce, and securing financing through the representatives of Italian banking and merchant houses resident in Lisbon. Through royal initiative, a system of maritime insurance took shape and helped to shield investors from catastrophic losses. Portuguese merchants traded in England, France, and the Low Countries and ventured into the Mediterranean. By the fifteenth century, Portugal had the economic experience and the maritime expertise to begin the African expansion.[6]

As an introduction to the early phases of European enterprises in Africa, it is worth quoting the comments made by A. G. Hopkins in his *Economic History of West Africa*:

> First, the Europeans who came to West Africa in the fifteenth and sixteenth centuries were interested in goods other than slaves. Second, this commerce continued even after the overseas slave trade was well under way. Third, there were marked regional differences in West Africa depending on the nature of trade with the Europeans. Fourth, European shipping services encouraged the growth of a new kind of long distance coastal trade in West Africa.[7]

His third point is especially noteworthy. Africa was so varied and Portuguese activity in different regions so distinct that it is difficult to generalize with any degree of accuracy. In order to assess the economic activities of the Portuguese in Africa and to place slave trading within its proper context, it is necessary to look at the African coast according to its geographical divisions:

Ceuta
The rest of Morocco
The Mauretanian coast and Arguin
Senegambia, the Upper Guinea coast, and the Cape Verde Islands
The Costa da Mina
Lower Guinea, Benin, and São Tomé
Kongo
Angola

The first Portuguese possession in Africa was Ceuta, flanked by Jebel Musa, the southern pillar of Hercules across the strait from Gibraltar. Ceuta's conquest was the result of a raid planned by King John I and his finance minister, João Afonso. Their motives were numerous, and many of them were long-standing. Expansion into Morocco offered enticing possibilities for solving or at least alleviating a number of significant economic concerns that Europe generally and Portugal particularly faced at the beginning of the fifteenth century. The nobility, from the greatest lords to the simplest knights, were particularly hard pressed. In the aftermath of the Black Death, when the population was reduced by a quarter to a third from its preplague peak, labor was expensive and scarce, especially because the growth of the cities, with greater opportunities brought about by the rise of trade and commerce, drained peasants from the countryside. With more goods available, the nobles needed money to purchase the luxury items that were becoming indispensable for their style of life, but their income was still based on the land and was tied up in fixed rents that could not be expanded easily. Because of inflation and frequent devaluations of the coinage, merchants and the crown needed more gold, and gold, as we saw in chapter 4, came principally from the sub-Saharan goldfields of Africa via the desert caravan routes. With the caravans a Muslim monopoly, Europeans could only secure gold through intermediaries. Portugal also had a chronic shortage of grain. Additional supplies could be obtained only by bringing new lands under cultivation or by purchase in foreign markets, and the latter intensified the need for gold. Sugar cultivation was certainly present in southern Portugal by 1400, and the sugar planters looked for new lands to extend their activities. Expansion of grain and sugar agriculture was also related to a demand for slaves, who could be used as cheap labor at a time when free laborers were demanding higher wages, and slaves could also be viewed as investments. In addition dyestuffs and other goods necessary for the textile industry were in demand, while the long-established high seas fishing fleets needed expanded fisheries.[8]

Possession of Ceuta gave the Portuguese a naval base on the Mediterranean and a trading position in North Africa. Morocco produced grain, particularly wheat and barley, while off the Moroccan coast were rich fishing grounds. Moroccan cloths were important and could be purchased and exported. Ceuta was tied in with the Saharan trading network, offering Sudanese gold and slaves. Sugar was produced in several areas of Morocco; Ceuta was one, and there were several others in the south. As it happened, not all the Portuguese aims in taking Ceuta were fulfilled. The Muslims diverted much of Ceuta's Saharan trade to other Moroccan ports, and the Portuguese were denied the full measure of what they had sought. Nevertheless, they decided to hold Ceuta and expand their attention to include the rest of the Moroccan Atlantic coast.[9]

After 1415 and throughout the fifteenth century, the Portuguese began to trade in the ports of Morocco's west coast. In Tangier, Salé, and other places, they began to engage in legitimate trade, facing competition from the Genoese but displacing them by midcentury. Slaves were trickling into Portugal, but they were mainly recruited by the traditional means: capture in war, corsair raids, and purchase in Moroccan slave markets. Slaves aside, in Morocco the trade mainly concerned other items. Probably the most important purchases of the Portuguese were wheat and barley. They also bought textiles, horses and cattle, and some Sudanese gold. Much of the grain was not taken home to Portugal; rather it was used as a medium of exchange in other markets farther to the south. On the simplest level, the Portuguese began a carrying trade linking various Moroccan ports, and the Moroccan goods were used in the West African trade. The Portuguese never lost the idea of further territorial conquest in Morocco and succeeded in taking some other towns, but at the same time they were content to act there as traders.[10]

After Ceuta was secured, a debate emerged in Portuguese ruling circles about future plans. Ceuta was a logical starting place for any of several further initiatives. There could be expansion eastward into the Mediterranean, but that would run afoul of the entrenched interests of Muslims and other Christians. There could be attempts on the Muslim kingdom of Granada, but nothing came of that beyond an unsuccessful Portuguese seige of Málaga in 1465. Morocco itself would be difficult to invade, and after some small successes, the Portuguese failed miserably at Tangier in 1537. That left the Atlantic and West Africa, which the Portuguese could use in approaching more closely to the goldfields. That was the plan they adopted; and it had the concurrence of the crown, the nobles, and the merchants, all of whom stood to gain.[11]

With West Africa as the major goal, the exploration of the coast continued. After Cape Bojador was passed in 1434, the Portuguese reached Cape Blanco in 1441. In 1443 Nuño Tristão, sailing beyond Cape Blanco, entered Arguin Bay to the southeast. In this period of the 1430s and 1440s, once southern Morocco had been passed, sailing masters found themselves passing along an inhospitable coast. This is the region where the Sahara reaches the Atlantic, inhabited in the fifteenth century by Islamized Berbers. Although there were few local products of note to buy, the coastal towns were linked with the Sudan by caravan routes, and the Portuguese sea traders were quick to realize that profits were to be made from trading the inhabitants themselves. Slaving began. In 1440–41 two Portuguese expeditions, one commanded by Antão Goncalves and the other by Nuño Tristão, took captives from among the Berbers and returned to Portugal with them. The first slaves brought directly back to Portugal arrived in 1441. The chronicler Azurara described the scene with a mixture of pity and complacency, as a group of slaves arrived in 1444.

> And these, placed all together in that field, were a marvelous sight; for amongst them were some white enough, fair to look upon, and well proportioned; others were less white like mulattoes; others again were black as Ethiops, and so ugly, both in features and in body, as almost to appear (to those who saw them) as images of the lower hemisphere. But what heart could be so hard as not to be pierced with piteous feelings to see that company? For some kept their heads low and their faces bathed in tears, looking one upon another; others stood groaning very dolorously, looking up to the height of heaven, fixing their eyes upon it, crying out loudly, as if asking help of the Father of Nature; others struck their faces with the palms of their hands, throwing themselves at full length upon the ground; others made their lamentations in the manner of a dirge, after the custom of their country. And though we could not understand the words of their language, the sounds of it right well accorded with the measure of their sadness.[12]

It is important to note that, except for a few blacks who were already slaves, these first captives were Berbers; the lands of the blacks still were farther to the south.[13]

The first group of slaves had been brought to the town of Lagos in southern Portugal. In 1444 Lanzarote de Freitas, the *almoxarife* (royal controller) of Lagos, assembled a group of investors (including the bishop of the Algarve) into a partnership and outfitted six caravels to go out and see what profits could be made. Because Prince Henry the Navigator had received grants giving him wide authority over the African coast and the Atlantic islands, no one legally could sail to West Africa without his license and without paying him one-fifth of the profits. Until his death in 1460 Henry personally organized only about one-third of the legal voyages. The other two-thirds received his authorization, and, of course, there were other illegal voyages. In the same period the pope granted the Portuguese Order of Christ, a crusading military order whose commander was Prince Henry, a monopoly over the spiritual efforts to be undertaken in the Atlantic regions. Thus Henry was in a position to reap the greatest benefits from African expansion. He could direct the course of expansion by means of his ability to grant or withhold licenses. He could direct missionary activity. Because most of the lands of the Order of Christ were located in the Algarve, Henry about this time moved his principal residence to the south, to a place near Sagres on the coast. There he could direct the voyages to the Atlantic and oversee his Portuguese lands and those of his order. An additional benefit, from Henry's point of view, was that the captives could be put to work on the order's vast estates in southern Portugal, chronically in need of labor. One of Henry's motivations may have been exploration for the sake of curiosity, but basic material considerations were far more important.[14]

In the 1440s Portuguese vessels on the African coast often engaged in slave raiding. The practice persisted occasionally after that, but by the 1450s it was becoming apparent that a less violent and more sophisticated means of acquiring slaves was evolving. The slave trade came to replace slave raiding. The events at Arguin after the Portuguese established a factory, or commission merchant's station, on the island exemplified the change. Even though Arguin was within the Sahara, local Berber merchants could provide the Portuguese with Sudanese goods and slaves, brought there via a branch route of the caravan network. In addition, the island could be used as a support base for voyages still farther to the south and for coastal fishing, an important aspect often overlooked in the story of Portuguese expansion.[15] The Venetian Cadamosto visited Arguin in the 1450s and reported that the factory provided some seven to eight hundred slaves for shipment back to Portugal each year. Valentim Fernandes, writing of the region in 1506–7, described the island as one league wide, two leagues long, and four leagues around.

> On the island, facing the continent and on a very high rock, is built a very beautiful and powerful fortress which belongs to the king of Portugal. This fortress is the site of important commerce, because the king maintains there a captain and a factor with other functionaries to guard the fortress. . . .
>
> At two leagues from Arguin there is another island [the Isle of Herons] with innumerable birds . . . the birds are given to the slaves to eat.[16]

The natives of the island were Azenegue Berbers, who traded far and wide, from Mali in the Sudan to Safi in Morocco. They purchased horses in Morocco and took them to Mali to exchange for gold and slaves from black Africa as well as other goods, identified by Valentim Fernandes as antelope skins, gum arabic, civet (obtained from the civet cat and used as a base for perfume), ostrich eggs, camels, cows, and goats. To buy these items from the Azenegues, the Portuguese imported cloth, saddles and stirrups, basins (no doubt copper ones), saffron, and wheat. The last was perhaps the most important. By the time of Fernandes, when India had been reached and commerce with Asia established, oriental goods had entered the list: cloves, pepper, ginger, red coral, and cornalines (Indian stones).[17]

From the base at Arguin, the Portuguese penetrated the African interior for a time. They had an inland trading station at Wadan, a crossroads for the caravan network, but it was ultimately unsuccessful. At Arguin itself the commercial opportunities were limited; it was never more than the terminus of a branch route off the main West African caravan paths. The availability of trade goods was greater in black Africa farther to the south; and by the mid-sixteenth century, when the developing Atlantic trade increased the volume of commerce, Arguin began to decline, especially because it had never achieved self-sufficiency.[18]

Between 1448 and 1460 the Portuguese reached the next section of the African coast: the area directly north and south of Cape Verde, where two major rivers, the Senegal and the Gambia, and two lesser ones, the Casamance and the Geba, flowed into the Atlantic. The Portuguese called this stretch the Cape Verde coast, and modern historians call its northern portion Senegambia. The first region discovered where sub-Saharan blacks lived, it was tied more closely with the commercial and political centers of the Sudan than any other coastal region. Although the region's economic importance for the Portuguese was surpassed later by places farther to the south, it did offer a significant slave trade and a less significant gold trade up to about 1505. With the Jolofs dwelling between the Senegal and the Gambia, the Portuguese traded horses for slaves; the Jolofs had already been trading horses for slaves with Arab and Sanhaja dealers. In time fewer slaves could be obtained in exchange for horses. In the 1450s a poor horse could be traded for 25 to 30 slaves; later a horse brought only 10 to 12 slaves; and by the early sixteenth century, only 5 slaves. The Portuguese took advantage of the navigability of the Senegal and sailed upriver sixty leagues for slave trading. Below the Jolof region the Portuguese established relations with the Mande people and others, exchanging horses for slaves, but that trade too declined rather quickly. In the great fairs at Cantor the Portuguese secured gold of great purity and in substantial quantities, and for it they traded a variety of products: horses, cloth, brass *manilhas* (semicircular pieces of brass, a standard trade item), caps and hats. On the Casamance River the Portuguese traded these same items and also iron; in return they received slaves, native cotton, and civet. Along the Geba River they found their first malaguetta pepper.[19]

Malaguetta, or grains of paradise, was a variety of pepper derived from two related plants, *Afromomium melegueta* and *Afromomium Granum-paradisi*. First traded in Europe in the thirteenth century, brought there via the trans-Saharan routes, malaguetta commanded high prices because of its scarcity. In the fifteenth and sixteenth centuries the Portuguese made great profits from the spice, which gave its name to the Costa da Malagueta (rather ambiguously called the Grain Coast in English) southeast from Sierra Leone.[20]

Below the Geba River as far as Sierra Leone, the coast was not particularly lucrative for trading, except for the gold in the region of the Scarcies River, but Sierra Leone itself was much more profitable. First discovered in 1461–62, the region drew increasing numbers of Portuguese after 1470. They obtained gold, slaves, and malaguetta in quantity, along with minor goods such as cobalt and exotic parrots, which fetched a high price back in Europe. To pay for these items, the Portuguese brought into Sierra Leone the same goods as elsewhere and also salt.[21]

The Portuguese were not often concerned with building colonies or even trading stations in this region; only in the islands were true colonies founded. The Cape Verde Islands filled the need for a factory, secure and easy to defend, and they also served for colonization. Economically, the Cape Verdes served a dual purpose: as an entrepôt for coastal trading, and as a stage for agricultural development by colonists from Portugal. The dyestuff orchilla, found growing wild in the Canaries, was transplanted to the Cape Verdes and used locally or sent back to Europe. Imported cultivars also included cotton and indigo. Livestock breeding became an important pursuit, and horses were bred for trade with the Jolofs of Senegambia. Salt was produced on one of the islands. Slavery affected the Cape Verde economy in two ways. First, slaves from the mainland served as labor on the islands, both in agriculture and in cloth manufacturing. The cloth produced there became an important export to the Guinea coast. Second, slaves were brought to the islands for reexport. This was a crucial part of the economy, and, in fact, most of the islands' production of agricultural and manufactured goods went not to Europe, but back to Africa to purchase more slaves. Records show that in 1513–15 nearly 3,000 slaves were brought to Santiago, the principal island of the Cape Verde group, on twenty-nine vessels. Probably a majority of the slaves were passed on to other markets.[22]

Purchasing slaves was the norm; few were captured. The Portuguese government tried two other ways of managing the mainland area opposite the Cape Verdes in the fifteenth century. One was direct royal control, and the other was to grant a concession to a person who would manage the trade of the region in return for a share of the proceeds.[23] In both cases, official policy was to sponsor settlement in the islands, but to prohibit permanent settlements on the mainland. The area was a rich one, not as rich as the Costa da Mina, but important enough for the crown to try to make sure that its profits were regular. Nonetheless, the temptation to unlicensed traders was great, and there soon emerged an illicit commerce carried out by *lançados* and *tangomaos*. Walter Rodney defined them:

> The former [term] takes its origin from *lançar*, "to throw," and refers to the fact that these white residents had "thrown themselves" among the Africans. A *tangomao* was . . . a white trader who had gone to the extreme of adopting the local religion and customs. . . . [24]

Although the government legislated against the *lançados* and the *tangomaos*, it was unable to eliminate them, and their actions would long continue. They were useful in the slave trade, acting as intermediaries in transferring slaves to the coastal markets.

One of the potentially most lucrative series of discoveries in West Africa took place between 1469 and 1475, as the east-west coast along the southern edge of the hump of the continent was surveyed. Here the explorers found themselves close to the gold-bearing region of Akan, and here they first were able to buy gold in great quantity. This was due to the efforts of Fernão Gomes, who in December 1469 received a five-year license from Afonso V to explore the coast south of Sierra Leone. Gomes paid the king two hundred *milreis* annually and was obliged by his contract to explore at least one hundred leagues of coastline per year. By the end of the contract, which had been extended for an additional year, the expeditions he sent out had mapped the coast to below the equator and beyond the point where the African coast begins its southward thrust. Of vital importance was the fact that the first expedition that Gomes sponsored, led by João de Santarém and Pero Escobar, had found gold available for purchase in the vicinity of Cape Three Points. Although the goldfields themselves were inland and not reached by the Portuguese, the availability of gold impelled them to dub the region "the mine," and that stretch of the shore became known as the Costa da Mina.[25]

Other discoveries in the same period led to the creation of a trading system covering the entire coast of Lower Guinea from Sierra Leone to the Bight of Biafra. The major components were the Gold Coast around Cape Three Points; the Niger Delta and Benin; and the islands of Fernando Po. Príncipe, and São Tomé. The region had been explored by the expeditions sent out by Gomes during 1469–75, during the period when he held the contract for exploration. His license expired in 1475, and just at that time European events diverted Portuguese royal attention from Africa until the death of Afonso V in 1481. The new king, John II, turned his attention to the problems of Africa, which had suffered from neglect for six years. The first priority was to protect the royal monopoly on trade in the region, which was being challenged by the Castilians and by unlicensed Portuguese traders. The Treaty of Alcaçovas, ending a Portuguese-Castilian war, gave Portugal a virtual monopoly in Africa. Portugal got a free hand to operate on the coast and in the Azores and the Madeiras, while Castilian control of the Canaries was ratified. Although Castile in return agreed to stop its own and foreign ships from intruding into the Portuguese sphere without specific Portuguese license, a treaty alone could not protect trade in Lower Guinea, and in addition to foreign interlopers there was the danger of unlicensed Portuguese traders. As a result, in December 1481 John II sent out an expedition to build a factory and fortress on the Costa da Mina. The mission's commander, Diogo de Azambuja, secured the agreement of the local Fante chief, Caramansa, and began construction of the complex named São Jorge da Mina, which soon became the key to Portuguese control of the region. Artisans brought from Portugal built the fortress from native stone on a rock mound at the mouth of the Benya River, from which it could protect the anchorage at the river's mouth, where ships of up to three hundred tons could anchor safely.[26]

The trade conducted at the Mina station provided the Portuguese with a large and steady flow of gold brought from the interior by African merchants. The Portuguese bought the gold and other products with goods they imported: metals, cloth, blue glass beads, and ornaments. One demand of the African traders deserves special note: they wanted slaves. On the Costa da Mina, slavery and the slave trade were established institutions, and the African merchants needed bearers to carry back the bulky imported goods. To solve this problem, the Portuguese had to offer them African slaves in partial exchange for the gold. Because they could not secure a sufficient number of slaves from Senegambia or other regions to the north, they had to look farther afield for sources of supply. These they found in the rivers of the Niger Delta, where they could buy slaves and return them to the Costa da Mina as part of the price they paid to buy gold.[27]

To illustrate the complexity of Portuguese trade in Africa, it is worth examining in detail the activities of their enclave at São Jorge da Mina. The key element at Mina was the acquisition of gold that the Africans brought to the coast. Much of the trading was done within the walls of the trade castle. For some years, however, the king of Commany refused to enter the courtyard; his trading was done under the shade of the trees at some distance from the walls. In all cases, the trading was conducted by the Portuguese factor and his assistants. Their primary aim was to secure a good price in gold for their merchandise. The African merchants measured gold dust with their fingers, and the Portuguese weighed larger pieces of gold on a set of balances. The factor then recorded the transaction and stored the gold in a large locked chest—the *arca com tres chaves*—until it was taken back to Lisbon. The amount of gold received yearly in the early sixteenth century was phenomenal. It has been estimated at 10 percent of the world's supply.[28] To pay for it the Portuguese imported a variety of trade goods.

Perhaps the most important Portuguese imports into Mina were the slaves from Africa farther to the south. These were brought mainly from the regions of the Niger Delta, Kongo, and Angola, after having been kept for a time and selected on the island of São Tomé. Other goods included metals. Copper was the most important, imported in the form of basins and *manilhas* of set value, but there was also metal hardware in lead, iron, and steel. Cloth purchased in North Africa and southern Portugal was also brought to Mina, and a lively trade in used clothing from Portugal was also important. Various shells were sold at Mina and beads of several varieties, called *coris* by the Portuguese. These should not be confused with *cowrie* shells, an import that served in several parts of West Africa as a currency. Wines were first brought in for the consumption of the Portuguese residents, but soon a demand for them grew among the Africans. They were accustomed to palm wine, an indigenous alcoholic beverage, but they developed a taste for the sweet varieties of Portuguese wines.[29]

The Mina station, like other Portuguese trade forts, attracted many Africans who came to live in the shadow of the wall and formed their own towns owing allegiance to the Portuguese commander. Close contact between Europeans and Africans brought about intermarriage and a gradual blending of culture for those living close to the fort, but European influence seldom penetrated very far into the interior. Portuguese activity at Mina was limited mainly to the fort and its surrounding territory. This was a common pattern in the Portuguese places in West Africa; trade, not cultural or territorial expansion, was their major emphasis. The trade forts never became important centers of missionary activity; in fact, aside from efforts made in Kongo, the Portuguese showed little commitment to the effort to spread Christianity. Gradually, too, Mina began to develop its own slave population, a further indication of its enclave status. Not all the slaves brought in were sold to the gold merchants, and many of those who remained were put to work as laborers and domestics in the fortress itself.[30]

In the first decades after the Portuguese reached the Niger Delta, that region seemed very promising. The Ijo, the first people the Portuguese encountered in the Niger Delta, had contact with the nearby interior kingdom of Benin, one of the most advanced of the West African states, but one that was oriented toward the Sudan and not toward the coast until the Portuguese came. As they traded in the delta, the Portuguese quickly began to receive intelligence about Benin, and John II sent emissaries headed by João Afonso d'Aveiro into the interior to seek out the king of Benin in 1486. D'Aveiro went first by sea to Ughoton, a delta town that had become the main base of Portuguese trading in the region, and then persuaded its chief, a tributary of the Oba (king) of Benin, to accompany him inland to Benin City.[31]

The high hopes for Benin, as a source of slaves and malaguetta and as a ground for missionary work, did not bear the anticipated fruit, although strong Benin pepper (*Piper guineense*, called by the Portuguese *pimento de rabo*) did bring profits in European markets. Plans for factories at Ughoton and Benin were not successful; they existed for a time and fell into disuse. Part of the reason for their failure was environmental: the Portuguese succumbed to tropical diseases in unacceptable numbers. The Oba of Benin, for his part, was not too interested in Portuguese missionary efforts, and, as for trade, the Portuguese soon found that Benin's ruler did not really control the peoples of the Niger Delta and could not guarantee a Portuguese monopoly in the region. Portugal continued to trade in the Niger Delta and at Benin City, but a new complication arose. The Oba established separate markets for male and female slaves in his kingdom, and soon it was virtually impossible to purchase men there. This was especially difficult for the Portuguese, who wanted male workers far more than female. Slaves continued to be available in Benin and in the Niger Delta into the seventeenth century, but they were not natives. Rather, they were people captured or otherwise acquired up the Niger River in today's northern Nigeria and brought to the coast by merchants of Benin.[32]

In 1492 a colony was established in the islands on São Tomé and Príncipe, settled by both voluntary and forced Portuguese colonists, including among the involuntary a number of young Jews, some of them Spaniards ousted from their homeland by the expulsion decree of the same year. The economy of São Tomé was based soon on sugar cane cultivation, for which the colonists needed slaves from the Niger Delta. The colonists also found that they could make a profit supplying slaves to São Jorge da Mina as well as to Lisbon. Portuguese policy was to allow the settlers at São Tomé and Príncipe to import a certain number of slaves, but traders coming directly from Portugal were to have the right to secure the bulk of the slaves. The islanders protested this limitation, and for years they tried to secure a monopoly on the slave trade in the region for themselves. By 1519 they had won their battle; henceforth slaves were purchased on the mainland, transported to the islands, and put to work temporarily in the production of sugar. After a period of "seasoning," the best of the slaves were shipped to São Jorge da Mina and sold there to the African gold merchants, who were in a position to enforce their refusal to buy any but the best and most perfect slaves. Other slaves were taken to the Cape Verde Islands, Madeira, and metropolitan Portugal; after about 1530 the traders of São Tomé began to ship the bulk of their slaves to American markets.[33] Writing of São Tomé in the first decade of the sixteenth century, Valentim Fernandes said that "there are on this island nearly two thousand slaves who cultivate and work the land, without counting the slaves of commerce of which there are sometimes nearly five or six thousand."[34]

Farther to the south, the kingdom of the Kongo at first looked like a promising field for Portuguese enterprise. The king was powerful, and initially there was hope that his kingdom could be converted. The Portuguese first gave him military aid, and he accepted Christianity for a time before reverting to his native religion. His son Afonso maintained his adherence to Catholicism and, on his father's death in 1506, defeated the Kongolese supporters of paganism. Thereafter Afonso began a close association with the Portuguese in economics and culture. He sent groups of Kongolese to be educated and trained in Portugal, and requested and received missionaries, teachers, and skilled craftsmen from Portugal to instruct the people of the Kongo. However, the mutual cooperation did not last too long, and the greatest obstacle to success seems to have been the slave trade. The price of the mission to the Kongo was paid for in part by slaves, but, more important, the Portuguese who began to arrive there about 1510 soon were neglecting their official duties and devoting a large portion of their attention to slave trading. The difficulties became apparent in only four or five years; by 1526 they had reached such great proportions that Afonso complained to Lisbon that "there are many traders in all corners of the country. They bring ruin to the country. Every day people are enslaved and kidnapped, even nobles, and even members of the king's own family."[35]

Large slave caravans journeyed from the interior to the capital. Afonso took care to prevent free Kongolese from being enslaved, but foreigners—such as

Teke, Hum, and Ambunda—were fair game. This is one more illustration of the tendency of all groups to avoid enslaving those considered to be members of their own societies. The great demands of the resident Portuguese for slaves, together with the practice of native Kongolese of enslaving other Kongolese, was sufficient cause for Afonso to stop the slave trade and expel all Portuguese in 1526. He soon rescinded his order, but at the same time he enacted stringent regulations. A team of inspectors, made up of one Portuguese and two Kongolese, was to examine each slave and to free any kidnapped native. Gradually, whites found themselves restricted to Mbanza Kongo (the capital) and the town of Mpinda. The greatest interior slave market was on the Stanley (Malebo) Pool on the Kongo (Congo) River, where the Hum people were sold. This area was called *pumbo*, from Mpundu, the Kongolese name for Stanley Pool, and slave traders there were called *pombeiros*. Originally the name had applied to the Portuguese who traded there, but after the whites were prohibited from entering the interior, the term came to apply to the African slaves of the Portuguese who traveled to the region and brought back the other blacks they purchased.[36]

On longer acquaintance, the Portuguese found that the Christianization of the Kongo was not going smoothly and that the country was valuable mainly as a source of slaves for São Tomé and Lisbon. Even this trade was difficult, and by the middle of the sixteenth century, the Portuguese developed contacts and obtained a more secure supply of slaves in Angola, a recently formed state south of the Kongo. Several factors account for the shift southward from the Kongo to Angola, a movement that became pronounced in the late sixteenth and early seventeenth centuries. Perhaps the most important factor was the Portuguese crown's taxation on the slaves its subjects bought in the Kongo; the Angolan trade was illicit and therefore untaxed. Many slaves were available in the Kongo— 4,000 to 5,000 each year in the 1530s—but it was cheaper and more convenient to acquire slaves in Angola, where they were easily available in coastal markets. Trading in the Kongo was hampered by the restrictions against enslaving Kongolese and the necessity of buying slaves from other groups in the interior.[37]

By the second quarter of the sixteenth century the Portuguese had established a well-functioning trading network centered on West Africa, ranging from Morocco to Angola. Its tendrils stretched from central Europe to India, and it was the key element in the economic underpinnings of the Portuguese empire. The great trade of the Portuguese was in Eastern spices, and to pay for those spices European goods were of little value; the Indians despised them. To get the spices, the Portuguese needed gold, which they could purchase from Africans, principally in the region of São Jorge da Mina. To buy gold there they needed a variety of items of exchange: slaves, metals, cloth, alcohol, horses, glass ornaments and mirrors, and shells. This last item requires some special comment. Shell currency, mainly cowries, was common in several African regions. However primitive it may appear at first glance, it was a rather sophisticated response to the need for a medium of exchange. Shells served as monetary units; their total number was limited; and the introduction of additional units was controlled by the rulers. The shells could not be counterfeited, and, unlike metal coins, they could not be shaved or clipped to any advantage. The Portuguese bought shells in India and used them for trade on the African coast. In North Africa they purchased cloth for sale in West Africa. They could provide alcoholic beverages from their own production in the home country and in Madeira. They could not obtain the metals they needed from their own mining. Copper, a metal easily worked, was especially favored in Africa, where it was already known but not available in large quantity. To secure copper, the Portuguese had recourse to the markets of the Low Countries, where they had been trading for a long time. European copper was experiencing a boom in production just at this time, due to the development of new mines in central Europe. German merchants took copper to Antwerp, where the Portuguese could use the profits of the spice and sugar trade to buy it and then use it to buy gold and other goods in Africa.[38]

The case that West African slavery was a development in response to European pressure was most forcefully put by Walter Rodney for the area he studied, the Upper Guinea coast, and he implied that the same was true for other areas.[39] Although the question is still a matter for scholarly research and debate, the present consensus is that slavery and slave trading were already present in many areas of West Africa well before the coming of the Europeans in the fifteenth century, and that African merchants and rulers welcomed the trading opportunities the Europeans offered. The Venetian Cadamosto, who visited Senegal in the 1450s, provided confirmation for this line of thought in his description of the king of "Senega."

> The king lives thus: he has no fixed income [from taxes]: save that each year the lords of the country, in order to stand well with him, present him with horses, which are much esteemed owing to their scarcity, forage, beasts such as cows and goats, vegetables, millet, and the like. The king supports himself by raids, which result in many slaves from his own as well as neighbouring countries. He employs these slaves [in many ways, mainly] in cultivating the land alloted to him: but he also sells many to the Azanaghi [and Arab] merchants in return for horses and other goods, and also to Christians, since they have begun to trade with these blacks.[40]

Recently John Fage studied the evidence for the entire West African coast, relying exclusively upon the testimony of eyewitnesses for the first two and a half centuries of European trade. His conclusions are similar in certain respects to the interpretations of social structure in the western Sudan in the Middle Ages: power was based on control of people, not of land. As Fage put it:

> it would seem, indeed, that the possession of men and women was both the source and the symbol of wealth and power, particularly perhaps because they seem to have been a scarce resource in relation to the amount of land and other resources available for exploitation. So, as foreign trade

increased, some of them—but men rather than women, for the latter paid biological interest—could serve as money with which, if the occasion arose, other commodities could be purchased.[41]

Many questions regarding the trade in African slaves probably will be answered in the next few years, as works in preparation become published and available.[42] It is already apparent that long-distance trade was well under way in West Africa before the Europeans arrived,[43] and we will no doubt find that Eugenia W. Herbert's interpretation—that the Portuguese adapted themselves to existing African trading networks—will be sustained.[44]

The slave trade was only one component of the Portuguese trading empire. The Portuguese quickly had moved beyond the stage of casual raiding to secure captives, and it was newcomers to Africa, such as the Englishman John Hawkins in the mid-sixteenth century, who still engaged in that primitive form of acquisition. The slaves the Portuguese bought were taken where they could be put to work—on plantations, sugar plantations above all—in the Atlantic islands and southern Portugal, or they were taken where they could be marketed—on the Costa da Mina, in Spanish mainland or Canarian markets, and in Italy. Until the middle of the sixteenth century, these markets could absorb only a limited number of slaves. It was only after New World plantations were established that the growth of the Atlantic slave trade would transform slave trading from a necessary but confined component of the Portuguese imperial economy into one of the greatest forced migrations the world has ever known.

In the story of the first century and a half of the African side of the transatlantic slave trade, the main participants were the Portuguese and the Spaniards; the minor ones were the Dutch, the French, and the English. The Portuguese monopolized the legal trade, supplying slaves to the Atlantic islands, to Europe, and to the Spanish and Portuguese colonies in the New World. They followed the pattern they had established in the fifteenth century with only minor variations in practice, although the total number of slaves shipped from Africa increased significantly. The greatest change that occurred was the intervention of other European slave traders. There were many illegal incursions into the Portuguese sphere along the West African coast, notably because it was almost impossible to control by the relatively small number of Portuguese naval vessels. Spaniards made clandestine raids from the Canaries, and in the 1560s John Hawkins made three raiding expeditions, the first English ones, during which he resorted to seizing slaves forcibly on his first voyage and aiding a native ruler in Sierra Leone to war on his neighbors to secure slaves for his third. Among the English, Hawkins was an exception, and it was only after 1650 that British slaving began in earnest. The French slave trade, too, did not get under way on a large scale until the late seventeenth century.[45] If the Portuguese had to face only minor annoyances from the Spanish, English, and French in this period, they confronted a much more formidable rival in the Dutch.

In the 1630s and 1640s the Dutch made serious threats to the very existence of the Portuguese possessions in Africa, America, and Asia. From 1580 to 1640 Spain ruled Portugal, and in the long war that the Dutch prosecuted against the Spanish crown, Portuguese strongholds were regarded as fair game. In 1630, after a period of clandestine raids in Spanish and Portuguese areas on both sides of the Atlantic, the Dutch took Pernambuco, by then a sugar-producing region on Brazil's northern coast. In Africa they took São Jorge da Mina, Angola, and Arguin. Within thirty years the Portuguese had regained the majority of their lost colonies, permanently losing only Mina and other Gold Coast ports, but the Dutch were to remain a major factor in the slave trade throughout the seventeenth and eighteenth centuries, when they and the other European powers used their possessions in the Caribbean islands for lucrative sugar ventures.[46]

Sugar, in fact, is the key to understanding the most important questions in the early history of the transatlantic slave trade: why such a trade developed, why the major states of Europe squabbled over it, and why black slaves came to constitute the vast majority of workers in it. Changes in the economies of major regions of the world since the fourteenth century certainly played their part, and we previously have mentioned some of those changes. Unquestionably, one of the most important involved the development of sugar production in the Atlantic islands.

SUGAR PLANTATIONS IN THE ATLANTIC ISLANDS

In the fifteenth century the Spaniards and the Portuguese established sugar plantations on the Atlantic islands off the west coast of Africa. These plantations turned out to be prototypes of the New World enterprises that began in the sixteenth century. As we have seen previously, the cultivation of sugar cane and the manufacture of refined sugar had a continuous history long before the fifteenth century. The production of sugar in the Muslim world and on the island and mainland areas of the Christian Mediterranean always involved large-scale establishments, but the use of slave labor was of small importance, even though there may have been occasional use of slaves. The three elements that were to characterize sugar plantations in the Americas were first seen in the Atlantic islands. These included large land holdings, a crop to be sold in the growing markets of Europe, and slave labor. The first two elements could be found in earlier sugar estates in the Near East and the Mediterranean. The third element—wholesale reliance on slave labor—was new. The first complete transformation took place on Madeira, the principal island of the Madeiras group. Madeira, therefore, might be considered the link between Mediterranean sugar production and the system that was to dominate New World slavery and society into the nineteenth century.[47]

As Europeans made the first tentative excursions into the Atlantic in the thirteenth and fourteenth centuries, they brought back little more than geographical knowledge of two groups of islands: the Canaries and the Madeiras. By 1339 a portolano sailing chart produced in Catalonia had accurately identified them. At first, Portuguese and Castilian ships put in at the islands for easily obtainable items such as wood and the red dye "dragon's blood," the resin of the dragon tree, and sailing masters used the islands occasionally as pirate bases. The Portuguese crown was not very interested in the islands until 1417, when the Castilians visited the Madeiras with a large force. Faced with potentially serious Castilian competition, John I of Portugal acted decisively. An expedition of some one hundred people, mostly from southern Portugal, sailed to the principal islands of the Madeiras, Madeira and Porto Santo, to establish permanent settlement. The leaders were two Portuguese, João Gonçalves Zarco and Tristão Vaz Teixeira, and an Italian, Bartolomeo Perestrello. All three were members of the lower nobility, as were some fourteen others. Zarco seems to have held more authority than the others, and he worked out the division of the islands. One-half of Madeira was allocated to Zarco, while Teixeira got the remaining half of Madeira and Perestrello the island of Porto Santo. Each was to be lord of his territory with the ability to parcel out lands to the other settlers. In 1433 King Duarte made his brother Prince Henry lord of the Madeiras for his lifetime. Henry in turn made the threefold division permanent by creating captaincies and awarding them to the three lords on a hereditary basis.[48]

The agricultural exploitation of the islands was first based on mixed farming and grazing, but quickly sugar became important. Prince Henry was responsible for the introduction of sugar cane in Madeira and secured cuttings, as well as Malvoisie grapevines from Crete, to be sent there. Teixeira planted the first sugar cane and processed a first crop of some one thousand pounds of sugar. Just where the cane came from is somewhat controversial. The two earliest sources, Duarte Pacheco Pereira and João de Barros, both state that Henry obtained cuttings and experts from Sicily, but Valentim Fernandes, who wrote in the early sixteenth century, reported that the prince sent to Valencia for cuttings. Bailey W. Diffie noted that in 1478 a Valencian sugar master received recognition in Madeira. But the Portuguese need not have gone so far afield. Sugar cane was being grown in southern Portugal early in the fifteenth century, and the Portuguese capture of Ceuta put them in proximity to Moroccan sugar fields.[49]

Even though the islands were uninhabited and fertile, and even though the first experiments with sugar were successful, the phenomenal growth of the islands did not happen overnight; careful and extensive preparation was needed. The islands had a dense cover of vegetation that had to be cleared before cultivation or even pasturing of animals was possible. The simple expedient of burning was adopted, and great fires rapidly did the work of years. There are even stories that some of the settlers had to flee into the sea or rivers to escape the clearing fires that had spread beyond their control, but in the wake of the burning, a fertilizing layer of ash covered the soil. Next, irrigation canals and terracing had to be constructed. That took more time, and it is likely that the settlers brought in technicians skilled in irrigation to direct the construction and slaves from the Canaries for the labor. In the interim before full-scale agriculture could be developed, the settlers sustained themselves on fish caught locally, and exported wood and dyestuffs to support themselves. By 1450 the efforts at taming the island were completed, and Madeira began to produce profits. Both Madeira and Porto Santo produced grain in abundance, far exceeding the demands of the local population. Porto Santo regularly exported wheat and barley to Portugal, and the wheat from the islands was also exported to the Saharan coast and black Africa to help underwrite the Portuguese coastal trade.[50]

The newly emerging sugar industry on Madeira received a boost in 1452 when the first water-powered sugar mill was constructed by a knight (*escudero*) in Prince Henry's service, Diogo de Teive. Teive was promised a monopoly on sugar crushing if he were successful, and his contracted payment to Henry was one-third of the profits in kind. If unsuccessful, Teive would be replaced by another contractor. If he could not keep up with demand, a second contractor would be allowed to construct a mill. Sugar turned out to be an immediate success, and, together with the growth of other agricultural pursuits, it helped to sustain a rapid increase in population. According to Cadamosto in 1455, there were 800 people living on the island of Madeira, and Azurara, writing in the same decade, noted 150 *moradores*. If *moradores* was used in the sense of householders, then the estimates of total population are about the same. In any case it is clear that soon the population rose dramatically. It passed 2,000 in the 1460s, and in this number were included the first slaves brought from Africa. By the beginning of the sixteenth century, the population stood at 15,000 to 18,000, and of that number 2,000 were slaves.[51]

The proportion of slaves among the inhabitants of the Madeiras probably reached a peak about this time. From the mid-fifteenth century, slaves had been brought in to meet the labor demands in the sugar industry. Some came from Morocco and the Berber lands immediately to the south; others were black Africans obtained from among the groups with whom the Portuguese were steadily making contact; and still others were Guanches from the Canaries. The use of slaves soon began to decline, and there were even proposals to expel the Guanches. Most of the sugar plantations were relatively small and were occupied and managed by their owners. None approached the size and scale of the later Brazilian and Caribbean plantations. This, of course, meant a limit on the number of slaves who could be employed. Population in Portugal was growing slowly in the sixteenth century, and as a consequence many free laborers left the mainland to go to Madeira, further depressing the market for slaves. In its early history Madeira was a precursor of the future American colonial areas, but by the early sixteenth century it resembled a province of Portugal.[52]

Sugar production and trade prospered. Shiploads of sugar were delivered to the large European markets: Lisbon, Seville, Antwerp, and cities in the Mediterranean. Although most of the plantations and mills were in the hands of Portuguese, most of the export trade was controlled by foreigners, many of them Italians resident in Portugal. The European demand for sugar was strong, and the lower costs of Madeiran sugar caused heavy competition for the longer established Mediterranean producers. We have already seen that in the face of this competition the Ravensburgers abandoned their Valencian operations, while Sicily and Cyprus suffered a decline in their sugar profits.[53]

Other Atlantic islands also produced sugar. It was introduced into the Azores, but it never became very profitable there because of the unfavorable climate. Grain and dyestuffs were always more important than sugar as exports from the Azores. As a result, only a few slaves were ever brought to the Azores.[54] Sugar was also introduced in the Cape Verde islands, but agriculture there concentrated on cereals and fruits and was complemented by cattle raising. São Tomé, which became a crucial entrepôt for the transatlantic slave trade, produced some sugar, as did the island of Fernando Po, but neither became very important as sugar producers. São Tomean sugar was regarded as poor, because the loaves into which it was shaped had a tendency to crumble, making them hard to market.[55]

The Portuguese were not the only Europeans who were developing the Atlantic islands in the fifteenth and sixteenth centuries. By the late fifteenth century Castile, too, had entered the field and had taken over the Canary Islands, where sugar did not take long to develop. The Europeans who began to land on one or another of the islands in the fourteenth century discovered that, unlike the other Atlantic islands, the Canaries had a native population, the Guanches, a Caucasian stone-age people perhaps akin to the Berbers. They were subdued by the Spanish and some of them were enslaved. Of these, a number were exported to Europe or the Madeiras, while others were employed on Canarian sugar plantations, as were blacks and Berbers from Africa. Sugar production probably reached a peak in the Canaries in the first quarter of the sixteenth century. The Welsers, a German banking family, invested in sugar cane in Palma on Grand Canary. They owned four plantations at the height of their activity before withdrawing in 1520. Sugar was used as an alternative currency in these years, an indication of its importance in the economy. In 1526, a year near the peak of the Canarian sugar boom, there were twenty-nine mills in the islands, compared with sixteen in Portuguese Madeira. A decline, made worse by an infestation of caterpillars in 1530, was soon apparent, and its most important probable cause was competition from other producers. Before the decline, however, the Canaries acted as a way station for Spanish sugar manufacturing, and sugar cane cuttings and sugar processing techniques were taken to Spanish possessions in the newly discovered Caribbean islands to be installed there.[56]

Though slave labor had not been a major feature of sugar cane agriculture in the Mediterranean, it may have been used there on occasion. Slaves came to be used in greater numbers on the farms and in the mills of the Atlantic islands, but there too free labor was often used, as Portuguese and Spaniards migrated to the newly discovered islands. The connection between slavery and sugar, though, had been planted. It would bear its bitter fruit in the Americas, where large tracts of land suitable for sugar cane production were brought under European control by the Spaniards in the Caribbean islands and on the mainland of North and South America, and by the Portuguese in Brazil. There the great distances separating the shores of the Atlantic would act as a barrier to large-scale European migration in a period when that continent's population had not yet reached great numbers. The native inhabitants of the American regions were put into service on sugar plantations, but the combination of epidemic diseases and forced labor reduced their numbers at an alarming rate. To replace them the Portuguese and the Spaniards, as a result of the contacts they had made with West Africa, had a supply of labor readily at hand; and thus they began the transatlantic slave trade, with all its vexing and persistent complications for the history of the Americas. Before and during the American trade, however, there was another vector of the black slave trade leading to Europe. We will examine the African presence in Renaissance Europe in the next chapter.

8

AFRICAN SLAVES IN EUROPE

As European commerce with the Atlantic islands and the West African coast developed from the fifteenth through the mid-seventeenth century, slave trading was an important aspect, but by no means was it the only or even the most profitable component of that trade. Nevertheless, as it grew it provided slaves for two distinct areas: Europe itself and the European colonial settlements on both sides of the Atlantic. We will defer the discussion of the development of African slavery in the Americas and deal with that story in chapter 9 and 10. In this chapter we will examine the use of African slaves in Europe during the first two centuries of the existence of the direct slave trade, as it was conducted by the Portuguese and, to a lesser extent, by other Europeans.

Two preliminary observations must be made. First the presence of black Africans was not new in the history of Mediterranean Europe. From classical times, if not before, small numbers of Africans had reached the shores of the inland sea, some traveling voluntarily, others having been forced to make the trip. By the ninth century at the latest, Muslim caravan traders had brought blacks from sub-Saharan Africa to the Mediterranean ports they controlled. The main object of their trade was to supply slaves to the Islamic world, and in consequence Islamic Spain received a relatively small but constant supply of African slaves throughout its existence. As the Christian kingdoms of Iberia grew, they all obtained some black slaves through channels of trade and, more significantly, through their reconquests of Muslim possessions in the peninsula. Nonetheless, the numbers of blacks slaves in the Crown of Aragon, Castile, and Portugal were always small before the fifteenth century. When Iberians held slaves or traded them in the Middle Ages, they were almost always dealing with "Moors," a generic term for Muslims, regardless of their ethnic origins. Blacks were unusual, though certainly present in this context. Some blacks also reached Christian Europe from the twelfth century onward via the links of trade that

Italian, southern French, and Catalan merchants established with North African ports. It was because of this trade linkage that there was a small presence of blacks in western Mediterranean Europe in the late Middle Ages, as we have mentioned in earlier chapters.

The second point to be noted was that during the first two centuries of the Atlantic slave trade, blacks were confined almost exclusively to the same European areas that they had been in the Middle Ages, and within those areas they were most numerous in Portugal and Spain. The Italian trade with North Africa continued to supply some black slaves to Italy, and others trickled into Italy from the Portuguese African ventures, but the numbers of blacks in Italy was never large.[1] In France there were fewer still, although some could be found in the Midi throughout these centuries. The court of the duke of Anjou had North African servants and slaves in the fifteenth century.[2] In England blacks were rarities until English slaving reached its full development in the late seventeenth century. Small numbers of blacks, or even single individuals, reached England by various means in the later Middle Ages, but that was unusual. Others were introduced as a result of the slaving voyages of John Hawkins in the second half of the sixteenth century, but he disposed of most of the slaves he had kidnapped by selling them in the Spanish-American possessions.[3] The countries of northern and eastern Europe may have seen blacks occasionally, but never in significant numbers until much later. Thus the history of the black presence in Europe in this period is mainly the story of blacks as slaves and freedmen in Portugal and Spain.

Portuguese slave trading soon became very complex, as traders took slaves from several places on the West African coast to markets where they could be sold. These included the Portuguese colonies in the Atlantic islands, the Costa da Mina (where the Portuguese sold Africans from farther south to the local black rulers and merchants), and Portugal itself. For the first four decades of its existence, the Portuguese slave trade was organized rather loosely. Shipmasters needed special licenses to make the voyages to Africa, and on their return they had to pay a certain percentage of their profits to the crown or to a royal designee. They could unload and sell their cargoes in various Portuguese cities, usually in the south. By the 1460s the trade was becoming more lucrative, and, as tighter regulation seemed essential, the crown in 1474 assumed full control over the trade of Guinea, as the Portuguese called the West African region.

Gradually the Portuguese crown began to center the administration of colonial trade in Lisbon, although slaves could still be unloaded in Setubal and some ports of the Algarve. Trade as a whole was directed by officials of the Guinea House in Lisbon; but in the 1480s as trade prospered and as the slave trade, in particular, grew in importance, King John II created a special office to handle the slave trade, called the Lisbon House of Slaves, the Casa dos Escravos de Lisboa, a division of the existing Guinea House. It was under the direction of the *almoxarife dos escravos*, a royal official charged with administering the trade, specifically with collecting of the royal dues. The slave trade was moving into a new phase of monopolies, and in 1486 the king awarded a monopoly of the slave trade in the area of Benin to the Florentine merchant Bartolomeo Marchione, who was to compensate the crown for his monopoly with an annual payment of over one million *reis*. The House of Slaves was to check on Marchione's dealings as well as on the slave trade in other African regions.[4]

The House of Slaves had its location near the Lisbon docks in close proximity to the Guinea House. It contained a prison for confining the newly arrived slaves before they were sold, offices for the administrators and record keepers of the trade, and, in addition, a cooperage for the construction of casks and barrels needed for royal vessels. The *almoxarife* had primary responsibility for the slave trade: he was charged with the official loading and unloading of the slave ships, with housing the slaves, with supervising their sale, with collecting royal duties on privately imported slaves, and with maintaining full financial records for the crown.[5]

The vessels engaged in the African trade were relatively small: caravels of fifty to one hundred tons, and *naus* or *navios*, ships of over one hundred tons. Their crews consisted of able and ordinary seamen, a scribe (a royal official assigned to each ship), a pilot, and a shipmaster. Often the ships carried an African interpreter to help conduct business on the coast, particularly in places where there was no regular Portuguese presence. Although these African interpreters were at first slaves, they had the possibility of becoming free. By the early years of the sixteenth century, blacks were also serving among the seamen on the slaving ships.[6]

On the voyage, landfall could be made at several sorts of slaving stations. Where the Portuguese had factories (such at Arguin and Ughoton), the exchanges were conducted between the royal officials on the spot and the ships' officials. Along the Upper Guinea coast, *lançados* and *tangomaos* collected slaves in coastal barracoons to await the slaving ships. In still other places, the ships anchored and dealt directly with local African merchants and rulers, in a process known as ship trade. In was in such places that African interpreters aboard the ships were particularly useful. Once the slaves had been collected, they suffered on the return voyage from several hardships. Those who passed through the holding areas at São Tomé were branded on their right arms, at first with a cross, later with the letter "G," signifying Guinea. Although after 1519 crown regulations specified treatment aboard ship, there were problems of food, water, clothing, and shelter that could cause disease and death for the slaves, especially during longer voyages. Those who died en route were dumped overboard. To control the recalcitrant, chains and manacles were carried. These generally did the required job, but insurrections were not unknown. In 1509, for example, a group of slaves from Arguin tried unsuccessfully to take over the ship that bore them.[7]

The *almoxarife* of the House of Slaves met each ship arriving in Lisbon from

Africa. Before a ship could be unloaded, the officials had to inspect its cargo and records. Once that was done, the fettered slaves were led through the streets to the House of Slaves, where they would be assigned a price determined by the heads of the House of Slaves and the Guinea House, together with their assistants. The variables used in setting the price were sex, age, physical condition, and health, all determined by careful examination by the royal officials, who affixed a parchment price tag by a string around the slave's neck. Then the royal import duties had to be paid, and previously sold slaves were released to their buyers. The others remained on hand for future sales. These sales were made to individuals or to wholesale contractors (*corretors*) who could remove the slaves and sell them in the public slave market of Lisbon or transport them elsewhere.[8]

Not all the slaves reached Lisbon in good enough condition to be sold immediately. The harsh conditions of the voyages caused an attrition due to disease, malnutrition, and physical or psychological injury. Those who arrived ill were examined by the officials and cured if possible. For those suffering severe maladies, a lower sale price could be set, and buyers could take their chances with the afflicted slaves. Still others could not be sold at any price. In such cases, the officials found private citizens to nurse them; if they recovered, those who had cared for them could buy them at a special low price. Many never recovered, and a callous and insalubrious practice was the random disposal of the bodies of dead slaves. They were usually taken outside the city walls, often just beyond St. Catherine's Gate, and unceremoniously dumped. This created a serious threat to public health, and in 1515, King Manuel I ordered the construction of a mass burial pit close to St. Catherine's Gate where all dead slaves were to be placed, with the pit periodically cleansed with quicklime. One Lisbon street, the Poço dos Negros, derived its name from the pit.[9]

It is virtually impossible to determine accurately the numbers of slaves involved in the Portuguese slave trade to Europe. The vessels that loaded slaves in West Africa did not bring all their cargoes back to Lisbon, despite royal efforts to centralize the trade. Many ships stopped off in the islands and disposed of some slaves as they did; others unloaded in Portuguese towns south of Lisbon; while still others sailed directly for Seville and other ports of Andalusia. A. C. de C. M. Saunders estimated that from 1441 to 1470 up to 1,000 slaves reached Lisbon yearly, and that from 1490 to 1530 between 300 and 2,000 slaves annually were brought to Lisbon.[10]

The slave trade, as we have seen, was a significant component of the imperial Portuguese economy, although it was not of primary importance. In the early sixteenth century, prices for individual slaves increased dramatically. In terms of income for the crown, the slave trade brought in less than seven million *reis* annually in the period from 1511 to 1513, whereas the spice trade from India in 1506 was estimated at fourteen to sixteen million *reis*, and the gold trade from Mina brought about forty-eight million *reis*. By the middle of the sixteenth century, the slave trade had grown in importance, as the revenues from gold and spices declined. The slave trade in midcentury, together with other African goods aside from gold, yielded some 34.7 million *reis*, whereas Mina's gold brought only 14 to 18.7 million *reis*, and the Indian trade was greatly reduced. To place this in another context, Saunders noted that none of this "matched the crown's income from taxation and monopolies in Portugal itself: 69,200,000 *rs.* in 1506, 234,500,000 *rs.* in 1559."[11]

Those African slaves who were destined to remain in Portugal made significant impressions on several social and economic aspects of the country, although their numbers were small. Saunders, in his recent and comprehensive history of blacks in Portugal in the first century of the Atlantic slave trade, found that the numbers of black slaves (32,370) and freedmen (2,580) in the mid-sixteenth century made up a relatively low percentage (2.5 to 3 percent) of the total Portuguese population of 1.2 to 1.4 million inhabitants. Their geographic concentration varied widely: up to 10 percent of the overall population in Lisbon and the Algarve, around 6 percent in other towns and cities, and much lower in the northern rural areas.[12] This distribution illustrates the primarily urban role that blacks played in Portugal's economy.

Slaveowners came from a wide range of the Portuguese population, and the work their slaves did reflected the owners' choices. The higher ranks of society made use of numbers of slaves as domestic servants, but in much smaller numbers than would become common later in the New World. Aside from domestic servants, other urban slaves worked for institutions, and among these, hospitals were significant, using slaves as cleaners and launderers. Owners of slaves could either supervise their work directly or rent them out to craftsmen and tradesmen. It was common for slave women to be employed as washerwomen and garbage and refuse collectors. Slave men worked on the docks as stevedores, and as laborers in the construction industry. Slaves with greater skill worked in the craft guilds, although the more prestigious of the guilds—those of swordmakers, goldsmiths, and lapidaries—restricted slave access to the higher ranks of membership. Blacksmiths and shoemakers offered seemingly unrestricted advancement to slaves, but hosiers and pastrymakers put bounds on the rise of their slaves. Sellers of water, vegetables, and processed food were often slaves, and the authorities regulated their activities because of considerations of public health.[13]

Although the urban pursuits of the Portuguese slaves were very similar to those of other Africans in colonial Latin American cities at the same period, the situation in agriculture was very different on the two continents. There is no evidence of slave use in plantation agriculture in Portugal, and when slaves were used on the land, they seem to have been concentrated in small numbers, relatively more in the south and decreasing in concentration toward the north. The great division seems to have been the Tagus River; slave use in agriculture was more common south of the river and much less frequent north of it.[14]

As was to be the case later along the west coast of South America, slaves in

Portugal were to be found as sailors, boatsmen, and ferrymen. We previously mentioned black seamen and interpreters on the trading vessels sailing to Africa. Back in Portugal the ferries on the Douro and the Tagus were often worked by black slaves,and the authorities took various steps to ensure steady performance of the slaves' duties.[15]

The treatment afforded to black slaves in Portugal had a number of repressive aspects, but blacks received treatment that was somewhat better than that accorded Muslim slaves. Throughout the fifteenth and sixteenth centuries there were actually two slave systems in Portugal: one of the blacks and the other, longer standing, of Muslims. The latter were treated more harshly than the blacks for two significant reasons: they were considered political enemies (and, indeed, most of them were prisoners of war, victims of piracy or land raids in Morocco), and they were religiously different, separated by a barrier of hostility from Portuguese Christian society. Most blacks, by contrast, had been animists before they were enslaved, and many of them were baptized and seemed to accept Christianity with a degree of willingness. They were well regarded by the Portuguese, and many regulations, as a result, gave them a better position than the Muslims. Some blacks were quite sincere in their religious conversions and took part in religious brotherhoods and confraternities. Some blacks, too, were trained for and admitted into holy orders, but such black clerics could only exercise their offices back in their homelands. Others entered Portuguese religious orders as lay brothers.[16]

The laws reflected the Portuguese differentiation between black and Muslim slaves. The Africans were punished less harshly for infringements of the curfew or for carrying weapons. Based on Roman and canon law and local customs, the Portuguese law codes of the fifteenth century (*Ordenações Afonsinos*) and later (the *Ordenações Manuelinos* of 1514 and the *Leis Extravagantes* collected in 1569) set the norms for the regulation of the civil life of the slaves, who were regarded as legally equivalent to poor free Portuguese. In addition, slaves convicted of crimes did not always receive the full legal penalty. Masters often intervened or purchased pardons for their slaves so that their economic usefulness would not be impaired.[17]

For those who sought an avenue out of slavery, several paths lay open. Flight was generally ineffective, primarily because a slave would have to reach Africa to find a haven. One party of slaves whose members seized a ship and tried to sail to Africa misjudged their position, put in to shore near Setubal, and were captured nearby. There were extradition treaties with Castile so that escaped slaves would be returned if they crossed the borders, and Portuguese agents could enter Castile to apprehend runaways. The laws also provided rewards for informers and penalties for those who aided fugitives.[18]

Manumission, as in other societies, was a popular and secure method of attaining freedom, and in Portugal by the sixteenth century the population of freed slaves amounted to some 10 percent of the slave population. The manumission document was called the *carta de alforria*, and it usually could be given only by the master himself, either in his lifetime or by will. Manumissions were sometimes freely given, but more often certain conditions had to be fulfilled: payment or an agreement for continued service after freed status had been attained.[19]

Of the blacks who fell victim to the Portuguese slave trade, only a minority actually arrived or remained in Portugal, as we have seen. In Africa the slave trade fed either the new Portuguese plantations in São Tomé, the Cape Verdes, and Madeira, or the African demand at São Jorge da Mina. Other slaves were sold to Castilians in the Canaries or on the mainland. Of those who were taken to Portugal, significant numbers were later taken and sold elsewhere in Europe, particularly in Spain but also in Italy.

Outside Portugal, perhaps Europe's highest number of slaves in the fifteenth and sixteenth centuries were concentrated in Seville, a city with a long and important history. By the late Middle Ages, it was probably the largest city of the Iberian Peninsula. Located in the lower valley of the Guadalquivir River, it dominated a large agricultural hinterland, and it was closely linked with the sea, as oceangoing vessels of the period could sail up the river as far as the city. The maritime connection was reinforced by the presence of a large community of Genoese and other Italian merchants who engaged in commercial transactions tying Seville closely with the Mediterranean and the Atlantic. Thus it is not surprising that when the Americas were reached at the end of the fifteenth century, Seville soon was able to gain a near monopoly on trade to the New World.[20]

Slavery was nothing new in late medieval and Renaissance Seville. The city had large numbers of slaves in the Muslim period before the mid-thirteenth century (black Africans among them). After the Christian reconquest of the region, most of the slaves in Seville were Muslim prisoners of war, the products of the constant skirmishing between Christians and Muslims in the waters of the western Mediterranean or along the land frontier separating Castile from the kingdom of Granada, the last remaining Muslim stronghold in Europe. In many of the reconquered cities there were periodic revolts of Muslims, and one common consequence of the quelled revolts was the enslavement of rebels and their transportation to other Castilian cities.[21]

In the Muslim period some Africans had entered Spain, and the trickle became larger in the fourteenth century as slaves and other trade items of the trans-Saharan caravans came to be sold in Europe by Spanish and Italian merchants who purchased them in North African ports. By the mid-fifteenth century, Castilians had begun to acquire West African black slaves, brought to Europe by the Portuguese. Until 1479, when Portugal got papal confirmation of her West African monopoly, Castilians too brought slaves back legally from African voyages, and even after that they occasionally secured illicit cargoes.[22]

In Seville, black and Muslim slaves were so numerous that some "compared the city to a giant chessboard containing an equal number of white and black chessmen.''[23] The presence of slaves may have been striking, but they were hardly as numerous as free citizens. Table 8.1 shows the numbers of slaves recorded in Seville's notarial records from 1453 to 1525. These figures require careful analysis. It should be observed that the notarial records are far more complete for the period 1501–25 because that was the period in which Spanish notaries were first required to preserve their registers. The higher figures for that period also reveal the quickening of the pace of the African slave trade. The figures for the latter two periods on the table also indicate a slightly greater number of male slaves, but the records mainly furnish evidence of slave sales rather than slave imports. Other studies provide more detailed records. In the period 1484–89 household records for approximately one-half of Seville's households reveal a total of 348 slaves, with a slight predominance of female slaves—188 women and 160 men. Records of baptisms in the parish of San Ildefonso between 1492 and 1500 indicate that of a total of 323 baptisms 34 were of slaves, or just over 10 percent.[24] A census in 1565 listed 6,327 slaves in a total population of 85,538, or some 7.4 percent of the total population, a lower percentage than Lisbon. The slaves enumerated in the 1565 count were not reported according to their ethnic origin, but after the mid-sixteenth century, blacks probably outnumbered slaves from all other ethnic groups.[25]

Table 8.1. Numbers of Slaves in the Notarial Records
of Seville, 1453–1525

Slave Groups	1453–1475			1476–1500			1501–1525		
	Male	Female	Total	Male	Female	Total	Male	Female	Total
Muslims	4	9	13	61	27	88	775	640	1415
Blacks	6	11	17	127	106	233	1660	1578	3238
Mulattoes	3	1	4	19	12	31	258	237	495
Canarians	1	1	2	33	33	66	58	28	86
American Indians	—	—	—	2	—	2	21	16	37
Totals	14	22	36	242	178	420	2772	2499	5271

Source: Alfonso Franco Silva, *La esclavitud en Sevilla y su tierra a fines de la edad media* (Seville, 1979), pp. 132–46.

After their arrival in Seville by sea or overland from Portugal, most slaves were sold to private buyers. Unlike Lisbon, Seville had no recognized slave market; rather, the slave dealer would parade his wares through the streets accompanied by an auctioneer who would arrange sales on the spot. The buyers, at least in the period 1484–89, were predominately from the artisan class. The slaves' prices varied according to age, sex, and physical condition, with children bringing the lowest prices. They needed lengthy care and training (and were subject to disease and death) before they could be put to work profitably. Domestic service was the usual lot of slaves when they were sold. Most comfortable households had at least two slaves, while the wealthier ones had greater numbers, much as their contemporaries in Italy did. For the late fifteenth century, in his study of slaves in half the neighborhoods of Seville, Antonio Collantes de Terán found 166 citizens who owned one slave, 49 who owned two, 16 who owned three, 7 who owned four, and 3 who owned five or six. In addition to domestic service, slaves were also used in smaller numbers in income-producing ventures. They worked in the soap factory and the municipal granary. They were porters and longshoremen, retail sellers in the streets and plazas, assistants for shopkeepers and merchants. Slaves acted as agents for their merchant-owners; some were even sent to the Spanish settlements in the Americas to conduct business. They were excluded from membership in the crafts guilds, but guild masters could and did employ them as helpers. They worked in Seville's printing shops and soap factories, and at least two weapon makers employed black slaves.[26]

The treatment of slaves varied according to the whims of their masters. Masters had full rights over their slaves and directed their conduct. Slaves were required to attend to religious duties, and manumission came for those who rendered meritorious service or accumulated enough money to purchase freedom. The emergence of a numerous group of mulattoes testifies to a high degree of concubinage, common law unions, and even occasional mixed marriages. Most domestic slaves lived in their masters' households, but many of those who worked outside the masters' homes lived apart in Seville's poorer districts.[27]

African slaves in Seville, as in contemporary Portugal, enjoyed a considerably better reputation than Muslim or Morisco slaves, who were considered recalcitrant, hostile, and liable to run away. The higher regard for blacks was translated into generally better treatment. Religion seems to have been the operative factor. With the increasingly hostile relations between Islamic and Christian states in the Mediterranean in the fifteenth and sixteenth centuries, the Christians directed considerable mistrust toward Muslims and even toward Moriscos, who though converted to Christianity were suspected of harboring Islam in their hearts. African blacks, on the other hand, if they had not been Muslims, were considered as good converts once baptized. This facilitated their acceptance by the whites and enabled them to become acculturated more easily. Baptism was a necessity for black slaves, whose masters then became responsible for ensuring their slaves' religious participation. Masters and their white friends acted as godparents for the children of slaves, and black slaves were buried in Christian cemeteries and at times even in family vaults in the churches. Slaves, especially those in the second generation and after, were often sincerely pious and participated fully in the religious life. In the parish of San Bernardo, as early as the late fourteenth century, the church set up the Hospital of Our Lady to serve the black population, whose members founded a black brotherhood or confraternity a few years later to run the hospital. San Bernardo was one of the most visible of the parishes where blacks and mulattoes lived in Seville. By the late sixteenth century many others lived in the parish of San Ildefonso, where they also had a religious brotherhood and where a street was named the Street of Mulattoes. Blacks were never completely accepted by the white population of Seville, especially by the lower classes who competed with them for jobs, but their religious devotion and participation in the religious life and festivals increased their acceptance.[28]

The blacks in Seville by the mid-fifteenth century had one of their ranks appointed as a city official (called the *mayoral*, or steward) to settle problems involving his fellow blacks, including relations with their masters and the city courts. By 1475 the black population was large enough for Ferdinand and Isabella to make the *mayoral* a royal official. The first incumbent was Juan de Valladolid, who was commonly called "the Negro count."[29]

Seville was a boom town in the late fifteenth and sixteenth centuries. There was a rapidly growing population, together with increasing crime and the emergence of an underworld. Despite the evidence of assimilation, slaves were feared, and the possibility of a Morisco-led urban slave revolt was constantly on the minds of the municipal authorities. To lessen the threat, individual masters were allowed to discipline their own slaves. The municipality also issued laws prohibiting slaves from carrying arms and limiting their right of assembly. Regardless of the paths to assimilation and manumission available to them, some slaves in Seville sought to flee. Royal and municipal officials pursued them, and the owners of fugitives often offered rewards for their return. Once a fugitive was recaptured he or she could never thereafter be freed, and this provision must have acted as a serious deterrent.[30]

Seville, as Ruth Pike noted, in its ethnic diversity more closely resembled the cities of the New World than other European cities,[31] but other cities in southern Spain had notable black populations as well. In the Andalusian town of Palos de la Frontera, for example, nearly 20 percent of the children born between 1568 and 1579 were black.[32] Mediterranean Europe had other cities in which slavery flourished in the period, even if they were not as racially mixed as Seville.

The city of Valencia was the capital of the kingdom of the same name, that together with the kingdom of Aragon and the county of Barcelona made up the Crown of Aragon (which also included the Balearic Islands and southern Italian possessions). Valencia was an important center for slavery in the fifteenth and sixteenth centuries. Because the Valencian government regulated and taxed the slave trade, its archives house today a fund of documents that reveal the varied facets of slave life and conditions in that kingdom. Unlike Seville, which fitted the pattern of Atlantic centers, Valencia still reflected the older pattern of slavery in the medieval Mediterranean. If slaves were not as numerous in Valencia as they were in Seville, they were more varied in their ethnic origins. The bulk of the slaves there were Muslim in origin, either from Valencia itself or from

North Africa. There were also other slaves from other provenances present in Valencia, brought there via the established slave trade routes.

Muslims came to be slaves in a variety of ways. Valencia had a large Muslim population at the time of its conquest in the thirteenth century. Many of these Muslims had been slaves while Valencia was still in Muslim hands; others had been enslaved at the time of the conquest. The descendants of these Muslims often continued as slaves. Children born to slave parents became slaves in their turn. Even though the offspring of free fathers and slave mothers were free by law, in practice they were usually considered slaves, too. Valencian Muslims could also face enslavement as the result of a variety of legal penalties. Free Muslims who tried to flee to North Africa could be enslaved. Homicide, adultery, prostitution, and robbing owners of their slaves could all be punished by enslavement. Debt slavery was also a possibility, the only voluntary form of slavery in Valencia. Debtors could sell themselves or their children to satisfy the debt, usually for a temporary term after which the pawn would become free again. As one example, a Muslim enslaved his son to a Jewish creditor until the sum the Muslim owed was satisfied.[33]

Other Muslim slaves later were acquired from outside the kingdom. Perhaps the most important method of enslavement was by capture in war. The constant Castilian skirmishing along the frontiers of Granada produced captives, who were often sold in Valencia. This trade peaked with the long war of conquest, from 1480 to 1492, which ended with the Castilian victory over Granada and a consequent addition of captured slaves to the market. Captives also came from the Spanish raids on North African ports such as Oran and Tripoli. Muslims who rebelled against Christian rulers in Aragon and Castile were subject to enslavement. Piracy increased their numbers; there was constant corsair activity along both shores of the Mediterranean, conducted by both Christians and Muslims. The victims of these pirate raids were held as slaves until and unless they were ransomed. The Portuguese, too, sold Muslim captives whom they had captured in North African raids. During the late fifteenth and early sixteenth century, some 40 to 150 slaves reached Valencia in normal years, with larger numbers arriving in the aftermath of significant Christian victories. Other Muslims reached Valencia from the eastern Mediterranean.[34]

Although Muslims probably constituted the most numerous element among the slaves in Valencia, there were a variety of other groups. Among them were some Jewish slaves—mainly from North Africa—who had fallen victim to pirate raids at sea or in North Africa; no Jews of Iberian origin were among them. Canarians, whose fate as slaves we shall examine in detail later, reached Valencia from Castilian sources. African blacks came from the Muslim slave trade or from the Portuguese African slave trade. As many as 500 or 600 black slaves reached Valencia in certain years, and Vicenta Cortés Alonso has found records of over 5,000 blacks who reached Valencia between 1482 and 1516. In addition, there were a few native Americans brought back from Spanish or Portuguese possessions in the New World, and, from 1512, a trickle of Asians, mainly Indians from the subcontinent, whom the Portuguese imported to Europe. All this means that slavery in Valencia, as in Seville, resembled a great ethnic mosaic, and in the course of time a significant racial mixture ensued.[35]

Owing to the fifteenth-century decline of Barcelona, Valencia was the most active commercial center in the peninsular Crown of Aragon. Merchants with slaves to sell used Valencia as their favored market. About one-third of the dealers listed in contemporary documents were from Valencia, whereas the rest included Castilians, Portuguese, Genoese, Florentines, Venetians, and other Italian merchants. When dealers introduced slaves into Valencia, they first rested them and then displayed them in a public place where potential buyers (including commission agents, *corredores*) could view them. Before they could be sold, the governmental formalities took place. Because the crown levied a tax of 20 percent on the sale of slaves, it designated a royal official, the *bayle general*, to collect the levies, and this official quickly acquired great competence over the lives of the slaves. Before slaves could be sold, they had to be registered with the *bayle*, and in the years of great influxes of slaves, the *bayle's* agents visited towns of the kingdom to determine if the slaveholders had registered their slaves and paid the requisite tax on them. Each slave entering the kingdom had to be brought before the *bayle* and his agents before he or she could be sold. In the presence of another crown official, the *alcaldí del rey*, the *bayle* (or his designee) questioned the slave, through translators if they were needed and available, to determine the slave's origin and the circumstances of his or her enslavement. The sellers had to swear that their slaves had been acquired as a result of good or just war.[36]

Slaves on occasion took advantage of the interview to claim that they were really freed and that their sale should not be permitted. The *bayle* took the slave's testimony and, after seeking confirmation from other witnesses, decided the slave's fate. Several examples will illustrate the procedures involved. In 1512 a Muslim merchant from Oran was on the verge of being sold when he testified in response to the inquiry of the *bayle* that he was free and had come to Valencia to serve a royal official. Officers and sailors of the ship that had brought him to Valencia testified in support of the Muslim's contention, and the *bayle* turned him over to the custody of a Valencian citizen until his story could be verified. In another case, a black woman claimed to have been freed by the will of her first master, but his heirs had sold her outside the kingdom in Málaga. After residing there a while she was sent back to Valencia, where four years later she was up for sale again. The *bayle* charged a local pharmacist to hold her until more evidence could be collected. In 1516 a man named Simón, twenty years old and branded, claimed to be free, but testimony held him to be a slave, and he was sold.[37]

Once the legal requirements were fulfilled, the *bayle* assessed a value for each slave. White slaves were considered the most valuable, and women more valuable than men. Canarian slaves were cheaper, while black slaves were the cheapest of all, because they were assumed to need more training. Blacks who had passed some time previously in a Muslim or Christian kingdom were more highly regarded because they were assumed to be more fully acculturated, and they commanded higher prices than the new arrivals. In general, younger slaves were cheaper than adults. Higher prices were assessed for those who were judged to possess desirable qualities: beauty, intelligence, or skills. When the price was set and the royal duties were paid by the slave's owner, the *bayle* issued a receipt noting the slave's name, condition, and place of capture. If the slave were to be exported from the kingdom, the receipt also listed the price, the name of the master, and where the slave was to be sold.[38]

After the pricing and the governmental formalities were completed, the dealers regained custody of their slaves. This was not the last interest the *bayle general* and his staff would have in them, though. He was also responsible for the pursuit and apprehension of fugitive slaves and for the sale of slaves that came to be owned by the crown. These were generally transgressors such as vagabonds, unlicensed beggars, and convicted adulterers, whose crimes were punished by enslavement, and recaptured runaway slaves.[39]

The buyers of slaves represented many of the classes in Valencian society: nobles, clergy, merchants, manufacturers, members of the learned professions, soldiers and military officers, and crown servants. Most slaves worked as domestic servants; others worked in all sectors of the economy. They were prohibited from being sailors or galley oarsmen, because of the suspicion that they might use their relative freedom to flee. Those owned by merchants, however, did have a wide freedom of movement as they worked as agents of their masters. Muslim slaves were especially valued because they could use their knowledge of Arabic to conduct trade with other Muslims.[40]

Masters exercised all the traditional rights over their slaves, who were considered to be totally dependent on them. Masters had the right to the produce of their slaves' labor, whether the slaves worked directly for the master or outside the home for other people. For injuries to the slave, the master was indemnified, and he had to pay for injuries his slave caused. Considered to have no independent legal rights, slaves could not be witnesses in court; they could not testify against their masters; and they could not initiate legal action on their own. In the fifteenth century a group of masters organized an insurance pact to protect themselves against the possible consequences of any crimes their slaves committed.[41]

Masters could dispose of their slaves as they wished: by sale, by testament, and by gift, as in 1491, when King Ferdinand gave his aunt three slaves taken from a Muslim ship. The special conditions of slavery in Valencia meant that the opportunities for a slave to attain freedom were relatively open. Many of the Muslim captives taken at sea and in land raids were held for ransom rather than as personal slaves. Once captured, the slaves had several possibilities for being ransomed. They were sold in the market like other slaves, but they would go free as soon as the sum set for their ransom was paid. Unfortunately, the money was not always immediately forthcoming. Relatives could bring money from North Africa, if they could obtain the required travel passes, or relatives could exchange themselves for the captives. If the captives could not have the money sent, they could become licensed beggars. Muslims on the other side of the Mediterranean conducted the same sort of business and captured Christians for ransom. Public and private exchanges periodically took place, and peace treaties between Christian and Muslim states often contained clauses calling for mutual repatriation of prisoners. Juan Batlle, a native of the kingdom of Valencia, had a brother held captive in North Africa. In 1491 he bought a Muslim slave from a Christian merchant and arranged with the merchant to take the slave to North Africa, find the brother, and exchange the slave for him. In 1494 Francisca Bos sent a Muslim slave to Oran in a German vessel, the slave to be exchanged for her husband who was being held there.[42]

For Muslims, flight was also a possibility. They could hope to reach the coast and, with luck, contact a Muslim ship. For blacks and other slaves from distant regions the possibility of flight was severely limited. In 1463 a crown agent in Barcelona ordered Guillem de Barberà, who held the castle of Sant Martí Sarroca, to return a black slave, twenty-five years old, who had fled his owner in Barcelona, the armorer Guillem Sobrer, and ended up in Barberà's castle. His status there was unclear, but he was described as "in the power of" Barberà, so he may not have attained even a temporary freedom.[43] For the blacks, there was little or no possibility of ransoming and hardly any way of getting back to their homeland if they were freed.

In setting the conditions of slavery in the newly conquered kingdom of Valencia in the thirteenth century, King James II had authorized slaves to be freed if they paid their masters their purchase price, but things did not always follow that easily. A common pattern was for owners to free slaves in their wills, either providing for their immediate manumission or for a future term of service to the owner's heirs. They had no control beyond the grave, though, and heirs were known on occasion to neglect to carry out the provisions of the will. Non-Christian slaves of Christian masters could be freed on the basis of baptism only if the master agreed. For Muslim slaves of Jewish masters, the crown became involved if the slave were baptized. Royal officials permitted the newly baptized Moor to work for a Christian until he could pay his ransom. If he could not do so within two months, the *bayle* canceled the debt and arranged to have the convert work for the king until he had repaid his ransom.[44] All this stemmed from the high degree of religious diversity in Valencia, because of the uneasy coexistence there of Christians, Jews, and Muslims, and the official favor for Christianity.

Black slavery continued in Valencia throughout our period, and in the sixteenth and seventeenth centuries blacks constituted about one-half of the total slave population. No large slave gangs were used, and slaves were usually assigned to domestic service or artisan work, with some masters even renting their slaves to others for determined periods.[45] Black freedmen were also present in Valencia from the fifteenth century onward. One group of them received a license in 1472 to establish a religious brotherhood, called the *cofradía* of Nuestra Señora de Gracia (Our Lady of Grace), one of whose functions was to dispense charity to the poor and sick. The members possessed a chapter house where they held their meetings, and they made an annual pilgrimage to the nearby monastery of St. Augustine.[46]

One aspect of slavery in Europe had a relatively short existence from the fourteenth to the sixteenth century: the phenomenon of Guanche slavery. The Guanches were the natives of the Canary Islands (though the term *Guanches* is at times applied only to natives of the island of Tenerife). When individual European captains with authorization from the Spanish crown undertook the conquest of the Canaries in various phases from the fourteenth to the early sixteenth century, they found the islands inhabited by natives akin to the Berbers of northwest Africa. Mainly subsisting from herding, only on the island of Grand Canary had they developed an agricultural economy. Politically they divided themselves into smaller or larger bands, and the Castilian absorption proceeded by securing treaties with some of the bands and conquering others. Only natives of the conquered bands could be enslaved legally, but the agents of the crown had to maintain constant vigilance to ensure that the conquerors did not violate the rules and enslave members of the treaty bands.[47]

The Castilians in time remade the Canaries along European lines, with cities, farms, and sugar plantations, but in the initial phases of the conquest of the individual islands the conquerors resorted to enslaving natives. They needed quick profits to pay for their expeditions, mainly financed on credit, and the sale of slaves was a quick way to make the profits necessary to repay the loans. Many enslaved Guanches were taken back to the peninsula and sold there; others remained in the islands and found themselves put to work by the Europeans. The conditions they lived under resembled, not surprisingly, those of the slaves in late medieval Spain.[48]

In obtaining slaves among the Guanches, the conquerors and colonists found a loophole that permitted them to enslave members of some treaty bands. If members of those groups rebelled or refused to carry out the terms of their treaties, they could be enslaved as "captives of second war" (*de segunda guerra*). For such captives, there were potential remedies for their condition. The most important was manumission. The process of manumission was similar to that practiced in Mediterranean Europe throughout the late Middle Ages, the most crucial component being the inclination of the master. Many documents state pious reasons for an owner's granting a slave's freedom, but in almost every case strings were attached: monetary payments, the promise of future payments, or future service (often a year's labor service). In 1528, Pedro de Vergara freed two Guanche slaves, Pedro and Juan de Abona, because they had become Christians and because each had paid him sixty Castilian *doblas*, a perfect example of the contemporary mixture of religious and economic motivations.[49]

Slaves generally were required to pay their masters for their manumission. Each slave controlled a *peculium*, a legal legacy from Roman times, but often he or she could not use this money to buy his freedom because de jure it belonged to the master. The most popular and effective method of obtaining freedom was for relatives or other members of the slave's band to offer financial aid. Free Guanches constantly aided their enslaved compatriots to obtain freedom, and numerous Guanche wills mentioned allotments for the redemption of other Guanches. These sums were left to executors charged with purchasing and freeing the designee. Money or goods could not be left directly to the slave, because any property he or she owned became part of the *peculium* and thus fell under the master's control. The executor could purchase the slave directly, or he could arrange an exchange for the slave in question, usually by purchasing a black slave and giving him to the master. Thus manumission usually was beyond the grasp of an individual slave, who needed the assistance of a third party. This also was more easily arranged for slaves who remained in the islands, because those who were sold in European markets were much more difficult for their relatives to trace.[50]

Because of the relatively small Guanche population, the fact that many bands were exempt (at least theoretically) from being enslaved, and the frequency of manumission, the natives of the Canaries did not make a substantial or a long-lasting addition to the international slave trade. They did not even fill the labor needs of the Canaries, and other sources of labor were necessary before the islands could be developed fully. So the Canaries witnessed the influx of other laborers, including a number of free Castilian workers. More substantial settlers often brought their own slaves with them. Berbers and black slaves were obtained from Castilian raids and trade along the West African coast, or were brought to the Canaries by Portuguese dealers. In the course of time, slaves came to be born in the islands. For a short period after the first Spanish contact with the Americas, Amerindians were sold in the Canaries. Their numbers were always few, and the trade soon stopped when the Spanish crown outlawed the slave trade in native Americans. In the early years of the sixteenth century, then, the Guanche slave trade to Europe ceased, as the Guanches increasingly assimilated European culture and intermarried with the colonists.[51]

In sum, the Atlantic slave trade to Europe never reached great numbers, and slaves specifically imported into Europe were increasingly little more than luxuries. They were helpful, perhaps, for artisans and small merchants and shopkeepers; more frequently they were domestics, and at times concubines. As a result, black slaves were rarities outside a few Spanish and Portuguese cities. We should mention, parenthetically to be sure, that several other varieties of slavery were present in Europe at this period. In Russia, the early modern period saw a great resurgence of slavery and patterns of peasant dependency. Western European states about this time instituted penal slavery in several varieties for people convicted of certain crimes. The condemned ended up as galley slaves, as forced miners, or as forced labor on public works. In addition, there was the continuing pattern of captivity and enslavement for ransom practiced by both Muslims and Christians in the Mediterranean, which we have mentioned in previous chapters.[52] We will not discuss these other varieties of slavery here because they do not relate to the main aim of this book, that of tracing the roots of New World slavery. It is likely that the slave trade from Africa to Europe would have dwindled and eventually died out, but in the sixteenth century the Atlantic slave trade developed a second route, this one to the Americas, that quickly came to eclipse the older route to Europe.

9

THE EARLY TRANSATLANTIC
SLAVE TRADE

The discovery of America and the subsequent European expansion into it inaugurated a new stage in the history of slavery. The vast numbers of slaves shipped across the Atlantic from Africa to the Americas transformed the social and physical complexion of the New World and in many American countries created problems of assimilation that have yet to be resolved. For the period before 1650 we have three major topics remaining in the book, and the next two chapters will cover them: first, the problem of labor supply for the new colonies and the different sources of labor the colonists experimented with before choosing black slaves; second, the Atlantic slave trade and its numbers; and, third (addressed in chapter 10), black slavery in the Latin American colonies.

We first must consider the alternatives to the use of black African slaves that were available to the various European colonists during this period. To do so we will discuss the separate cases of the Spaniards and the Portuguese, and mention the slightly later English development, omitting the Dutch and the French, whose stories come later. Basically, the story in each case is one of failure to fill labor requirements by using sources other than black slaves. Free white labor was out of the question. Settlers were in short supply in the first centuries after the discovery of America; and free Europeans, whether Portuguese, Spanish, or English, were not accustomed to doing gang labor in the Old World and would not willingly cross the Atlantic to do something they would refuse to do at home. The Spaniards and the Portuguese attempted at first to use Amerindians, and the English, who occasionally enslaved Amerindians, initially made use of indentured servants from the British Isles. By 1650, however, at least in the Iberian colonies, only blacks could be legally slaves, although they were not the only victims of coerced labor, and about that time the English colonists in North America and the Caribbean were beginning to develop black slavery in their colonies.

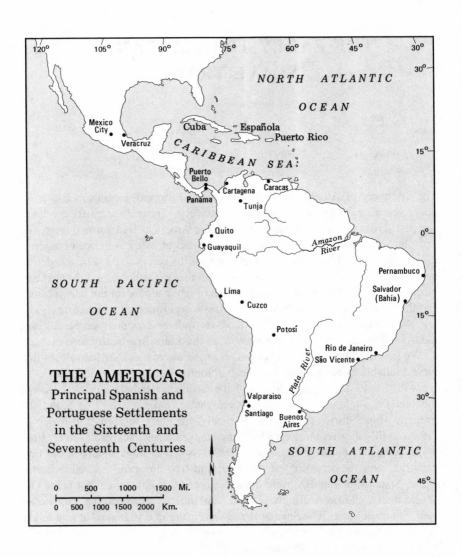

120°   105°   90°   75°   60°   45°   30°

30°

NORTH   ATLANTIC

OCEAN

Mexico
City
Veracruz

Cuba   Española
              Puerto Rico

15°

CARIBBEAN   SEA

Puerto
Bello
Panama   Cartagena   Caracas
              Tunja

Quito
Guayaquil

Amazon
River

0°

SOUTH   PACIFIC

OCEAN

Lima
Cuzco

Pernambuco

Salvador
(Bahia)

15°

Potosí

Rio de Janeiro
São Vicente

Plata River

THE AMERICAS
Principal Spanish and
Portuguese Settlements
in the Sixteenth and
Seventeenth Centuries

Valparaiso
Santiago
Buenos
Aires

30°

SOUTH   ATLANTIC

OCEAN

45°

| 0 | 500 | 1000 | 1500 | Mi. |

| 0 | 500 | 1000 | 1500 | 2000 | Km. |

N

So far in this book we have examined the history of slavery as it was practiced in the societies of the Old World. Philip D. Curtin, one of the deans of the new school of slavery studies, has written of the sea change that slavery as an institution underwent as it developed on the American side of the Atlantic.

[C]ontinuity with Mediterranean slavery was only part of the story. The institution of slavery that continued in the New World became far different from slavery as it was practiced in Europe, the Muslim world, or in sub-Saharan Africa. . . . While it may have begun as a means of labor recruitment, it changed and became a new kind of institution, where the bundle of property rights in the masters' hands was far more elaborate, all inclusive, and permanent than its model in Europe. The old European slavery, in short, had suffered a sea change. Whatever its precedents in the Old World, the reality by the beginning of the eighteenth century was actually another kind of institution, not borrowed from the European past, nor yet an institution found in some overseas society and adopted to European use. It had roots in Europe, but was nevertheless so profoundly modified through time that it became a new invention, devised for a new situation—the highly specialized plantation society.[1]

In the remaining two chapters we will trace the ebb and flow of the tides that brought about this sea change. The continuities and changes that can be observed in European colonial society in the Americas from 1492 to around 1650 set the foundations for the plantation societies of the New World, with their heavy or exclusive reliance on slave labor and with substantial modifications in the practice of slavery.

LABOR SUPPLY—
ALTERNATIVES TO BLACK SLAVES

When Christopher Columbus made the first successful Atlantic crossing and return since the Vikings, he was not looking for a New World, despite a commonly held impression. His Spanish sponsors were seeking a new route to the spice markets of Asia, and if Columbus in the process found territories that could be claimed for the crown of Castile, that was all to the good. The first voyage of Columbus was not something new and totally unprecedented; rather, his action was the logical culmination of over a century of Iberian ventures into previous unknown parts of the Atlantic. By 1492 the Portuguese and the Spaniards had a firm knowledge of the West African coast and of the principal islands of the eastern Atlantic, and rumors already circulated of additional islands to the west of the Canaries and the Azores. After leaving the Andalusian coast, Columbus followed prevailing winds to the Canaries, where the expedition put in and refitted. Then they began the epochal voyage that was to change world history, and after some thirty-three days at sea they reached land in the Bahamas.[2]

The first contact with the New World has taken on mythic importance in popular history,[3] but the discoverers themselves took it rather matter-of-factly. Columbus constantly focused his attention on profit-making ventures, and, because of the experience he had gained living among the Portuguese, slavery was one of the first things he considered. Soon after he landed, he composed a letter to Ferdinand and Isabella that specifically addressed the possibility of enslaving the islanders. He captured seven natives to take back with him.

> these people are very simple as regards the use of arms, as your High-
> nesses will see from the seven I have caused to be taken, to bring home
> and learn our language and return; unless your Highnesses should order
> them all to be brought to Castille, or to be kept as captives on the same
> island; for with fifty men they all can be subjugated and made to do what
> is required of them.[4]

Columbus's first expedition encountered Arawaks, one of the two major groups inhabiting the Caribbean islands. They were less hostile and warlike than the cannibalistic Caribs, and by the end of his first voyage Columbus had transferred his slaving intentions to the Caribs, whom he had not yet personally encountered but about whom the stories were sufficiently derogatory to make him believe they could be legally enslaved.[5]

During Columbus's second voyage to the Caribbean, the policy of enslave-ment he had mentioned during his first voyage grew in significance. Toward the end of 1494 the first native uprising against the Europeans took place. After the Spaniards had quelled it, they collected some sixteen hundred captives. The majority were divided among the Spaniards on the island, and about five hun-dred were sent back to Spain in the four ships of Antonio de Torres in early 1495. Columbus explained to the royal couple that

> there are now sent with these ships some of the cannibals, men and women
> and boys and girls. These Their Highnesses can order to be placed in
> charge of persons so that they may be able better to learn the language,
> employing them in forms of service, and ordering that gradually greater
> care be given to them than other slaves. . . . [To] take some of the men
> and women and send them home to Castile would not be anything but well,
> for they may some day be led to abandon that inhuman custom which they
> have of eating men, and there in Castile, learning the language, they will
> more readily receive baptism and secure the welfare of their souls.[6]

Michele Cuneo, who returned to Spain on the same ships, related that some two hundred captives died on the voyage and that their bodies were dumped over-board. Cuneo believed that the cold weather encountered when they approached Europe caused the deaths. Disease is a more likely explanation, as we will see later. Cuneo went on to say: "We landed all the [remaining] slaves at Cádiz, half of them sick. They are not people suited to hard work, they suffer from the cold, and they do not have a long life."[7]

Although Columbus never abandoned his firm belief that he had reached Asia, he soon came to realize that the lands he found did not fit the traditional descriptions of that continent. Nonetheless, he was keen to make the new Spanish possessions profitable, hence his efforts to establish a slave trade, to extract gold, and to encourage European agricultural ventures. The slave trade in Caribbean and mainland natives was not to last long, and gold extraction in the islands was to prove not much more profitable. European agriculture was another proposition, even though it too failed to prosper immediately and experienced a number of false starts. The first commercially important European crop to be introduced in the new lands was sugar cane, which Columbus brought on his second voyage, along with other European plants including wheat, barley, and grapevines. The initial plantings were not a success. Sugar cane failed at first, because the first planters tried to grow it in small plots, and, in the absence of refineries, they could process it only into molasses, not granular sugar. The labor of natives proved ineffective, and Spaniards abandoned the fields and farms to rush to the gold fields on Española when they were discovered.[8]

In the decades following Columbus's first contact with the New World, Spanish policy underwent fundamental shifts as further lands were explored and conquered. By the 1540s Spaniards had expanded their control over the Caribbean islands, conquered the Aztecs of Mexico and the Incas of Peru, and established strongholds in Central America and the northeastern portion of South America. They quickly abandoned the idea that they could establish a commercial network of factories as the Portuguese had in West Africa and Asia. Such a trading system was not suitable for the different conditions of the New World, a fact the Portuguese readily appreciated; their Brazilian colony followed a pattern similar to that of the Spanish-American colonies, rather than their own African and Asian factory system. In the New World there were no preexisting trading centers with goods that could be exchanged for European items for later sale in European markets. Successful and profitable development required strenuous efforts to subdue the natives, to mine the mineral wealth of the North and South American continents, and to begin the production of commercial crops that could be sold in Europe. The model the Spaniards used was based in part on the experience of their own reconquest of the Muslim lands in southern Spain, during which they had distributed the newly acquired lands among the leaders of the conquering armies, and in part on their exploitation of the Canary Islands, where they had subdued the natives and used the new lands for plantation agriculture. They followed, then, their own recent colonial history as a guide in their actions in the Americas.

One of the first profit-making ventures was the production of sugar cane, a crop that offered numerous advantages. The soil and climate of many regions of the American possessions were well suited to sugar growing. Moreover, Spaniards and Portuguese had experience with sugar growing in the Atlantic islands and at home, and they were in the forefront of refining technology. Labor was the only questionable factor in the equation. The production of refined sugar, from planting to shipping the finished product, was arduous, as we know from previous chapters. Rapidly it became apparent that there were steep barriers to the employment of native labor on a large scale. The most important factor was their sharp demographic decline, a consequence of excessive mortality in the face of disease, war, and the social disruption that accompanied the conquest. At the same time, the Spanish rulers considered the natives as their subjects, with certain safeguards placed on them and prohibitions established regarding the manner in which they could be exploited. Two major obstacles therefore faced the Spanish colonists in their attempts to use native labor: depopulation and royal regulation. We will examine both in their turn.

The older histories gave stirring accounts of the Spanish conquests in the New World, and, to account for the rapid success of the conquistadores, their authors trotted out such explanations as the assumed natural superiority of the white races (although this was tempered in the works of William H. Prescott and others by Protestant antipathy for Catholicism), technological advantage (iron, steel, and gunpowder versus stone weapons), and horses (which frightened the natives and gave the Europeans mobility and striking power). A more recent, ecological explanation stresses the differences that time and isolation had wrought in the Western Hemisphere. Because of their isolation from the rest of the world, the Americas were free of numbers of diseases that were endemic elsewhere. These probably included influenza, smallpox, measles, malaria, plague, and perhaps even the common cold.[9] Scholars reconstructing the disease history of early colonial Latin America are unable to determine precisely what diseases were causing the problems. Diagnosis of disease was not well developed in the sixteenth century, and the records commonly lump diseases in such a way as to make it almost impossible to assign a specific cause. What is clear, however, is that the suffering was great among the Amerindians and that smallpox was the chief villain.

When a previously unknown disease enters an unexposed population, it is particularly virulent at the outset and affects the population in a harsh and devastating manner. Smallpox, for example, was a common disease of childhood in fifteenth-century Europe, Asia, and parts of Africa. Children exposed to it suffered and were scarred by it, but they typically recovered and thereby acquired immunity to subsequent attacks. Those individuals who were particularly susceptible to the disease died from it before they produced children of their own. When smallpox entered the New World, it encountered a population that had never been exposed and that had built up no natural immunities, either on the individual or societal level. Thus it affected them in a particularly brutal fashion, as people of all ages fell sick at the same time, not just children, as in

Europe. During the course of the disease, there often were not enough well people to care for the stricken. Furthermore, the victims typically do not become delirious and unconscious of their fate but remain fully aware of the horrible course of the affliction. Because it was unfamiliar, no one knew what to do to ease the pain and suffering. Perhaps as important was the psychological devastation accompanying the disease. People throughout history have been able to deal with known evils and gradually to develop defensive mechanisms to soften the mental suffering. In the Americas, the advent of virulent smallpox and other new diseases was too rapid for the afflicted to accommodate themselves mentally to what must have seemed inexplicable torments. For the Amerindian population there is evidence that despair exacerbated the physical suffering of disease and added to the mortality. As if this were not enough, the diseases struck in a many-pronged attack, and those who escaped one disease were liable to fall to another.[10]

In addition to facing the simultaneous impact of multiple diseases, previously unexposed people of childbearing years succumbed along with children and the elderly. Because many adults died, the demographic losses that mortality caused during the acute phases of the epidemics could not be made up by an increased birthrate once the crises had passed. Beyond this, in the case of the native American population, the new political and economic structure that the Spaniards imposed meant that many people were uprooted from their long-established patterns of social organization and were put to work in mines and in unfamiliar agricultural activities. That reorganization disrupted the fundamental bases of the indigenous society, and the insecurity that afflicted the uprooted weakened their ability to withstand disease. As a consequence, it is not surprising that disastrous demographic losses ensued.[11]

What may be surprising is the scale of those losses. The history of population is difficult to study, especially for the Americas, where no demographic records were kept and where the European conquerers only began to keep systematic records quite some time after the conquest and then only for the areas under their control. Modern estimates of the demographic decline vary widely.[12] The pre-conquest population has been placed anywhere from 13.3 million to 90–112 million; by 1650, according to the same estimates, it stood somewhere between 4.5 and 10 million. To date, precision has not been attained with regard to these estimates, and it probably never will be, but there are two generalizations that can be accepted with assurance: one, there was a serious decline in population, and two, the demographic history of certain regions is far better known than others. The best studied regions are the Caribbean, the central valley of Mexico, and Peru. The island of Española, the principal scene of early European activity in the Caribbean, may have had the most dramatic decline: by 1570 only a few hundred natives remained, out of a population that had numbered anywhere from one hundred thousand to several million before 1492. Mexico has been intensively studied by Woodrow W. Borah and Sherburne F. Cook, together with other members of the so-called Berkeley school of demographic historians associated with them. For central Mexico their figures show the following estimated decline.[13]

1519	25.3 million
1523	16.8 million
1548	6.3 million
1568	2.6 million
1580	1.9 million
1595	1.3 million
1605	1.0 million

Noble David Cook, in his demographic study of colonial Peru, found a similar but less dramatic decline and offered the following estimates.[14]

1520	3,300,574
1530	2,738,673
1540	2,188,626
1550	1,801,425
1560	1,513,396
1570	1,290,680
1580	1,106,662
1590	968,197
1600	851,994
1610	754,024
1620	671,505
1630	601,645

However much the details may vary, as scholars make new discoveries and offer new interpretations, it is clear that everywhere in the New World the indigenous population declined severely in the aftermath of European expansion.

The Spaniards had not caused those losses deliberately. There is no episode in Spanish (or Portuguese) colonial history equivalent to the proposal of the British commander Sir Jeffrey Amherst to send blankets formerly used by smallpox victims to the Amerindians involved in Pontiac's rebellion of 1763.[15] The worst that can be said of the Iberians is that they inadvertently introduced the diseases and made their impact greater by disrupting the New World societies. As Eric Wolf commented:

Pleaders of special causes ascribed the decimation of the Indian population to Spanish cruelty, but the Spaniards were neither more nor less cruel than other conquerors, past or present. . . . The chief factor in this disaster appears to have been not conscious maltreatment of the Indian but the introduction of new diseases to which the Indians were not immune.[16]

The Spaniards did not want to kill off the native population—just the opposite, in fact—they wanted to put them to work. In their attempt to do so, they encountered difficulties that convinced them that native labor was not well suited for the most lucrative ventures they proposed for the New World. One of the greatest difficulties, from the colonists' viewpoint, was that the Spanish imperial government took measures intended to protect the Amerindians from exploitation. These measures were never totally effective, but they reflected the humanitarian impulses of the home government and hindered the colonists who tried to extract the maximum labor possible from the Amerindians.

In the early years of colonization, a thriving slave trade in native Americans developed throughout the Caribbean and the adjacent mainland. In fact, the original plans for Cortés's expedition to Mexico, as conceived by the governor of Cuba who authorized it, was to seek gold and slaves, not conquest or settlement. The first Spanish policy established by Queen Isabella claimed the native population as vassals subject to the crown of Castile, and who therefore could not be enslaved. By 1495, however, those natives captured in "just war" could be enslaved, and Spaniards were allowed to purchase captives held as slaves by other native groups. The Laws of Burgos in the early sixteenth century, although they proposed fair treatment for the Amerindians, followed Aristotelian doctrine in declaring them to be natural slaves. In Charles V's reign, several laws limited the ability of the colonists to enslave natives or practice other forms of forced labor. Nonetheless, laws prohibiting indigenous slavery—and laws generally—were difficult to enforce in the New World, and colonists were able to evade them on various pretexts.[17]

The attempts to use Amerindians as slaves were not especially effective, particularly because of the demographic losses. The *encomienda* system was a second effort, initially developed to provide for the Christianization of the natives, that allowed the colonists to marshal labor. Under *encomienda*, a number of native families were "commended" to a colonist (the *encomendero*), who undertook their assimilation to the new colonial system by grouping them in a central village and providing for their religious education. In return for this, the *encomendero* was entitled to the use of their labor. Problems soon arose, as *encomenderos* mistreated the people entrusted to them and began to treat their *encomiendas* as if they were landed estates. In addition, declining populations reduced the value of the original grants in many cases. The crown and its officials back in Spain, made aware of the abuses by a long series of complaints by Spaniards on the spot, began to curtail the settlers' authority over the indigenous population. First, native slavery was declared illegal in 1542, and in 1550 the system of *encomienda* labor was abolished. Passage of these laws did not end the previous practices overnight, but at midcentury a new system for providing native labor came to be used. This was *repartimiento*, a system under which Spaniards who could demonstrate a need for labor would be provided with Amerindian workers on a rotational basis from nearby communities; in Peru the *mita* system served the same function. The Spaniards were expected to provide decent working conditions for the *repartimiento* laborers and to pay them a determined wage; but, again, practice diverged from legal doctrine, and because of abuses the crown ended the *repartimiento* system except for mine labor.[18]

Given the rapidly declining native population and the equally rapidly expanding need for labor in the colonies, Spaniards in the Indies very quickly began to report the high death rate the natives were suffering and to question the excessive reliance upon native labor, even before it was known that the crown would restrict the exploitation of native laborers. Bartolomé de las Casas was one of the most eloquent spokesmen for the plight of the Amerindians, and in 1516 he suggested that white and black slaves be imported as laborers to relieve the burdens shouldered by the natives. Las Casas's suggestion that slaves replace Amerindians in colonial fields, mines, and workshops gave the weight of his prestige to the beginnings of the organized slave trade, and his reputation, quite properly, has suffered for it. Although later in his life he repented of his earlier views and recognized that the arguments he put forth for the improved treatment of the indigenous people could apply equally to the blacks, he never published his revised views. They appeared only in posthumous editions of his writings. The intellectual and ecclesiastical attacks on the exploitation of the native laborers were strengthened by the insistence of the Spanish colonists that Amerindians were unsuited for intensive labor and that blacks, who in their view had a much higher capacity for work, should replace them. A constant stream of letters from the Indies reached Spain bearing the message that one black could do the work of four to eight Amerindians.[19]

The Portuguese in Brazil faced similar problems of labor supply. Although Brazil had been discovered in 1500, for some thirty years no serious attempt was made to settle it. Attention could not easily be spared from Portugal's lucrative African and Asian ventures, and Brazil did not offer immediate advantages. There were no dense populations and well-organized societies in Brazil similar to the Aztecs or Incas. Until the late seventeenth century, there was no lure of Brazilian gold. During those thirty years, Portuguese ships called at points along the coast where they bartered trade goods—chiefly iron weapons—with the coastal peoples for brazilwood, which yielded dyes of various red hues. The Portuguese faced competition, however, from French captains who began to take their ships to the same coast and challenge the Portuguese, in addition to allying themselves with some of the native groups.[20]

In 1534 King John III directed Portuguese efforts to colonize Brazil, because if he had not, French or other foreign interlopers might have established permanent settlements and challenged Portugal's claims. He divided the coast into a series of twelve captaincies (*capitanias*), each under the control of a Portuguese donatary (*donatário*), who usually was a member of the lower nobility. The captaincies varied in size from thirty to one hundred leagues along the coast, stretching without well-defined limits into the interior. In this early period only a few of the captaincies thrived, especially Pernambuco in the northeast, and São Vicente in the south.[21] In 1549 the king sent Brazil's first governor-general to the new captaincy of Bahia, which was under direct crown supervision. By 1565, the French, who had established themselves at Rio de Janeiro, were expelled, bringing all Brazil under exclusive Portuguese control.[22]

Portuguese settlers—both from the home country and from the Azores and Madeira—crossed the Atlantic in the early colonial period to establish themselves in Brazil, enough of them to begin to transform the landscape, but not in sufficient numbers to provide the labor needed. At first they continued the process of barter with the local groups to gain food and labor. However, as sugar planting and other agricultural ventures grew, the settlers found that they needed more and more labor. Many of the native Brazilians were hunters and gatherers and were not accustomed to agricultural labor. Others, such as the Tupinambá, did practice manioc agriculture, but it was exclusively a female occupation; Tupinambá men were not accustomed to continual agricultural labor. Few of the local people, agriculturists or hunters and gatherers, were inclined to submit to organized and difficult labor for long periods under the barter system. Because that system could no longer supply the Portuguese with the labor they needed, they began to resort to several methods of coercion to obtain local labor. One was to directly exploit the natives as chattel slaves. Intertribal warfare was common among the indigenous Brazilians, and the Portuguese found they could purchase or "ransom" prisoners. They also raided villages directly for slaves. The Jesuits tried a second method, that of collecting people into protected villages (aldeias) and attempting to turn them into peasants on the European model. Finally, efforts were made to force the natives into becoming wage laborers. The Amerindians resisted, at times successfully, all such efforts, and in time the twin impediments to large-scale slavery—royal restrictions and demographic decline due to disease, barriers the Spaniards also faced—began to impel the Brazilian settlers to reduce their reliance on native workers and to seek new sources of labor.[23]

The crown in Lisbon consistently issued rules and regulations designed to protect Brazil's native population. The earliest surviving rule is that of 1511, issued to a ship trading for brazilwood, which enjoined the crew, under the threat of stiff punishment, not to harm the people they encountered. In 1548, at the time of the first appointment of a governor-general in Brazil, the crown issued a *regimento* (regulation) specifying fair treatment for the Amerindians. King Sebastian III provided the first rules specifically dealing with native slavery in 1570. Natives were not to be enslaved, unless they had been taken captive in a "just war," which could only be declared by the king or by the governor. There were loopholes; those who warred against Portuguese settlers or who were cannibals could be enslaved. King Philip I (Philip II of Spain, who had gained the Portuguese throne in 1580) declared that just wars could only be sanctioned by the king.[24]

Philip II of Portugal (Philip III of Spain) in 1605 strengthened the prohibition on enslaving Amerindians, and in 1609 he enacted even more far-reaching legislation. All Amerindians in Brazil, whether Christian or pagan, were declared to be free. Because their work was to be secured voluntarily and paid for, forced labor was abolished. Jesuits were given charge over them, and any Portuguese attempting to enslave them was to be punished. This legislation brought forth strong opposition among the colonists in Brazil, and two years later the king backed down. He gave the governor, if he were faced with armed native resistance, the ability to call a council meeting to decide whether an armed response would be just, and, before any war could be conducted, prior permission had to be obtained from Lisbon. In emergencies war could be waged without royal approval, but the prisoners taken could not be sold until the royal permission was obtained. The law also allowed Portuguese settlers to go into the native areas to "rescue" those captured and condemned to death: they could temporarily enslave those they rescued, usually for a term of ten years.[25] The settlers found ways to evade the new limitations on enslaving natives. Even the Jesuits had to allow the Portuguese to use the labor of protected Amerindians at times.[26]

As we have seen, the Portuguese were, through most of the sixteenth century, virtual monopolists on the Atlantic shores of Africa, and it is not surprising that Portuguese settlers in Brazil were attracted to the needs that could be served by importing African blacks. This was especially the case in the Brazilian regions of Bahia and Pernambuco, where the soils permitted sugar growing, and in Rio de Janeiro.[27] Between 1575 and 1600 sugar production expanded rapidly in Brazil. The European market for sugar meant prosperity for the Brazilian sugar industry and that it could survive the problems, such as temporary droughts and the depredations of English pirates (who captured sixty-nine sugar ships in the period 1589–91 alone). By 1600 Brazilian sugar was bringing in greater profits than the Asian spice trade.[28]

The expansion of sugar was accompanied by the introduction of increasing numbers of black slaves from Africa. As the demand for sugar grew, the expanding need for labor was filled by the importation of black slaves; that importation allowed sugar production to be expanded further; and additional demand for slaves arose. The importation of black slaves into Brazil was first legalized in 1549, but it was not until 1570 that blacks began to be imported in great numbers. This transition was due to changing demands on the part of the European settlers, who turned away from the use of indigenous labor for the reasons we have already mentioned: because of the demographic decline of the Amerindians as they succumbed to European diseases and their activities in resisting European advance by fleeing and fighting against the Europeans; because of the control and protection of the Jesuits; and because of the actions of the crown in legislating against Amerindian slavery.[29] The transition to the predominant use of black slaves in the Brazilian sugar industry began around the mid-1580s and was substantially complete by the early decades of the seventeenth century.

English settlement was on the periphery of the Spanish and Portuguese colonial world and was not important in the period before 1650. The English colonies in Barbados and on the North American continent began over a century later than the Iberian ones, and the colonists did not turn to large-scale slavery until the later seventeenth century. The early history of slavery in the early English colonies is not nearly as clear as that in the Iberian settlements. English relations with the Amerindians were different, primarily because those they encountered were relatively few in numbers and their social organizations were not as advanced as the highland peoples the Spaniards encountered. Native Americans suffered from high mortality rates due to disease and were never very important in the English slave system, even though they were enslaved in various English North American colonies.[30] As a consequence, the English colonists faced problems of labor supply similar to those of the Spaniards and Portuguese. In the early years, the English made use of English indentured servants, but several factors rendered their use less than satisfactory: their terms of service were limited; they could not be exploited to the extent slaves could be; and once their period of service was over they caused problems of assimilation.[31] Some blacks taken to the English colonies as slaves in the early seventeenth century were manumitted and became free farmers, but the free black community virtually disappeared by the eighteenth century, when laws placing all blacks in servile status became common.[32]

It took the English planters over a century to turn to a more exclusive reliance on black slaves, and only after 1650 did black slavery come to be well entrenched. Various explanations have been advanced for this relatively slow transition.[33] In reviewing such arguments, C. Duncan Rice offered an inclusive interpretation. He asserted that

> it seems unlikely that the tardiness with which the slavery of Africans emerged in the English colonies is only the reflection of a yeoman reluctance to enslave foreign races. . . . A major explanation for the slowness with which the institution of slavery crystallized in Barbados, Virginia and the other English colonies was that the numbers of blacks imported in the first forty years of settlement was too tiny to make their separation into a distinct legal category feasible. In turn, a principal reason why these blacks were initially so few was that the English settlers lacked the means to buy them. In the early seventeenth century, they had no commercial contacts in West Africa, and could get blacks only by buying them at ruinous prices from the Dutch merchants who had smuggled them at the expense of the Portuguese. It was principally this factor which forced the English to rely in the early stages of settlement on white indentured servants. Like Indians, these had certain disadvantages, mainly the tendencies to riot, murder their masters or run away. The English attempts to use cheap non-black labour, like the Spanish ones, came to

nothing. As soon as increased capital and better commercial contacts gave them the opportunity, they too moved towards using black labour, probably spurred on by the threat to law and order posed by the growing numbers of landless and masterless whites who had served their terms. They were fortunate in that this coincided with the collapse of Portuguese power and the decline of the Dutch, which enabled them to break into the Guinea trade on their own behalf.[34]

Although the origins and timing of their decisions differed, each of the first three colonial powers ultimately came to the same conclusion: black slaves were the best choice for labor in the New World. The idea that black slaves from Africa possessed numerous advantages was common among the European colonists in the New World, and they frequently stated that the labor of one black was worth that of several Indians.[35] Although we do not know if the colonists had a complete understanding of all the variables involved, especially in the early years, black labor did offer several advantages. Many of the Africans came from societies that practiced large-scale agriculture—as we saw in chapter 6—and were accustomed to the labor discipline inherent in such pursuits, unlike many Amerindians. Many blacks, too, knew metal working, especially in iron, a field of endeavor alien to the native Americans, who used metal primarily for decorative rather than productive purposes. Black slaves were not covered by the restrictions on exploitation that the colonial powers established for the native Americans. Africans had been born in a region that shared a pool of several diseases with the Europeans. Therefore, they were less susceptible to the European-borne diseases that were devastating the native population of the Americas and to certain tropical diseases. Epidemiologically, there was an advantage to the use of Africans. The fateful choice—that Africans were to be preferred to Indians as laborers—assured the development of the transatlantic slave trade.

THE SLAVE TRADE

Even as the policies of the first European colonists were forming, the slave trade in African blacks was developing.[36] Blacks began to go to the new colonial possessions almost from the start, and free blacks as well as slaves made the voyage. Tradition, perhaps apocryphal, holds that at least one black was on Columbus's initial voyage. It is more likely that Spaniards on the second voyage brought slaves with them. Queen Isabella limited the trade to Christian slaves, either those born in Spain or naturalized and baptized there. In 1501 royal decrees prohibited Jews, Muslims, *conversos* (Christian converts of Jewish origins), or Moriscos (Christian converts of Muslim origin) from going to the New World.[37] The Spanish crown had recently completed, so it was believed, a campaign to make Spain almost totally Christian, by forcing all of Spain's Jews and most of the Muslims to abandon their old religions for Christianity, or leave the kingdom. This brought an end to the religious plurality that had characterized Spain's medieval history, and Ferdinand and Isabella wanted to prevent such plurality from developing in the newly conquered lands overseas. In 1503 Isabella prohibited the slave trade.[38]

Some slaves had continued to slip through after 1503, usually in special shipments authorized by Ferdinand. This trickle grew after 1513, when the licensing system was introduced. Those who secured a license and paid a fee could ship slaves legally to the Indies. The crown in this fashion could satisfy part of the colonial demand for labor and at the same time provide itself another source of income.[39]

In 1518 the Hieronymite friars on Española called for the importation of blacks directly from Africa, thus arguing for a change in policy. In the first stages of the slave trade, the crown had specified that only *ladinos* (Christianized, Spanish-speaking slaves) should be allowed passage to the Indies. Specifically to be avoided was the transportation of the Muslim Wolofs from Guinea, who might introduce the dreaded religious plurality into Spanish America. The Hieronymites were calling for the importation of *bozales* (unacculturated slaves). In the New World the term *bozal* generally was used to describe an African newly introduced into European-controlled area, whereas *ladino* at first was used for a slave who had been born in Spain or who had resided there long enough to acquire the language before he or she was taken to the Indies. Later, *ladino* came to be used for designating the level of assimilation of the slave, whether he or she had been assimilated in Spain or in Spanish territory overseas, and *criollo negro* was used to describe an American-born black. As time passed, *ladino* and *criollo negro* came to be used indiscriminately. It soon became apparent that in some respects the colonists preferred *bozales* to *ladinos*: they could be molded more easily into the Spanish pattern. All the *bozales* were black, and their skin color would aid in their identification and control. Many of the *ladinos* in the early period were mulattoes or Moriscos and could escape detection more easily.[40]

The licensing system was characteristic of the Spanish policy of regulating as much as possible every aspect of colonial development and administration. The policy was never totally successful, but neither was it ever totally abandoned. Even after licensing was introduced in 1513, it was apparent that there was a greater demand for slaves than could be supplied. In 1518 Charles V gave exclusive slaving licenses to Laurent de Gouvenot, one of his Flemish favorites, and to Jorge de Portugal. Gouvenot received permission to ship 4,000 slaves over a five-year period, and Jorge de Portugal received permission for 400. Gouvenot sold his licenses to Genoese merchants. The Genoese, with a flourishing merchant community in Seville, already were involved in the slave trade and would remain so. Licensed slaves were to be taken from Guinea or any other part of Africa and shipped to Cuba, Española, Jamaica, Yucatán, or Mexico (this last after 1523). These initial licenses set a pattern that lasted for over a century. They established an annual quota, a fee for each slave, acquisition in specified African zones (thus permitting *bozales* to be shipped), and delivery directly to the Americas, bypassing Spain. When the first licenses ran out in 1528, Heinrich Ehinger and Hieronymous Seiler, agents of the German banking firm of the Welsers, received a new license on similar terms.[41]

After the licenses of Ehinger and Seiler expired, a new period began, lasting from 1532 to 1589, during which the merchants and officials of Seville, members of the Consulado and the Casa de Contratación, regulated the slave trade. Licenses granted by the Casa could be obtained in a variety of ways: some by purchase, some by royal grant, and some as repayments for forced loans to the government. Rolando Mellafe has listed the groups who received the licenses in ascending order of their importance in the trade. Crown and church officials could take their slaves with them, free of duty, when they left Spain to fill official positions in the New World. Conquerors and other participants in the conquest were sometimes granted licenses in recompense for the services they had performed for the crown. Institutional grants of slave licenses often went to corporate groups in the Americas such as urban councils, hospitals, monasteries, and convents. Individuals could get licenses for various reasons: rendering exceptional service to the crown, occupying a position at court, being a member of the Council of the Indies or the Casa de Contratación, or by securing a special grant from the king.[42]

In practice the licensee did not actually deliver the slaves to America; he usually sold part or all of his block of licenses to merchants, who then resold them. Genoese merchants in Seville controlled the trade until midcentury. Eventually the Portuguese traders, who were familiar with West and Central Africa and whose country controlled important African trading centers, secured the licenses. Once they got them, they were able to deliver the slaves to the New World.[43]

The Portuguese were also in a position to transport far more slaves than provided for by the number of licenses for slaves delivered in Seville. Smuggling was a constant problem in the sixteenth century, and its prevalence renders virtually impossible any attempt to determine the exact numbers of slaves delivered. Contraband trade was relatively easy, because at the same time that the Portuguese were shipping slaves to Spanish America, they were also providing them to Portuguese colonists in Brazil. Portuguese slave licenses for trade to Brazil were only one-half the cost of Spanish licenses for slaves bound for the Spanish colonies, and, as a result, the Portuguese listed many of the slaves taken from the African coast as bound for Brazil. Once in American waters, the slave ships would head for Spanish-American ports, and their masters would claim that their ships had been diverted and damaged by storms. Because Spanish port officials were legally bound to render aid to distressed ships, they allowed the Portuguese to land and sell their cargoes. In this way unlicensed slaves were introduced into the Spanish-American markets, contravening official regulations and enriching the Portuguese slavers as well as the port officials they no doubt bribed.[44]

From the inception of the slave trade, Portuguese had been involved in it, due in large part to their control of the slave collection points in Africa. Until the 1580s, Spanish officials of the Casa de Contratación in Seville tried to limit the role of the Portuguese by insisting that all slaves to the New World be carried in ships sailing with the annual fleets from Spain to America. The officials of Seville were unsuccessful in this, only in part because of the contraband trade, and by 1580 the stage was set for the Portuguese to assume an even greater role.

In that year King Philip II of Spain took advantage of a Portuguese dynastic crisis to secure the throne of Portugal for himself; thereafter, from 1580 to 1640, Philip II and his successors ruled jointly over Portugal and Spain. Because these years were ones of a high demand for black slaves in the New World, the Portuguese traders were in an excellent position to prosper from the new arrangement. Philip saw numerous benefits to be obtained from a more highly regulated trade and in 1580 began to sign contracts with Portuguese *rendeiros*, wholesale contractors in the African trade, in return for a royal share in the business. There were three major areas of slaving in the 1580s: the Cape Verde Islands, São Tomé, and Angola. Philip signed contracts for the supply of slaves from these three regions either with individuals or partners. In return for their licenses, the *rendeiros* would pay the crown a percentage of their profits, one-fourth for the contracts on the Cape Verdes and São Tomé, and one-third on those of Angola. In addition, the license holders were granted an important concession: they could deliver their human cargoes to American ports in ships sailing on their own, outside the normal annual fleets of the Carrera de Indias.[45]

From 1580 to 1595 the Portuguese gradually expanded their participation, even though they had not yet received a monopoly. Contracts to non-Portuguese for slaves as yet undelivered were still outstanding, and it was not until 1595 that the new *asiento* system of exclusive contracts emerged. This system was established in a contract signed with Pedro Gómez Reinel in 1594 and 1595. He was obliged to deliver 4,250 live slaves to the Indies each year; to do so he could sell the licenses freely to subcontractors at a price not to exceed thirty ducats per slave, and in return he was to pay the crown 100,000 ducats annually. Gómez Reinel was required to post a bond of 150,000 ducats to make sure that he carried out his bargain; he would have the exclusive right to sell individual slave licenses during the term of his *asiento*. Navigation laws were liberalized; ships could sail outside the convoy system; all slaves were to be taken first to Cartagena but Gómez Reinel's agents could take them on to be sold in other places. A series of *asentistas* succeeded Gómez Reinel, and the system lasted, with a brief interruption from 1609 to 1615, until 1640 when Portugal rebelled against Spain.[46]

The documents produced in the administration of the *asientos* and preserved for historians allow our first detailed picture of the transatlantic slave trade. In particular the regulations that were established and the legal cases that developed permit a more complete understanding of the intricacies of the trade. Enriqueta Vila Villar has studied the records and offered new information and new conclusions. Those who wished to participate in the trade had to comply with a set of legal requirements that were quite complex. The shippers (*cargadores*) purchased licenses from the *asentista*, usually in lots of eighty or more, but at times in smaller or much larger numbers. The purchasers of the licenses occasionally could command sufficient capital to make the deal on their own, but usually shares were sold to groups of investors who would form temporary companies to share the expenses and divide the profits. A crucial participant was the ship's master, who held shares of the stock and who had full charge of the ship and its cargo during the voyage. The ships were usually Spanish or Portuguese. Regulations required the use of Iberian-built and owned ships, but later in the period of the *asientos*, vessels of Dutch or English manufacture engaged in the trade as well. The striking feature of the ships involved was that they were quite small. Most were less than one hundred tons burden; others were larger, but very few exceeded two hundred tons. The *asientos* specified that 1.2 *piezas* (a *pieza* equaled one adult male) could be carried for each ton, but sometimes more were loaded. The slavers preferred small ships, because the initial capital investment was less and because smaller ships could maneuver in and out of shallow rivers and estuaries more easily.[47]

Once the ship was obtained and its crew embarked, it first had to proceed to Seville to be inspected and registered by the Casa de Contratación. The first requirement was to present the slaving licenses already purchased and to obtain an official register from the Casa. The ship then underwent three separate inspections. First the conditions and carrying capacity of the ship were determined, as well as its gear and artillery. The latter was necessary because slave ships sailed outside the convoy system and had to provide their own defenses. Next the interior was inspected, and the officials specified the provisions the ship should carry. The final inspection was done to determine if the first two had been performed properly and if the special requirements imposed by the first two sets of inspectors had been fulfilled. When all three inspections were completed the ship was cleared to sail for Africa.[48]

The crew, composed of Spaniards and Portuguese, had to plan for a long voyage. The quickest voyages generally took a year and a half, and slower ones could last up to four years. The first stage was down the African coast to one of the Portuguese slaving stations. Santiago in the Cape Verde Islands was the closest, but international piracy conducted by the French, Dutch, and English, beginning in the 1570s and culminating in Sir Anthony Sherley's capture of Santiago in 1596, rendered it less attractive than the more distant stations. The island of São Tomé was more isolated from the raids of other Europeans, and it was linked with its main source of slaves, the kingdom of the Kongo, through

Mpinda, a port near the mouth of the Zaire River. In the late sixteenth and the early seventeenth centuries São Tomé was reaching its rather short-lived peak, based on slaving and sugar growing. Still farther south was Angola, whose principal city, São Paulo de Luanda, became the most important slaving center in the first half of the seventeenth century.[49]

At times it took a ship a year or more to obtain a cargo of slaves, depending on the state of local market conditions. Long stays on Africa's Atlantic coast were hard on crews and vessels alike. The men fell victim to tropical diseases, and worms attacked the wood of the hull, especially in Angolan anchorages. When the ship's cargo of slaves was complete, a resident agent of the *asentista* visited the ship. He required that the slaves be unloaded onto small boats bobbing on the water around the ship, while he went on board to search for any hidden slaves. Then he counted the slaves as they reboarded the ship from the boats and turned a copy of his register over to the master, who then could begin the second stage of the trip, across the Atlantic to America.[50]

Dependent as the vessels were on wind and ocean currents, the voyage to America usually took two months or more. The shorter, quicker route was from São Tomé or the Cape Verdes northward to the westward-flowing equatorial current. If the trip originated at Luanda, one of two long and arduous passages could be chosen. The first called for sailing close to the wind, with frequent tacking, northward through the Gulf of Guinea to the equatorial current. The second was to sail to the west until the other side of the Atlantic was reached.[51]

The slaves, miserably crammed below decks, with no way of knowing their fate, suffered regardless of how long the voyage took. There were almost always some slaves who died on the voyage, victims of overcrowding, disease, or malnutrition. The ships usually loaded more slaves than the licenses provided, to cover eventual losses on the trip. Vila Villar provided the accounting in table 9.1 of licenses, loadings, and slaves delivered in Veracruz in the early seventeenth century.[52]

Clearly many unlicensed slaves were loaded in Africa and in most cases fewer slaves were unloaded than began the voyage (table 9.1); losses in transit continued through the centuries of the Atlantic slave trade. For the ships Vila Villar studied, the average number of slaves carried was 248.3, and the average loss in slaves was 22.3 percent. The losses varied considerably. The four ships of 1620 and 1621 delivered all the slaves they had loaded in Africa, whereas the one ship of 1611 compiled the poorest record, losing over one-half. The reasons for the losses on the Atlantic crossing are complex, and historians are still trying to assess them. It is clear that problems of disease began to arise even before the slaves boarded the vessels. Slaves in Africa usually were brought from the interior to holding areas along the coast. On their way to the coast they may well have traversed areas where they encountered unfamiliar diseases. While being held awaiting sale and embarkation, they were crowded into miserable camps in which slaves from several areas were confined long enough for a disease any one

Table 9.1. The Slave Trade to Veracruz, 1605-1621

Year [a]	Number of Ships	Slaves Loaded in Africa	Slaves Unloaded in Veracruz	Number of Licenses Registered
1605	2	572	381	280
1606	1	200	165	120
1608	7	1,876	1,461	910
1609	3	604	545	480
1611	1	313	151	169
1616	1	235	172	180
1617	1	170	120	150
1618	5	992	628	800
1619	2	570	350	400
1620	1	464	464	150
1621	3	817	817	370
Undated	2	330	297	280
Total	29	7,143	5,551	4,289

Source: Enriqueta Vila Villar, *Hispanoamérica y el comercio de esclavos* (Seville, 1977), p. 139.

[a] Records not available for 1607, 1610, 1612-15.

of them contracted to be spread to others. Often the slave ships coasted from one slave market to another while full cargoes were collected. New slaves placed on board often brought new diseases with them. On the transatlantic voyage the crowded and unsanitary conditions allowed ill slaves to infect others. If the vessel ran low on food or water or both, new maladies would arise.[53]

Other reasons besides mortality accounted for some of the decline in numbers of slaves during the crossing. One cause would be the attacks of pirates, who seized slaves to sell them themselves. Legal slaving ships could also have put into illegal ports to drop off slaves without paying duties on them. Customs officials at the legal ports could be bribed to report smaller numbers than actually arrived. Nonetheless, the most dramatic reason for the decline in numbers was fatal disease.

Conditions were unspeakable in the holds of the ships, as the testimony of many observers indicates. The cleric Alonso de Sandoval left one sad description, asserting that one-third of the slaves usually died on the voyage. They were

so crowded, in such disgusting conditions, and so mistreated, as the very ones who transport them assure me, that they come by six and six, with collars around their necks, and these same ones by two and two with fetters on their feet, in such a way that they come imprisoned from head to feet, below the deck, locked in from outside, where they see neither sun nor moon, [and] that there is no Spaniard who dares to stick his head in the hatch without becoming ill, nor to remain inside for an hour without the risk of great sickness. So great is the stench, the crowding and the misery of that place. And the [only] refuge and consolation that they have in it is [that] to each [is given] once a day no more than a half bowl of uncooked corn flour or millet, which is like our rice, and with it a small jug of water and nothing else, except for much beating, much lashing, and bad words. This is that which commonly happens with the men and I well think that some of the shippers treat them with more kindness and mildness, principally in these times. . . . [Nevertheless, most] arrive turned into skeletons.[54]

Not as much is known about the early slave trade to Brazil as to the Spanish colonies, although the life of the slaves on shipboard was no less horrifying. We do know that two principal means of supply existed. One was the traditional means by which a merchant in Lisbon secured licenses and contracted with the master of a slave ship to pick up the slaves at one of the stations in Africa and take them to Brazil. After 1558 each planter in Brazil got the right to import up to 120 slaves per year, ostensibly to resupply his own needs for agricultural labor. Katia Mattoso has argued persuasively that 120 slaves per year would be far more than even the largest planters needed for their own sugar mills, and that they probably sold the excess numbers to smaller proprietors and thereby gained additional sources of income.[55]

Three Brazilian ports, each with a fine natural harbor, supplied the demands for slaves in the regions where Portuguese development was most advanced. Recife, farthest to the north, supplied the region of Pernambuco. Bahia, the early colonial capital in the northeast, received slaves for the sugar plantations in the region of the bay of Todos os Santos. Rio de Janeiro, in the south, had an early significance that later developed into first-rank importance.[56]

The slave supply to Brazil was relatively unhindered up to 1580, the year Philip II of Spain became the king of Portugal. Spain was facing rebellion in the Netherlands, and after the Spanish and Portuguese crowns were joined, the Dutch began to attack Portuguese possessions. The Dutch later turned from harassment to conquest. Beginning in the 1620s, the Dutch West India Company seized Portuguese possessions on both sides of the Atlantic: Bahia from 1624 to 1625, Pernambuco from 1630 to 1654, Angola and São Tomé from 1641 to 1648, and São Jorge da Mina from 1638 on. (Mina was a slave importing center, as we saw in chapter 7.) After the Portuguese broke from Spain in 1640, they turned their full attention to regaining the positions occupied by the Dutch. They were successful everywhere but at São Jorge da Mina, the important gold trading station on the coast of Guinea. However, the Dutch after 1648 allowed the Portuguese to trade at Mina.[57]

One of the most difficult problems in the history of the Atlantic slave trade is to determine the numbers of slaves who were forced to make the voyage and survived it. In the period before the Spanish crown began to issue licenses, there are no firm figures at all, and not until the period of the Portuguese *asientos* do figures become available. Throughout the first century and a half of the American slave trade, the twin problems of unlicensed voyages and misrepresentations of the licensed shipments preclude real certainty. Nonetheless, it is possible to provide some estimates of the volume of the Atlantic slave trade. The first comprehensive effort to quantify it was made by Philip D. Curtin, who published *The Atlantic Slave Trade: A Census* in 1969, which he clearly labeled as a preliminary accounting subject to changes as scholars examined other evidence. His conclusions aroused controversy, because his estimate of the total movement of blacks across the Atlantic in the four centuries of the trade was just over nine and one-half million.[58] Some of the attacks on Curtin's figures came from those who felt that reducing the figures, from the fifteen to twenty million that was commonly accepted before Curtin wrote, would diminish modern horror at the sufferings the slaves had endured. Curtin was also criticized, or chided, by historians of demography, who felt the figures he proposed for individual periods or places could be improved through further work, even though Curtin himself had made the same point. Later scholars have reexamined specific components of the Atlantic slave trade and come to higher estimates than Curtin for those components. This led J. E. Inikori to put forward an estimate of 13,392,000 for the total slave trade and James Rawley to make an estimate of 11,345,000.[59] The latest scholar to revise Curtin's figures on the basis of the most recent studies is Paul E. Lovejoy, who criticized Inikori's assumptions and pointed out errors of calculation in Rawley's figures. After careful assessments, Lovejoy arrived at an estimate of 9,778,500, a figure remarkably close to that of Curtin.[60]

For the period from the fifteenth century through 1650, the best estimates are that that over 350,000 slaves arrived in the ports of Spanish America and some 250,000 arrived in Brazil (table 9.2). The trade to the French and British islands of the Caribbean and to British North America was just getting under way by 1650, with fewer than 25,000 delivered there. These figures must remain tentative, but for a variety of reasons they may never be firmer. As Vila Villar showed (see table 9.1), far more slaves were loaded in African ports than were delivered. Part of the discrepancy was because of the losses in transport of 15 to 25 percent or even more. Also, the licenses were granted for a specified number of *piezas de Indias* (*pieças* in Portuguese), that is, adult men in their prime. In practice, women, handicapped adult men, old men, and adolescents counted as less than a full *pieza*. More individuals, therefore, could be shipped legally than even the licenses indicated. We have no way of estimating illegal shipments.

Ultimately Brazil would absorb more black slaves than any other part of the New World, but the Portuguese slave trade to Brazil began later than the trade to Spanish America. Brazil, as we saw, did not become a vital area for the importation of slaves until the last decade of the sixteenth century. The slow

Table 9.2. Estimated Total Volume of the Atlantic Slave Trade, 1451–1650

Period	Europe	Atlantic Islands	São Tomé	Spanish America	Brazil	British Caribbean	French Caribbean	British North America	Total
1451–1475	12,500	2,500	—	—	—	—	—	—	15,000
1476–1500	12,500	5,000	1,000	—	—	—	—	—	18,500
1501–1525	12,500	5,000	25,000	—	—	—	—	—	42,500
1526–1550	7,500	5,000	18,800	12,500	—	—	—	—	43,800
1551–1575	2,500	5,000	18,800	25,000	10,000	—	—	—	61,300
1576–1600	1,300	2,500	12,500	56,000	40,000	—	—	—	112,300
1601–1625	300	—	12,500	148,800	100,000	—	—	200	261,800
1626–1650	300	—	6,300	111,600	100,000	20,700	2,500	1,200	242,600
Total	49,400	25,000	94,900	353,900	250,000	20,700	2,500	1,400	797,800

Sources: Philip D. Curtin, *The Atlantic Slave Trade: A Census* (Madison, 1969); Enriqueta Vila Villar, *Hispanoamérica y el comercio de esclavos* (Seville, 1977); Paul E. Lovejoy, "The Volume of the Atlantic Slave Trade: A Synthesis," *Journal of African History* 23 (1982): 473–501.

development of settlements in the early years of the century, and the continued reliance on Indian labor meant that relatively few slaves were being imported. The direct slave trade to Brazil became legal in 1549, but only after 1570 did the trade become substantial, thereafter gaining rapidly after its slow beginning. Curtin estimated that 10,000 slaves were taken to Brazil between 1551 and 1575; this number increased to 40,000 in the last quarter of the sixteenth century; and in each of the first two quarters of the seventeenth century 100,000 Africans were introduced, for an estimated total of 250,000 for the period up to 1650.[61] After 1650 the annual importation into Brazil surpassed that into Spanish America.

To sum up the efforts to quantify the Atlantic slave trade, the combined estimates—based on Curtin, Vila Villar, and Lovejoy—come to 628,500 slaves delivered in the Americas up to 1650. During the same period, 169,300 slaves were delivered to Europe, the Atlantic islands, and São Tomé.[62] We should also probably add an additional figure to cover those slaves shipped to Spanish America before 1526 and to Brazil before 1650 and to cover those others illegally entered, but it is virtually impossible to make estimates for those portions of the trade.

When the American destination of those hundreds of thousands of African slaves was finally reached after the Atlantic crossing, their ships anchored and the landing formalities were carried out. In Spanish-American ports, two officials visited each ship, and their inspection echoed the procedures that had been performed before the departure from Africa. They came out to the ship, ordered the slaves placed on boats standing alongside, and had two of their assistants search the vessels for any hidden slaves. The slaves were then reloaded on board and counted. When this was done, the legal formalities were completed and the master turned his surviving slaves over to the local factors. The first days on American soil for the newly arrived slaves were spent in warehouses or encampments where they were fed, rested, cleaned up, and were given some medical treatment. Those who reached Brazil were confined in huts in compounds in the towns. After a period of ten to fifteen days they were either delivered to prior purchasers or offered for sale, either by auction or by direct arrangements between purchasers and sellers.[63] Those who had survived the horrors of the oceanic voyage were then on the verge of beginning their lives as slaves in the New World.

10
SLAVERY IN
EARLY COLONIAL LATIN AMERICA

Once the slaves reached the Americas, they faced an unknown future and a variety of fates that they could not foresee. One idea that must be abandoned is that the slave buyers intended to use their purchases only for hard, unskilled labor. Many slaves did suffer lives of unrelenting toil in the fields, mills, and mines after having been deprived of human dignity, physical comfort, and legal rights. Others, though they remained slaves, found that less burdensome situations awaited them and that their talents and skills, which they either brought with them or acquired later, afforded them a better life than that of the unskilled workers.[1] Latin American slavery in the first century and a half of its existence was not monolithic, and among the slaves a hierarchy based on skill and the consequent advantages to their owners soon developed. Slavery in the Portuguese and Spanish territories had from the beginning, and retained, a complex development. Even if Spanish and Portuguese laws and regulations were the same for all slaves, it is possible to see the creation both in Brazil and the Spanish colonies of two systems: one for the domestics, artisans, and assistants of all sorts; and another for the gang slaves on the plantations and in the mines.[2] The first was a continuation of the pattern of acquiring slaves as supplemental laborers and domestics that was practiced in the medieval Christian states of the Mediterranean; the second stemmed from the more recent pattern of plantation slavery in the Atlantic islands. This distinction never was enunciated fully, but the conditions and prospects for slaves differed considerably, depending on the occupations to which they were assigned. Still others won their freedom, and from the beginning of the colonial period a free black population developed.

None of this could be known by the unfortunate captives aboard the stinking slave ships as they were taken ashore at a totally unfamiliar port and handed over by the white seamen to another group of whites. Some of the slaves would be put to work almost immediately close by the place they disembarked in coastal

Brazil, the Caribbean islands, or the Spanish mainland. Others faced still farther journeys: a lengthy trip to Panama, the Pacific, and eventually to Peru; or an overland passage to the Valley of Mexico. The occupations to which their owners assigned them were the first indication of what the rest of their lives would hold for them.

In the early decades of the conquest and subordination of Mexico and Peru, blacks—both slave and free—participated as auxiliaries of the Spanish conquerors. In this role they were particularly valuable. They served as soldiers and occupied an intermediate position between the Spaniards and the indigenous population. A black freedman, Juan Garrido, participated in the conquest of Mexico, and black slaves accompanied the expeditions to Peru. In the early pacification of Chile, Juan Valiente, a black slave from Mexico, rose to become an infantry captain and secured an *encomienda* for himself. He sent money back to Mexico to purchase his freedom, but the money never reached his owner, who was still trying to force his slave's return when Valiente died in battle. The blacks' assimilation of European culture, more rapid than that of the native Americans, made them very useful in the postconquest restructuring of colonial society. In fact, many of the first blacks in mainland Spanish America were used to fill the gap between the demand for skilled laborers, assistants, and troopers and the available supply of Europeans. In this aspect, unlike plantation slavery, the slave system of Spanish America resembled that of medieval and Renaissance Italy, Spain, or Portugal.[3]

Nevertheless, one of the most significant reasons for bringing slaves to the Americas in the first century and a half of the colonial period was that their labor was needed on sugar plantations. For many Africans who survived the Middle Passage, life on a sugar estate and labor in the cane fields or in the mill was their first, and for many their last, experience in the New World.

New World sugar plantations began with the first Spanish colonies.[4] In 1502 the Spanish crown sent out an expedition with over two thousand men under the new governor, Nicolás de Ovando, charged with developing the settlements in the Caribbean islands. In 1503 Pedro de Atienza and Miguel Ballester combined to attempt sugar production on Española. Atienza brought plantings of cane, and together the two men built a processing plant to make molasses in the town of Concepción de la Vega. Their modest beginnings inspired other colonists to attempt similar operations. The refining of the cane juice into sugar was tried, with initially unimpressive results. Only in 1515 were the first steps taken to build a true sugar mill on the island. In that year Gonzalo de Vellosa, a surgeon who had at his disposal sixty-seven native laborers and some territory in the uplands, imported technical experts from the Canaries to begin construction of a sugar mill. Their advice was that Vellosa's land, labor, and capital were all too meager to support a full-scale mill complex. Thereafter, Vellosa sought partners and found them in Cristóbal and Francisco de Tapia, who had acquired capital and land in the coastal plain, and by 1517, using the most up-to-date technology available, the mill was in operation.[5]

Larger-scale production of cane sugar was then possible, but rapid expansion depended on support from the crown and colonial officials. When Charles V became king in 1516, he reviewed the situation on Española and, impressed by samples of sugar and other colonial goods the colonists sent him, charged his new governor, Rodrigo de Figueroa, with supporting the efforts of the sugar manufacturers. Figueroa had Charles's authorization to grant privileges and, more important, loans to prospective sugar manufacturers. The king also encouraged sending experts from the Canaries to the Caribbean, exempted technological equipment from taxation, and allowed on-the-spot production of the copper ware necessary in the refining process. Progress was rapid. By 1520 some forty mills were under construction, with six already in operation, and in 1522 Jean Florin made the first recorded exportation of sugar from America to Europe, a twenty-five-ton shipload. Thereafter there were upheavals in the sugar manufacturing of Española, but thirty-four mills were in operation from the 1530s to the 1570s. Just as in the slave trade, the Genoese of Seville were heavily involved in the New World sugar industry.[6]

The Caribbean islands had several advantages for sugar production over Mediterranean Europe and the Spanish and Portuguese islands in the eastern Atlantic. The tropical climage meant that freezing weather, which occasionally threatened Mediterranean fields, was not present. In some parts of the Caribbean, rainfall provided sufficient water for the crops without irrigation. Elsewhere, water from streams that could easily be diverted for irrigation was present and more reliable than on the Atlantic islands. In addition, forests covering parts of the islands could be harvested for fuel to fire the refineries' boilers.

Sugar production first spread from Española to the island of Puerto Rico, where construction of mills—again with royal loans—from the 1530s to the 1550s established the industry. Jamaica had mills in production by 1519. Cuban sugar development was slow in the sixteenth century, even though cane probably was first taken to the island in 1511. There were several proposals to begin production in Cuba, but obstacles delayed it until the 1570s, when several mills were built in the region of the Bahía Honda, near Havana. However, the Cuban industry only began to prosper when production spread to eastern Cuba near Santiago in the last years of the sixteenth century.[7]

Part of the reason for the slow development of sugar production in the Caribbean, and for the slowness of other development as well, was the relative stagnation of the region following the conquest of Mexico in the 1520s and of Peru in the 1540s. These mainland areas were richer; their natives' levels of civilization and political and economic development were higher; and their potential for profits was greater than that of the Caribbean islands. As a consequence, many European emigrants left the islands to pursue their fortunes on the mainland.

Mexico was conquered first, and quickly after its conquest sugar began to be grown and processed there. In one of his letters to Charles V, Hernando Cortés described the market of Tenochtitlán, the Aztec capital. Among the products sold there, he noted, were honey and a sort of sugar made from the *maguey* plant. Cortés was fully aware of the potential of sugar cane, because he had come to the Caribbean in 1504 at the age of nineteen and had witnessed the beginning of sugar production in the islands. When he wrote his fourth letter to Charles V he asked that seeds and cuttings of European plants, including sugar cane, be sent to Mexico. He did not have to wait long, for in the late 1520s he was building two *ingenios* (water mills) in Tuxtla, in the region of Veracruz. The Tuxtla mills took some ten years to become operational, due in no small part to intrigues and lawsuits Cortes had to face, which diverted his attention. In the 1530s and 1540s the conqueror also built mills on his lands in the vicinity of Cuernavaca and contracted with Genoese merchants to exchange sugar directly for slaves. Other colonists began to build mills, aided by land grants from the crown, although direct royal loans were not available to them. The great expansion of the Mexican sugar industry took place in the second half of the sixteenth century, and by 1600 there were more than forty licensed mills in operation, possibly with the addition of other small, unlicensed ones.[8]

Sugar in Peru probably arrived with the conquerors or shortly after the conquest. By the end of the sixteenth century sugar plantations were common in several parts of the colony, where suitable soils and water for irrigation could be found. In the seventeenth century labor for the sugar estates came from salaried workers—not *mita* labor—and black slaves.[9]

The New World sugar estates followed the same pattern and used the same techniques as those in the Atlantic islands, which were themselves little different from earlier Mediterranean models, except for a greatly increased use of slave labor. First there was the land, by no means all of which would be devoted to sugar cane cultivation, since part would be woodland that was to provide the fuel for the mill; part would be preserved for the production of food for the workers and the animals; and part would be pasture lands for the animals of the mill, both draft animals and those raised for food. The remainder would be the cane fields and the irrigation works. At a suitable place on the property the buildings of the estate would be located. They consisted of housing for the workers as well as the warehouses and the mill complex itself, with a water mill (*ingenio*) or an animal-powered mill (*trapiche*) for crushing the cane, a boiling house (*casa de calderas*), and a refinery (*casa de purgar*). Many of the sugar plantations had their own churches and fortifications.

Slaves performed all the steps necessary to produce the cane and then manufacture sugar from it, and Amerindians often provided supplementary, unskilled labor. It is not an exaggeration to state that sugar production would not have reached the heights it did without the contributions of black slaves, both common laborers and specialists. The majority of the slaves were unskilled, and they were divided into teams directed by overseers (often slaves themselves), who woke the field hands well before dawn and set them to work at their appointed tasks. For most of the slaves, the work was unrelenting, debilitating, and stultifying. Almost from the beginning, however, some favored slaves found themselves assigned to tasks with more responsibility, for which skill and not brute force was needed.

In Mexico and other mainland areas, much of the skilled labor of sugar manufacturing seems to have been done by Spaniards, with black slaves only occasionally occupying technical positions. On the Caribbean island of Española the records of the *ingenio* of Santiago de Paz for 1547, in contrast, indicate a heavy concentration of black slaves occupying skilled posts. In his study of that plantation, Robert S. Haskett found that there were 72 slaves, 46 of them men and 26 women. Their labor was supplemented by 50 *repartimiento* natives. Of the black men, 44 were identified by some occupational title. These included an overseer, a sugar master, a master of cooling foam, 5 boiler tenders, a refiner, 5 press operators, a miller, and others also concerned with sugar making. Still others had skills ancillary to direct production: a carter, a smith, a boxmaker, an oxherd, 2 shepherds, and 4 stockmen.[10] This description contrasts with Ward Barrett's analysis of the Mexican sugar plantations of the Cortés family, for which he found that Spaniards held most of the skilled posts.[11] This discrepancy may be explained by the fact that the Caribbean islands were something of a backwater in the decades following the conquest of Mexico, when many Spaniards left the islands to seek greater opportunity in New Spain. Perhaps the owner of Santiago de Paz could not find Spaniards for the posts on his *ingenio* and turned instead to black slaves. Santiago de Paz may have been unusual in its heavy proportion of skilled slaves, but it was not unusual on many sugar plantations for some black slaves to be skilled workers. That slaves occupied skilled positions in the sugar mills was no guarantee that they necessarily had easier lives than the field hands. Working conditions in the mills were harsh, so much so that the Spanish crown prohibited the use of natives in them.

Black slavery in Brazil lasted longer than elsewhere in the Americas, and the slave trade to that country ultimately accounted for about 40 percent of the black slaves imported into the Americas. During our period, the black slaves of Brazil were mainly used in sugar production. Sugar in Brazil, from the late sixteenth century and especially during the boom of the seventeenth century, dominated the northeastern coastal regions, particularly in the lands surrounding the Bahia de Todos os Santos (the *Recôncavo*) and the region of Pernambuco (the *Várzea*). The crown made land grants (*sesmarias*) to favored settlers, many of whom set up sugar mills (*engenios* in Portuguese) and planted sugar crops. Because the grants often contained more land than the mill owners could manage to work themselves, many of them subdivided part of their holdings and made leasing or sharecropping arrangements with cane growers (*lavradores de cana*). These white settlers produced a sugar cane crop on the lands they held and turned a fourth or a third of that crop over to the mill owner for refining into marketable sugar.[12]

Both mill owners and cane growers employed slaves in a variety of ways. They all had household slaves, who were physically better treated than those working in the fields and mills. Sexual liaisons often developed between the masters and their female household slaves, and their mulatto offspring helped to resupply the labor needs of the household staff. The bulk of the laborers lived in barracks close to the mills, not in the master's house. Among them were field workers who grew the cane, and other slaves produced food for the people and animals of the estates, and raised draft horses and oxen. The slaves working in the sugar mills had harsher lives still, and because of numerous constraints upon them, seldom were sufficient numbers of new slaves being born and surviving to adulthood from among these workers. Plantation owners seem not to have felt that it was an economic proposition to raise young mill workers, and they chose to work the plantation slaves unmercifully and to purchase replacements for them when they became incapable of work or died.[13]

Life for all the slaves on the sugar plantations was difficult, but the mill workers endured the worst conditions. They toiled in hellish conditions doing work that was physically demanding and dangerous. This description was provided by a traveler in 1649:

> And in these mills (during the season of making sugar) they work both day and night, the work of immediately supplying the canes into the mill being so perilous as if through drowsiness or heedlessness a finger's end be but engaged between the posts, their whole body inevitably follows, to prevent which, the next Negro has always a hatchet ready to chop off his arm, if any such misfortune should arrive.[14]

In the seventeenth century, colonial writers referred to Brazil as a "paradise for mulattoes, a purgatory for whites, and a hell for blacks."[15]

Brazil's sugar mills were true hell for the black refinery workers, but it is unlikely that anywhere was a true paradise for mulattoes—and even if Brazil was a purgatory for whites, it was a profitable one for those in the northeast of the colony, and for the merchants and shippers of Europe. It was also lucrative for the privateers of England, France, and Holland, who harassed the vessels carrying their cargoes of sugar across the Atlantic. Between 1562 and 1568, for example, the English pirates John Hawkins and John Lovell took thirty-one ships along the Portuguese trade routes.[16] Despite these continuing depredations, Brazil developed as a phenomenally prosperous colony with a large range of commercial and social activities based on the underpinnings of sugar and the labor of black slaves.

The sugar estates, combining agricultural production with mechanized processing, had numerous and varied positions to fill. The same range of occupations did not exist in most other large-scale agricultural enterprises. Some slaves were used on grain-producing estates, on indigo plantations, and on cattle and sheep ranches; but they were not needed in the same numbers as they were on the sugar estates, and there were fewer opportunities for any of them to learn specialized skills.[17] Slaves were also used in other important agricultural undertakings. Shortly after the conquest of Peru, a number of small farms were established around the centers of Spanish production. Called *chácaras* or *estancias*, these truck farms produced a variety of crops and raised animals for sale in the town markets. Typically, the work force consisted of a few black slaves, who either lived on the *chácaras* or in nearby towns and whose labor was supplemented at harvest time by Amerindian labor. In the late sixteenth century, Peruvian agriculture grew in size and importance, and the black slave population increased accordingly. Peruvian estates usually were not devoted to a single crop, although on the south coast some were specialized producers of wine grapes and elsewhere there were sugar plantations. Many agriculturists combined several small holdings with a diversified farming and stock-raising regime. As the local governors began to carry out royal decrees limiting native labor, the work of black slaves became more important. In the 1580s and 1590s the authorities forbade the use of Amerindians in sugar mills and vineyards and in 1601 also excluded them from work in the olive groves. This meant that blacks were in greater demand for agriculture in Peru, and it also helps to explain the quickening of the slave trade into Peru after about 1580.[18]

The region of Caracas in the seventeenth century made increasing use of black slaves in the cacao industry. The cacao planters first used *encomienda* labor, but the importation of black slaves began in the early years of the seventeenth century and grew substantially as a consequence of the cacao boom of the 1630s and 1640s.[19]

The mines from Mexico to Chile were great magnets for slave labor, and in them slaves encountered the harshest environments and the highest death rates of all slave occupations. Mining for precious metals, as we saw in the previous chapter, began soon after the initial Spanish settlements in the Caribbean islands. The first silver mines in central Mexico began to be exploited in the 1530s and 1540s, particularly in the Zacatecas area discovered in 1546. Labor there was provided mainly by natives under *encomienda* and later *repartimiento*, with some addition of black slaves. Black slaves were present from the founding of Zacatecas as a city, but records concerning them only become abundant after 1650. The silver deposits in the region of Parral, over 1,500 miles north of Mexico City, were discovered as early as 1550, but in the 1630s the discovery of much richer deposits brought a boom to the area. Labor in the Mexican mining districts was mainly provided by Amerindians. Nevertheless, black and mulatto slaves were valued components of the labor force, especially in the Zacatecas mines, because they could be retained permanently, whereas the natives had the right to temporary terms of service. Slaves in mining were also used in seventeenth-century Colombia, and the greatest demand for slaves in the early settlements of Chile developed because they were needed for labor in the mines. In the rich South American mines of Potosí, black slaves supplemented indigenous labor.[20]

Slaves also worked in transport on land and sea. They were carters and muleteers, sailors and galley oarsmen. For land transport, carts were used when roads permitted, but for mountainous regions mule-trains were clearly superior to the alternatives: native porters or llamas in the Andes. A typical mule-train in Peru would be headed by a Spaniard, who had charge of ten to twenty mules and one black for each three mules. In Mexico, black teamsters often were sold along with the animals when pack trains changed hands.[21]

Many black slaves (and later free people of color) worked in providing food for the markets and tables of the colonial towns. They were fishermen on the boats that plied the Peruvian coastline; they were bakers and confectioners in the cities. In Peru they worked in *pulperías*, establishments that combined the functions of grocery stores and taverns. Peter Boyd-Bowman found one Mexican reference to a black slave who was an innkeeper in sixteenth-century Puebla.[22]

Even though the majority of the slaves in the New World were unskilled laborers, others learned artisan techniques from the Europeans or brought with them skills they had learned in Africa, such as weaving and iron working. As previously mentioned, it was a decided advantage for a slave to know or learn some skill.

Black slaves were used, along with Amerindians, in the cloth-weaving factories (*obrajes*) that sprang up in Mexico, and they were generally used for the operations that required skill, while the native workers provided the unskilled labor. Such skilled slaves were more highly valued and as a result better treated. Some masters even allowed them to work for others and to save part of what they earned to purchase their freedom. There were clear advantages for the masters as well: skilled slaves were more profitable; they were useful helpers in the artisan shops; and they could be hired out for wages paid to their owners. In the early decades of Peru's conquest, artisans were the second largest group of slaveowners, their numbers surpassed only by the *encomenderos*. When possible, artisans bought previously trained slaves, while others trained their slaves in artisan techniques through apprenticeship. Such skills were immediately useful to both the slaves and their owners, and, with freedom, skilled workers formed the elite of the free black and mulatto population.[23]

Most, but not all, of the artisan pursuits were urban, but there were some rural artisan occupations in which blacks worked. The skilled trades on the sugar plantations have been mentioned already. Slaves also worked on or near the Peruvian vineyards to make pottery and leather containers for wine. Many estates had slave carpenters and masons. Nonetheless, opportunities were restricted in the countryside, and it was in the cities that talented slaves found more extensive outlets for their skills.

In the towns slaves were employed in all aspects of the construction industry. They hewed timber from the forests and stone from the quarries; they worked as brick and tile makers; they were blacksmiths. When the materials were prepared, other slaves used them to construct houses, stores and warehouses, public buildings, churches, monasteries, hospitals, and even fortifications. Still other slaves were tanners and leatherworkers. Some artisan crafts were more difficult for them to enter; these included the lucrative occupations of gold and silver-smithing, tailoring, and dress and hat making. Slaves were surely employed even in these professions, but usually only as helpers, for the European members of the guild hierarchy, jealous of their privileges, did not allow easy access for slaves into the ranks of the masters. In early colonial Mexico, slaves were not permitted to work in silk making or glove manufacture, and their labor was restricted in millinery and printing. Frederick Bowser discovered 121 skilled slaves among the records of slave sales in Peru in the period from 1560 to 1650, and the accompanying list of their occupations gives a good idea of the range of artisanal activities pursued by slaves.[24]

Tailor	16	Carpenter	6
Sawyer	12	Candlemaker	4
Brickmaker	12	Hosier	3
Hatmaker	12	Wheelwright	3
Blacksmith	10	Potter	2
Cobbler	9	Carder	2
Charcoal maker	8	Boilermaker	2
Leatherworker	8		

Twelve other skilled slaves from this group each followed a different occupation. James Lockhart uncovered cases in which Spaniards in Peru assembled special teams of skilled slaves, together with their tools, for sale as a unit.[25]

Thus we can see that slaves were put to a variety of uses in colonial Latin America. The foregoing discussion also helps to dispel the idea that all black slaves were used as unskilled labor in the homes, fields, and mines of their Iberian owners. Nonetheless, that black slaves were used with great frequency as domestic servants will come as no surprise. In the New World, just as in all the other slaveowning societies we have examined, those who could afford slaves purchased them to act as servants, buying as many as the owners' means would permit. Early in the colonial period Amerindians often were used as domestics, but as time passed the majority of the household servants came to be blacks. Cut off from their homelands, they were regarded as more pliant and reliable than the Amerindians, who retained close and therefore potentially threatening ties with their native communities. Many of the black domestic slaves were owned by Spanish women who taught them the necessary skills and supervised their labor, as they served as maids and nurses, cooks and launderers, gardeners and other functionaries. Wealthy and pretentious slaveowners had troops of armed and liveried slaves who escorted their masters and mistresses through the streets with displays of great pomp. Institutional owners as well as private ones employed black slaves. These included the monasteries, convents, and hospitals, where slaves did much of the ordinary work and also served as personal servants for the members of the religious orders. They also served in governmental offices; sometimes they were owned directly by the institution, but more often they were rented from private owners or owned by crown and local officials.[26]

For a picture of a land- and slaveowner of moderate standing, we are fortunate to have accounts of Juan de Castellanos. Born in the Spanish province of Seville, Castellanos was a soldier in his early life, later became a priest, and died in 1607 as the curate of the town of Tunja in present-day Colombia. He owned houses in town and farms in the nearby countryside, along with oxen, horses, and a thousand sheep. He also owned over thirty slaves when he died, and among the provisions of his will we can see precise details concerning them. Four of the slaves were the most favored; they probably were his household servants. Two women, Maria and Francisca, were described as *negras*, most likely African-born, and were given their freedom. Agustín, a *negro criollo*, meaning he had been born in the colonies, was left to the church of Tunja. A *mulata* named Francisca had been lent to relatives of Castellanos; he gave them permission to free her if they wished. Andrés was a slave born in Santo Domingo; he could purchase his freedom for 180 pesos paid to Castellanos's estate. Miguel, a *criollo*, could buy his freedom for 150 pesos. Among the slaves were several complete and incomplete families. One was composed of Pedro Congo, his wife Isabel, and their three sons. A certain Francisco had married Isabel "la Chica," and they lived together with her son. Another named Francisco had been given to Castellanos's nephew. Francisco was not to be sold, and Castellanos authorized his nephew to free the slave by the terms of his will or sooner if he wished. The same nephew received by bequest a slave shepherd and all Castellanos's sheep. The remaining slaves were listed by name but no special provisions were made for them.

Castellanos left money in his will to purchase masses for the souls of the slaves who died on his estate, and he also made provisions for the material concerns of the slaves still living. In his will the priest of Tunja gave his slaves various bequests of clothing and also specified what property they owned in their own right, acquired as gifts or otherwise, so that no questions of ownership would arise. Maria, whom he freed, owned several mares among her master's herd and some washing troughs and jewels. Francisca, the *mulata*, had a mare she inherited from her dead mother; she was to receive either it or its foal.[27]

In his will, Castellanos appeared as a fairly benevolent slaveowner, but it is impossible to tell how typical he was. Many more studies on the individual level are needed before we can be sure of the answers; but, despite the present gaps in the record, many scholars have addressed the question of whether Latin America's slave systems were harsher or milder than the systems in the non-Iberian areas.

During a critical period for the study of slavery—the 1940s through the 1960s—a prominent interpretation postulated slavery in Portuguese America and, by implication, in Spanish America as more benign than that in the English colonies and later in the United States. This view rested in large part on the work of Gilberto Freyre, who in three widely read books published in English between 1946 and 1959 described slavery and race relations in Brazil as relatively mild and benign due to the lack of institutional or social bars to racial mixing, and from this evidence he postulated a truly democratic racial blending in the Portuguese world. American scholars followed his lead and drew sharp distinctions between what they considered milder Latin American slavery and the harsher slavery of North America; they stressed what they considered an easier position of nonwhites in a multiracial society after emancipation. The most influential work was Frank Tannenbaum's *Slave and Citizen*, published in 1947, which argued that royal legislation based on Roman law, the influence of the Catholic church, and the attitudes of the white settlers in Latin America made for a far more benevolent slave system and more egalitarian racial relations than in North America. Tannenbaum's ideas helped set the basis of interpretation for Stanley M. Elkins' *Slavery*, published in 1959, and for Herbert S. Klein's *Slavery in the Americas*, published in 1967.[28]

The pendulum began to fall in the other direction in 1963 when C. R. Boxer published *Race Relations in the Portugese Colonial Empire, 1415–1825*, a work based on Boxer's extensive familiarity with the archival sources, materials which Freyre had mainly neglected. Boxer highlighted the harsh features that could be found in the Portuguese slave system and attacked the idea of Portuguese colonial society as lacking color bars. In 1971 Carl N. Degler, in *Neither Black nor White*, argued that many similar features of slavery were present in both Brazil and North America and that the greatest differences related to the easier acceptance of mulattoes in Brazil. A. J. R. Russell-Wood contributed to the debate in an article in 1978 tracing persistent Portuguese justifications for slavery during the colonial period, and Stuart B. Schwartz has shown that the Brazilian whites held stereotypes of blacks that hauntingly echo those of the antebellum American South.[29]

The recent scholarly debate leads us to question seriously the impression of a relatively benevolent Latin American slave system. It also cautions us to be aware of the complexities of slavery in the Iberian colonies: variations in time, variations in place and ecological niche, and variations in the tasks assigned to slaves. The household slaves of the Portuguese governor-general of Bahia led far different lives from those of the cane cutters in the nearby fields of the *Recôncavo*. The thirty slaves of the curate of Tunja and the slaves in the mines elsewhere in Colombia were all subject to the same laws, but their lives were quite distinct. At the same time that there were harmonious relations, there also were serious tensions. That is clear both from the efforts of the Latin American slaveholders to devise both positive and negative means of social control for the black and mulatto population, and from the efforts of the slaves and freedmen to evade those measures.

As the numbers of slaves in the colonies rose, the Spanish crown, the church, and the local officials promulgated rules designed to assimilate the slaves into colonial society (albeit as subordinates) and to ameliorate their conditions of life and work (so long as their economic usefulness would not be compromised). Slaves were allowed to marry; indeed, it was a necessary corollary of their Christianization. As they were to be baptized, they had to be allowed the sacrament of marriage, which additionally would give them a more settled life and render them more docile. The crown limited the punishments masters could inflict on their slaves and attempted to reserve major punishments for the courts and civil authorities. In spite of the twin pressures of church and state, masters only grudgingly relinquished their power to punish. The government could intervene in cases of abuse, but it did so infrequently. Masters at times disrupted family life by selling married slaves, and cases are few in which the church or government was able to stop the practice.

Christianization and Hispanization went hand in hand. D. M. Davidson identified three aims of this policy:

> it would influence the development of a society where shared religious and cultural values produced a slave regime based on consent; it would provide certain outlets for slave tensions and discontent through religious ritual and social activities; and it would offer slaves spiritual equality in the City of God in return for deference and obedience to their masters in this world.[30]

The first efforts at assimilation would involve baptism, performed if the slave had not been made a Christian before leaving Africa, and language training, informally conducted by masters and other slaves. We can examine other aspects of the policy by looking at marriages and manumissions.

Slave marriages were allowed both in royal and canon law, and both crown and church officials in the colonies supported slaves' rights to marry. From as early as 1524 the Spanish crown had specified that of all slaves shipped to the New World, one-third were to be female. Bowser found that in the records of the slaves sold in Lima from 1560 to 1650, 24.5 percent of *bozales* sold were female. Although the ratio between male and female slaves was lopsided, there were some legally recognized slave marriages. As in so many aspects of the slave experience in the Americas, rural slaves had a more difficult time than those in the cities. Many agricultural establishments had far more male slaves than female, and hence the opportunities for marriage were more restricted. Even in the towns there were sometimes obstacles to slave marriage. Church councils and church leaders consistently supported the propositions that slaves should be permitted to marry, that once married they should not be denied conjugal rights, and that slave families should remain intact. Nevertheless, despite the law and clerical pressure, and despite the fact that stable families would produce slave children owned by the masters, some slaveowners did everything they could, including physical punishment, to prevent their slaves from marrying. Marriage, of course, reduced the flexibility of the masters to sell their workers or move them to different locations. Some owners of married slaves prohibited them from exercising their conjugal rights and sold their children in defiance of the laws. Shrewd slaves, faced with their masters' obstinance, could occasionally get ecclesiastical courts or the Inquisition to intervene on their behalf. Not all masters, of course, discouraged marriage for their slaves; some even encouraged slave marriages and preferred to own married couples.[31]

From the beginning of the colonial period in Latin America, both racial mixing and miscegenation could be observed in the New World, and there are several factors to account for the two phenomena. The first was the unbalanced ratio of women to men among both the European and the African population in the early colonial period. A white male in the New World had the widest choice of marriage and sexual partners. He could choose a white woman, some of whom were living in the American colonies from nearly the beginning, despite the persistent myth that conquest and settlement were all-male occupations. Instead, or perhaps in addition, a European man could choose an Amerindian or black woman as a concubine or wife. Children produced by such unions would be known as *mestizos* in the case of white-Amerindian mixing, or *mulatos* if the parents were white and black.

It was far more difficult for a black slave to secure a sexual partner or a wife of his own race. First of all, the imbalance in the sex ratio in the transatlantic slave trade meant that there were at least three or four times more black males than females in the Americas. The total number of female slaves in the available pool was further reduced by masters taking black women as concubines or wives. Many of the slave women ended up in households in the towns, while in the countryside there were far more men than women. The combined circumstances meant that many black men sought personal alliances with Amerindian women, for anything from short-term liaisons to legal marriage. Blacks could derive advantages from marriage to native women. Early in the colonial period it was possible to make a legal case that the fact of marriage of a slave to a free Amerindian woman would thereby permit him to attain freedom. Even after that loophole was closed, the children of such marriages would be free. The imperial government, in its continual but ineffective attempt to keep the races separate, legislated against black cohabitation with the natives, but it was to no avail. Blacks and Amerindians continued to produce offspring, generally called *pardos* or *zambos*.

After the first generation, the children of parents of different races themselves produced children whose complex racial background was indicated by still other terms in the rich vocabulary of Spanish colonial society, which had as many as forty-six specific designations for such offspring. For example, the children of a black and *mestizo* couple were called *mestizos prietos*. When *pardos* and Amerindians produced offspring, these were called *mulatos lobos*. In addition, sale documents for slaves often used other terms to record variations in skin color: *atezado* (blackened), *prieto* (blackish), *pardo* (dark, dusky), *moreno* (dark brown), *loro* (tawny), *membrillo* (quince), or *color de membrillo corcho* (the color of cooked quince).[32] The terminology in colonial Brazil was similar and

> included the designations of *branco* [white], *pardo* [mulatto], and *preto* [black]. . . . To these should be added less well-defined terms such as *mestiço cabra, crioulo, trigueiro, escuro*, or *moreno*. Sometimes it was felt that a single word was inadequate to describe the degree of blackness or whiteness of an individual and the writer would resort to such phrases as *corado bastamente* (lit: 'fairly coloured'), *de cor fechada* (lit: 'of a closed colour'), *de cor equivoca* (lit: 'of a dubious colour'), *ao parecer branco* (lit: 'white to all appearances'), or to a tribal rather than racial descriptions such as *de cor Fula* (lit: 'of the colour of the Fulah').[33]

Mameluco or *mestiço* designated the child of European and Amerindian parents in colonial Brazil.[34]

Reflecting the influence of Roman law on the medieval and early modern Spanish and Portuguese law codes, it was possible for slaves to attain freedom through manumission, but the two ordinary forms of manumission—by self-purchase or by the master's testament—indicate that freedom was almost always dependent on the master's wishes. If permission were granted, slaves could purchase their own freedom, or others could buy it for them. Monetary payments were not always involved. Exceptional services performed by slaves for their masters or the state could gain them their freedom. Many of the Africans who accompanied Pizarro and Almagro in the conquest of Peru won their freedom for having fought alongside the Spaniards. The legal formalities for manumission were slight; they did not require a court appearance, only that both parties present themselves before a notary to file a document of manumission, known as a *carta de libertad* in the Spanish empire and a *carta de alforria* in the Portuguese. In the case of manumission by testament, the master's executors would be expected to file the *carta* with a notary. In most cases agreeing or refusing to permit slaves to be freed was the master's prerogative, but masters could be forced by the civil authorities to free their slaves, usually when they were convicted of having mistreated them. The state could also reward a slave's signal acts with freedom.[35]

The chances for manumission varied according to time, place, and the personal characteristics of the slave involved. In periods of economic crisis, for example, a temporary surplus of labor could arise, and masters who could not sell their excess slaves might allow them to purchase freedom on relatively easy terms. In general, however, several circumstances made the path to freedom easier for some slaves. Urban slaves were more likely to be freed than rural ones, mulattoes more likely than pure blacks, and women and children more likely than adult men. For Mexico City in 1576–77, Colin Palmer's archival research revealed a total of 435 free Afro-Americans. Of these, 307, or 70.6 percent, were women. Of these free women 87 percent were mulattoes, and of the men 85 percent.[36] Frederick Bowser, analyzing the patterns of manumission in Mexico City from 1580 to 1650, found that 62 percent of the cases dealt with women and children, and only 8 percent of the manumissions involved men in their working prime. For Peruvian slaves in the period 1560–1650, Bowser found a similar pattern: 67 percent of those freed were female, and only 3 percent were males aged 16 to 35 years.[37] In a period when miscegenation was common, many of the manumissions involved slaves who were biologically related to their masters or who were related to those who purchased their freedom for them.

In addition to granting outright freedom, some manumission documents showed that the masters at times insisted that the newly freed slave perform specified services for a determined period as a condition of freedom. Other *cartas de libertad* could be written to indicate that a future schedule of payments was to be met. This was an anticipation of the system of *coartación*, which in the eighteenth and nineteenth centuries allowed slaves to buy their freedom on the installment plan.[38]

Because manumission was frequent and because some blacks were in the New World from the earliest period of European colonization, a distinctive group of free people of color soon developed. Many of them had marketable skills, and they and their children often prospered. Although they were subject to discriminatory legislation at times and to hostility on the part of some whites, they had their own social ties and religious brotherhoods to offer them a feeling of community. Regrettably, the limitations of space do not permit us to examine in detail the free black and mulatto population, one of the most interesting in colonial society.[39]

If the practice of allowing marriages and manumissions could be considered positive means of social control, the negative corollary was the system of punishment. Slavery is by its very definition coercive, and nothing reveals that characteristic more than the physical punishments suffered by the slaves. Whipping and branding were common punishments for malefactors: the former for ordinary transgressions, the latter for more serious ones. Rolando Mellafe has provided an account of the scale of punishments for fugitive slaves.

> Punishments to be meted out to runaways were stipulated [by government officials]. If a slave was absent for four days, he was to receive a total of

fifty lashes. For eight days and a distance of a league (three miles) from the city, the punishment was one hundred lashes and an iron shackle of twelve pounds, on one foot for two months. If the slave fled for a period of less than four months outside the city, but without becoming involved with cimarrones [organized fugitives], he would receive one hundred lashes for the first offense and banishment for the second. If he had joined the cimarrones, another hundred lashes was added. An absence of more than six months and the committing of some offense, whether or not with the cimarrones, was punishable by death.[40]

Some persistent male runaways were castrated, and hanging was the normal mode of capital punishment. Another punishment was *pringar*, also practiced in Andalusia back in Spain, which consisted of the dropping of molten fat or pitch onto the slave's naked flesh. The government physically mutilated certain convicted slaves, and masters could bind their slaves with iron fetters, chains, and stocks.[41]

Fugitive slaves were apparently among the greatest problems that the slave-owners and the public officials had to confront. Bowser studied 502 criminal cases in the period from 1560 to 1650 in Peru and found that the convictions were based on the crimes noted in the accompanying tabulation.[42]

Running away	270
Theft	81
Assault	72
Murder	36
Drunk and disorderly	14
Possession of weapons	10
Resisting arrest	6
Aiding runaways	6
Jailbreak	4
Rape	2
Vandalism	1

The elevated number of convictions of fugitives is a firm indication that the process of assimilation and the attempts at amelioration of the slaves' conditions of life were at best only partially successful. Slaves were still mistreated and slave families disrupted by individual masters, and there was nothing the law could do to ease the harsh conditions in the mines and on the sugar plantations. Despite all the initiatives to create a docile labor force, some slaves would not accept their condition, and slave resistance lasted as long as slavery.

Flight was the most widely practiced method of resistance. If the Spaniards and Portuguese found the Americas a land of opportunity, their slaves discovered more limited opportunities of their own. Within two years of the introduction of the first slaves into the Americas, fugitives were causing problems for colonial officials. True, the black runaway could not hope to regain his homeland, but there were possibilities for asylum in the sparsely settled and poorly policed areas of the Caribbean islands and the mainland. This remained true for centuries, because there were always isolated lands in the backwoods, in the mountains, and in the jungles. Runaways might be taken in by unreduced Indian tribes, and those with talent could find Europeans willing to make use of their talents, regardless of their fugitive status.[43]

In the early seventeenth century, the slave Josef Criollo fled from Lima, reached Mexico, and lived there three years before being apprehended and sold to a new master.[44] Usually fugitives did not get so far away, and most were caught close by the familiar places where they had lived. Flight was often a successful method of obtaining better treatment or a change of owner. Slaves were chronically in short supply, and those who needed them would be willing to take the risk inherent in purchasing or retaining a fugitive in order to ensure labor service. Strict punishments were prescribed for fugitives and those who aided them, but often slaves were not punished as severely as the law allowed. Their masters intervened for them, possibly out of humane feelings and probably from a desire to avoid having their slaves harmed and thus reduced in usefulness.[45]

Masters could reclaim apprehended slaves in return for a payment to those who had caught them. In Mexico during the course of the sixteenth century, the fee for apprehension went up from two pesos to fifty. If the master refused to pay, or if ownership of the slave could not be determined, the slave was assigned for a one-year period to a temporary master, and when the year elapsed he was sold by public officials, who then would compensate the person who had caught him.[46]

Other slaves sought to escape totally from Spanish or Portuguese control. Some banded together to establish settlements and societies in vacant lands of difficult access. Perhaps many succeeded, but we may never know, because most of the documents relate to the runaways who were recaptured and the revolts that failed. We do know that most of the blacks brought from Africa were men, and many of them had been captives in war, sometimes high-ranking ones, if their own statements are to be believed. This was both an advantage and a disadvantage for them. They profited from their military experience but they lacked women, a necessary ingredient in the recipe for founding new, self-sustaining societies. At first they also lacked arms, food, and other supplies. They found it difficult, if not impossible, to maintain themselves without recourse to European or Amerindian settlements, which they plundered for their needs, thus reinforcing their outlaw status. They engaged in two essential types of guerrilla activity, although the aims of each blended imperceptibly into one another. One was attempted revolt to free all slaves and to dislodge and drive out the Europeans; the other, more widespread, was designed to secure an independent state away from European centers.

Black slaves first took part in an uprising when they aided the Amerindians of Española in their revolt against the Spaniards in 1519. Three years later some forty black slaves owned by Diego Columbus (Christopher Columbus's son) rose on their own on the island. After some initial success in their actions against isolated farms, they met determined resistance and eventual defeat when Columbus raised a volunteer force in Santo Domingo, crushed the band, and executed the survivors.[47]

Other insurrections and lesser raids took place throughout the European-controlled areas. Mexico's first slave rebellion was quelled in 1537 when Viceroy Antonio de Mendoza discovered a plot designed to free the slaves in the colony. He promptly arrested the ringleaders, forced their confessions, and executed them. Mendoza's quick action ended the immediate threat, but white colonists never forgot the incident and continued to fear a recurrence. Their fears were justified; two other revolts shook Mexico in the 1540s. In 1548 Mendoza placed a night curfew on blacks in Mexico City, forbade the sale of arms to them, and outlawed public assemblies of three or more blacks. Mendoza's successor as viceroy, Luis de Velasco, continued Mendoza's policies and extended them in 1553 by establishing a militia, the Santa Hermandad, so named because it resembled the fifteenth-century Castilian rural police force, designed to check the activities of the cimarrons, as the runaways were called. These actions failed to stifle the revolts; they continued in Mexico even after the end of our period.[48]

The colonies in Central America, where opportunities for rebellion were certainly present, also experienced widespread slave resistance. Development along the coasts from Honduras to Panama lagged behind that of Mexico, Peru, and the Caribbean islands. There were relatively few Spaniards or colonial settlements in the region, and the rugged terrain and abundant vegetation made the country ideal for clandestine settlements and guerrilla activity. Gold and silver deposits promised wealth for the producers, but chronic labor shortages hindered development. Along the Olancho and Guayape rivers in the 1540s were the most promising deposits, but in 1542 the black slave laborers revolted and drove out the Spaniards for a time. The Central American region got a bad reputation in official Spanish circles, in part because of the constant attacks of cimarrons well into the seventeenth century. It was also deemed too expensive to garrison and pacify, because early economic development was weak. Hence it proved very difficult for settlers in the region to obtain and keep slaves.[49] During the same period, slaves revolted and formed communities in Venezuela.[50]

Peru also experienced persistent threats from cimarrons, who operated mainly in the area of Lima in relatively small bands. The Peruvian environment was not lush enough to support hidden settlements, and relations between blacks and Amerindians were usually hostile; there would be no amalgamation of communities of fugitives there. The cimarron bands raided isolated settlements, looted and kidnapped, and captured pack trains. Nevertheless, they never seriously threatened the colony, and the Peruvian Santa Hermandad, even though rife with corruption and inefficiency, generally held the bandits in check.[51]

The story was different in Mexico and Brazil, where cimarrons developed true communities, called *palenques* by the Spaniards and *ladeiras, mocambos*, and *quilombos* by the Portuguese. These fugitive communities lasted for considerable periods and exacted a great toll in lives and resources before they were finally vanquished. The best known fugitive community in Mexico was never defeated, and its leaders secured an accommodation with the Spanish authorities after troops failed to conquer the fugitives. This was the early seventeenth-century *palenque* of the Yanguicos near Mount Orizaba. The eastern region of the colony of New Spain in Mexico was troubled by cimarrons at the end of the sixteenth century. The activities of the cimarrons were especially challenging because from their settlements they could easily attack the colony's main lifeline, the road from Veracruz to Mexico City. One attempt to pacify the region failed in 1606, and the cimarrons carried out a daring and successful raid on a wagon train in 1609. The same year the viceroy decided to take more stringent action against them and sent a force under Pedro Gonzalo de Herrera to settle the problem. Herrera left Mexico City with 100 Spanish soldiers and marched to Veracruz, where he raised some 250 additional troops before proceeding into cimarron territory. At the same time, the cimarrons continued their raids, and after one attack they took a captured Spaniard to their headquarters. His account is the most complete description of one of the Mexican *palenques*. The captive was brought before the ruler (variously called Ñaga, Ñanga, or Yanga), reportedly an African prince who had fled his owner thirty years before and thereafter assembled a band consisting of eighty adult men with twenty-four black and Indian women and numerous children. The group lived from raiding and farming, moving their village from time to time to avoid detection. They practiced Christianity and their town had a chapel. Yanga governed the settlement, and the warriors, comprising over half the men, were led by an Angolan. Apparently secure in their ability to elude or resist the pacification forces, Yanga released his Spanish captive with instructions to deliver an arrogant letter to Herrera.

Herrera and his men fought some skirmishes in Yanga's territory, but they were unable to engage the main cimarron force. After several exchanges of messages, the two sides reached an accommodation. Yanga agreed to stop the harassment of the colonists, to return the slaves who had escaped most recently, to assist in the capture of fugitive slaves in return for a payment, and to aid the crown against any foreign attack. In return the viceroy promised that long-standing members of Yanga's community would be freed and that the *palenque* would receive a charter as a town under its own government and a Spanish magistrate (*justicia mayor*). Yanga and his descendants would rule the town as its governors. The crown would pay for outfitting a church, and Yanga would permit Franciscan missionaries to live within the town, which received the official name San Lorenzo de los Negros and prospered at least through the seventeenth century.[52] This was an isolated incident, although doubtless other cimarron settlements escaped official knowledge and thus the pages of recorded history. By no means did the pacification of Yanga's group bring an end to cimarron activity in Mexico; that lasted throughout the colonial period.

In Brazil comparable developments were also taking place, but on a far larger scale. The growth of Brazil's sugar economy and the great influx of black slave labor to run it began after 1550. Conditions on the plantations and in the mills were harsh, as we know from earlier discussions. Despite royal and church efforts to alleviate the suffering, there was little that could be done to ease the physical torment that sugar workers had to endure, and many slaves resorted to flight to escape the conditions that the colonial authorities themselves often described as hellish. The successful fugitives often banded together and established communities—*mocambos*—that became at times quite populous and extensive and that were able to withstand the punitive expeditions mounted against them. In the first half of the seventeenth century, the Brazilian authorities tried various methods to control the fugitives. Various local governments licensed bush captains (*capitãos do campo*) and paid them on a commission basis according to the number of slaves they captured and returned. The policy was only partially successful, because the bands of slave catchers were generally not large enough to tackle whole communities and often resorted to capturing any black they encountered, fugitive or not. Attempts to use Amerindians in cooperative ventures against the runaways also fell short of the intended goal. After 1637 any person returning a fugitive could collect the bounty, but the failure of governmental attempts to quell the fugitive slave problem permitted the *mocambos* to survive.[53]

The most impressive of the *mocambos* was Palmares in the province of Pernambuco, a settlement that apparently got started in the early years of the seventeenth century.[54] The Portuguese sent a military expedition against it in 1612 with little success. Dutch expeditions in the 1640s reported that the *mocambo* consisted of several small villages and two larger ones, with a combined population estimated at 11,000. A European account of one of the larger towns in 1645 reported that it was

> half a mile long, its street six feet wide and running along a large swamp, tall trees alongside. . . . There are 220 *casas*, amid them a church, four smithies and a huge *casa de conselho*; all kinds of artifacts are to be seen. . . . (The) king rules . . . with iron justice, without permitting any *feticeiros* among the inhabitants; when some Negroes attempt to flee, he sends *crioulos* after them and once retaken their death is swift and of the kind to instill fear, especially among the Angolan Negroes; the king also has another *casa*, some two miles away, with its own rich fields. . . . We asked the Negroes how many of them live (here) and we

were told some 1,500 inhabitants all told. . . . This is the Palmares *grandes* of which so much is heard in Brazil, with its well-kept lands, all kinds of cereals, beautifully irrigated with streamlets.[55]

By 1677 Palmares was a collection of at least a dozen settlements stretching over sixty leagues. It was ruled by an elected king who governed by a set of laws and regulations probably drawn from several political traditions from the Kongo-Angola region. The Europeans made several attempts to subdue Palmares, in an effort to stop the raids the fugitives conducted and to prevent even more slaves from fleeing, but the blacks were able to hold out until they were defeated and their king killed in 1694. During its existence of nearly a century, the rulers of Palmares were able to use resilient African techniques to integrate and govern an internal population that included people from a wide variety of African ethnic and linguistic groups as well as those who had assimilated European culture. The accomplishment looms larger because it was done while facing outside military pressure bent on the destruction of the community as a whole.[56]

Fascinating and spectacular as these cimarron communities were, they still involved only a fraction of the slaves in the Americas. The majority did not run away and thus remained inside the slave system. Most who escaped slavery did so legally, through manumission.

SLAVERY'S CONTINUING LEGACIES

By 1650 slavery was well established in the New World, and we can see clearly that it had its antecedents in the Old World from Roman times onward and drew also on cultural traditions from the Christian world, Islam, and Africa. In the early history of the European colonies in the Americas we have seen the existence of two varieties of slavery: small-scale slavery, in which a limited number of slaves were recruited to fill the gaps between needs and available supplies of domestic and artisan labor; and large-scale gang slavery, for the sugar plantations and mines. Both types were practiced in the New World during the first one and a half centuries of the existence of European settlement. From the beginning, slaves were brought to the Americas for supplementary artisan labor and domestic labor. Spanish and Portuguese settlers were few; their numbers were tiny in comparison with the vast numbers of the Amerindians. In the early years, the role of blacks as the companions and auxiliaries of the conquerors and settlers was a real one, and many blacks worked closely with the conquerors, occupying an intermediary role between the Europeans and the native population. By the seventeenth century, however, things were changing. There were more European settlers. The indigenous population had declined, and those who remained were collared tightly in a mesh of rules and regulations and other means of control. There was by then a sizable mulatto and *mestizo* population, the descendants of slavers and slaves, conquerors and conquered, who came to fill the intermediary role for which some black slaves had previous been imported. Thereafter, most blacks were imported solely for their labor value, for the work they could do in the plantations, mines, and other large-scale establishments. Plantations and mines had drawn slaves destined for gang labor from the beginning. After the middle of the seventeenth century, however, slavery became ever more closely associated with the needs of the plantations, and the importations of slaves were primarily to fill that demand. New World slavery became more exclusively gang slavery.

The same sort of demand for gang laborers was also found in the English colonies in North America, which, from the late seventeenth century on, increasingly imported slaves. Interesting as it is, we cannot go on to discuss that, nor can we go on to discuss the later development of Latin American slavery. An ample number of outstanding studies exist for that part of the story, and this book will have served its purpose if the background of American slavery is now clearer.

Together, continuity and change make up history. Throughout this book we have stressed continuity and change in the persistence of slavery. By continuing the story of slavery through the first century and a half after the discovery of America, we have been able to show how slavery's Old World roots sent up shoots and new branches in the New World. Slavery in the New World was of the same root stock as that of the Old, but the slaveholders of the Americas neglected certain branches, lopped off others, and encouraged only those they considered particularly useful.

The slave systems of the New World showed great continuity with the Old World patterns. In fact, all the general features that persisted in slavery from Roman times onward were introduced in the Americas. Only those features that had a restricted development, in time or geographic locale, were missing. We do not find eunuchs as a special group in the New World, only as victims of punishment. We do not find slaves as administrators. But we do find virtually everything else. We find slave and free blacks as soldiers: they participated in the early wars of conquest, and in defense against English and Dutch intruders, and later formed special military units in Brazil. We find slaves as sexual partners. We can trace the laws that governed slavery back through the late medieval and early modern European codes to their Roman origins. Obviously, law in the Spanish and Portuguese colonies was based on the prevailing law in the metropolitan areas. This law in turn was based on Roman laws that were rediscovered in the Middle Ages, and revived and incorporated into the colonial codes. We can trace the conditions slaves lived under back through the centuries, their prospects for manumission and the mechanisms of those manumissions, and the problems of assimilation for the slaves who won their freedom—all these had their origins in the slave systems of the Old World.

The use of slaves and their procurement as additional labor for the unfilled needs of a system of basically free labor was the same in the medieval Mediterranean as in the New World. In the New World, unlike the European and Muslim worlds of the Middle Ages, there also existed the system of gang labor for the plantations. Here the precedents were more recent, although their distant origins could be seen in the latifundia of Roman times. However, the Muslims used plantation slavery only in a few restricted places during a few short periods, and the Europeans hardly used it at all before the establishment of the sugar plantations on the islands on the eastern side of the Atlantic, which got their start in the fifteenth century.

Even though Old World slavery ultimately underwent a sea change as it moved to the new environment of the Americas, the similarities are as striking as the differences. New World slavery was a logical outcome of patterns well established in Europe, the Near East, and Africa for over a millennium and a half. Its peculiar development in the eighteenth and nineteenth centuries is due primarily to the emphasis on gang slavery during that period. Regardless of real or perceived differences between the systems of the various European groups in the Americas, slavery there in the two centuries before its final abolition was as harsh a system as the world has known. Slavery of any variety is abhorrent, but the particularly grueling conditions that the eighteenth- and nineteenth-century New World slaves endured came primarily from the significance and dominance of gang slavery. Thus, although the culmination of the slave system in the Americas—from the seventeenth century to the nineteenth—was due to the special social and economic circumstances of the societies of the New World, it is unlikely that that system would have developed as it did without the Old World roots.

NOTES

NOTES

CHAPTER 1. THE PROBLEM OF SLAVERY

1. The most complete analysis of slavery worldwide and across time is Orlando Patterson, *Slavery and Social Death: A Comparative Study* (Cambridge, Mass., and London, 1982). See also James L. Watson, ed., *Asian and African Systems of Slavery* (Berkeley and Los Angeles, 1980), particularly the first two essays: James L. Watson, "Slavery as an Institution, Open and Closed Systems," pp. 1–15; and Jack Goody, "Slavery in Time and Space," pp. 16–42. See also Vicenta Cortés Alonso, "Algunas ideas sobre esclavitud y su investigación," *Bulletin de l'Institut Historique Belge du Rome* 44 (1974): 127–44.

2. Sean O'Callaghan, *The Slave Trade Today* (New York, 1961); Jonathan Derrick, *Africa's Slaves Today* (London, 1975).

3. Moses I. Finley, *Ancient Slavery and Modern Ideology* (New York, 1980), p. 74.

4. Pierre Dockès, *Medieval Slavery and Liberation*, trans. Arthur Goldhammer (Chicago, 1982), pp. 4–5.

5. Patterson, *Slavery and Social Death*, p. 5.

6. Dockès, *Medieval Slavery*, p. 7.

7. Finley, *Ancient Slavery and Modern Ideology*, p. 77; also see Watson, "Slavery as an Institution," pp. 3–9. Patterson uses the phrase "natal alienation" to describe this situation.

8. The corollary is that blacks were not regarded as inferior during classical times. See Frank Snowden, *Blacks in Antiquity: Ethiopians in the Greco-Roman Experience* (Cambridge, Mass., 1970); and Frank Snowden, "Ethiopians in the Greco-Roman World," in *The African Diaspora: Interpretive Essays*, ed. Martin L. Kilson and Robert I. Rotberg (Cambridge, Mass., 1976), pp. 11–36.

9. David Brion Davis, *The Problem of Slavery in Western Culture* (Ithaca, 1966), pp. 31–35. By the same author, *Slavery and Human Progress* (New York, 1984), not available when this volume was prepared.

10. Patterson, *Slavery and Social Death*, p. 340.

11. Thomas Wiedemann, ed., *Greek and Roman Slavery* (Baltimore and London, 1981), selection 126 (*Digest* 32,99, citing Paulus), pp. 122–23.

12. Moses I. Finley, "Slavery," *International Encyclopedia of the Social Sciences* (New York, 1968), 14:310.

13. See Goody, "Slavery in Time and Space," pp. 17–18.

14. Dockès, *Medieval Slavery*, pp. 4–10.

15. H. J. Nieboer, *Slavery as an Industrial System: Ethnological Researches*, 2d ed. (The Hague, 1900).

16. Evsey D. Domar, "The Causes of Slavery or Serfdom: A Hypothesis," *Journal of Economic History* 30/1 (1970): 18–32. The quotation is on p. 21.

17. Ibid.

18. Orlando Patterson, "The Structural Origins of Slavery: A Critique of the Nieboer-Domar Hypothesis from a Comparative Perspective," in *Comparative Perspectives on Slavery in New World Plantation Societies*, ed. Vera D. Rubin and Arthur Tuden, Annals of the New York Academy of Sciences, vol. 292 (New York, 1977), p. 33. Patterson here used ancient Greece as a case study, while suggesting the modes of analysis he would later use in the massive study, *Slavery and Social Death*, published five years later.

19. Goody, "Slavery in Time and Space," pp. 22, 24.

20. Finley, *Ancient Slavery and Modern Ideology*, p. 86.

21. Greek slavery, except for a few remarks about it and comments on Aristotle's views concerning it, is excluded from this book.

22. Finley, *Ancient Slavery and Modern Ideology*, p. 86.

23. Immanuel Wallerstein, *The Modern World-System: Capitalist Agriculture and the Origins of the European World-Economy in the Sixteenth Century* (New York and London, 1974); Eric R. Wolf, *Europe and the People without History* (Berkeley and Los Angeles, 1982).

24. Goody stresses the point, "Slavery in Time and Space," pp. 24, 41. The idea is explicit or implicit in most of the recent studies.

25. Eugene D. Genovese, *The World the Slaveholders Made* (New York, 1969), p. 98.

26. Henri Lévy-Bruhl, "Théorie de l'esclavage," in his *Quelques problèms du très ancien droit romain* (Paris, 1934); reprinted in *Slavery in Classical Antiquity: Views and Controversies*, ed. Moses I. Finley (Cambridge, Eng., and New York, 1960; reprint, 1969), pp. 151–69; particularly pp. 154–56.

27. The outstanding survey of Western intellectual attitudes toward slavery is Davis, *The Problem of Slavery*. For summaries of the views of the earliest group of abolitionists, see Colin A. Palmer, *Slaves of the White God: Blacks in Mexico, 1570–1650* (Cambridge, Mass., and London, 1976), pp. 167–72; and Charles R. Boxer, *Salvador de Sá and the Struggle for Brazil and Angola, 1602–1686* (London, 1952), pp. 236–40.

28. Dockès, *Medieval Slavery*, pp. 210–12.

29. Watson, "Slavery as an Institution," pp. 6–7, 9.

CHAPTER 2. THE RISE AND DECLINE OF
THE ROMAN SLAVE SYSTEM

1. For Greek slavery generally, see the recent interpretive work by Moses I. Finley, *Ancient Slavery and Modern Ideology* (New York, 1980); the comprehensive collection of sources edited and annotated by Thomas Wiedemann, *Greek and Roman Slavery* (Baltimore and London, 1981); and the essay collection edited by Moses I. Finley, *Slavery in Classical Antiquity: Views and Controversies* (Cambridge, Eng., 1960; reprint, 1969). All three contain excellent bibliographical citations. See also Victoria Cuffel, "The Classical Greek Concept of Slavery," *Journal of the History of Ideas* 27 (1966): 323–42; and David Brion Davis, *The Problem of Slavery in Western Culture* (Ithaca, 1966), pp. 66–73. For other ancient Mediterranean societies, see Isaac Mendelsohn, *Slavery in the Ancient Near East* (New York, 1949), and E. E. Urbach, *The Laws Regarding Slavery as a Source for the Social History of the Period of the Second Temple, the Mishnah, and Talmud* (London, 1964; reprint, New York, 1979). There is a flourishing school of Soviet studies on ancient slavery, discussed in Finley, *Ancient Slavery and Modern Ideology*. Most of their studies have appeared only in Russian, but an exception is the translation of Elena M. Shtaerman and M. K. Trofimova, *La shiavitù nell' Italia imperiale, I–III sècolo* (Rome, 1975).

2. Wiedemann, ed., *Greek and Roman Slavery*, selection 1 (*Digest*, 1, 5, from Florentius, *Institutes*, bk. 9), p. 15.

3. Keith Hopkins, *Conquerors and Slaves*, vol. 1 of *Sociological Studies in Roman History*

(New York and Cambridge, Eng., 1978), pp. 1-96; Moses I. Finley, *The Ancient Economy* (Berkeley and Los Angeles, 1973), p. 70. Several ancient writers commented on the process. See Wiedemann, ed., *Greek and Roman Slavery*, selection 141 (Appian), pp. 133-35; selection 142 (Suetonius), p. 135; and selection 143 (Livy), p. 135.

4. Finley, *Ancient Slavery and Modern Ideology*, p. 86.

5. Ibid, pp. 132-37; Pliny (*Letters*, 3, 19) discussed the relative advantages of concentrated versus dispersed holdings; in Wiedemann, ed., *Greek and Roman Slavery*, selection 146, pp. 137-38.

6. The figures are from Hopkins, *Conquerors and Slaves*, pp. 66, 102. P. A. Brunt, *Italian Manpower, 225 B.C.-A.D. 14* (Oxford, 1971), p. 124, cited 3,000,000 slaves in a total population of 7,500,000.

7. William V. Harris, *War and Imperialism in Republican Rome, 327-70 B.C.* (Oxford, 1979), pp. 54-104, confronts the economic motivations for Rome's expansion, partly in opposition to numerous scholars who would deny that the Romans were motivated by economic concerns. See also Hopkins, *Conquerors and Slaves*, passim; Finley, *Ancient Economy*, pp. 71, 73, 80, 156; William L. Westermann, *The Slave Systems of Greek and Roman Antiquity* (Philadelphia, 1955), pp. 63-64, 84. In 209 B.C. Scipio Africanus took Carthago-Novo (modern Cartagena) in Spain from the Carthaginians. He sent back to Rome up to 2,000 skilled slaves to work in the area of military supply. See William L. Westermann, "Industrial Slavery in Roman Italy," *Journal of Economic History* 2 (1942): 149-63, especially p. 152. Livy's list of enslavements from 297-293 B.C. appears in Harris, *War and Imperialism*, p. 59 n. 4.

8. Finley, *Ancient Slavery and Modern Ideology*, pp. 82-83; Finley, *Ancient Economy*, p. 32. On Egypt, see Iza Biezunska-Malowist, *L'esclavage dans l'Egypte gréco-romaine*, 2 vols. (Warsaw, 1974, 1977); id., "Le travail servile dans l'agriculture de l'Egypte romaine," *Ve Congrès d'Histoire Economique* (Leningrad, 1974).

9. Wiedemann, ed., *Greek and Roman Slavery*, selection 229, pp. 199-207; Peter Green, "The First Sicilian Slave War," *Past and Present* 20 (1961): 10-29; W. G. G. Forrest and T. C. W. Stinton, "The First Sicilian Slave War," *Past and Present* 22 (1962): 87-91: Moses I. Finley, *Ancient Sicily to the Arab Conquest*, vol. 1 of *A History of Sicily* (New York, 1968), pp. 139-44; Arnold J. Toynbee, *Hannibal's Legacy: The Hannibalic War's Effects on Roman Life*, 2 vols. (London, 1965), 2:321-27; Joseph Vogt, *Ancient Slavery and the Ideal of Man*, trans. Thomas Wiedemann (Cambridge, Mass., 1975), pp. 26, 39, 53-54. I have followed Wiedemann on the spelling of Eunous's name; other scholars spell it "Eunus." For the wider context, see Gerald P. Verbrugge, "Slave Rebellion or Sicily in Revolt?" *Kokalos* 20 (1974): 46-60; and William L. Westermann, "Slave Maintenance and Slave Revolts," *Classical Philology* 40 (1945): 1-29.

10. Wiedemann, ed., *Greek and Roman Slavery*, selection 230, pp. 207-15; Toynbee, *Hannibal's Legacy*, 2:327-31; Finley, *Ancient Sicily*, pp. 144-46.

11. Wiedemann, ed., *Greek and Roman Slavery*, selections 231-32, pp. 215-22; Finley, *Ancient Sicily*, pp. 146-47; Michael Grant, *Gladiators* (New York, 1968), pp. 14-16, 25; Z. Rubensohn, "Was the Bellum Sparticium a Slave Insurrection?" *Rivista de Filologia* 99 (1971): 290-99; P. A. Brunt, *Social Conflicts in the Roman Republic* (New York, 1971), pp. 114-115; Keith Hopkins, *Death and Renewal*, vol. 2 of *Sociological Studies in Roman History* (Cambridge, Eng., 1983), pp. 1-30.

12. Pierre Dockès, *Medieval Slavery and Liberation*, trans. Thomas Goldhammer (Chicago, 1982), pp. 62-64.

13. Lucius Junius Moderatus Columella, *On Agriculture (Res rustica)*, 3 vols. (vol. 1, ed. and trans. H. Boyd; vols. 2-3, ed. and trans. E. S. Forster and E. H. Hellner) (Loeb Classical Library, Cambridge, Mass., and London, 1941, 1954-55), 1:100-101. On Roman agriculture generally, see K. D. White, *Roman Farming* (Ithaca, 1970). On rural slavery, see the thorough discussion of the ancient sources by William Emerton Heitland, *Agricola: A Study of Agriculture and Rustic Life in the Greco-Roman World from the Point of View of Labour* (Cambridge, Eng., 1920; reprint, 1970).

Heitland's interpretations, however, are now often dated. Richard Duncan-Jones has used Columella's writings to analyze agricultural profitability; see *The Economy of the Roman Empire: Quantitative Studies*, 2d ed. (Cambridge, Eng., 1982), pp. 33-59.

14. Marcus Terentius Varro, *On Agriculture (Res rustica)*, ed. and trans. William Davis Hooper and Harrison Boyd Ash (Loeb Classical Library, Cambridge, Mass., and London, 1934), pp. 224-27. Varro's description of slaves as *instrumenti vocale* recalls Aristotle's phrase: "the slave can be classified as an [animate] tool assisting activity," Wiedemann, ed., *Greek and Roman Slavery*, p. 117.

15. Wiedemann, ed., *Greek and Roman Slavery*, selection 201 (Plutarch, *Cato the Elder*), p. 182.

16. Marcus Porcius Cato, *On Agriculture (De agri cultura)*, ed. and trans. William Davis Hooper and Harrison Boyd Ash (Loeb Classical Library, Cambridge, Mass., and London, 1934), p. 9. Westermann, in *Slave Systems*, p. 76, represents Cato as suggesting that "when [the slaves] fell ill the rations were to be reduced as a measure of economy." That is a misstatement. Cato, in fact, said that rations were to be increased for field workers during the summer, when they expended greater physical effort, and field workers at all times were to receive larger rations than slaves with less demanding work (pp. 70-71).

17. Columella, *On Agriculture*, 1:90-93.

18. J. C. Fitzgibbon, "Ergastula," *Classical News and Views* 20 (1976): 55-59. Many scholars, following Columella, take the *ergastulum* to mean a prison, perhaps underground, to confine the slaves when they were not working. See, for example, Dockès, *Medieval Slavery*, p. 69. Robert Etienne, however, has argued that the *ergastulum* was not a place, but a group of slaves, possibly chained, at hard labor on the latifundia in the early period of Roman expansion. "Recherches sur l'ergastule," *Actes du colloque 1972 sur l'esclavage (Besançon)* (Paris, 1972), pp. 249-66.

19. Varro, *On Agriculture*, pp. 226-29.

20. Columella, *On Agriculture*, 1:94-95. For comments on Roman slave breeding, see Finley, *Ancient Slavery and Modern Ideology*, p. 130, and A. H. M. Jones, "Ancient Empires and the Economy: Rome," *Third International Conference of Economic History, 1965* (published Paris, 1970), pp. 81-104, reprinted in A. H. M. Jones, *The Roman Economy: Studies in Ancient Economic and Administrative History*, ed. P. A. Brunt (London, 1974), pp. 114-39 (p. 128 on slave breeding). Slave breeding in the Americas much later should be considered quite different, because of the masters' deliberate interference in the personal lives of the their slaves.

21. Columella, *On Agriculture*, 1:82-85.

22. Finley, *Ancient Economy*, p. 83; Finley, *Ancient Slavery and Modern Ideology*, pp. 91-92. Hopkins believes that slave prices steadily rose; his view is in contrast to that of many other scholars (*Conquerors and Slaves*, pp. 110, 158-63). For a list of slave prices, see Duncan-Jones, *Economy of the Roman Empire*, pp. 348-50.

23. Westermann, *Slave Systems*, pp. 6, 29, 84, 96; M. L. Gordon, "The Nationality of Slaves under the Early Roman Empire," *Journal of Roman Studies* 14 (1924): 93-111 (reprinted in Finley, ed., *Slavery in Classical Antiquity*, pp. 171-89). On the origins of slaves, W. W. Buckland, *The Roman Law of Slavery: The Conditions of the Slave in Private Law from Augustus to Justinian* (Cambridge, Eng., 1908), pp. 397-436; Ramsey MacMullen, *Roman Social Relations, 50 B.C. to A.D. 284* (New Haven and London, 1974), pp. 13-14. For kidnapping and fraudulent enslaving of free persons, see Brunt, *Social Conflicts*, pp. 116-19. After Constantine, the rescuer could raise an exposed child as free or slave. See Buckland, *Roman Law of Slavery*, p. 608; Wiedemann, ed., *Greek and Roman Slavery*, selections 111-112, 114-115, 119, 121-124; pp. 113-15, 117-20. The Roman commerce in slaves has not been studied often, but preliminary assessments have been provided by Wayne E. Boese, "A Study of the Slave Trade and the Sources of Slaves in the Roman Republic and the Early Roman Empire" (Ph.D. diss. University of Washington, 1973); and William V. Harris, "Towards a Study of the Roman Slave Trade," in *The Seaborne Commerce of Ancient Rome: Studies in Archeology and History*, ed. J. H. D'Arms and E. C. Kopff, vol. 36 of *Memoirs*

of the American Academy of Rome (Rome, 1980). See also the comments of J. P. V. D. Balsdon, *Romans and Aliens* (Chapel Hill, 1979), pp. 78–79.

24. Jones, "Slavery in the Ancient World," p. 11; Henri Lévy-Bruhl, "Théorie de l'esclavage," in his *Quelques problèmes du très ancien droit romain* (Paris, 1934), pp. 15–34 (reprinted in Finley, ed., *Slavery in Classical Antiquity*, pp. 151–69); Wiedemann, ed., *Greek and Roman Slavery*, selection 125, pp. 120–21.

25. For a short, penetrating discussion of the role of war in Roman gang-slavery and the diversity within Roman slavery, see Keith Hopkins, "Slavery in Classical Antiquity," in *Caste and Race: Comparative Approaches*, ed. Anthony de Reuck and Julie Knight (London, 1967), pp. 166–77.

26. A. H. M. Jones, *The Later Roman Empire, 284–602: A Social, Economic and Administrative Survey*, 2 vols. (Norman, Okla., 1964), 2:851. Finley asserted that slaveowners in Rome made up a larger percentage of the free population than in the American South (*Ancient Economy*, p. 79). Wiedemann suggested that one or two slaves was the normal number for an average household, *Greek and Roman Slavery*, pp. 99–100.

27. Jones, *Later Roman Empire*, 2:851–52.

28. Comments on slaves and sex, both heterosexual and homosexual, can be found in most of the recent books cited in this chapter. See also Sarah B. Pomeroy, *Goddesses, Whores, Wives and Slaves: Women in Classical Antiquity* (New York, 1975), pp. 192–93; Beert C. Verstraete, "Slavery and the Social Dynamics of Male Homosexual Relations in Ancient Rome," *Journal of Homosexuality* 5/3 (1980): 227–36.

29. Jones, *Later Roman Empire*, 2:691, 860; R. H. Barrow, *Slavery in the Roman Empire* (London, 1928), pp. 105–16; Westermann, *Slave Systems*, pp. 15, 73, 120; Wiedemann, ed., *Greek and Roman Slavery*, selections 108, 130–33, 137, 192; pp. 111–12, 125–28, 130, 177.

30. Finley, *Ancient Economy*, p. 82.

31. Dockès, *Medieval Slavery*, p. 156.

32. Ibid., pp. 155–56; Moses I. Finley, "Technological Innovation and Economic Progress in the Ancient World," *Economic History Review*, 2d series, 18 (1965): 29–45, especially 43–44. See also Finley, *Ancient Slavery and Modern Ideology*, p. 182 n. 47, citing, among others, H. W. Pleket, "Technology and Society in the Greco-Roman World," *Acta Historiae Neerlandica* 2 (1967): 1–22; and id., "Technology in the Greco-Roman World: A General Report," *Talanta* 5 (1973): 6–47. Westermann, "Industrial Slavery," pp. 156–57; A. H. M. Jones, "Slavery in the Ancient World," in *Slavery in Classical Antiquity*, ed. Finley, pp. 6–7; T. F. Carney, *The Economics of Antiquity: Controls, Gifts and Trade* (Lawrence, Kans., 1973), p. 126. The quotation is from Finley, *Ancient Economy*, p. 82.

33. Vogt, *Ancient Slavery*, pp. 105, 107, 109–11, 114–16, 123–26; Jones, *Later Roman Empire*, 2:997; Hopkins, *Conquerors and Slaves*, pp. 76–79, 123–25.

34. P. R. C. Weaver, *Familia Caesaris: A Social Study of the Emperor's Freedmen and Slaves* (Cambridge, Eng., and New York, 1972), pp. 5–8; Jones, *Later Roman Empire*, 1:435, 2:836; Barrow, *Slavery in the Roman Empire*, p. 149; Wiedemann, ed., *Greek and Roman Slavery*, selection 168, pp. 161–62. On slaves and the aqueducts, see Wiedemann, ed., *Greek and Roman Slavery*, selection 167 (Fontinus, *The Aqueducts of Rome*), pp. 159–61. See also Orlando Patterson's analysis of the *familia Caesaris* in *Slavery and Social Death: A Comparative Study* (Cambridge, Mass., and London, 1982), pp. 300–308.

35. Barrow, *Slavery in the Roman Empire*, pp. 146, 148; Jones, *Later Roman Empire*, 1:365, 2:614, 647; Westermann, *Slave Systems*, p. 102; Finley, *Ancient Economy*, p. 101; Wiedemann, ed., *Greek and Roman Slavery*, selections 58–63, pp. 65–68.

36. Westermann, *Slave Systems*, p. 105; Wiedemann, ed., *Greek and Roman Slavery*, selection 65, pp. 68–69. Special clothing for freedmen was suggested, too, and also rejected, although the felt freedman's cap was frequently mentioned.

37. Wiedemann, ed., *Greek and Roman Slavery*, selection 187, p. 174.

38. Ibid., selection 178, p. 168.

39. Ibid., selections 180, 209; pp. 169–71, 188–89. See also A. N. Sherwin-White, *Racial Prejudice in Imperial Rome* (Cambridge, Eng., 1967), pp. 83–84.

40. Wiedemann, ed., *Greek and Roman Slavery*, selection 190, pp. 175–76. It is hard to understand how Joseph Vogt could state that "Vedius Pollio . . . was allowed to punish his slaves by throwing them into his fishpond with complete impunity . . . ." (*Ancient Slavery*, p. 104).

41. Barrow, *Slavery in the Roman Empire*, p. 152; Westermann, *Slave Systems*, pp. 79, 108.

42. Barrow, *Slavery in the Roman Empire*, pp. 100–103; Buckland, *Roman Law of Slavery*, pp. 187–238; Finley, *Ancient Economy*, p. 64; Hopkins, *Conquerors and Slaves*, pp. 125–26.

43. MacMullen, *Roman Social Relations*, pp. 92–93.

44. John A. Crook, *Law and Life of Rome* (Ithaca, 1967), p. 29.

45. MacMullen, *Roman Social Relations*, p. 115; Westermann, *Slave Systems*, pp. 1. 57, 74–75; Wiedemann, ed., *Greek and Roman Slavery*, selections 52, 54–55; pp. 61–64.

46. Wiedemann, ed., *Greek and Roman Slavery*, selections 67–68, pp. 69–70.

47. On fugitives, see the reference to the Roman state's "carefully defined procedures to ensure the swift recovery of runaways," Wiedemann, ed., *Greek and Roman Slavery*, selection 212 (*Digest*, 11, 4.1, Ulpian), p. 190. On branding, see Paul-Marie Duval, *La vie quotidienne en Gaul pendant la paix romaine, Ier–IIIe siècles après J. C.* (Paris, 1952), pp. 31–33; Wiedemann, ed., *Greek and Roman Slavery*, selection 218, pp. 193–94. On the metal collars, ibid., selections 219–21, p. 194.

48. Balsdon, *Romans and Aliens*, p. 89.

49. For emancipation, see Westermann, *Slave Systems*, pp. 5, 18, 27, 71, 75, 95; Barlow, *Slavery in the Roman Empire*, pp. 173–74, 177–80, 190–92, 195; MacMullen, *Roman Social Relations*, pp. 104–5; Weaver, *Familia Caesaris*, pp. 62–63; Finley, *Ancient Economy*, p. 171; Hopkins,, *Conquerors and Slaves*, pp. 115–31; Wiedemann, ed., *Greek and Roman Slavery*, selections 29–45, pp. 50–56; selection 69, pp. 70–72; selections 203–4, p. 184. On freedmen, see Susan Treggiari, *Roman Freedmen in the Late Republic* (Oxford, 1969); A. M. Duff, *Freedmen in the Early Roman Empire* (Oxford, 1928; reprint, Cambridge, Eng., 1958). On the continuing obligations of freedmen to their former masters, see Wiedemann, ed., *Greek and Roman Slavery*, selections 29–37, 40–45; pp. 53–56; Crook, *Law and Life of Rome*, pp. 51–55.

50. Wiedemann, ed., *Greek and Roman Slavery*, selection 32 (*Digest*, 40, 1), p. 52.

51. Balsdon, *Romans and Aliens*, pp. 87–88.

52. Buckland, *Roman Law of Slavery*, pp. 598–603.

53. The most famous limitations of manumissions were those of Augustus. See Wiedemann, ed., *Greek and Roman Slavery*, selections 6, 71; pp. 29–30, 72–73. See also Balsdon, *Romans and Aliens*, pp. 86–87.

54. Pliny provided a farm, and later a manager for it, to his former nurse. Wiedemann, ed., *Greek and Roman Slavery*, selection 136, pp. 129–30.

55. Petronius, *The Satyricon and the Fragments*, trans. John Sullivan (Harmondsworth, Eng., and Baltimore, 1965). Paul Veyne, "Vie de Trimalcion," *Annales: E. S. C.* 16 (1961): 213–47. On p. 213 Veyne said: "As imaginary as it is, this life merits being taken seriously. We are going to try an experiment: to consider Trimalchio as an actual person and to place his biography among the others available from the period. The *Satyricon* . . . [is] an excellent historical document." Sherwin-White places this work of Petronius in the larger context of aristocratic disdain for freedmen. (*Racial Prejudice in Imperial Rome*, pp. 84–86). See also John H. D'Arms, *Commerce and Social Standing in Ancient Rome* (Cambridge, Mass., 1981), pp. 97–120.

56. Petronius, *Satyricon*, p. 45.

57. Ibid., p. 62.

58. Ibid., p. 63.

59. Ibid., pp. 65–66.

60. Ibid., pp. 68–69.

61. Ibid., p. 86.

62. Ibid., p. 82.

63. Wiedemann, ed., *Greek and Roman Slavery*, selection 49, p. 59.

64. Moses I. Finley, *Aspects of Antiquity: Discoveries and Controversies* (New York, 1968), p. 162.

65. Petronius, *Satyricon*, p. 46.

66. For general discussions, see Dockès, *Medieval Slavery*, pp. 145–49; and Davis, *Problem of Slavery*, pp. 62–90.

67. Examples include "handmaid of the Lord," Luke 1: 38, for *ancilla domini*, slave of the Lord; and "the good and faithful servant," Matthew 25: 21, for slave. Vogt, *Ancient Slavery*, pp. 142–47.

68. Augustine's attitudes have been widely reported. See, for example, Davis, *Problem of Slavery*, pp. 87–88.

69. Wiedemann, ed., *Greek and Roman Slavery*, selection 242 (Augustine, *Commentary on Psalm 99*, 7), pp. 245–46.

70. Charles Verlinden, *L'esclavage dans l'Europe médiévale*, vol. 1: *Péninsule ibérique—France* (Bruges, 1955), 1:37–38; Jones, *Later Roman Empire*, 2:931.

71. Verlinden, *Esclavage*, 1:40–41; Westermann, *Slave Systems*, pp. 154–55; Finley, *Ancient Economy*, p. 101; Wiedemann, ed., *Greek and Roman Slavery*, pp. 50–51.

72. Hopkins, *Conquerors and Slaves*, p. 118. Patterson carried this view a bit further: "manumission, by providing one of the major incentives for slaves, reinforced the master-slave relationship" (*Slavery and Social Death*, p. 341).

73. Hopkins, *Conquerors and Slaves*, p. 118.

74. Wiedemann, ed., *Greek and Roman Slavery*, selection 208, p. 187.

75. For the decline, see Finley, *Ancient Economy*, pp. 84–93; Verlinden, *Esclavage*, 1:27–31; Jones, *Later Roman Empire*, 2:795–97, 801–3, 815; Westermann, *Slave Systems*, pp. 101–2, 120, 140–41. For pre-fifth-century German slavery, see E. A. Thompson, "Slavery in Early Germany," *Hermathena* 89 (1957): 17–29 (reprinted in Finley, ed., *Slavery in Classical Antiquity*, pp. 191–203).

76. A. H. M. Jones, "The Roman Colonate," *Past and Present* 13 (1958): 1–13 (reprinted in Jones, *Roman Economy*, pp. 293–307); Marc Bloch, *Slavery and Serfdom in the Middle Ages*, trans. William R. Beer (Berkeley and Los Angeles, 1975), pp. 1–31; Paul Petit, *Pax Romana*, trans. James Willis (London, 1976), pp. 247–49).

77. Jones, *Later Roman Empire*, 2:796.

78. Here it is appropriate to quote a general statement that fits the situation of the late Roman West perfectly: "When a slave system experienced a major economic slump . . . masters found themselves with capital tied up in assets—their slaves—which generated earnings that were either less than their maintenance costs or much less than what could be earned from other investments. In such situations the best way for masters to liquidate was to encourage the slaves to buy their freedom. When, as was usually the case, this could be done without losing the services of most of the ex-slaves, all the better." Orlando Patterson, *Slavery and Social Death*, pp. 285–86.

79. Finley, *Ancient Economy*, pp. 84–93—the quotation is on p. 93; Finley, *Ancient Slavery and Modern Ideology*, pp. 126–49. See also John Percival, "Seigneurial Aspects of Late Roman Estate Management," *English Historical Review* 84 (1969): 449–73.

80. Anne Hadjinicolaou-Marava, *Recherches sur la vie des esclaves dans le Monde Byzantin* (Athens, 1950), pp. 76–77, 97–100.

81. Ibid., pp. 86–87, 90–91.

82. Ibid., pp. 12–20, 70–71.

83. Rodolphe Guilland, "Les eunuques dans l'Empire Byzantin: Étude de titulature et de prosopografie byzantines," *Études Byzantines* 1 (1943): 197–238; id., "Fonctions et dignites des eunuques," *Études Byzantines* 2 (1944): 185–225. On the subject of eunuchs in the Roman Empire, see Hopkins, *Conquerors and Slaves*, pp. 172–96.

84. *The Digest of Justinian*, trans. Charles H. Munro, 2 vols. (London, 1904–1909); *The Institutes of Justinian*, trans. J. B. Moyle, 5th ed. (Oxford, 1913); *The Civil Law, Including the Twelve Tables, the Institutes of Gaius, the Rules of Ulpian, the Opinions of Paulus, the Enactments of Justinian, and the Constitutions of Leo*, ed. S. P. Scott (Cincinnati, 1932; reprint, New York, 1973).

CHAPTER 3. SLAVERY IN EARLY MEDIEVAL EUROPE

1. The history of the transition from slavery to serfdom in medieval Europe had its classic historian in Marc Bloch. Several of his essays are collected in *Slavery and Serfdom in the Middle Ages*, trans. William R. Beer (Berkeley, Los Angeles, and London, 1975). In those essays, and in his other writings cited in this chapter, Bloch laid out in magisterial detail the progression of changes for France and other parts of Europe. The first essay in the collection, "How and Why Ancient Slavery Came to an End," pp. 1–31, provides an excellent beginning point for this chapter. Bloch was killed by the Germans in 1944 for his activities in the French Resistance, and since then two generations of scholars, following his lead, have introduced a number of detailed changes in Bloch's interpretations. The current dean of the historians of slavery in Europe is the Belgian scholar Charles Verlinden, whose numerous and excellent studies, mainly institutional, are cited throughout the present book. The latest interpretive work is Pierre Dockès, *Medieval Slavery and Liberation*, trans. Arthur Goldhammer (Chicago, 1982). For another classic, see Max Weber, *The Agrarian Sociology of Ancient Civilizations*, trans. R. I. Frank (Atlantic Highlands, N. J., 1976).

2. E. A. Thompson, "Slavery in Early Germany," in *Slavery in Classical Antiquity: Views and Controversies*, ed., Moses I. Finley, (Cambridge, Eng., 1960; reprint, 1969); E. A. Thompson, *The Visigoths in the Time of Ulfila* (Oxford, 1966), pp. 38–41; Alfons Dopsch, *The Economic and Social Foundations of European Civilization* (New York, 1969), p. 45.

3. E. A. Thompson, "Peasant Revolts in Late Roman Gaul and Spain," *Past and Present* 2 (1952): 11–23; J. M. Wallace-Hadrill, *The Long-Haired Kings and Other Studies in Frankish History* (New York, 1962), pp. 27–28.

4. Charles Verlinden, *L'esclavage dans l'Europe médiévale*, vol. 1: *Péninsule ibérique— France* (Bruges, 1955), 1:61–62.

5. Georges Duby, *The Early Growth of the European Economy: Warriors and Peasants from the Seventh to the Twelfth Century*, trans. Howard B. Clarke (Ithaca, 1974), p. 31.

6. Ralph Arnold, *A Social History of England, 55 B.C. to A.D. 1215* (London and Toronto, 1967), pp. 123, 251; P. D. King, *Law and Society in the Visigothic Kingdom* (Cambridge, Eng., 1972), pp. 90, 161–62; Robert Latouche, *The Birth of Western Economy: Economic Aspects of the Dark Ages*, trans. E. M. Wilkinson (New York, 1961), pp. 70–71.

7. Verlinden, *Esclavage*, 1:80, 729–31; Dopsch, *Economic and Social Foundations*, pp. 232–33; Arnold, *Social History of England*, pp. 135, 176; King, *Law and Society*, pp. 131, 196, 198. A commonplace is that the most active slave traders were Jewish. How much this belief is a product of records originally written by Christians and then interpreted by modern Christian historians should be examined. King (*Law and Society*, p. 199 n. 1) tells us that "the actual evidence of Jewish slave-trading in the Visigothic kingdom is slim. . . . "On the dramatic decree of 694 by King Erwig reducing all unconverted Jews in the Visigothic kingdom to slavery, see Roger Collins, *Early Medieval Spain: Unity in Diversity, 400–1000* (News York, 1983), pp. 135–37, 143. Whether the law was enforced is open to question. On slavery and the Frankish conquest of southern Gaul, see Samuel Dill, *Roman Society in Gaul in the Merovingian Age* (London, 1926; reprint, New York, 1966), p. 104.

8. Arnold, *Social History of England*, pp. 176; King, *Law and Society*, pp. 172–74; Duby, *Early Growth*, pp. 42–43.

9. *The Burgundian Code: Book of Constitutions or Law of Gundobad, Additional Enactments*, trans. Katherine Fischer Drew (Philadelphia, 1949; reprint, 1972), pp. 24–25, 41–42, 44.

10. Dill, *Merovingian Age*, p. 48.

11. King, *Law and Society*, pp. 170–71.

12. Marc Bloch, *Feudal Society*, trans. L. A. Manyon, 2 vols. (Chicago, 1964), 2:361–62.

13. King, *Law and Society*, p. 48.

14. Gregory of Tours, *History of the Franks*, ed. and trans. Ernest Brehaut (New York, 1916; reprint, 1973), pp. 106–8.

15. King, *Law and Society*, p. 171. In the Merovingian kingdom, children of unauthorized liaisons between slaves of two masters were divided, two-thirds for the woman's master, one-third for the man's. This could mean that several children were separated physically, or that each child owed the two masters dues in the same ratio. Verlinden, *Esclavage*, 1:692.

16. Dopsch, *Economic and Social Foundations*, pp. 233, 253; King, *Law and Society*, p. 182.

17. Cited in Arnold, *Social History of England*, p. 251.

18. Verlinden, *Esclavage*, 1:94–95, 704; King, *Law and Society*, pp. 164–67.

19. King, *Law and Society*, p. 75; Verlinden, *Esclavage*, 1:92. Bloch, *Feudal Society*, 1:255–56, reports that slaves of the Franks could not serve in the host, although they could be found among the lords' armed retainers.

20. Dockès, *Medieval Slavery*, pp. 148–49.

21. Quoted by Duby, *Early Growth*, p. 42.

22. On the church and slavery, see Verlinden, *Esclavage*, pp. 99–100, 702–5; Dopsch, *Economic and Social Foundations*, pp. 250–51, 267, 272; King, *Law and Society*, p. 151; Latouche, *Birth of Western Economy*, p. 304; Duby, *Early Growth*, pp. 32–33.

23. Dopsch, *Economic and Social Foundations*, p. 233; Arnold, *Social History of England*, pp. 177, 252; Verlinden, *Esclavage*, 1:95; King, *Law and Society*, pp. 179–81; Bloch, *Feudal Society*, 1:258. The freeing at the crossroads was reminiscent of the Roman lares cult, "which was closely associated with crossroads and intersections," and in which "the Roman freedmen played a disproportionate role." Orlando Patterson, *Slavery and Social Death: A Comparative Study* (Cambridge, Mass., and London, 1982), p. 215.

24. King, *Law and Society*, pp. 160–61; Verlinden, *Esclavage*, 1:85; Bloch, *Feudal Society*, 1:259.

25. King, *Law and Society*, pp. 160–62, 164, 169–70; Verlinden, *Esclavage*, 1:80–81, 83, 85; Dopsch, *Economic and Social Foundations*, p. 235.

26. King, *Law and Society*, pp. 162–63; Verlinden, *Esclavage*, 1:81, 678–79. Bloch (*Feudal Society*, 2:338) reported that "some of these found their way into the ranks of the early vassals."

27. Duby, *Early Growth*, p. 40.

28. Ibid., p. 32; Latouche, *Birth of Western Economy*, pp. 68–70.

29. Guy Fourquin, *Le paysan d'Occident au Moyen Age* (Paris, 1972), p. 40; Duby, *Early Growth*, pp. 38–40, 71; Latouche, *Birth of Western Economy*, pp. 71–72.

30. Latouche, *Birth of Western Economy*, pp. 68–69. The best treatment is that of Pierre Dockès, *Medieval Slavery*, pp. 138–44, in which he criticizes the views of previous scholars.

31. From the Paderborn Capitulary, A.D. 785, in H. R. Loyn and John Percival, eds., *The Reign of Charlemagne: Documents on Carolingian Government and Administration* (London, 1975), p. 52.

32. From the Capitulary of Aix, A.D. 802–3, ibid., p. 83.

33. Synod of Frankfurt, A.D. 794, ibid., p. 60; Double Capitulary of Thionville, A.D. 805, ibid., p. 87.

34. Guy Fourquin, *Lordship and Feudalism in the Middle Ages*, trans. Iris and A. L. Lytton Sells (New York, 1976), pp. 42–45; Fourquin, *Paysan d'Occident*, pp. 69–72; Duby, *Early Growth*, pp. 85–87; Latouche, *Birth of Western Economy*, pp. 182, 199.

35. Fourquin, *Lordship and Feudalism*, p. 45. For a sound, short summary of peasant life under Charlemagne, see Pierre Riché, *Daily Life in the World of Charlemagne*, trans. Jo Ann McNamara (Philadelphia, 1978), pp. 101–11.

36. B. H. Slicher van Bath, *The Agrarian History of Western Europe, 500–1850* (London, 1963), p. 46.

37. Fourquin, *Le paysan d'Occident*, p. 50.

38. Latouche, *Birth of Western Economy*, p. 39.

39. Slicher van Bath, *Agrarian History*, pp. 43–47; Georges Duby, *Rural Economy and Country Life in the Medieval West*, trans. Cynthia Postan (Columbia, S.C., 1968), pp. 37–39; Dopsch, *Economic and Social Foundations*, pp. 234–35; Verlinden, *Esclavage*, 1:83.

40. Slicher van Bath, *Agrarian History*, pp. 70–71; Latouche, *Birth of Western Economy*, p. 271; March Bloch, *Land and Work in Medieval Europe: Selected Papers*, trans. J. E. Anderson (New York, 1969), pp. 169–85; Lynn White, Jr., *Medieval Technology and Social Change* (Oxford, 1962); Albert C. Leighton, *Transport and Communication in Early Medieval Europe, A.D. 500–1100* (Newton Abbot, Eng., 1972).

41. Gino Luzzatto, *An Economic History of Italy from the Fall of the Roman Empire to the Sixteenth Century*, trans. Philip Jones (London, 1961; reprint, 1968), p. 30; Dopsch, *Economic and Social Foundations*, pp. 234–35; Duby, *Rural Economy*, p. 154.

42. Duby, *Early Growth*, pp. 168, 172; Fourquin, *Lordship and Feudalism*, pp. 173–74; Charles Verlinden, "L'origin de Sclavus-Esclave," *Bulletin Ducagne: Archivum Latinitatis Medii Aevi* 17 (1942): 37–128.

43. Bloch, *Feudal Society*, 1:262. For the change generally, ibid., 1:257–64. Bloch, *Land and Work*, pp. 177–78; Luzzatto, *Economic History of Italy*, pp. 42–43.

44. Marc Bloch, *French Rural History: An Essay on Its Basic Characteristics*, trans. Janet Sondheimer (Berkeley and Los Angeles, 1966), pp. 77–83, 86–89; Bloch, *Feudal Society*, 1:256, 260, 263; Bloch, *Land and Work*, pp. 136–68; Duby, *Rural Economy*, pp. 218–19; Slicher van Bath, *Agrarian History*, pp. 49–50; Verlinden, *Esclavage*, 1:733; Fourquin, *Lordship and Feudalism*, pp. 174–77. See Dockès: "The war of the mills itself makes clear where the interest of the peasant as against that of the masters lay: the smashing of the hand mill took eight centuries! No historian denies that this war was waged, and yet in the end only Bloch drew the unavoidable conclusion: technological progress was the fruit of harsh coercion by the lords. Perhaps the image of this war that sticks most firmly in the mind is that of the abbot who paved the hall of his monastery with confiscated mill-stones." (*Medieval Slavery*, pp. 180–81.)

45. Bloch, *French Rural History*, pp. 91–93; Dockès, *Medieval Slavery*, p. 183.

46. Bloch, *Feudal Society*, 1:265.

47. Georges Duby, "Medieval Agriculture, 500–1500," in *The Fontana Economic History of Europe*, ed. Carlo M. Cipolla, vol. 1 (London, 1972), pp. 184–86; Duby, *Rural Economy*, p. 221; Fourquin, *Lordship and Feudalism*, p. 177.

48. Peter F. Foote and David M. Wilson, *The Viking Achievement: A Survey of the Society and Culture of Early Medieval Scandinavia* (New York and Washington, 1970), pp. 65–78; Joan Dist Lind, "The Ending of Slavery in Sweden: Social Structure and Decision Making," *Scandinavian Studies* 50 (1978): 57–71.

49. Henry R. Loyn, *Anglo-Saxon England and the Norman Conquest* (New York, 1963), pp. 85–88, 350–52; R. H. Bautier, *The Economic Development of Medieval Europe*, trans. Heather Karolyi (London, 1971), p. 81; Austin Lane Poole, *From Domesday Book to Magna Carta, 1087–1216*, 2d ed. (Oxford, 1964), pp. 40–41; Frank M. Stenton, *Anglo-Saxon England*, vol. 2 of *The Oxford History of England*, 3d ed. (Oxford, 1971), pp. 314, 476–77, 479–80, 515; Arnold, *Social History of England*, p. 308; Duby, *Rural Economy*, pp. 193–94; Bloch, *Feudal Society*, 1:270–71; Forquin, *Lordship and Feudalism*, p. 189; Latouche, *Birth of Western Economy*, p. 282.

50. Joseph F. O'Callaghan, *A History of Medieval Spain* (Ithaca and London, 1975), pp. 165–66; see Luis García de Valdeavellano, "Las instituciones feudales de España," appendix to the Spanish translation of F. L. Ganshof, *El Feudalismo* (Barcelona, 1963), pp. 229–305; id., *Curso de historia de las instituciones españolas*, 2d ed. (Madrid, 1970), pp. 245–56.

51. Luzzatto, *Economic History of Italy*, pp. 44, 57, 93; Duby, *Early Growth*, p. 148.

52. Verlinden, *Esclavage*, 1:66, 672, 677; *Laws of the Alamans and Bavarians*, trans. Theodore John Rivers (Philadelphia, 1977), p. 79.

53. A. R. Lewis, *Naval Power and Trade in the Mediterranean, A.D. 500–1100* (Princeton,

1951), pp. 13, 50; Dopsch, *Economic and Social Foundations*, pp. 232-33; Verlinden, *Esclavage*, 1:66-72, 670-71, 676-77; Bautier, *Economic Development*, 24, 32.

54. Duby, *Early Growth*, pp. 103-4.

55. Verlinden, *Esclavage*, 1:221-23; Lewis, *Naval Power and Trade*, pp. 45, 48; Maurice Lombard, *The Golden Age of Islam*, trans. Joan Spencer (Amsterdam, 1975), p. 233.

56. Bloch, *Feudal Society*, 1:66; Lewis, *Naval Power and Trade*, p. 180; Bautier, *Economic Development*, p. 27; Verlinden, *Esclavage*, 1:706.

57. Verlinden, *Esclavage*, 1:216-18, 706-11, 718; Renée Doehardt, *Le haut Moyen Age occidental: Économies et sociétés* (Paris, 1971), p. 290; Riché, *Daily Life*, pp. 116-17; Bloch, *Feudal Society*, 1:66; Bautier, *Economic Development*, p. 40; Duby, *Early Growth*, p. 108; Latouche, *Birth of Western Economy*, pp. 162-63.

58. Doehardt, *Haut Moyen Age*, pp. 290-91; Bautier, *Economic Development*, p. 107; Verlinden, *Esclavage*, 1:218-20, 731-32. But see Bloch, *Feudal Society*, 1:5, on Fraxinetum.

59. Duby, *Early Growth*, pp. 144-45, 153.

60. Lewis, *Naval Power and Trade*, p. 116.

61. Loyn and Percival, eds., *Reign of Charlemagne*, p. 129.

62. Luzzatto, *Economic History of Italy*, pp. 35, 51; Lewis, *Naval Power and Trade*, 178.

63. Luzzatto, *Economic History of Italy*, p. 53; Christopher Brooke, *Europe in the Central Middle Ages, 962-1154* (New York, 1964), p. 81; Frederic C. Lane, *Venice: A Maritime Republic* (Baltimore and London, 1973), pp. 7-8, 26; Lewis, *Naval Power and Trade*, pp. 219, 223.

64. Brooke, *Central Middle Ages*, pp. 79-81, 215; Bloch, *Land and Work*, p. 203; Lombard, *Golden Age of Islam*, pp. 233; Duby, *Early Growth*, pp. 129-30.

65. Lombard, *Golden Age of Islam*, pp. 44, 196-98; E. Ashtor, *A Social and Economic History of the Near East in the Middle Ages* (Berkeley and Los Angeles, 1976), pp. 106-107; Stuve Bolin, "Mohammed, Charlemagne and Ruric," *Scandinavian Economic History Review* 1 (1953): 5-39.

66. Bautier, *Economic Development*, p. 96; see Duby, *Early Growth*, pp. 141-42, on Spanish Christians shipping Muslim slaves to France.

CHAPTER 4. SLAVERY IN THE WORLD OF ISLAM

1. Moses I. Finley, *The Ancient Economy* (Berkeley and Los Angeles, 1973), p. 71.

2. "Slavery and concubinage with slave women were taken for granted" among the Arabs before the rise of Islam. Joseph Schacht, *An Introduction to Islamic Law* (Oxford, 1964), p. 7.

3. Maurice Lombard, *The Golden Age of Islam*, trans. Joan Spencer, (Amsterdam, 1975), p. 167.

4. On the persistence of Islamic slavery into this century, see Sean O'Callaghan, *The Slave Trade Today* (New York, 1961); and the more recent book by Jonathan Derrick, *Africa's Slaves Today* (London, 1975).

5. Reinhart Dozy, *Spanish Islam: A History of the Moslems in Spain*, trans. Francis Griffin Stokes (London, 1913; reprint, 1972), p. 236; Charles Verlinden, *L'esclavage dans l'Europe médiévale*, vol. 1: *Péninsule ibérique—France* (Bruges, 1955), 1:181-83, 188-90.

6. Verlinden, *Esclavage*, 1:211-14, 216-21, 225.

7. Ibid., 1:185-87, 192-96, 202-5, 207, 237-38; Dozy, *Spanish Islam*, pp. 429-30.

8. Verlinden, *Esclavage*, 1:209, 237. 239.

9. Charles Emmanuel Dufourcq, *La Espagne catalane et le Maghrib aux XIIIe et XIVe siècles* (Paris, 1966), pp. 74-76.

10. Reuben Levy, *The Social Structure of Islam* (2d ed. of *The Sociology of Islam*) (Cambridge, Eng., 1965), pp. 75-76; R. Brunschvig, "Abd," in *Encyclopedia of Islam*, 2d ed. (Leiden, 1960), 1:24-40; Schacht, *Introduction to Islamic Law*, p. 127.

11. Quoted in Levy, *Social Structure of Islam*, p. 75.

12. Tacitus, *On Britain and Germany* (*Agricola* and *Germania*), trans. Harold Mattingly (Baltimore, 1948; reprint, 1964), p. 120.

13. Lombard, *Golden Age of Islam*, p. 198. Verlinden (*Esclavage*, 1:214) says that these figures refer only to European slaves in Córdoba!

14. Lombard, *Golden Age of Islam*, pp. 195, 201, 233; Verlinden, *Esclavage*, 1:221; S. D. Goitein, *A Mediterranean Society: The Jewish Communities of the Arab World as Portrayed in the Documents of the Cairo Geniza*, 3 vols. (Berkeley and Los Angeles, 1967-78), 1:137-38; A. R. Lewis, *Naval Power and Trade in the Mediterranean, A.D. 500-1100* (Princeton, 1951), pp. 45, 48; Robert Mantran, *L'expansion musulmane (VIIe-XIe siècles)* (Paris, 1969), especially p. 143.

15. A. Mez, *Die Renaissance des Islams* (Heidelberg, 1922), p. 156; Lombard, *Golden Age of Islam*, pp. 199-200.

16. "That your right hand owns" was a euphemism for slaves. *Koran*, sura 4, sec. 40, in *The Koran Interpreted*, trans. Arthur J. Arberry, 2 vols. in 1 (New York, 1955), 1:106.

17. Quoted in Levy, *Social Structure of Islam*, p. 221.

18. N. J. Coulson, *A History of Islamic Law*, Islamic Surveys no. 2 (Edinburgh, 1964), pp. 43-45, 50; Levy, *Social Structure of Islam*, pp. 77-79; Maxime Rodison, "Histoire économique des classes sociales dans le monde musulmane," in *Studies in the Economic History of the Middle East*, ed. M. A. Cook (New York and London, 1970), pp. 139-43.

19. Goitein, *Mediterranean Society*, 1:345.

20. *Koran*, Arberry trans., sura 24, sec. 30, 2:50.

21. Lombard, *Golden Age of Islam*, p. 18; S. D. Goitein, "Slaves and Slavegirls in the Cairo Geniza Records," *Arabica* 9 (1962): 1-20.

22. Levy, *Social Strucure of Islam*, p. 77; Goitein, *Mediterranean Society*, 1:94, 135, 143, 145. In the Abbasid period, slave girls were often trained to play chess. Muhammad Manazir Ahsan, *Social Life under the Abbasids, 170-289 A.H.—786-902 A.D.* (London and New York, 1979), p. 215.

23. Goitein, *Mediterranean Society*, 1:78, 133-34, 164.

24. Ibid., 1:139, 143-44, 2:257; Marshall G. S. Hodgson, *The Venture of Islam: Conscience and History in a World Civilization*, 3 vols. (Chicago and London, 1974), 2:127; Mez. *Renaissance des Islams*, pp. 161-62.

25. Evariste Lévi-Provençal, *Histoire de l'Espagne musulmane*, 3 vols. (Paris, 1950), 3:178-79, 209, 314-17.

26. Levy, *Social Structure of Islam*, pp. 64, 79-80, 111; Schacht, *Introduction to Islamic Law*, pp. 127, 166.

27. *Koran*, Arberry trans., sura 4, sec. 25, 1:104.

28. Gustav E. von Grunebaum, *Classical Islam: A History, 600-1258*, trans. Katherine Watson (Chicago, 1970), p. 80.

29. Hodgson, *Venture of Islam*, 2:143-44; Goitein, *Mediterranean Society*, 2:349.

30. Goitein, *Mediterranean Society*, 2:349.

31. Ibid., 1:132; Levy, *Social Structure of Islam*, p., 77; Lombard, *Golden Age of Islam*, pp. 197, 200.

32. The quotation from Jahiz is in Verlinden, *Esclavage*, 1:213.

33. *Koran*, Arberry trans., sura 24, sec. 30, 2:50.

34. Levy, *Social Structure of Islam*, p. 80. A famous case in Islamic jurisprudence was "the case of the six slaves," concerning the freeing of slaves by their master's will. Ali ibn-Uthman, Medina's governor, had the slaves draw lots and permitted the freeing of only two, stating that a person could dispose of only one-third of his property by will. There is no indication that this was more than an isolated incident. Coulson, *Islamic Law*, p. 65.

35. Levy, *Social Structure of Islam*, p. 81; S. D. Goitein, *Studies in Islamic History and Institutions* (Leiden, 1966), pp. 179-80; Paul G. Fomand, "The Relations of the Slave and the Client to the Master or Patron in Medieval Islam," *International Journal of Middle Eastern Studies* 2 (1971): 59-66. F. E. Peters suggested that clientage was not an automatic benefit for the newly enfranchised. Rather, it was highly desirable and eargerly sought; without it, the freed slave's position was precar-

ious. See Peters, *Allah's Commonwealth: A History of the Near East, 600-1100 A.D.* (New York, 1973), p. 47.

36. Goitein, *Studies*, p. 197 n. 3.

37. For comments on slave domestics, see Ahsan, *Social Life under the Abbasids*, pp. 155, 168.

38. E. Ashtor, *A Social and Economic History of the Near East in the Middle Ages* (Berkeley and Los Angeles, 1976), pp. 38, 66-67, 150; von Grunebaum, *Classical Islam*, p. 101. Beginning in the tenth century, the conditions of peasants approached that of the medieval European serfs. Ashtor, *Social and Economic History of the Near East*, pp. 182-83.

39. Ashtor, *Social and Economic History of the Near East*, p. 166; Graham W. Irwin, ed., *Africans Abroad: A Documentary Survey of the Black Diaspora in Asia, Latin America, and the Caribbean during the Age of Slavery* (New York, 1977), pp. 106-7; Mohamed Talbi, "Law and Economy in Ifriqiya (Tunisia) in the Third Islamic Century: Agriculture and the Role of Slaves in the Country's Economy," in *The Islamic Middle East, 700-1900: Studies in Economic and Social History*, ed. A. L. Udovitch (Princeton, 1981), pp. 209-49. I am grateful to Michael Morony of UCLA for giving me an advance copy of Talbi's manuscript in French.

40. Alexandre Popovic, *La révolte des esclaves en Iraq au IIe/IXe siècle* (Paris, 1976);Ashtor, *Social and Economic History of the Near East*, pp. 115-21. It must be noted that a recent historian of Islam, M. A. Shaban, emphatically denied that the Zanj were slaves. "It was not a slave revolt. It was a *zanj*, i.e. a Negro revolt." *Islamic History: A New Interpretation*, 2 vols. (Cambridge, Eng., 1971, 1976), 2:101. Shaban asserted that the most famous historian of the revolt, Theodore Nöldeke, mistakenly labeled it as a slave revolt, and that later historians have followed Nöldeke's interpretation without reexamining it. See Theodore Nöldeke, "A Servile War in the East," in *Sketches from Eastern History*, trans. John Sutherland Black (London, 1892; reprint, Beirut, 1963), pp. 146-75; also reprinted in Irwin, ed., *Africans Abroad*, pp. 78-99. The question remains unresolved; all other authorities that I have consulted call the Zanj slaves, and Shaban himself in his first volume implied that it was a slave revolt (1:106).

41. Ashtor, *Social and Economic History of the Near East*, pp. 121-31.

42. "The fact must be emphasized that the conditions of life of the Zanj slaves were absolutely exceptional for medieval Muslim society." Popovic, *Révolte des esclaves*, p. 65.

43. David Ayalon, *L'esclavage du Mamelouk* (Jerusalem, 1951); *Studies on the Mamluks of Egypt (1250-1517)* (London, 1977); and *The Mamluk Military Society* (London, 1979). See also Patricia Crone, *Slaves on Horses: The Evolution of the Islamic Polity* (Cambridge, Eng., 1980); Daniel Pipes, *Slave Soldiers and Islam: The Genesis of a Military System* (New Haven, 1981); Jere L. Bacharach, "African Military Slaves in the Medieval Middle East: The Cases of Iraq (869-955) and Egypt (868-1171)," *International Journal of Middle East Studies* 13/4 (1981): 471-95. See also the comments of Orlando Patterson, *Slavery and Social Death: A Comparative Study* (Cambridge, Mass., and London, 1982), pp. 308-14.

44. Verlinden, *Esclavage*, 1:213-15; William Montgomery Watt, *A History of Islamic Spain* (Edinburgh, 1966), pp. 58, 85-86.

45. Edmund O. von Lippmann, *Geschichte des Zuckers, seiner Darstellung und Verwendung* (Leipzig, 1890); Noël Deerr, *The History of Sugar*, 2 vols. (London, 1949-50); Wallace K. Aykroyd, *The Story of Sugar* (New York, 1967). The latter book was published in London in 1967 as *Sweet Malefactor: Sugar, Slavery, and Human Society*.

46. Lippmann, *Geschichte des Zuckers*, pp. 92-105. For an overview of sugar's labor requirements, see J. H. Galloway, "The Mediterranean Sugar Industry," *Geographical Review* 67/2 (1977): 177-94.

47. Wilhelm von Heyd, *Histoire du commerce du Levant au Moyen-Age*, trans. Furey Reynaud, 2 vols. (Leipzig, 1885-86; reprint, Amsterdam, 1967), 2:680-82. On the later history of slaves in the region, see Ashtor, *Social and Economic History of the Near East*, pp., 115-21.

48. Heyd, *Commerce du Levant*, 2:685; Lombard, *Golden Age of Islam*, p. 167; Ashtor, *Social and Economic History of the Near East*, p. 62; Deerr, *History of Sugar*, 1:86-87. For Morocco,

see Paul Berthier, *Les anciennes sucreries du Maroc et leurs réseaux hydraliques: Étude archéologique et d'histoire économique, un episode de l'histoire de la canne à sucre* (Rabat, 1966). For a summary of sugar's spread, see Sidney M. Greenfield, "Plantations, Sugar Cane and Slavery," *Historical Reflections/Réflexions Historiques* 6/1 (1979): 85–119.

49. Ashtor, *Social and Economic History of the Near East*, pp. 157, 199, 245; Saleh Hamarneh, "Sugarcane Cultivation and Refining under the Arab Muslims during the Middle Ages," *Annals of the Department of Antiquities, Hashemite Kingdom of Jordan* 22 (1977–78): 12–19. See also Andrew M. Watson, "The Arab Agricultural Revolution and Its Diffusion, 700–1000," *Journal of Economic History* 34 (1974): 8–35. Sugar may also have been cultivated in Turkey; see Claude Cahen, *Pre-Ottoman Turkey* (London, 1968), p. 158.

50. Ashtor, *Social and Economic History of the Near East*, pp. 306–7, 319; Goitein, *Mediterranean Society*, 1:252, 264. For references to sugar by Jewish traders, see S. D. Goitein, *Letters of Medieval Jewish Traders* (Princeton, 1973), pp. 18, 26, 98, 158, 191, 195, 238.

51. Bernard Lewis, *Race and Color in Islam* (New York, 1971). See also his later, shorter, "The African Diaspora and the Civilization of Islam," in *The African Diaspora: Interpretive Essays*, ed. Martin L. Kilson and Robert I. Rotberg (Cambridge, Mass., and London, 1976), pp. 37–56. See also J. O. Hunwick, "Black Africans in the Islamic World: An Understudied Dimension of the Black Diaspora," *Tarikh* 5 (1978): 20–40.

52. Raymond Mauny, *Les siècles obscurs de l'Afrique noire: Histoire et archéologie* (Paris, 1971), pp. 141–42; Nehemia Levtzion, *Ancient Ghana and Mali* (London, 1973), p. 126.

53. Levtzion, *Ancient Ghana and Mali*, pp. 124–52, has an excellent discussion of the trade. The most comprehensive account of the trans-Saharan trade, although it deals with a later period and relies heavily on British sources, is Abu Boahen, *Britain, the Sahara, and the Sudan, 1788–1861* (Oxford, 1964). For the pre-Islamic evidence, see R. C. C. Law, "The Garamantes and Transsaharan Enterprise in Classical Times," *Journal of African History* 8 (1967): 181–200; and E. W. Bovill, *The Golden Trade of the Moors*, 2d ed. (London, 1970), pp. 31, 36, 41–42. See also Timothy F. Garrard, "Myth and Metrology: The Early Trans-Saharan Gold Trade," *Journal of African History* 23 (1982): 443–61; John T. Swanson, "The Myth of Trans-Saharan Trade during the Roman Era," *International Journal of African Historical Studies* 8/4 (1975): 582–600. The best quantitative survey of the Saharan slave trade is Ralph A. Austen's "The Trans-Saharan Slave Trade: A Tentative Census," in *The Uncommon Market: Essays in the Economic History of the Atlantic Slave Trade*, ed. Henry A. Gemery and Jan S. Hogendorn (New York, 1979), pp. 23–76. See also Raymond Mauny, "Les deux Afriques," in *Les grandes voies maritimes dans le monde, XVe–XIXe siècles* ed. Michel Mollat (Colloque international d'histoire maritime, 7th, Vienna, 1965) (Paris, 1965), pp. 179–83. Two particular components of the trade are covered by Michael Brett, "Ifriqiya as a Market for Saharan Trade from the Tenth to the Twelfth Century A.D.," *Journal of African History* 10 (1969): 347–64; and B. G. Martin, "Kanem, Bornu, and the Fazzan: Notes on the Political History of a Trade Route," *Journal of African History* 10 (1969): 15–27.

54. J. C. Anene, "Liaison and Competition between Land and Sea Routes in International Trade from the Fifteenth Century: The Central Sudan and North Africa," in, *Grandes voies maritimes*, ed. Mollat, pp. 191–99; Anthony G. Hopkins, *An Economic History of West Africa* (New York, 1973), p. 85.

55. Hopkins, *Economic History of West Africa*, p. 86.

56. Nehemia Levtzion, "The Early States of the Western Sudan to 1500," in *History of West Africa*, ed. J. F. A. Ajayi and Michael Crowder, 2d ed., 2 vols. (London, 1976), 1:143.

57. Anene, "Central Sudan and North Africa," p. 194; H. J. Fisher, "The Eastern Maghrib and the Central Sudan," in *The Cambridge History of Africa*, ed. Roland Oliver, vol. 3 (Cambridge, Eng., 1977), pp. 276–78.

58. Ibn-Battuta, *Travels in Asia and Africa*, trans. and ed. H. A. R. Gibb (New York, 1927; London, 1929; reprint, New York, 1969), pp. 317–19; Claude Meillassoux, "L'itinéraire d'Ibn Battuta, de Walata à Malli," *Journal of African History* 13 (1972): 389–95.

59. S. Daniel Neumark, "Trans-Sahara Trade in the Middle Ages," in *An Economic History*

of Tropical Africa, ed. Z. A. Konczacki and J. M. Konczacki, 2 vols. (London, 1977), 1:129-30; Levtzion, "Early States," pp. 142, 144; Levtzion, *Ancient Ghana and Mali*, p. 124; Hopkins, *Economic History of West Africa*, pp. 47-48; Ivan Hrbek, "Egypt, Nubia, and the Eastern Sudan," in *Cambridge History of Africa*, 3:83, 88-90.

60. Mauny, "Les deux Afriques," p. 178.

61. Hrbek, "Egypt, Nubia," pp. 71-72, 88-90; Nehemia Levtzion, "The Western Maghrib and the Sudan," in *Cambridge History of Africa*, 3:376.

62. Levtzion, *Ancient Ghana and Mali*, pp. 127-29; Neumark, "Trans-Sahara Trade," pp. 127-28; Marc Bloch, *Land and Work in Medieval Europe*, trans. J. E. Anderson (New York and Evanston, 1969), pp. 186-229; Fernand Braudel, "De l'or du Soudan à l'argent d'Amérique," *Annales: E.S.C.* 1 (1946): 9-22; Robert S. Lopez, "Back to Gold, 1252," *Economic History Review* 9 (1956): 219-40; Andrew M. Watson, "Back to Gold—and Silver," *Economic History Review* 20 (1967): 1-34; H. C. Krueger, "Genoese Trade with North-West Africa in the Twelfth Century," *Speculum* 8 (1933): 377-95; Vitorino de Magalhães Godinho, "I Mediterraneo saariano e as caravanas de ouro," *Revista de História* 11 (1955): 307-53, and 12 (1956): 59-107; Vitorino de Magalhães Godinho, *L'économie de l'empire portugais au XVe et XVIe siècles* (Paris, 1969); Marian Malowist, "Quelques observations sur le commerce de l'or dans le Soudan occidental au Moyen Age," *Annales: E.S.C.* 25/6 (1970): 1630-36.

63. Levtzion, "Early States," pp. 142-43; Neumark, "Trans-Sahara Trade," pp. 128-30. For the long-term history of one of the gold regions, see Philip D. Curtin, "The Lure of Bambuk gold," *Journal of African History* 14 (1973): 623-31.

64. Valentim Fernandes, *Description de la Côte occidentale d'Afrique (Sénégal au Cap de Monte, Archipels)*, ed. T. Monod, A. Teixeira da Mota, and R. Mauny (Bissau, 1951), p. 89; P. F. de Morães Farias, "The Silent Trade: Myth and Historical Evidence," *History in Africa* 1 (1974): 9-24.

65. Hubert Deschamps,, *Historie de la traite des noirs de l'antiquité à nos jours* (Paris, 1971), pp. 29-33; Bovill, *Golden Trade*, pp. 101-2.

66. Austen, "Trans-Saharan Slave Trade," p. 68.

CHAPTER 5. SLAVERY IN LATE MEDIEVAL EUROPE

1. Speros Vryonis, Jr., *Byzantium: Its Internal History and Relations with the Muslim World: Collected Studies* (London, 1971), 9:234.

2. For the Crusades, see Kenneth M. Setton, ed., *A History of the Crusades*, 2d ed., 5 vols. (Madison, 1969-); Stephen Runciman, *A History of the Crusades*, 3 vols. (Cambridge, Eng., 1951-54); and Hans Eberhard Mayer, *The Crusades* (New York and Oxford, 1972).

3. Charles Verlinden, *The Beginnings of Modern Colonization: Eleven Essays with an Introduction*, trans. Yvonne Freccero (Ithaca and London, 1970), pp. 79-80.

4. Meron Benvenisti, *The Crusaders in the Holy Land* (New York, 1972), pp. 20, 217-18.

5. Mayer, *Crusades*, p. 151.

6. Ibid., p. 178; J. S. C. Riley-Smith, *The Feudal Nobility and the Kingdom of Jerusalem, 1117-1277* (Hamden, Conn., 1973), pp. 62-63, 76, 88, 258.

7. Fulcher of Chartres, *A History of the Expedition to Jerusalem, 1095-1125*, trans. Frances Rita Ryan, ed. Harold S. Fink (Knoxville, 1969), p. 130.

8. William of Tyre, *A History of Deeds Done beyond the Sea*, trans. and ed. Emily Atwater Babcock and A. C. Krey, 2 vols. (New York, 1943), 2:6.

9. Jonathan Riley-Smith, *The Knights of St. John in Jerusalem and Cyprus, c. 1050-1310*, vol. 1. of *A History of the Order of the Hospital of St. John of Jerusalem*, ed. Lionel Butler (London and New York, 1967), pp. 425-27, 434; Wilhelm von Heyd, *Histoire du commerce du Levant au Moyen-Age*, trans. Furey Reynaud, 2 vols. (Leipzig, 1885-86; reprint, Amsterdam, 1967), 2:684; Mayer, *Crusades*, p. 163. Wallace K. Aykroyd (*The Story of Sugar* [New York, 1967]) generally has accurate information, but he is mistaken when he says that in Syria and Palestine "Western Europeans, represented by the Crusaders, saw and tasted sugar for the first time." (p. 13.) Many other

Westerners had known sugar at home for over a century, but the Crusades did popularize sugar and created a demand for it in the West.

10. Jean Richard, *The Latin Kingdom of Jerusalem*, trans. Janet Shirley, 2 vols. (Amsterdam, 1979), p. 73: Joshua Prawer, *The Crusaders' Kingdom: European Colonialism in the Middle Ages* (New York, 1972), pp. 363–64.

11. Riley-Smith, *Knights of St. John*, p. 446; Richard, *Latin Kingdom*, p. 125. See also Benvenisti, *Crusaders in the Holy Land*, p. 254, on archeological ruins of sugar factories.

12. Noël Deerr, *The History of Sugar*, 2 vols. (London, 1949–50), 1:76–77; Richard, *Latin Kingdom*, p. 351; Joshua Prawer, "Étude de quelques problèmes agraires et sociaux d'une seigneurie croisée au XIIIe siècle," *Byzantion* 22 (1952): 5–61; Verlinden, *Modern Colonization*, p. 20; James Westfall Thompson, *Economic and Social History of the Middle Ages (300–1300)*, 2 vols. (New York, 1928; reprint, 1959), pp. 362, 424; Edmund O. von Lippmann, *Geschichte des Zuckers, seiner Darstellung und Verwendung* (Leipzig, 1890), p. 181.

13. Saladin's armies destroyed sugar mills in Tiberias and Acre, something Saladin himself regretted. Richard, *Latin Kingdom*, p. 176.

14. Heyd, *Commerce du Levant*, 2:686; Thompson, *Economic and Social History*, p. 423.

15. David Jacoby, "Citoyens, sujets et protégés en Chypre," *Byzantinische Forschungen* 5 (1977): 174–777; Freddy Thiriet, *La Romanie vénitienne au Moyen Age: Le développement et l'exploitation du domaine colonial vénitien (XIIe–XVe siècles)* (Paris, 1959), p. 333; Gino Luzzatto, *Studi di storia economica veneziana* (Padua, 1954), pp. 117–23; Gino Luzzatto, *Storia economica di Venezia dall'XI al XVI sècolo* (Venice, 1961), pp. 54, 64, 196; Frederic C. Lane, *Venice: A Maritime Republic* (Baltimore and London, 1973), pp. 144–45; Mayer, *Crusades*, pp. 231–32, 237, 239; Verlinden, *Modern Colonization*, pp. 19–20, 97n. I wish to thank David Jacoby for his suggestions on this topic.

16. Deerr, *History of Sugar*, 1:79, 83; Verlinden, *Modern Colonization*, pp. 96–97; Thiriet, *Romanie vénitienne*, pp. 417–18.

17. Ibn-Hauqal, quoted by Deerr, *History of Sugar*, 1:76.

18. Quoted by Deerr, *History of Sugar*, 1:77.

19. Verlinden, *Modern Colonization*, p. 20; Deerr, *History of Sugar*, 1:76–77; Richard, *Latin Kingdom*, p. 351.

20. Carmelo Trasselli, "Producción y comercio del azúcar en Sicilia del siglo XIII al XIX," *Revista Bimestre Cubana* 72 (1957): 138–41. The article was also published as "Produzione e commercio delle zucchero in Sicilia dal XII al XIX sècolo," *Economia e Storia* 2 (1955).

21. The mistaken statement is found in Lippmann, *Geschichte des Zuckers*, pp. 217–18, and Deerr, *History of Sugar*, 1:77, 2:536. Verlinden follows Lippmann and Deerr (*Modern Colonization*, p. 20). The definitive statement on the mill is by Moacyr Soares Pereira, *A origem dos cilindros na moagem da cana: Investigacão em Palermo* (Rio de Janeiro, 1955). Of later writers, José Pérez Vidal supports Pereira totally in *La cultura de la caña de azúcar en el Levante español* (Madrid, 1973), pp.63–65, while J. H. Galloway leans toward Pereira's case in "The Mediterranean Sugar Industry," *Geographical Review* 67/2 (1977): pp. 186–87.

22. Trasselli reported that only free workers were employed in the Sicilian sugar industry, "Producción y comercio," p. 135. Verlinden's citation of the rental of a Turkish slave to work for a Sicilian sugar plantation owner in 1462 probably represents only an exception. Charles Verlinden, *L'esclavage dans l'Europe médiévale*, vol. 2; *Italie—Colonies italiennes du Levant—Levant latin—Empire byzantin* (Bruges, 1977), 2:231.

23. Gerald A. J. Hodgett, *A Social and Economic History of Medieval Europe* (New York, 1974), p. 196; Deerr, *History of Sugar*, 1:79.

24. Fernand Braudel, *The Mediterranean and the Mediterranean World in the Age of Philip II*, trans. Siân Reynolds, 2 vols. (New York, 1972), 1:168–230.

25. Dennis Mack Smith, *Medieval Sicily, 800–1713*, vol. 2 of *A History of Sicily* (London, 1968), p. 15.

26. Christopher Brooke, *Europe in the Central Middle Ages, 962–1154* (New York, 1964), pp. 116–17.

27. Eugene H. Byrne, "Genoese Trade with Syria in the Twelfth Century," *American Historical Review* 25 (1920): 206.

28. Verlinden, *Modern Colonization*, p. 91.

29. Iris Origo, *The Merchant of Prato: Francesco de Marco Datini, 1335–1410* (New York, 1957), pp. 90–91.

30. G. Pistarino, "Fra liberti e schiave a Genova nel Quattrocento," *Anuario de Estudios Medievales* 1 (1964): 353–55.

31. Joseph and Frances Gies, *Merchants and Moneymen: The Commercial Revolution, 1000–1500* (New York, 1972), pp. 244, 257.

32. Michel Balard, "Remarques sur les esclaves à Gênes dans la seconde moitié du XIIIe siècle," *Mélanges d'Archéologie et d'Histoire* 80 (1968): 627–80, especially 651–53; Giovanna Balbi, "La schiavitù a Genova tra i sècoli XII e XIII," in *Mélanges offerts à René Crozet*, ed. Pierre Gallais and Yves-Jean Riou, 2 vols. (Poitiers, 1966), 2: 1025–29, especially 2:1029; Domenico Gioffrè, *Il mercato degli schiavi a Genova nel sècolo XV* (Genoa, 1971), pp. 89–90; Lane, *Venice*, p. 51; Jacques Heers, *Esclaves et domestiques au Moyen-Age dans le monde méditerranéen* (Paris, 1981), pp. 135–41.

33. Iris Origo, "The Domestic Enemy: The Eastern Slaves in Tuscany in the Fourteenth and Fifteenth Centuries," *Speculum* 30 (1955): 321–66, especially 340–44.

34. Balbi, "Schiavitù a Genova," 2:1028.

35. Origo, *Merchant of Prato*, p. 93.

36. Ibid.

37. Ibid.

38. Jacques Heers, *Gênes au XVe siècle: Activité économique et problèmes sociaux* (Paris, 1961), p. 554.

39. Pistarino, "Liberti e schiave," pp. 361–62.

40. Gioffrè, *Mercato degli schiavi*, p. 96

41. Ibid., pp. 100–104; Pistarino, "Liberti e schiave," p. 362.

42. Origo, "Domestic Enemy," pp. 345–46; Pistarino, "Liberti e schiave," p. 361.

43. Origo, "Domestic Enemy," p. 346.

44. Heers, *Gênes*, p. 554.

45. Balard, "Esclaves à Gênes," pp. 651–52, 664–66.

46. Origo, "Domestic Enemy," p. 333: Lane, *Venice*, pp. 333, 347.

47. Gioffrè, *Mercato degli schiavi*, pp. 90–91.

48. Balard, "Esclaves à Gênes," pp. 673–74.

49. Origo, "Domestic Enemy, pp. 333–34, 340.

50. Ibid., pp. 334–36.

51. Lane, *Venice*, p. 206.

52. Origo, *Merchant of Prato*, p. 92.

53. Ibid.

54. Origo, "Domestic Enemy," p. 331

55. Balbi, "Schiavitù a Genova," 2:1029; Heers, *Gênes*, pp. 554–56.

56. Pistarino, "Liberti e schiave," p. 364.

57. Origo, "Domestic Enemy," p. 345.

58. Balbi, "Schiavitù a Genova," 2:1027–28.

59. Balard, "Esclaves à Gênes," p. 678.

60. Ibid., p. 676; Verlinden, *Modern Colonization*, p. 91; Heers, *Gênes*, pp. 554–55.

61. R. H. Bautier, *The Economic Development of Medieval Europe*, trans. Heather Karolyi (New York, 1971), p. 101. See also Lane, *Venice*, p. 60.

62. Balbi, "Schiavitù a Genova," 2:1025–29.

63. Balard, "Esclaves à Gênes," p. 680.

64. Andrew S. Ehrenkreutz, "Strategic Implications of the Slave Trade between Genoa and Mamluk Egypt in the Second Half of the Thirteenth Century," in *The Islamic Middle East, 700–1900: Studies in Economic and Social History*, ed. A. L. Udovitch (Princeton, 1981), pp. 335–45. See also Elena C. Skrzinskaja, "Storia della Tana," *Studi Veneziana* 10 (1968): 3–45.

65. Balard, "Esclaves à Gênes," pp. 630, 634–49.

66. Origo, "Domestic Enemy," p. 336.

67. Michael E. Mallett, *The Florentine Galleys in the Fifteenth Century, with the Diary of Luca de Maso degli Albrizzi, Captain of the Galleys, 1429–1430* (Oxford, 1967), pp. 114, 127–29.

68. On the Black Death, see William H. McNeill, *Plagues and Peoples* (Garden City, N.Y., 1976), pp. 151–70; William M. Bowsky, ed., *The Black Death: A Turning Point in History?* (New York, 1971); Philip Ziegler, *The Black Death* (New York, 1969). The Black Death in England had a notable impact on the conditions of rural workers. In its aftermath the remaining peasants were able to throw off the last vestiges of serfdom. See R. H. Hilton, *Bond Men Made Free: Peasant Movements and the English Rising of 1361* (London, 1973); id., *The English Peasants in the Late Middle Ages* (Oxford, 1975).

69. Origo, "Domestic Enemy," p. 324.

70. Lane, *Venice*, p. 133.

71. Gioffrè, *Mercato degli schiavi*, pp. 13–15, 17–22, 27, 31–32, 36–37.

72. Origo, "Domestic Enemy," p. 332; Lane, *Venice*, pp. 332–33.

73. Lane, *Venice*, pp. 332–33.

74. Charles Verlinden, *L'esclavage dans la Europe médiévale*, vol. 1: *Péninsule ibérique— France* (Bruges, 1955), 1:105–06, 108–09, 116–18, 122, 128–29, 135–38, 172–74,; J. Font Ruis, "La sociedad en Asturias, León y Castilla en los primeros siglos medievales," in *Historia social y económica de España y América*, ed. Jaime Vicens Vives, 5 vols. (Barcelona, 1957–), 2:319–20.

75. Verlinden, *Esclavage*, 1:546–47, 550; Verlinden, *Modern Colonization*, pp. 38–39.

76. Verlinden, *Esclavage*, 1:548–49, 551–59, 589, 593.

77. Verlinden, *Modern Colonization*, pp. 37–38.

78. James W. Brodman, "Military Redemptionism and the Castilian Reconquest, 1180–1250," *Military Affairs* 44 (1980): 24–27; Verlinden, *Esclavage*, 1:606–10.

79. Jaime Vicens Vives, with Jorge Nadal, *An Economic History of Spain*, trans. Frances M. López-Morillas (Princeton, 1969), pp. 148–49.

80. Verlinden, *Esclavage*, 1:251–73.

81. Robert I. Burns, S. J., *Islam under the Crusaders: Colonial Survival in the Thirteenth-Century Kingdom of Valencia* (Princeton, 1973). p. 111; Robert I. Burns, S. J., *The Crusader Kingdom of Valencia*, 2 vols. (Cambridge, Mass., 1967), 1:2, citing Muntaner, *Crónica catalana*, ch. 13.

82. Burns, *Islam under the Crusaders*, p. 351.

83. Ibid., pp. 109–10, 407; Burns, *Crusader Kingdom*, 1:22, 128.

84. Charles Emmanuel Dufourcq, *La Espagne catalane et le Maghrib aux XIIIe et XIVe siècles* (Paris, 1966), pp. 72–73; Burns, *Islam under the Crusaders*, pp. 109–10, 250, 252, 260; Verlinden, *Esclavage*, 1:292-95.

85. John Boswell, *The Royal Treasure: Muslim Communities under the Crown of Aragon in the Fourteenth Century* (New Haven and London, 1977), pp. 49-56, 313, 316-17; Burns, *Islam under the Crusaders*, pp. 111—12, 128; Burns, *Crusader Kingdom*, 1:115; Verlinden, *Esclavage*, 1:291–92, 300.

86. Burns, *Crusader Kingdom*, pp. 248-52.

87. J. A. Doering, "La situación de los esclavos a partir de las Siete Partidas," *Folia Humanistica* 4 (1966):337-61; E. N. van Kleffens, *Hispanic Law until the End of the Middle Ages* (Edinburgh, 1968).

88. Thomas F. Glick, *Islamic and Christian Spain in the Early Middle Ages* (Princeton, 1979),

pp. 77–78; S. M. Imamuddin, *Some Aspects of the Socio-Economic and Cultural History of Muslim Spain, 711–1492 A.D.* (Leiden, 1965), pp. 88–89; Pérez Vidal, *Cultura de la caña*, pp. 11–13.

89. Pérez Vidal, *Cultura de la caña*, pp. 14–15, 37–38, 41–45.

90. Antonio H. de Oliveira Marques, *History of Portugal*, 2 vols. (New York, 1972), 1:140; Henrique Gomes de Amorim Parreira, "História do açúcar em Portugal," *Anais: Estudos da História da Geografia da Expansão Portuguesa* 7 (1952): 18.

91. Galloway, "Mediterranean Sugar Industry," pp. 182–88; L. A. G. Strong, *The Story of Sugar* (London, 1954), pp. 22–31.

92. Francesco Balducci Pegolotti, *La Practica della Mercatura*, ed. Allan Evans, (Cambridge, Mass., 1936), pp. 297, 362–65.

CHAPTER 6. SLAVERY IN
SUB-SAHARAN AFRICA TO 1650

1. For the best introduction, see Paul E. Lovejoy, *Transformations in Slavery: A History of Slavery in Africa* (Cambridge, Eng., 1983). I am grateful to Professor Lovejoy for providing me with a copy of the page proofs for his book before publication. Two major compendia are Suzanne Miers and Igor Kopytoff, eds., *Slavery in Africa: Historical and Anthropological Perspectives* (Madison, 1977), particularly the editors' "Introduction: African 'Slavery' as an Institution of Marginality," pp. 3–81; and Claude Meillassoux, ed., *L'esclavage en Afrique précoloniale* (Paris, 1975). Miers and Kopytoff seek to establish a generic form of African slavery, whereas Meillassoux seeks to establish a Marxist perspective. For criticisms of the views of Miers and Kopytoff and Meillassoux, and for other interpretations, see Paul E. Lovejoy, "Indigenous African Slavery," *Historical Reflections/Réflexions Historiques* 6 (1979): 19–61; Martin A. Klein, "The Study of Slavery in Africa," *Journal of African History* 19 (1978):559–609; Frederick Cooper, "The Problem of Slavery in African Studies," *Journal of African History* 20 (1979): 103–25; Martin A. Klein and Paul E. Lovejoy, "Slavery in West Africa," in *The Uncommon Market: Essays in the Economic History of the Atlantic Slave Trade*, ed. Henry A. Gemery and Jan S. Hogendorn (New York, 1979), pp. 181–212; Paul E. Lovejoy, "Slavery in the Context of Ideology," in *The Ideology of Slavery in Africa*, ed. Paul E. Lovejoy (Beverly Hills and London, 1981), pp. 11–38. A new collection is Claire C. Robertson and Martin A. Klein, eds., *Women and Slavery in Africa* (Madison, 1983).

2. The best collection is that of Nehemia Levtzion and J. F. P. Hopkins, eds., *Corpus of Arabic Sources Relating to West Africa* (Cambridge, Eng., 1981).

3. Paul E. Lovejoy and Steven Baier, "The Desert-Side Economy of the Central Sudan," *International Journal of African Historical Studies* 8/4 (1975): 551–81.

4. Raymond Mauny, *Les siècles obscurs de l'Afrique noire: Histoire et archéologie* Paris, 1971), pp. 141–42; S. Daniel Neumark, "Trans-Saharan Trade in the Middle Ages," in *An Economic History of Tropical Africa*, ed. Z. A. Konczacki and J. M. Konczacki, 2 vols. (London, 1977), p. 129; Hubert Deschamps, *Histoire de la traite des noirs de l'antiquité à nos jours* (Paris, 1971), p. 25; Nehemia Levtzion, *Ancient Ghana and Mali* (London, 1973). See also the materials on the trans-Saharan trade cited in chapter 4, especially Ralph A. Austen's figures on the volume of the slave traffic.

5. Humphrey J. Fisher, "The Eastern Maghrib and the Central Sudan," in *The Cambridge History of Africa*, ed. Roland Oliver, vol. 3 (Cambridge, Eng., 1977), p. 238. For other accounts, see Mauny, *Siècles obscurs*, pp. 141–43; Deschamps, *Traite des noirs*, p. 25.

6. Fisher, "Eastern Maghrib and Central Sudan," p. 239; Levtzion, *Ancient Ghana and Mali*, pp. 3–15; Sharon E. Nicholson, "The Methodology of Historical Climate Reconstruction and Its Application to Africa," *Journal of African History* 20 (1979): 31–49.

7. Levtzion, *Ancient Ghana and Mali*, pp. 4–10, et passim. Claude Meillassoux, "The Role of Slavery in the Economic and Social History of Sahelo-Sudanic Africa," in *Forced Migration: The Impact of the Export Slave Trade on African Societies*, ed. J. E. Inikori (New York, 1982), 74–99; this article was first published as "Role de l'esclavage dans l'histoire de l'Afrique occidentale," *An-*

thropologie et sociétés 2 (1978):117–48. On Mali and Songhay, see also Marian Malowist, "The Social and Economic Stability of the Western Sudan in the Middle Ages," *Past and Present* 33 (1966): 3:15; and the response by Anthony G. Hopkins, "The Western Sudan in the Middle Ages: Underdevelopment in the Empires of the Western Sudan," *Past and Present* 37 (1967): 149–56.

8. Philip D. Curtin, *Economic Change in Precolonial Africa: Senegambia in the Era of the Slave Trade* (Madison, 1975), p. 153.

9. Lovejoy, *Transformations in Slavery*, pp. 15–18; Lovejoy, "Indigenous African Slavery," p. 25.

10. Klein and Lovejoy, "Slavery in West Africa," p. 183.

11. Jack Goody, *Technology, Tradition, and the State in Africa* (London, 1971), pp. 24–27, 29–30; Levtzion, *Ancient Ghana and Mali*, p. 14; Meillassoux, "Role of Slavery," 76–83.

12. Goody, *Technology*, pp. 34–37; 47–51, 68–69, 72; Robin Law, *The Horse in West African History: The Role of the Horse in the Societies of Precolonial West Africa* (Oxford, 1980), pp. 48, 54, 76–77; see map on p. 42. See also Humphrey J. Fisher, " 'He Swalloweth the Ground with Fierceness and Rage': The Horse in the Central Sudan, I. Its Introduction," and "II. Its Use," *Journal of African History* 13 (1972): 369–88, and 14 (1973): 355–79.

13. Law, *Horse in West African History*, pp. 44, 48–50, 54–55.

14. Ibid., pp. 61–63. For other instances, see Allan G. B. Fisher and Humphrey J. Fisher, *Slavery and Muslim Society in Africa: The Institution in Saharan and Sudanic Africa and the Trans-Saharan Trade* (Garden City, 1971), pp. 71, 81. Although the Fishers do bring in earlier material, their main emphasis in this book is the nineteenth century.

15. Levtzion and Hopkins, eds., *Corpus* (al-Zuhri), p. 198.

16. Ibid. (al-Idrisi), p. 112. See also John Spenser Trimingham, *A History of Islam in West Africa* (London and New York, 1962), pp. 62–63.

17. John Hunwick, "Songhay, Borno, and Hausaland in the Sixteenth Century," in *History of West Africa*, ed. J. F. A. Ajayi and Michael Crowder, 2 vols., 2d ed. (New York, 1976), 1:270; Fisher and Fisher, *Slavery and Muslim Society*, pp. 71–72; Fisher, "Horse in the Central Sudan, I," p. 382.

18. Fisher and Fisher, *Slavery and Muslim Society*, p. 24.

19. Ibid., pp. 23, 28, 31–37.

20. Dierk Lange, "Progrès de l'Islam et changement politique au Kanem du XIe au XIIIe siècle," *Journal of African History* 19 (1978): 495–513. See also Michael Brett, "Ifriqiya as a Market for Saharan Trade from the Tenth to the Twelfth Century A.D.," *Journal of African History* 10 (1969): 347–64; and B. G. Martin, "Kanem, Bornu, and the Fazzan: Notes on the Political History of a Trade Route," *Journal of African History* 10 (1969): 15–27.

21. Fisher and Fisher, *Slavery and Muslim Society*, p. 85; Lovejoy, *Transformations in Slavery*; Miers and Kopytoff, *Slavery in Africa*, pp. 3–81.

22. Lovejoy, *Transformations in Slavery*, pp. 13–15; Fisher and Fisher, *Slavery and Muslim Society*, pp. 119–20.

23. Levtzion and Hopkins, eds, *Corpus* (al-Sharishi), p. 153.

24. Ibid. (ibn-Battuta), p. 287.

25. Ibid. (ibn-Battuta), p. 300.

26. Ibid. (ibn-battuta), pp. 290–97.

27. Fisher and Fisher, *Slavery and Muslim Society*, p. 12.

28. Levtzion and Hopkins, eds., *Corpus* (ibn-Battuta), p. 302.

29. Hunwick, "Songhay, Borno, and Hausaland," pp. 278–79. Leo Africanus, *History and Description of Africa*, 3 vols. (London, n.d.; reprint, New York, n.d.), 1:128, 3:829–30.

30. Lovejoy, *Transformations in Slavery*, pp. 31–32. M. Tymowski, "Les domaines des princes du Songhay (Soudan occidental)," *Annales: E. S. C.* 25/6 (1970): 1637–58. Emmanuel Terray, "Long-Distance Trade and the Formation of the State: The Case of the Abron Kingdom of Gyaman," *Economy and Society* 3 (1974): 315–45. Levtzion, *Ancient Ghana and Mali*, pp. 117–20;

Nehemia Levtzion, "The Western Maghrib and Sudan," in *Cambridge History of Africa*, 3:388, 446-47. Nehemia Levtzion, "The Early States of the Western Sudan to 1500," in *History of West Africa*, ed. Ajayi and Crowder, 1:139; Fisher and Fisher, *Slavery and Muslim Society*, pp. 152-53.

31. Hunwick, "Songhay, Borno, and Hausaland," p. 278; Fisher and Fisher, *Slavery and Muslim Society*, p. 141.

32. Levtzion and Hopkins, eds., *Corpus* (al-Quazwini), p. 178; Ivan Hrbek, "Egypt, Nubia, and the Eastern Deserts," in *Cambridge History of Africa*, 3:71-72; Ivor Wilks, "The Mossi and Akan States to 1800," in *History of West Africa*, ed. Ajayi and Crowder, 1:427-29; Deschamps, *Traite des noirs*, p. 28; Fisher, "Eastern Maghrib and Central Sudan," p. 279; Fisher and Fisher, *Slavery and Muslim Society*, p. 138; Terray, "Long-Distance Trade and the Formation of the State," p. 338; Lovejoy, *Transformations in Slavery*, pp. 32-33.

33. Levtzion and Hopkins, eds., *Corpus* (al-Qazwini), p. 178.

34. Levtzion, "Early States," p. 139; Levtzion, "Western Maghrib and Sudan," p. 430.

35. Levtzion and Hopkins, eds., *Corpus* (al-Umari), p. 265.

36. Levtzion, "Early States," p. 139; Levtzion, "Western Maghrib and Sudan," p. 386; Levtzion, *Ancient Ghana and Mali*, pp. 112-14.

37. Abdullah Smith, "The Early States of the Central Sudan," in *History of West Africa*, ed. Ajayi and Crowder, 1:193; Ade Obayemi, "The Yoruba and Edo-speaking Peoples and Their Neighbours before 1600," in ibid., p. 259.

38. J. Suret-Canale and Boubacar Barry, "The Western Atlantic Coast to 1800," in *History of West Africa*, ed. Ajayi and Crowder, 1:465, 468. Walter Rodney, *A History of the Upper Guinea Coast, 1545-1800* (Oxford, 1970); J. D. Fage, "Slaves and Society in Western Africa, c. 1445-1700," *Journal of African History* 21 (1980): 289-310.

39. Levtzion, *Ancient Ghana and Mali*, pp. 111-12.

40. Fisher, "Eastern Maghrib and Central Sudan," p. 438.

41. Levtzion, "Western Maghrib and Sudan," p. 271.

42. Levtzion and Hopkins, eds. *Corpus* (al-Maqrizi), pp. 351, 355.

43. Ibid. (al-Maqrizi), p. 356; Trimingham, *History of Islam in West Africa*, p. 32; Hrbek, "Egypt, Nubia," p. 90; Levtzion, "Western Maghrib and Sudan," p. 376.

44. Levtzion and Hopkins, eds., *Corpus* (al-Maqrizi) p. 355.

45. Ibid., (ibn-Battuta), p. 300.

46. Fisher and Fisher, *Slavery and Muslim Society*, p. 155; Levtzion, "Western Maghrib and Sudan," pp. 376, 394-395; Hrbek, "Egypt, Nubia," p. 90.

47. Jean Pierre Olivier de Sardan, "Captifs ruraux et esclaves imperiaux du Songhay," in Meillassoux, ed., *L'esclavage en Afrique précoloniale*, pp. 99-134, especially 111-15. But see the criticism of his approach by Klein, "Study of Slavery," p. 603.

CHAPTER 7. AFRICA AND THE ATLANTIC ISLANDS

1. Jacques Heers, *Gênes au XVe siècle: Activité économique et problèmes sociaux* (Paris, 1961), pp. 473-82; Raymond Mauny, *Les siècles obscurs d'Afrique noire: Histoire et archéololgie* (Paris, 1970), p. 219.

2. Charles Verlinden, *L'esclavage dans l'Europe médiévale*, vol. 1: *Péninsule ibérique— France* (Bruges, 1955), 1:546-47, 550.

3. Nehemia Levtzion and J. F. P. Hopkins, eds., *Corpus of Arabic Sources Relating to West Africa* (Cambridge, Eng., 1981) (al-Umari), pp. 272-73.

4. On the nautical revolution see Carlo M. Cipolla, *Guns, Sails, and Empires: Technological Innovation and the Early Phases of European Expansion, 1400-1700* (New York, 1965); Richard W. Unger, *The Ship in the Medieval Economy, 600-1600* (London and Montreal, 1980); J. H. Parry, *The Discovery of the Sea* (Berkeley and Los Angeles, 1981).

5. E. G. R. Taylor, *The Haven-Finding Art* (London, 1965).

6. Vitorino de Magalhães Godinho, *A economia dos descobrimentos henriquinos* (Lisbon,

1962), pp. 75-81; see also the general accounts in Charles R. Boxer, *The Portuguese Seaborne Empire, 1425-1825* (New York, 1969); Bailey W. Diffie and George D. Winius, *Foundations of the Portuguese Empire* (Minneapolis, 1977); Antonio H. de Oliveira Marques, *History of Portugal,* 2 vols. (New York, 1972); J. D. Fage, "Slavery and the Slave Trade in the Context of West African History," *Journal of African History* 10 (1969): 393-404; and J. D. Fage, "Slaves and Society in Western Africa, c. 1445-1700," *Journal of African History* 2 (1980): 289-310.

7. Anthony G. Hopkins, *An Economic History of West Africa* (New York, 1973), p. 89.

8. Godinho, *Descobrimentos henriquinos,* pp. 69-81.

9. Ibid., pp. 82-116. For the events of the conquest itself, see H. V. Livermore, "On the Conquest of Ceuta," *Luso-Brazilian Review* 2 (1965): 3-13.

10. Godinho, *Descobrimentos henriquinos,* pp. 109-16; Nehemia Levtzion, *Ancient Ghana and Mali* (London, 1973), p. 132; Robert Ricard, *Études sur l'histoire des portugais au Maroc* (Coimbra, 1955), pp. 93-94; Robert Ricard, "Le commerce de Berbérie et l'organization économique de l'empire portugais aux XVe et XVIe siècles," *Annales de l'Institut d'Études Orientales* 2 (1936): 266-90; Heers, *Gênes,* pp. 480-82.

11. Godinho, *Descobrimentos henriquinos,* pp. 129-31.

12. Gomes Eannes de Azurara, *The Chronicle of the Discovery and Conquest of Guinea,* trans and eds., Charles Raymond Beazley and Edgar Prestage, 2 vols. (London, 1896-1899), 1:81.

13. A. C. de C. M. Saunders, *A Social History of Black Slaves and Freedmen in Portugal, 1441-1555* (Cambridge, Eng., 1982), p. 5.

14. Godinho, *Descobrimentos henriquinos,* pp. 188-89; Verlinden, *L'esclavage,* 1:617; Marques, *History of Portugal,* 1:158.

15. Godinho, *Descobrimentos henriquinos,* pp. 187-93; Marques, *History of Portugal,* 1:158-59; J. D. Fage, *A History of West Africa,* 4th ed. (Cambridge, Eng., 1969), p. 51; Valentim Fernandes, *Description de la Côte d'Afrique de Ceuta au Sénégal,* trans. and eds., P. de Cernival and T. Monod (Paris, 1938), pp. 61-71.

16. Fernandes, *Description,* pp. 61-65.

17. Ibid.; Heers, *Gênes,* p. 481.

18. Godinho, *Descobrimentos henriquinos,* p. 192; Fage, *History of West Africa,* p. 57; John William Blake, *West Africa: Quest for God and Gold* (Totowa, N.J., 1977); Vitorino de Magalhães Godinho, *L'économie de l'empire portugais au XVe et XVIe siècles* (Paris, 1969), pp. 181-185. On Senegambia generally, but mostly for the later period, see Philip D. Curtin, *Economic Change in Precolonial Africa: Senegambia in the Era of the Slave Trade* (Madison, 1975).

19. Godinho, *Descobrimentos henriquinos,* pp. 193-96; Robin Law, *The Horse in West African History: The Role of the Horse in the Societies of Precolonial West Africa* (Oxford, 1980) pp. 48, 51-52.

20. Godinho, *Descobrimentos henriquinos,* pp. 198-201.

21. Ibid., pp. 196-201.

22. Curtin, *Senegambia,* pp. 221-23; Law, *Horse in West African History,* pp. 52-53; T. Bentley Duncan, *The Atlantic Islands: Madeira, the Azores, and the Cape Verdes in Seventeenth-Century Commerce and Navigation* (Chicago, 1972), p. 198. For a general history, see António Carreira, *Cabo Verde: Formação e extinção de uma sociedade escravocrata* (Lisbon and Bissau, 1972).

23. For a full discussion, see Godinho, *Descobrimentos henriquinos,* pp. 204-8.

24. Walter Rodney, *A History of the Upper Guinea Coast, 1545-1800* (Oxford, 1970), p. 74.

25. John Vogt, *Portuguese Rule on the Gold Coast, 1469-1682* (Athens, Ga., 1979), pp. 6-8.

26. Ibid., pp. 20-31. São Jorge da Mina is often called Elmina, an English corruption of the original.

27. Ibid., pp. 71-72; Godinho, *Descobrimentos henriquinos,* p. 202.

28. Vogt, *Gold Coast,* pp. 59-92; Godinho, *L'empire portugais,* pp. 175-243.

29. Vogt, *Gold Coast,* pp. 63-64, 67-71.

30. Ibid., p. 57.

31. Alan F. C. Ryder, *Benin and the Europeans: 1485–1897* (London, 1969), pp. 24–32; E. J. Alagoa, "The Niger Delta States and their Neighbours to 1800," in *History of West Africa*, ed. J. F. A. Ajayi and Michael Crowder, 2d ed., 2 vols., (London, 1976), 1:358–59; J. D. Fage, "Slavery and the Slave Trade in the Context of West African History," *Journal of African History* 10 (1969):393–404.

32. Ryder, *Benin*, pp. 31–75; Godinho, *Descobrimentos henriquinos*, pp. 203–4.

33. Joseph C. Miller, "The Slave Trade in Congo and Angola," in *The African Diaspora: Interpretive Essays*, ed. Martin L. Kilson and Robert I. Rotberg, (Cambridge, Mass., and London, 1976), pp. 79–82. On São Tomé specifically, see Robert Garfield, "A History of São Tomé Island, 1470–1655" (Ph.D. dissertation, Northwestern University, 1971); Marian Malowist, "Les débuts du système de plantations dans la periode des grandes découverts," *Africana Bulletin* 10 (1969): 9–30; John L. Vogt, "The Early São Tomé-Príncipe Trade with Mina, 1500–1540," *International Journal of African Historical Studies* 6/3 (1973): 453–67.

34. Fernandes, *Description*, p. 121.

35. Georges Balandier, *Daily Life in the Kingdom of the Kongo from the Sixteenth to the Eighteenth Century*, trans. Helen Weaver, (New York, 1968), pp. 42–63; Jan Vansina, *Kingdoms of the Savanna* (Madison, 1966; reprint, 1975), pp. 45–58.

36. Vansina, *Kingdoms of the Savanna*, pp. 47, 53; Jan Vansina, "Long-Distance Trade Routes in Central Africa," *Journal of African History* 3 (1962): 375–90. The derivation of *pombeiro* appears on p. 378.

37. David Birmingham, *Trade and Conflict in Angola: The Mbundu and their Neighbours under the Influence of the Portuguese, 1483–1790* (Oxford, 1966), pp. 25–26, 32; Joseph C. Miller, *Kings and Kinsmen: Early Mbundu States in Angola* (Oxford, 1975); Miller, "Slave Trade," pp. 84–92.

38. On the copper trade, see Eugenia W. Herbert, "The West African Copper Trade in the Fifteenth and Sixteenth Century," unpublished paper presented at the Fourteenth International Congress of Historical Sciences, San Francisco, 1975; id., *Red Gold of Africa: Copper in Precolonial History and Culture* (Madison, 1983). The Portuguese also bought central-European silver in Antwerp for use in India, where silver enjoyed a high value in relation to gold. J. A. van Houtte, "The Rise and Decline of the Market of Bruges," *Economic History Review*, 2d series, 19 (1966): 29–47, especially p. 43. For an overview of the imports to the West African coast, see Paul E. Lovejoy, *Transformations in Slavery: A History of Slavery in Africa* (Cambridge, Eng., 1983), pp. 103–6. See also John L. Vogt, "Notes on the Portuguese Cloth Trade in West Africa, 1480–1540," *International Journal of African Historical Studies* 8/4 (1975): 623–51.

39. Rodney, *Upper Guinea Coast*, pp. 71–82, 95–106.

40. Cadamosto, *The Voyages of Cadamosto*, trans. and ed. G. R. Crone (London, 1937), p. 30.

41. Fage, "Slaves and Society," p. 309.

42. The impact of the slave trade on Africa and Africans is still far from fully assessed. See J. E. Inikori, ed., *Forced Migration: The Impact of the Export Slave Trade on African Societies* (New York, 1982).

43. Ivor Wilks, "A Medieval Trade Route from the Niger to the Gulf of Guinea," *Journal of African History* 3 (1962): 337–41; J. D. Fage, "Some Remarks on Beads and Trade in Lower Guinea in the Sixteenth and Seventeenth Centuries," *Journal of African History* 3 (1962): 343–47; Vansina, "Long-Distance Trade," pp. 375–90.

44. Eugenia W. Herbert, "Portuguese Adaptation to Trade Patterns: Guinea to Angola," *African Studies Review* 17 (1974): 411–23.

45. James A. Rawley, *The Trans-Atlantic Slave Trade: A History* (New York, 1981), pp. 105–8, 149–51; Colin Palmer, *Human Cargoes: The British Slave Trade to Spanish America, 1700–1739* (Urbana, 1981), pp. 3–5. On the Spanish rivalry, see Antonio Rumeu de Armas, *España en el Africa atlántica* (Madrid, 1956). John W. Blake, ed., *Europeans in West Africa, 1450–1560*, 2 vols. (London, 1942).

46. Rawley, *Trans-Atlantic Slave Trade*, pp. 79–103; Ernst van den Boogart and Pieter C.

Emmer, "The Dutch Participation in the Atlantic Slave Trade, 1596-1650," in *The Uncommon Market: Essays in the Economic History of the Atlantic Slave Trade*, ed. Henry A. Gemery and Jan S. Hogendorn (New York, 1979), pp. 353-75; Johannes Postma, "The Dimension of the Dutch Slave Trade from Western Africa," *Journal of African History* 13 (1972): 237-48.

47. Sidney M. Greenfield, "Madeira and the Beginnings of New World Sugar Cane Cultivation and Plantation Slavery: A Study in Institution Building," in *Comparative Perspectives on Slavery in New World Plantation Societies*, ed. Vera D. Rubin and Arthur Tuden, Annals of the New York Academy of Sciences, vol 292 (New York, 1977), pp. 536-52.

48. Ibid., pp. 537-40; Godinho, *Descobrimentos henriquinos*, p. 165; Sidney M. Greenfield, "Plantations, Sugar Cane and Slavery," *Historical Reflections/Réflexions Historiques* 6 (1979): 85-119, especially pp. 98-99; Charles Verlinden, *The Beginnings of Modern Colonization: Eleven Essays with and Introduction*, trans. Yvonne Freccero (Ithaca and London, 1970), p. 14.

49. Greenfield, "Madeira and the Beginnings," p. 544; Noël Deerr, *The History of Sugar*, 2 vols. (London, 1949-50), 1:100; Diffie and Winius, *Portuguese Empire*, pp. 306-7; Joel Serrão, "Le blé des îles atlantiques: Madere et Açores aux XVe et XVIe siècles," *Annales: E. S. C.* 9 (1954): 337-41.

50. Greenfield, "Madeira and the Beginnings," pp. 543-44; Godinho, *Descobrimentos henriquinos*, pp. 167-68; Greenfield, "Plantations," pp. 99-100; Pierre Chaunu, "Le Maroc et l'Atlantique (1450-1550)," *Annales: E. S. C.* 11 (1956): 361-65; Marques, *History of Portugal*, 1:153.

51. Greenfield, "Madeira and the Beginnings," p. 544; Greenfield, "Plantations," pp. 102-3; Verlinden, *Modern Colonization*, p. 216; Diffie and Winius, *Portuguese Empire*, p. 306; Marques, *History of Portugal*, 1:154; Deerr, *History of Sugar*, 1:100.

52. Godinho, *Descobrimentos henriquinos*, pp. 167-68; Marques, *History of Portugal*, 1:238; Virginia Rau, "The Madeiran Sugar Cane Plantations," in *From Reconquest to Empire: The Iberian Background to Latin American History*, ed. Harold B. Johnson (New York, 1970), pp. 75-77; For more detailed accounts of Madeiran sugar production, see Virginia Rau and Jorge Borges de Macedo, *O açúcar da Madeira nos fins do século XV: Problemas de produção e comercio* (Funchal, 1962); and Fernando Jasmins Pereira, *O açucar madeirense de 1500 a 1537: Produção e preços* (Lisbon, 1969). On the proposal to expel the Guanches, see Lothar Siemens Hernández and Liliana Barreto de Siemens, "Los esclavos aborígenes canarios en la isla de Madera (1455-1505)," *Anuario de Estudios Atlánticos* 20 1974):111-43.

53. Rau, "Madeiran Sugar Cane Plantations," pp. 78-82; Frederick C. Lane, *Venice: A Maritime Republic* (Baltimore and London, 1973), pp. 297-98.

54. Greenfield, "Plantations," pp. 108-10; Godinho, *Descobrimentos henriquinos*, p. 168; Marques, *History of Portugal*, 1:158, 239-40; Serrão, "Le blé," pp. 337-41.

55. Deerr, *History of Sugar*, 1:101-2, 260; Godinho, *Descobrimentos henriquinos*, p. 176; Greenfield, "Plantations," pp. 111-16; Malowist, "Système de plantations," pp. 9-30.

56. For a general account of the Canaries, see John Mercer, *The Canary Islanders: Their Prehistory, Conquest and Survival* (London, 1980). On the sugar cane industry, see Guillermo Camacho y Pérez-Galdos, "El cultivo do la caña de azúcar y la industria azucarera en Gran Canaria (1510-1535)," *Anuario de Estudios Atlánticos* 7 (1961): 1-60; Vitorino de Magalhães Godinho, "A economia das Canarias nos séculos XIV e XV," *Revista de História* 4 (1952): 311-20.

CHAPTER 8. AFRICAN SLAVES IN EUROPE

1. See chapter 5.

2. Charles Verlinden, *L'esclavage dans l'Europe médiévale*, vol. 1: *Péninsule iberique—France* (Bruges, 1955), pp. 762-65, 846-52; Françoise Piponnier, *Coutume et vie sociale: La cour d'Anjou, XIVe et XVe siècles* (Paris and The Hague, 1970), pp. 240-43.

3. The historiography of blacks in England is well developed, but of course most works treat later periods. See Anthony J. Baker, *African Link: British Attitudes to the Negro in the Era of the Atlantic Slave Trade* (London, 1978); Edward Scobie, *Black Brittania: A History of Blacks in Britain*

(Chicago, 1972; F. O. Shyllon, *Black Slaves in Britain* (London, 1974); id. *Black People in Britain, 1555–1833* (London, 1977); James Walvin, *Black and White: The Negro in English Society, 1555–1945* London, 1973); id., *The Black Presence: A Documentary History of the Negro in England, 1555–1860* (London, 1971); Paul Edwards and James Walvin, "Africans in Britain, 1500–1800," in *The African Diaspora: Interpretive Essays,* ed. Martin L. Kilson and Robert I. Rotberg, (Cambridge, Mass., and London, 1976), pp. 172–204. On the slaves Hawkins brought back, see Shyllon, *Black Slaves in Britain,* p. 3; and P. E. H. Hair, "Protestants as Pirates, Slavers, and Proto-missionaries: Sierra Leone, 1568 and 1582," *Journal of Ecclesiastical History* 21 (1970): 203–24.

4. John L. Vogt, "The Lisbon Slave House and African Trade, 1486–1521," *Proceedings of the American Philosophical Society* 117 (1973): 1–16; A. C. de C. M. Saunders, *A Social History of Black Slaves and Freedmen in Portugal, 1441–1555* (Cambridge, Eng., 1982), pp. 8–10.

5. Vogt, "Lisbon Slave House," p. 5.

6. Saunders, *Black Slaves and Freedmen,* pp. 11–12.

7. Ibid., pp. 12–15.

8. Ibid., pp. 15–19; Vogt, "Lisbon Slave House," pp. 9–10.

9. Saunders, *Black Slaves and Freedmen,* pp. 16, 110; Vogt, "Lisbon Slave House," pp. 11–12; A. H. de Oliveira Marques, *Daily Life in Portugal in the Late Middle Ages,* trans. S. S. Wyatt (Madison, 1971), p. 273.

10. Saunders, *Black Slaves and Freedmen,* pp. 17–25.

11. Ibid., pp. 31–33.

12. Ibid., pp. 47–61.

13. Ibid., pp. 62–68, 72–80; Verlinden, *Esclavage,* 1:838.

14. Saunders, *Black Slaves and Freedmen,* pp. 69–71. 86–87.

15. Ibid., pp. 71–72.

16. Ibid., pp. 149–65.

17. Ibid., pp. 113–33.

18. Ibid., pp. 134–138.

19. Ibid., pp. 138–48.

20. Ruth Pike, *Enterprise and Adventure: The Genoese in Seville and the Opening of the New World* (Ithaca, 1966); Jacques Heers, *Gênes au XVe siècle: Activité économique et problèmes sociaux* (Paris, 1961).

21. Miguel Angel Ladero Quesada, "La esclavitud por guerra a fines del siglo XV: El caso de Málaga," *Hispania* 27 (1967): 63–88; José Maria Robasco Valdés, "Dos aspectos de la esclavitud morisca: Málaga, 1569," in *Homenaje al Doctor Juan Reglà Campistol,* vol. 1 (Valencia, 1975), pp. 293–302; Ana Maria Vera Delgado, "Revuelta mudéjar de 1500–1501: El destino de los vencidos" (Actas del Congreso de Historia de Andalucía, 1976), in *Andalucía medieval,* vol. 2 (Córdoba, 1978), pp. 387–93; Mercedes García Arenal, "Los moriscos de la región de Cuenca segun los censos establecidos por la Inquisición en 1589 y 1594," *Hispania* 138 (1978): 151–99.

22. Ruth Pike, *Aristocrats and Traders: Sevillian Society in the Sixteenth Century* (Ithaca, 1972), p. 174.

23. Ibid., p. 170.

24. Antonio Collantes de Terán Sánchez, "Contribución al estudio de los esclavos en la Sevilla medieval," in *Homenaje al Profesor Carriazo,* ed. Luis Núñez Contreras, vol. 2 (Seville, 1972), pp. 109–21.

25. Ibid., p. 172; Alfonso Franco Silva, *La esclavitud en Sevilla y su tierra a fines de la edad media* (Seville, 1979), pp. 132–46. A condensation of Franco Silva's book appeared as *Los esclavos de Sevilla* (Seville, 1980).

26. Pike, *Aristocrats and Traders,* pp. 183–85; Franco Silva, *Esclavitud en Sevilla,* pp. 193–97; Collantes de Terán, "Contribución," pp. 111–12; Pike, *Enterprise and Adventure,* p. 40.

27. Ruth Pike, "Sevillian Society in the Sixteenth Century: Slaves and Freedmen," *Hispanic American Historical Review* 47 (1967): 344–59.

28. Pike, *Aristocrats and Traders*, pp. 173, 186-88; Juan Aranda Doncel, "Estructura de la población morisca en tres parroquias sevillanas: San Julián, San Román y Santa Lucía," *Boletín de la Real Academia de Córdoba de Ciencias, Bellas Artes y Nobles Artes* 45 (1976): 77-84.

29. Pike, *Aristocrats and Traders*, pp. 174, 180-81;

30. Franco Silva, *Esclavitud en Sevilla*, pp. 203-10.

31. Pike, *Aristocrats and Traders*, pp. 191-92. For later references, see Antonio Domínguez Ortiz, "La esclavitud en Castilla durante la Edad Moderna," *Estudios de Historia Social de España* 2 (1952): 367-428.

32. Vicenta Cortés Alonso, "La población negra de Palos de la Frontera (1568-1579)," in *Actas y Memorias del XXXVI Congreso Internacional de Americanistas, Sevilla, 1964*, vol. 3 (Seville, 1966), pp. 609-18.

33. Vicenta Cortés Alonso, *La esclavitud en Valencia durante el reinado de los Reyes Católicos, 1479-1516* (Valencia, 1964), pp. 29-31, 40-47.

34. Ibid., pp. 29-33, 39, 50-53, 55.

35. Ibid., pp. 33, 53-63; P. E. H. Hair, "Black African Slaves at Valencia, 1482-1516: An Onamastic Inquiry," *History in Africa: A Journal of Method* 7 (1980): 119-39; A. Teixeira da Mota, "Entrée d'esclaves noirs à Valence (1445-1482): Le remplacement de la voie saharienne par la voie atlantique," *Revue française d'histoire d'outremer* 66/1-2 (1979): 195-210; Jacqueline Guiral, "Les relations commerciales du Royaume de Valence avec la Berberie au XVe siècle," *Mélanges de la Casa de Velázquez* 10 (1974): 114-16; Vicenta Cortés Alonso, "Procedencia de los esclavos negros en Valencia (1482-1516)," *Revista española de Antropología Americana* 7 (1972): 123-51. On Jewish slaves in the Mediterranean world generally, see Jacques Heers, *Esclaves et domestiques au Moyen-Age dans le monde méditerranéen* (Paris, 1981), pp. 67-69.

36. Cortés Alonso, *Esclavitud en Valencia*, pp. 65-70, 87, 99, 107, 114-15, 118, 120; Vicente Graullera Sanz, *La esclavitud en Valencia en los siglos XVI y XVII* (Valencia, 1978), pp. 57-68.

37. Cortés Alonso, *Esclavitud en Valencia*, pp. 121-22.

38. Ibid., pp. 103-6, 130; Claude Carrère, *Barcelone: Centre économique a l'époque des difficultés, 1380-1462*, 2 vols. (Paris and The Hague, 1967), 1:484.

39. Cortés Alonso, *Esclavitud en Valencia*, pp. 79, 82, 91.

40. Ibid., pp. 124-27, 130. The prohibition on slaves serving as sailors and galley oarsmen seems not to have been general in early modern Spain. Some 2,000 slaves served on the ships of the Great Armada of 1588. (Archivo General de la Marina [Museo Naval, Madrid], manuscript 471, folios 174-78 v.) In 1603 the king paid 200 ducats to don Diego López de Aro for two Turkish slaves that López de Aro consigned to the galleys. (Archivo General de Simancas, *Consejo y Juntas de Hacienda, legajo* 431.)

41. Ibid., pp. 131-33; Miguel Gual Camarena, "Un seguro contra crímines de esclavos en el siglo XV," *Anuario de Historia de Derecho Española* 23 (1953): 247-58.

42. Cortés Alonso, *Esclavitud en Valencia*, pp. 132-36, 138-40.

43. Jaime Sobrequés Callicó, ed., *Catálogo de la cancillería de Enrique IV de Castilla, Señor del Principado de Cataluña, Lugartenencia de Juan de Beaumont, 1462-1464* (Barcelona, 1975), document 836, pp. 163-64.

44. Cortés Alonso, *Esclavitud en Valencia*, pp. 136-37.

45. Graullera Sanz, *Esclavitud en Valencia*, pp. 135, 137-43, 171-73.

46. Miguel Gual Camarena, "Una cofradía de negros libertos en el sigo XV," *Estudios de la Edad Media en la Corona de Aragón* 5 (1952): 457-66.

47. Manuela Marrero Rodríguez, *La esclavitud en Tenerife a raíz de la conquista* (La Laguna de Tenerife, 1966), pp. 17-18, 23-24, 26-27.

48. Ibid., pp. 31-33, 54-55; Antonio de la Torre y del Cerro, "Los canarios de Gomera vendidos como esclavos en 1489," *Anuario de Estudios Americanos* 7 (1950): 47-72.

49. Marrero Rodríguez, *Esclavitud en Tenerife*, pp. 29, 34-35.

50. Ibid., pp. 80-81, 84, 88, 96, 104. One lucky native of Gomera won his freedom from slavery in Gibraltar when the bishop of the Canaries intervened and secured the aid of Castile's royal coun-

cil. (Archivo General de Simancas, *Registro General del Sello*, 21 January 1491, folio 74.)

51. Marrero Rodríguez, *Esclavitud en Tenerife*, pp. 45–53, 55, 102–3.

52. For slavery in Russia, see Richard Hellie, *Slavery in Russia, 1450–1725* (Chicago, 1982); Richard Hellie, "Recent Soviet Historiography on Medieval and Early Modern Russian Slavery," *Russian Review* 35 (1976): 1–32. For penal slavery, see Orlando Patterson, *Slavery and Social Death: A Comparative Study* (Cambridge, Mass., and London, 1982), pp. 44–45; Johan Thorsten Sellin, *Slavery and the Penal System* (New York, 1976); Michael R. Weisser, *Crime and Punishment in Early Modern Europe* (Sussex, 1979); Ruth Pike, *Penal Servitude in Early Modern Spain* (Madison, 1983). For Mediterranean piracy and slavery in the period, see Fernand Braudel, *The Mediterranean and the Mediterranean World in the Age of Philip II*, trans. Siân Reynolds, 2 vols, (New York, 1972–73), 2:865–91; Ellen G. Friedman, "Christian Captives at 'Hard Labor' in Algiers, 16th–18th Centuries," *International Journal of African Historical Studies* 13/4 (1980): 616–32; Ellen G. Friedman, *Spanish Captives in North Africa in the Early Modern Age* (Madison, 1983); Stephen Clissold, *The Barbary Slaves* (Totowa, N.J., 1977).

CHAPTER 9. THE EARLY
TRANSATLANTIC SLAVE TRADE

1. Philip D. Curtin, "Slavery and Empire," in *Comparative Perspectives on Slavery in New World Plantation Societies*, ed. Vera D. Rubin and Arthur Tuden, Annals of the New York Academy of Sciences, vol 292 (New York, 1977), pp. 9–10.

2. John H. Parry, *The Spanish Seaborne Empire* (New York, 1966), p. 44; *The Discovery of the Sea* (Berkeley and Los Angeles, 1981), p. 199. Just which of the Bahama Islands Columbus first reached is disputed.

3. A classic statement of this viewpoint is given by Adam Smith in *The Wealth of Nations*.

4. C. R. Markham, ed., *The Journal of Christopher Columbus (during His First Voyage, 1492–93) and Documents Relating to the Voyages of John Cabot and Gaspar Corte Real*, (Hakluyt Society Publications, 1st series, vol. 86 (London, 1893; reprint, n.d.), pp, 38,41.

5. Carl Ortwin Sauer, *The Early Spanish Main* (Berkeley and Los Angeles, 1966), p. 35.

6. Cecil Jane, trans. and ed., *Select Documents Illustrating the Four Voyages of Columbus*, vol. 1: *The First and Second Voyages*, Hakluyt Society Publications, 2d series, vol. 65 (London, 1930), pp. 88–89. See also Troy S. Floyd, *The Columbus Dynasty in the Caribbean, 1492–1526* (Albuquerque, 1973), p. 28.

7. Quoted in Sauer, *Early Spanish Main*, pp. 87–88.

8. Ibid., p. 209; Mervyn Ratekin, "The Early Sugar Industry in Española," *Hispanic American Historical Review* 34 (1954): 1–3; Fernando B. Sandoval, *La industria del azúcar en Nueva España* (Mexico City, 1951), p. 11; Floyd, *Columbus Dynasty*, pp. 84–85.

9. The best available summary of these views is Alfred W. Crosby, Jr., *The Columbian Exchange: Biological and Cultural Consequences of 1492* (Westport, Conn., 1972). See also Percy M. Ashburn, *The Ranks of Death: A Medical History of the Conquest of America* (New York, 1947); Eric Wolf, *Sons of the Shaking Earth* (Chicago, 1959), pp. 195–97; and William H. McNeill, *Plagues and Peoples* (Garden City, 1976), pp. 176–91.

10. Crosby, *Columbian Exchange*, pp. 35–36.

11. Ibid., pp. 35–63.

12. For a general synthesis of the scholarly opinion, see Nicolás Sánchez-Albornoz, *The Population of Latin America*, trans. W. A. R. Richardson (Berkeley and Los Angeles, 1974), pp. 37–85; William M. Denevan, ed., *The Native Population of the Americas in 1492* (Madison, 1976). For Mexico, see Charles Gibson, *The Aztecs under Spanish Rule* (Stanford, 1964), pp. 5–6, 136–47, 448–51, 460–62.

13. Woodrow W. Borah and Sherburne F. Cook, *The Aboriginal Population of Central Mexico on the Eve of the Spanish Conquest* (Berkeley and Los Angeles, 1963), pp. 4, 88. See also William T. Sanders, "The Population of the Central Mexican Symbiotic Region, the Basin of Mexico, and the Teotihuacan Valley in the Sixteenth Century," in Devenan, ed., *Native Population*, pp. 85–150.

14. Noble David Cook, *Demographic Collapse: Indian Peru, 1520-1620* (Cambridge, Eng., 1981), p. 94.

15. Wilbur R. Jacobs, "British-Colonial Attitudes and Policies toward the Indian in the American Colonies," in *Attitudes of Colonial Powers toward the American Indian* ed. Howard Peckham and Charles Gibson (Salt Lake City, 1969), p. 83.

16. Wolf, *Sons of the Shaking Earth*, pp. 195-96.

17. On Amerindian slavery, see Silvio Zavala, *Los esclavos indios in Nueva España* (Mexico City, 1967); id., "Los esclavos indios en Guatemala," *Historia Mexicana* 19/4 (1970): 459-65; William L. Sherman, *Forced Native Labor in Sixteenth-Century Central America* (Lincoln, 1979); Peggy K. Liss, *Mexico under Spain, 1521-1556; Society and the Origins of Nationality* (Chicago and London, 1975); David L. Radell, "The Indian Slave Trade and Population of Nicaragua during the Sixteenth Century," in *Native Population*, ed. Devenan, pp. 67-76; Marie Helmer, "Note sur les esclaves indiens au Pérou (XVIe siècle)," *Bulletin de la Faculté des Lettres de Strasbourg* 43/7 (1965): 683-90; Jacques Lafaye, "L'église et l'esclavage des Indiens de 1537 à 1708," *Bulletin de la Faculté des Lettres de Strasbourg* 43/7 (1965): 191-203; Jean-Pierre Berthe, "Aspects de l'esclavage des Indiens en Nouvelle-Espagne pendant la première moitié du XVIe siècle," *Journal de la Société des Américanistes* 54/2 (1965): 189-209.

18. The classic work on *encomienda* is Leslie Byrd Simpson, *The Encomienda in New Spain: The Beginnings of Spanish Mexico*, rev. ed. (Berkeley and Los Angeles, 1966).

19. Colin A. Palmer, *Slaves of the White God: Blacks in Mexico, 1570-1650* (Cambridge, Mass., 1976), p. 8; Stuart B. Schwartz, "Indian Labor and New World Plantations: European Demands and Indian Responses in Northeastern Brazil," *American Historical Review* 83/1 (1978): 76-77. On Las Casas, see the many studies by Lewis Hanke, among them *The Spanish Struggle for Justice in the Conquest of America* (Philadelphia, 1949; reprint, Boston, 1965); *Aristotle and the American Indians: A Study in Race Prejudice in the Modern World*, rev. ed. (Bloomington, 1975); *All Mankind Is One: A Study of the Disputation between Bartolomé de las Casas and Juan Ginés de Sepúlveda in 1550 on the Intellectual and Religious Capacity of the American Indians* (De Kalb, Ill., 1974).

20. Charles Ralph Boxer, *The Portuguese Seaborne Empire, 1415-1825* (New York, 1969), pp. 85-86; John Hemming, *Red Gold: The Conquest of the Brazilian Indians* (London, 1978), pp. 8-13. The French frequently took some Amerindians back to France, ibid., pp. 12-13. Schwartz, "Indian Labor," pp. 47-48.

21. Boxer, *Portuguese Seaborne Empire*, p. 86; Hemming, *Red Gold*, pp. 36-37.

22. Boxer, *Portuguese Seaborne Empire*, pp. 86-87; Hemming, *Red Gold*, pp. 38-41. The full name of the early colonial capital of Brazil was Salvador da Bahia de Todos os Santos; it is usually called Bahia and occasionally Salvador.

23. Boxer, *Portuguese Seaborne Empire*, pp. 87-88; Schwartz, "Indian Labor," pp. 45, 50; Alexander Marchant, *From Barter to Slavery: The Economic Relations of Portuguese and Indians in the Settlement of Brazil, 1500-1580* (Baltimore, 1942).

24. Mathias C. Kiemen, *The Indian Policy of Portugal in the Amazon Region, 1614-1693* (Washington, D.C., 1954), pp. 3-5; Hemming, *Red Gold*, pp. 151,313.

25. Kiemen, *Indian Policy*, pp. 6-8. On the Jesuits, see Hemming, *Red Gold*, pp. 97-118, 313-17.

26. Boxer, *Portuguese Seaborne Empire*, pp. 92-94, 96; Schwartz, "Indian Labor," pp. 50-57; Hemming, *Red Gold*, pp. 57-118; Dauril Alden, "Black Robes versus White Settlers: The Struggle for 'Freedom for the Indians' in Colonial Brazil," in *Attitudes of the Colonial Powers*, ed. Peckham and Gibson, pp. 19-45; Stuart B. Schwartz, *Sovereignty and Society in Colonial Brazil: The High Court of Bahia and its Judges, 1609-1751* (Berkely and Los Angeles, 1973), pp. 122-39.

27. Boxer, *Portuguese Seaborne Empire*, pp. 90-92; Celso Furtado, *The Economic Growth of Brazil: A Survey from Colonial to Modern Times*, trans. Ricardo W. de Aguiar and Eric Charles Drysdale (Berkeley and Los Angeles, 1963), pp. 43-46.

28. Boxer, *Portuguese Seaborne Empire*, pp. 104-5.

29. James A. Rawley, *Trans-Atlantic Slave Trade: A History* (New York and London, 1981), pp. 27–28.

30. Jacobs, "British-Colonial Attitudes," p. 82.

31. E. S. Morgan, "Slavery and Freedom: The American Paradox," *Journal of American History* 59 (1972): 5–29; David W. Galenson, *White Servitude in Colonial America: An Economic Analysis* (Cambridge, Eng., and New York, 1981).

32. An important analysis of this transition in one region is that of T. H. Breen and Stephen Innes, *"Myne Owne Ground:" Race and Freedom on Virginia's Eastern Shore, 1640–1676* (New York and Oxford, 1980). For references to slavery in British North American before 1650, see Willie Lee Rose, ed., *A Documentary History of Slavery in North America* (New York, 1976), pp. 15–17, 22–23. The standard account of the English Caribbean beginnings is R. S. Dunn, *Sugar and Slaves: The Rise of the Planter Class in the English West Indies, 1624–1713* (Williamsburg, 1972).

33. The literature on this is extensive. See, for example, Winthrop D. Jordan, *White over Black: American Attitudes toward the Negro, 1550–1812* (Chapel Hill, 1968); Oscar and Mary Handlin, "Origins of the Southern Labor System," *William and Mary Quarterley*, 3rd series, 7 (1950): 199–222; Carl N. Degler, "Slavery and the Genesis of the Southern Labor System," *Comparative Studies in History and Society* 2 (1959): 49–66, 488–95. A convenient collection of extracts is provided by Raymond Starr and Robert Detweiler, eds., *Race, Prejudice and the Origins of Slavery in America* (Cambridge, Mass., 1975).

34. C. Duncan Rice, *The Rise and Fall of Black Slavery* (New York, 1975), pp. 25–26.

35. On this point, Schwartz ("Indian Labor," pp. 76–77) surveys the evidence, cites a number of sources, and concludes: "There was . . . a remarkable similarity among all the colonial regimes in the New World in the low value placed on Indian laborers in comparison with Africans . . . the similarity of opinion among all the New World slaveholding regimes suggests that there was a comparative advantage, especially in the formative period of slaveholding, in the use of African rather than Indian slaves and that this advantage was based on productivity in terms of return on investment." See also the discussion by Frederick Bowser, *The African Slave in Colonial Peru, 1524–1650* (Stanford, 1974), pp. 110–124.

36. There are two classic works on the slave trade to the Spanish Indies: J. A. Saco, *Historia de la esclavitud de la raza africana en el Nuevo Mundo, y en especial en los países Américo-Hispanos*, 2d ed., 3 vols. (Havana, 1937–43); Georges Scelle, *La traite négriere aux Indes de Castille: Contrats et traités d'assiento*, 2 vols. (Paris, 1905-6). See also Henri Lapeyre, "La trata de negros con destino a la América española durante los últimos años del reinado de Carlos V, 1544–1555," *Cuadernos de Investigación Histórica* 2 (1978): 335–39. Although most stress the period after 1650, there are several important general accounts of the transatlantic slave trade: Basil Davidson, *The African Slave Trade: Precolonial History, 1450–1850* (Boston and Toronto, 1961), also published as *Black Mother* (London, 1961) Philip D. Curtin, *The Atlantic Slave Trade: A Census* (Madison, 1969); Christopher Fyfe, "The Dynamics of African Dispersal: The Transatlantic Slave Trade," in *The African Diaspora: Interpretive Essays*, ed. Martin L. Kilson and Robert I. Rotberg, (Cambridge, Mass., and London, 1976), pp. 57–74; Enriqueta Vila Villar, *Hispanoamérica y el comercio de esclavos* (Seville, 1977); Herbert S. Klein, *The Middle Passage: Comparative Studies in the Atlantic Slave Trade* (Princeton, 1978); Henry A. Gemery and Jan S. Hogendorn, eds., *The Uncommon Market: Essays in the Economic History of the Atlantic Slave Trade* (New York, 1979); UNESCO, *The African Slave Trade from the Fifteenth to the Nineteenth Century* (Paris, 1979); Rawley, *Atlantic Slave Trade*; Colin Palmer, *Human Cargoes: The British Slave Trade to Spanish America, 1700–1739* (Urbana, 1981); J. E. Inikori, ed., *Forced Migration: The Impact of the Export Slave Trade on African Societies* (New York, 1982).

37. Rolando Mellafe, *Negro Slavery in Latin America*, trans. J. W. S. Judge (Berkeley and Los Angeles, 1975), pp. 14–15.

38. Ibid., pp. 15–16; Ruth Pike, *Enterprise and Adventure: The Genoese in Seville and the Opening of the New World* (Ithaca, 1966), pp. 55–56.

39. Mellafe, *Negro Slavery*, p. 38; Pike, *Enterprise and Adventure*, p. 56.

40. For a discussion of race in colonial Latin America, see Magnus Mörner, *Race Mixture in the History of Latin America* Boston, 1967).

41. Mellafe, *Negro Slavery*, pp. 38-41; Pike, *Enterprise and Adventure*, pp. 57-59; Palmer, *Slaves of the White God*, p. 9; Floyd, *Columbus Dynasty*, p. 184; Ralph H. Vigil, "Negro Slaves and Rebels in the Spanish Possessions, 1503-1558," *The Historian* 33 (1971): 637-55.

42. Mellafe, *Negro Slavery*, pp. 38-40, 42-43; Pike, *Enterprise and Adventure*, pp. 60-67.

43. Mellafe, *Negro Slavery*, p. 40.

44. Ibid., pp. 41-42; Enrique Otte and Conchita Ruiz-Burruecos, "Los Portugueses en la trata de esclavos negros de las postrimerías del siglo XVI," *Moneda y Crédito* 85 (1963): 3-40; Françoise Latour de Veiga Pinto, with A. Carreira, "Portuguese Participation in the Slave Trade: Opposing Forces, Trends of Opinion within Portuguese Society, Effects on Portugal's Socioeconomic Development," in UNESCO, *African Slave Trade*, pp. 119-47.

45. Vila Villar, *Commercio de esclavos*. pp. 24-25. A portion of her findings were published in English as "The Large Scale Introduction of Africans into Veracruz and Cartagena," in *Comparative Perspectives on Slavery*, ed. Rubin and Tuden, pp. 267-80.

46. Vila Villar, *Comercio de esclavos*, pp. 27, 32-35; Mellafe, *Negro Slavery*, pp. 44-45; Gonzalo Aguirre Beltrán, "The Slave Trade in Mexico," *Hispanic American Historical Review* 24 (1944): 415-16.

47. Vila Villar, *Comercio de esclavos*, pp. 128-31, 133, 141; Curtin, *Atlantic Slave Trade*, pp. 22-24; Pierre and Huguette Chaunu, *Séville et l'Atlantique*, 8 vols. (Paris, 1955-60), 1:310-13.

48. Vila Villar, *Comercio de esclavos*, 143-44.

49. Ibid., pp. 144-145.

50. Ibid., pp. 146-47.

51. Ibid., p. 147.

52. Ibid., p. 139.

53. Philip D. Curtin, "Epidemiology and the Slave Trade" *Political Science Quarterly* 83 (1968): 190-216; Klein, *The Middle Passage*, pp. 73-94; Joseph C. Miller, "Morality in the Atlantic Slave Trade: Statistical Evidence on Causality," *Journal of Interdisciplinary History* 11/3 (1981): 385-423; and the sources cited in these three works. The statistics Curtin, Klein, and Miller cite are from later than our period, but the mechanisms they discuss surely operated from the beginning of the trade. See also Kenneth F. Kiple and Virginia Himmelsteib King, *Another Dimension to the African Diaspora: Diet, Disease, and Racism* (Cambridge, Eng., 1981).

54. Alonso de Sandoval, *De Instauranda Aethopum Salute* (originally published Seville, 1627), ed. Angel Valtierra (Bogotá, 1956), pp. 107-8.

55. Katia M. de Queiros Mattoso, *Être esclave au Brésil, XVIe-XIXe* (Paris, 1979), pp. 60-61. True slave merchants only emerged in Brazil in the second half of the seventeenth century. Ibid., p. 61.

56. Rawley, *Trans-Atlantic Slave Trade*, pp. 27-28.

57. Leslie B. Rout, Jr., "The African in Colonial Brazil," in *African Diaspora*, ed. Kilson and Rotberg, pp. 137-39. Pierre Verger, *Flux et reflux de la traite des nègres entre le Golfe de Benin et Bahia de Todos os Santos du XVIIe au XIXe siècle* (Paris and the Hague, 1968); John Vogt, *Portuguese Rule on the Gold Coast, 1469-1682* (Athens, Ga., 1979), pp. 144-93.

58. Curtin's exact figure was 9,566,100 within a possible range of from eight to ten and one-half million.

59. J. E. Inikori, "The Origin of the Diaspora: The Slave Trade from Africa," *Tarikh*, 5, 6 (1978):1-19; and his introduction to *Forced Migration*; Rawley, *Trans-Atlantic Slave Trade*, p. 428.

60. Paul E. Lovejoy, "The Volume of the Atlantic Slave Trade: A Synthesis," *Journal of African History* 23 (1982):473-501.

61. Curtin, *Atlantic Slave Trade*, pp. 116, 119.

62. These estimates for the European trade (797,800 slaves delivered by 1650 to the areas the Europeans controlled) should be compared with Ralph A. Austen's figures (table 4.1), which show some 900,000 slaves making the trans-Saharan crossing in the same period.

63. Vila Villar, *Comercio de esclavos*, pp. 153–54; Aguirre Beltrán, "Slave Trade In Mexico," p. 413; Mattoso, *Être esclave*, pp. 61, 73, 77–88. For slave trading in one Spanish American town, see Carlos Sempat Assadourian, *El tráfico de esclavos de Córdoba de Angola a Potosí, siglos XVI–XVII* (Córdoba, Argentina, 1966). For an account of the terrible conditions on land once the slaves were unloaded, see David L. Chandler, "Health Conditions in the Slave Trade of Colonial New Granada," in *Slavery and Race Relations in Latin America*, ed. Robert Brent Toplin (Westport, Conn., 1974), pp. 51–88; id., *Health and Slavery in Colonial Colombia* (New York, 1981).

CHAPTER 10. SLAVERY IN
EARLY COLONIAL LATIN AMERICA

1. Despite the enormous and growing literature on Latin American slavery, there are still many unanswered questions. A survey of the field and an agenda for research was provided over ten years ago by Frederick Bowser, "The African in Colonial Spanish America: Reflections on Research Achievements and Priorities," *Latin American Research Review* 7 (1972): 77–92. A great deal of work has been done since then, a part of it by Bowser himself, but his article still has validity. More research is in progress, and it will expand and clarify many as yet obscure points. Already it is possible to reject such blanket statements as Immanuel Wallerstein's comment on the relations of slaves and sugar in the New World: "Slaves, however, are not useful in large-scale enterprises whenever skill is required." *The Modern World-System: Capitalist Agriculture and the Origins of the European World-Economy in the Sixteenth Century* (New York, 1974), pp. 88. We will see many counterexamples in this chapter.

2. The distinctiveness of the plantation system is stressed by Sidney W. Mintz, *Caribbean Transformations* (Chicago, 1974), pp. 43–130.

3. Peter Gerhard, "A Black Conquistador in Mexico," *Hispanic American Historical Review* 58/3 (1978): 451–59; James Lockhart, *Spanish Peru: A Colonial Society* (Madison, 1968), pp. 171–72; Frederick Bowser, *The African Slave in Colonial Peru, 1524–1650* (Stanford, 1974), pp. 5–10; William F. Sater, "The Black Experience in Chile," in *Slavery and Race Relations in Latin America*, ed. Robert Brent Toplin, (Westport, Conn., 1974), p. 16; Peter Boyd-Bowman found a letter written by Valiente's owner, Alonso Valiente, a citizen of Puebla in Mexico, that sheds light on the slave's circumstances and the breakdowns in communications that could occur in a large, sparsely settled empire. Alonso Valiente asserted: "About eight years ago . . . having in my possession one Juan Valiente, a Negro, as my slave, and wishing to treat him kindly and having confidence that he would conduct himself properly, I granted him permission before Alonso de Sopuerto, notary public of the city of Veracruz, to go to Guatemala and Peru and wherever else he might wish to go and earn a soldier's pay like a free man, earning whatever might be his share, provided that he keep an accounting of it and bring it all back to me within four years; and though the said Juan Valiente did not do so nor keep his promise, I, having trust in him, did, when the time was up, send him another authorization, but in all this time I have received no word from him. I therefore commission you the said Pedro Mexia my nephew to demand a reckoning from my slave Juan Valiente of all he has earned during this time and to take possession of it, and if the said Negro should desire his freedom, you, Pedro Mexia, are empowered to agree to a fair price and to execute a letter of freedom and of quitclaim, but should he desire not to be free, and neither he nor anyone on his behalf pay the ransom you ask of him, then you may either bring him or send him back to me in New Spain or else sell him for whatever price you see fit," Peter Boyd-Bowman, "Negro Slaves in Early Colonial Mexico," *The Americas* 26 (1969): 150–151.

4. Many scholars have worked on sugar in Spanish America, see: Fernando B. Sandoval, *La industria del azúcar en Nueva España* (Mexico City, 1951); Troy S. Floyd, *The Columbus Dynasty in the Caribbean, 1491–1526* (Albuquerque, 1973); Mervyn Ratekin, "The Early Sugar Industry in Española," *Hispanic American Historical Review* 34 (1954): 1–19; Robert S. Haskett, "Santiago de Paz: Anatomy of a Sixteenth-Century Caribbean Sugar Estate," *UCLA Historical Journal* 1 (1980): 51–79; Ward Barrett, *The Sugar Hacienda of the Marqueses del Valle* (Minneapolis, 1970);

G. Michael Riley, *Fernando Cortés and the Marquesado in Morelos, 1522–1547: A Case Study in the Socioeconomic Development of Sixteenth-Century Mexico* (Albuquerque, 1973).

5. Ratekin, "Early Sugar Industry," pp. 3–7; Carl Otwin Sauer, *The Early Spanish Main* (Berkeley and Los Angeles, 1966), pp. 209–10.

6. Ratekin, "Early Sugar Industry," pp. 10–12; Ruth Pike, *Enterprise and Adventure: The Genoese in Seville and the Opening of the New World* (Ithaca, 1966), pp. 128–44. See Floyd, *Columbus Dynasty*, on the use of Amerindians on the sugar estates and on slave raiding to supply them: pp. 112, 132–34, 176, 184, 224, 263n.50.

7. Sauer, *Early Spanish Main*, p. 210; Noël Deerr, *The History of Sugar*, 2 vols. (London, 1949–50), 1:123–26; Sandoval, *Industria del azúcar*, p. 14; Floyd, *Columbus Dynasty*, pp. 224–26; Pike, *Enterprise and Adventure*, p. 139; Enriqueta Vila Villar, *Historia de Puerto Rico (1600–1650)*, (Seville, 1974).

8. Sandoval, *Industria del azúcar*, pp. 21, 23–51; Riley, *Cortés and the Marquesado*, p. 64; Barrett, *Sugar Hacienda*, p. 11; Pike, *Enterprise and Adventure*, p. 65.

9. Nicholas P. Cushner, *Lords of the Land: Sugar, Wine, and Jesuit Estates of Coastal Peru, 1600–1767* (Albany, 1980).

10. Haskett, "Santiago de Paz," pp. 65–70, 76–77.

11. Barrett, *Sugar Hacienda*, pp. 74–78.

12. Stuart B. Schwartz, *Sovereignty and Society in Colonial Brazil: The High Court of Bahia and Its Judges, 1609–1751* (Berkeley and Los Angeles, 1973), pp. 95–121; Schwartz, "Free Farmers in a Slave Economy: The *Lavradores de Cana* of Colonial Bahia," in *Colonial Roots of Modern Brazil: Papers of the Newberry Library Conference*, ed. Dauril Alden (Berkeley and Los Angeles, 1973). Schwartz has worked extensively and intensively on aspects of slavery and sugar in colonial Brazil. See also his "The Mamumission of Slaves in Colonial Brazil: Bahia, 1684–1745," *Hispanic American Historical Review* 54/4 (1974): 603–35; Ward Barrett and Stuart B. Schwartz, "Comparación entre dos economías azucareras colonials: Morelos, Mexico y Bahía, Brasil," in *Haciendas, latifundios y plantaciones en América latina*, ed. Enrique Florescano, (Mexico City, 1975), pp. 532–72. Schwartz's forthcoming book is *Sugar Plantations and the Formation of a Brazilian Society* (Cambridge University Press). An important work that appeared too late for incorporation into this book is Robert Edgar Conrad, *Children of God's Fire: A Documentary History of Black Slavery in Brazil* (Princeton, 1983).

13. Leslie B. Rout, Jr., "The African in Colonial Brazil," in *The African Diaspora: Interpretive Essays*, ed. Martin L. Kilson and Robert I. Rotberg (Cambridge, Mass., and London, 1976), pp. 147–50.

14. Richard Flecknoe, *A Relation of Ten Years Travels in Europe, Asia, Affrique, and America* (London, 1656), pp. 79–80, cited in C. R. Boxer, *Salvador de Sá and the Struggle for Brazil and Angola, 1602–1686* (London, 1952), p. 234.

15. Boxer, *Salvador de Sá*, p. 235.

16. A. Teixeira da Mota, F. Mauro, and J. Borges de Macedo, "Les routes portugaises de l'Atlantique," *Anuario de Estudios Atlánticos* 25 (1968): 137; regarding the English in the 1580s, see Kenneth R. Andrews, *Elizabethan Privateering: English Privateering during the Spanish War, 1585–1603* (Cambridge, Eng., 1964), pp. 200–221.

17. For a magisterial overview of early Mexican economic development, see François Chevalier, *Land and Society in Colonial Mexico: The Great Hacienda*, trans. Alvis Eustis (Berkeley and Los Angeles, 1970). On the limited use of slaves on indigo plantations in Central America, see Murdo J. MacLeod, *Spanish Central America: A Socioeconomic History, 1520–70* (Berkeley and Los Angeles, 1973), p. 190. Boyd-Bowman, "Negro Slaves in Early Colonial Mexico," p. 146, reported that one-fourth of the slaves of known occupation in the Mexican city of Puebla and its region worked on ranches; more were teamsters.

18. Bowser, *African Slave in Colonial Peru*, pp. 88–90; Lockhart, *Spanish Peru*, p. 31; Colin A. Palmer, *Slaves of the White God: Blacks in Mexico, 1570–1650* (Cambridge, Mass., 1976), pp. 186–87.

19. Robert J. Ferry, "Ecomienda, African Slavery and Agriculture in Seventeenth Century Caracas," *Hispanic American Historical Review* 61/4 (1981): 609-36.

20. John S. Fox, "The Beginning of Spanish Mining in America: The West Indies and Castilla de Oro" (Ph.D. dissertation, University of California, Berkeley, 1940); P. J. Bakewell, *Silver Mining and Society in Colonial Mexico: Zacatecas, 1546-1700* (Cambridge, Eng., 1971), pp. 122-125; P. W. Powell, *Soldiers, Indians and Silver: The Northward Advance of New Spain, 1550-1600* (Berkeley and Los Angeles, 1952), pp. 14, 109-11; Jorge Chapa, "The Political Economy of Labor Relations in the Silver Mines of Colonial Mexico," Institute for the Study of Social Change, Working Papers Series, no. 105 (Berkeley, 1978); Robert C. West, *The Mining Community in Northern New Spain: The Parral Mining District*, Ibero-Americana, vol. 30 (Berkeley and Los Angeles, 1949), pp. 47-56; Vincent Mayer, Jr., "The Black on New Spain's Northern Frontier: San José de Parral, 1631 to 1641," Occasional Papers of the Center for Southwest Studies, no. 2 (Durango, Col., 1974); Peter Marzahl, *Town in the Empire: Government, Politics, and Society in Seventeenth-Century Popoyán* (Austin, 1978), pp. 25-27, 45-46; Sater, "Black Experience in Chile," pp. 23-25; Lewis Hanke, *The Imperial City of Potosí: An Unwritten Chapter in the History of Spanish America* (The Hague, 1956), pp. 24-27, 33.

21. Bowser, *African Slave in Colonial Peru*, pp. 96-100; Lockhart, *Spanish Peru*, p. 184; Boyd-Bowman, "Negro Slaves in Early Colonial Mexico" p. 137, 146.

22. Bowser, *African Slave in Colonial Peru*, pp. 106-8; Lockhart, *Spanish Peru*, pp. 31, 122, 184; Boyd-Bowman, "Negro Slaves in Early Colonial Mexico," p. 146.

23. On artisan labor, see Bowser, *African Slave in Colonial Peru*, pp. 125-35; Lockhart, *Spanish Peru*, pp. 31, 122, 182-84; Palmer, *Slaves of the White God*, p. 45.

24. Bowser, *African Slave in Colonial Peru*, p. 135.

25. Lockhart, *Spanish Peru*, p. 184.

26. Bowser, *African Slave in Colonial Peru*, pp. 100-105; Lockhart, *Spanish Peru*, pp. 159-63, 181; Palmer, *Slaves of the White God*, p. 43.

27. Vicenta Cortés Alonso, "Los esclavos domésticos en América," *Anuario de Estudios Americanos* 24 (1967): 955-83.

28. The best available survey of this material is A. J. R. Russell-Wood, "Africans and Europeans: Historiography and Perceptions of Reality, ch. 1 in *The Black Man in Slavery and Freedom in Colonial Brazil* (New York, 1982), pp. 1-26. See also Gilberto Freyre, *The Masters and the Slaves: A Study in the Development of Brazilian Civilization*, trans., Samuel Putnam (New York, 1946); id., *The Mansions and the Shanties*, trans. and ed., Harriet de Onis (New York, 1963); id., *New World in the Tropics: The Culture of Modern Brazil* (New York, 1959); Frank Tannenbaum, *Slave and Citizen: The Negro in the Americas* (New York, 1947); Stanley M. Elkins, *Slavery: A Problem in American Institutional and Intellectual Life* (Chicago, 1959); Herbert S. Klein, *Slavery in the Americas: A Comparative Study of Virginia and Cuba* (Chicago, 1967).

29. C. R. Boxer, *Race Relations in the Portuguese Colonial Empire, 1415-1815* (Oxford, 1963); Carl N. Degler, *Neither Black nor White: Slavery and Race Relations in Brazil and the United States* (New York, 1971); A. J. R. Russell-Wood, "Iberian Expansion and the Issue of Black Slavery: Changing Portuguese Attitudes, 1440-1770," *American Historical Review* 83/1 (1978): 16-42; Stuart B. Schwartz, *Sugar Plantations*. Donald Gray Eder reminds us that "it must not be forgotten that it was the Tannenbaum thesis that first asked the right questions, thereby expanding the parochial study of one region's peculiar institution to include the experience of other cultures throughout the New World." "Time under the Southern Cross: The Tannenbaum Thesis Reconsidered," *Agricultural History* 50/4 (1976): 600-14. The quotation is on the last page. A useful set of articles is contained in Laura Foner and Eugene D. Genovese, eds., *Slavery in the New World: A Reader in Comparative History* (Englewood Cliffs, N.J., 1969).

30. D. M. Davidson, "Negro Slave Control and Resistance in Colonial Mexico, 1519-1650," *Hispanic American Historical Review* 46 (1966): 241-42.

31. Bowser, *African Slave in Colonial Peru*, pp. 254-67; Palmer, *Slaves of the White God*, pp. 56-60; Russell-Wood, *Black Man*, p. 173.

32. Rolando Mellafe, *Negro Slavery in Latin America*, trans. J. W. S. Judge, (Berkeley and Los Angeles, 1975), p. 119; Palmer, *Slaves of the White God*, p. 62; Davidson, "Negro Slave Control," pp. 239-40; Boyd-Bowman, "Negro Slaves in Early Colonial Mexico," p. 137; Oriol Pi-Sunyer, "Historical Background to the Negro in Mexico," *Journal of Negro History* 42 (1957): 241, 243.

33. Russell-Wood, *Black Man*, p. 25.

34. Ibid., p. 30.

35. Mellafe, *Negro Slavery*, p. 119; Palmer, *Slaves of the White God*, p. 172; Leslie B. Rout, Jr., *The African Experience in Spanish America: 1502 to the Present Day* (New York, 1976), pp. 87-93; Russell-Wood, *Black Man*, p. 32.

36. Palmer, *Slaves of the White God*, p. 179.

37. Frederick Bowser, "The Free Person of Color in Mexico City and Lima: Manumission and Opportunity, 1580-1650," in *Race and Slavery in the Western Hemisphere: Quantitative Studies* ed., Stanley L. Engerman and Eugene D. Genovese (Princeton, 1975), p. 350; Bowser, *African Slave in Colonial Peru*, p. 291.

38. Hubert H. S. Aimes, "Coartación: A Spanish Institution for the Advancement of Slaves into Freedmen," *Yale Review*, old series 17 (1909): 412-31.

39. Bowser, "Free Person of Color," and numerous references in the other studies cited in this chapter. For the brotherhoods of slaves and free blacks in Brazil, see Russell-Wood, *Black Man*, pp. 128-60, especially 142-43, 153-54, and 190.

40. Mellafe, *Negro Slavery*, p. 106.

41. Palmer, *Slaves of the White God*, p. 50.

42. Bowser, *African Slave in Colonial Peru*, p. 172.

43. Ralph H. Vigil, "Negro Slaves and Rebels in the Spanish Possessions, 1503-1558," *The Historian* 33/4 (1971): 637-55, is a convenient survey of the actions of the early fugitives and rebels in Mexico. For Brazil, see Russell-Wood, *Black Man*, pp. 190-93.

44. Bowser, *African Slave in Colonial Peru*, p. 190.

45. Rout, *African Experience in Spanish America*, pp. 102-3.

46. Robert L. Brady, "The Domestic Slave Trade in Sixteenth Century Mexico," *The Americas* 24 (1968): 282.

47. Vigil, "Negro Slaves and Rebels," p. 643.

48. Davidson, "Negro Slave Control" p. 243-44. For increasing tensions in seventeenth-century Mexico involving blacks, see Jonathan I. Israel, *Race, Class and Politics in Colonial Mexico, 1610-1670* (London, 1975), pp. 67-75. For a general study of the fugitive slave communities, see Richard Price, ed., *Maroon Societies: Rebel Slave Communities in the Americas* (Garden City, 1973).

49. MacLeod, *Spanish Central America*, pp. 58, 158, 190-91, 430n.

50. Angelina Pollak-Eltz, "Slave Revolts in Venezuela," in *Comparative Perspectives on Slavery in New World Plantation Societies*, ed. Vera D. Rubin and Arthur Tuden, Annals of the New York Academy of Sciences, vol. 292 (New York, 1977), pp. 439-45; especially 439-40.

51. Bowser, *African in Colonial Peru*, pp. 195-221; the evidence for Chile has been surveyed by Sater, "Black Experience in Chile," pp. 29-32.

52. Davidson, "Negro Slave Control," pp. 246-50.

53. Stuart B. Schwartz, "The *Mocambo*: Slave Resistance in Colonial Bahia," *Journal of Social History* 3 (1970): 313-33.

54. R. K. Kent, "Palmares: An African State in Brazil," *Journal of African History* 6 (1965): 161-75.

55. Ibid., p. 167, citing Carneiro.

56. Ibid., pp. 169-74.

SELECTED BIBLIOGRAPHY

SELECTED BIBLIOGRAPHY

GENERAL AND INTERPRETIVE WORKS; BIBLIOGRAPHICAL GUIDES

Bloch, Marc. *Slavery and Serfdom in the Middle Ages.* Translated by William R. Beer. Berkeley and Los Angeles, 1975.

Cortés Alonso, Vicenta. "Algunas ideas sobre esclavitud y su investigación." *Bulletin de l'Institut Historique Belge du Rome* 44 (1974): 127–44.

Davis, David Brion. *The Problem of Slavery in Western Culture.* Ithaca, 1966.

———. *Slavery and Human Progress.* New York, 1984.

Dockès, Pierre. *Medieval Slavery and Liberation.* Translated by Arthur Goldhammer. Chicago, 1982.

Domar, Evsey, D. "The Causes of Slavery or Serfdom: A Hypothesis." *Journal of Economic History* 30/1 (1970): 18–32.

Finley, Moses I. *Ancient Slavery and Modern Ideology.* New York, 1980.

———. "Slavery." In *International Encyclopedia of the Social Sciences*, 14: 307–13. New York, 1968.

Lévy-Bruhl, Henri. "Théorie de l'esclavage." In his *Quelques problèms du très ancien droit romain.* Paris, 1934. Reprinted in *Slavery in Classical Antiquity: Views and Controversies*, pp. 151–69, edited by Moses I. Finley, Cambridge, Eng., and New York, 1960; reprint, 1969.

Nieboer, H. J. *Slavery as an Industrial System: Ethnological Researches.* 2d ed. The Hague, 1900.

Patterson, Orlando. *Slavery and Social Death: A Comparative Study.* Cambridge, Mass., and London, 1982.

———. "The Structural Origins of Slavery: A Critique of the Nieboer-Domar Hypotheses from a Comparative Perspective." In *Comparative Perspectives on Slavery in New World Plantation Societies*, Annals of the New York Academy of the Sciences, edited by Vera D. Rubin and Arthur Tuden, 292:12–33. New York, 1977.

Verlinden, Charles. *The Beginning of Modern Colonization: Eleven Essays with an Introduction.* Translated by Yvonne Freccero. Ithaca and London, 1970.

———. *L'esclavage dans l'Europe médiévale.* Vol. 1, *Péninsule ibérique—France.* Vol. 2, *Italie—Colonies italiennes du Levant—Empire byzantin.* Bruges, 1955, 1977.

Watson, James L., ed. *Asian and African Systems of Slavery.* Berkeley and Los Angeles, 1980.

Wiedemann, Thomas, ed. *Greek and Roman Slavery.* Baltimore and London, 1981.

Wolf, Eric, R. *Europe and the People without History.* Berkeley and Los Angeles, 1982.

The most comprehensive bibliographical guide has been provided by Joseph C. Miller. See his *Slavery: A Comparative Teaching Bibliography* (Waltham, Mass. 1977); and the supplements appearing periodically in the journal *Slavery and Abolition* from 1980. Miller plans to compile a new bibliography encompassing the original publication and the updated supplements.

THE ROMAN PERIOD (CHAPTER 2)

Blasdon, J. P. V. D. *Romans and Aliens*. Chapel Hill, 1979.

Barrow, R. H. *Slavery in the Roman Empire*. London, 1928.

Biezunska-Malowist, Iza. *L'esclavage dans l'Egypte gréco-romaine*. 2 vols. Warsaw, 1974, 1977.

———. "Le travail servile dans l'agriculture de l'Egypte romaine," *Ve Congrès d'Histoire Economique*. Leningrad, 1974.

Bloch, Marc. *Slavery and Serfdom in the Middle Ages*. Translated by William R. Beer. Berkeley and Los Angeles, 1975.

Boese, Wayne E. "A Study of the Slave Trade and the Sources of Slaves in the Roman Republic and the Early Roman Empire." Ph.D. dissertation, University of Washington, 1973.

Brunt, P. A. *Italian Manpower, 225 B.C.–A.D. 14*. Oxford, 1971.

Buckland, W. W. *The Roman Law of Slavery: The Conditions of the Slave in Private Law from Augustus to Justinian*. Cambridge, Eng., 1908.

———. *Social Conflicts in the Roman Republic*. New York, 1971.

Carney, T. F. *The Economics of Antiquity: Controls, Gifts and Trade*. Lawrence, Kans., 1973.

Cato, Marcus Porcius. *On Agriculture (De agri cultura*. Edited and translated by William Davis Hooper and Harrison Boyd Ash. Loeb Classical Library. Cambridge, Mass., and London, 1934.

Columella, Lucius Junius Moderatus. *On Agriculture (Res rustica)*. 3 vols. Vol. 1, edited and translated by H. Boyd; vols. 2–3, edited and translated by E. S. Forster and E. H. Hellner. Loeb Classical Library. Cambridge, Mass., and London, 1941, 1954–55.

Crook, John A. *Law and Life of Rome*. Ithaca, 1967.

Cuffel, Victoria. "The Classical Greek Concept of Slavery." *Journal of the History of Ideas* 27 (1966): 323–42.

D'Arms, John H. *Commerce and Social Standing in Ancient Rome*. Cambridge, Mass., 1981.

Davis, David Brion. *The Problem of Slavery in Western Culture*. Ithaca, 1966.

Dockès, Pierre. *Medieval Slavery and Liberation*. Translated by Thomas Goldhammer. Chicago, 1982.

Duff, A. M. *Freedmen in the Early Roman Empire*. Oxford, 1928; reprint, Cambridge, Eng., 1958.

Duncan-Jones, Richard. *The Economy of the Roman Empire: Quantitative Studies*. 2d ed. Cambridge, Eng., 1982.

Duval, Paul-Marie. *La vie quotidienne en Gaul pendant la paix romaine, Ier—IIIe siècles après J.C.* Paris, 1952.

Etienne, Robert. "Recherches sur l'ergastule." *Actes du colloque 1972 sur l'esclavage (Besançon)*, pp. 249–66. Paris, 1972.

Finley, Moses I. *The Ancient Economy*. Berkeley and Los Angeles, 1973.

———. *Ancient Sicily to the Arab Conquest*. Vol. 1, *A History of Sicily*. New York, 1968.

———. *Ancient Slavery and Modern Ideology*. New York, 1980.

———. *Aspects of Antiquity: Discoveries and Controversies*. New York, 1968.

———. ed. *Slavery in Classical Antiquity: Views and Controversies*. Cambridge, Eng., 1960; reprint, 1969.

———. "Technological Innovation and Economic Progress in the Ancient World." *Economic History Review*, 2d series, 18 (1965): 29–45.

Fitzgibbon, J. C. "Ergastula." *Classical News and Views* 20 (1976): 55–59.

Forrest, W. G. G., and T. C. W. Stinton. "The First Sicilian Slave War." *Past and Present* 22 (1962): 87–91.

Gordon, M. L. "The Nationality of Slaves under the Early Roman Empire." *Journal of Roman Studies* 14 (1924): 93–111. Reprinted in Finley, ed., *Slavery in Classical Antiquity*, pp. 171–89.

Grant, Michael. *Gladiators*. New York, 1968.

Green, Peter. "The First Sicilian Slave War." *Past and Present* 20 (1961): 10–29.

Guilland, Rodolphe. "Les eunuques dans l'empire Byzantin: Étude de titulature et de prosopografie byzantines." *Études Byzantines* 1 (1943): 197–238.

———. "Fonctions et dignités des eunuques." *Études Byzantines* 2(1944):185–225.

Hadjinicolaou-Marava, Anne. *Recherches sur la vie des esclaves dan le Monde Byzantin.*Athens, 1950.

Harris, William V. "Towards a Study of the Roman Slave Trade." in *The Seaborne Commerce of Ancient Rome: Studies in Archeology and History*, edited by J. H. D'Arms and E. C. Kopff. Vol. 36, *Memoirs of the American Academy of Rome*. Rome, 1980.

———. *War and Imperialism in Republican Rome, 327–70 B.C.* Oxford, 1979.

Heitland, William Emerton. *Agricola: A Study of Agriculture and Rustic Life in the Greco-Roman World from the Point of View of Labour*. Cambridge, Eng., 1920; reprint, 1970.

Hopkins, Keith. *Conquerors and Slaves*. Sociological Studies in Roman History, vol. 1. New York and Cambridge, Eng., 1978.

———. *Death and Renewal*. Sociological Studies in Roman History, vol. 2. Cambridge, Eng., 1983.

———. "Slavery in Classical Antiquity." In *Caste and Race: Comparative Approaches*, edited by Anthony de Rueck and Julie Knight, pp. 166–77. London, 1967.

Jones, A. H. M. "Ancient Empires and the Economy: Rome." *Third International Conference of Economic History, 1965*, pp. 81–104. Paris, 1970. Reprinted in A. H. M. Jones, *The Roman Economy: Studies in Ancient Economic and Administrative History*, edited by P. A. Brunt, pp. 114–39. London, 1974.

———. *The Later Roman Empire, 284–602: A Social, Economic and Administrative Survey*. 2 vols. Norman, Okla., 1964.

———. "The Roman Colonate." *Past and Present* 13 (1958): 1–13. Reprinted in Jones, *Roman Economy*, pp. 293–307.

Justinian. *The Digest of Justinian*. Translated by Charles H. Munroe. 2 vols. London, 1904, 1919.

———. *The Institutes of Justinian*. Translated by J. B. Moyle. 5th ed. Oxford, 1913.

———. *The Civil Law, Including the Twelve Tables, the Institutes of Gaius, the Rules of Ulpian, the Opinions of Paulus, the Enactments of Justinian, and the Constitutions of Leo*. Edited by S. P. Scott. Cincinnati, 1932; reprint, New York, 1973.

Lévy-Bruhl, Henri. "Théorie de l'esclavage." In his *Quelques problèmes du très ancien droit romain*, pp. 15–34. Paris, 1934. Reprinted in Finley, ed., *Slavery in Classical Antiquity*, pp. 151–69.

MacMullen, Ramsey. *Roman Social Relations, 50 B.C. to A.D. 284*. New Haven and London, 1974.

Mendelsohn, Isaac. *Slavery in the Ancient Near East*. New York, 1949.

Patterson, Orlando. *Slavery and Social Death: A Comparative Study*. Cambridge, Mass., and London, 1982.

Percival, John. "Seigneurial Aspects of Late Roman Estate Management." *English Historical Review* 84 (1969): 449–73.

Petit, Paul. *Pax Romana*. Translated by James Willis. London, 1976.

Petronious. *The Satyricon and the Fragments*. Translated by John Sullivan. Harmondsworth, Eng., and Baltimore, 1965.

Pleket, W. H. "Technology in the Greco-Roman World: A General Report." *Talanta* 5 (1973): 6–47.

———. "Technology and Society in the Greco-Roman World." *Acta Historiae Neerlandica* 2 (1967): 1–22.

Pomeroy, Sarah B. *Goddesses, Whores, Wives and Slaves: Women in Classical Antiquity*. New York, 1975.

Rubensohn, Z. "Was the Bellum Sparticium a Slave Insurrection?" *Rivista de Filologìa* 99 (1971): 290–99.

Sherwin-White, A. N. *Racial Prejudice in Imperial Rome*. Cambridge, 1967.

Shtaerman, Elena M., and M. K. Trofimova. *La schiavità nell' Italia imperiale, I–III sècolo*. Rome, 1975.

Snowden, Frank. *Blacks in Antiquity: Ethiopians in the Greco-Roman Experience*. Cambridge, Mass., 1970.

———. "Ethiopians in the Greco-Roman World." In *The African Diaspora: Interpretive Essays*, edited by Martin L. Kilson and Robert I. Rotberg, pp. 11–36. Cambridge, Mass., 1976.

Thompson, E. A. "Slavery in Early Germany." *Hermathena* 89 (1957): 17–24. Reprinted in Finley, ed., *Slavery in Classical Antiquity*, pp. 191–203.

Toynbee, Arnold J. *Hannibal's Legacy: The Hannibalic War's Effects on Roman Life.* 2 vols. London, 1965.

Treggiari, Susan. *Roman Freedmen in the Late Republic.* Oxford, 1969.

Urbach, E. E. *The Laws Regarding Slavery as a Source for the Social History of the Period of the Second Temple, the Mishnah, and Talmud.* London, 1964; reprint, New York, 1979.

Varro, Marcus Terentius. *On Agriculture (Res rustica).* Edited and translated by William Davis Hooper and Harrison Boyd Ash. Loeb Classical Library. Cambridge, Mass., and London, 1934.

Verbrugge, Gerald P. "Slave Rebellion or Sicily in Revolt?" *Kokalos* 20 (1974): 46–60.

Verstraete, Beert C. "Slavery and the Social Dynamics of Male Homosexual Relations in Ancient Rome." *Journal of Homosexuality* 5/3 (1980): 227–36.

Veyne, Paul. "Vie de Trimalcion." *Annales: E. S. C.* 16 (1961):213–47.

Vogt, Joseph. *Ancient Slavery and the Ideal of Man.* Translated by Thomas Wiedemann. Cambridge, Mass., 1975.

Weaver, P. R. C. *Familia Caesaris: A Social Study of the Emperor's Freedmen and Slaves.* Cambridge, Eng., and New York, 1972.

Westermann, William L. "Industrial Slavery in Roman Italy." *Journal of Economic History* 2 (1942): 149–63.

———. "Slave Maintenance and Slave Revolts." *Classical Philology* 40 (1945): 1–29.

———. *The Slave Systems of Greek and Roman Antiquity.* Philadelphia, 1955.

White, K. D. *Roman Farming.* Ithaca, 1970.

Wiedemann, Thomas, ed. *Greek and Roman Slavery.* Baltimore and London, 1981.

SLAVERY IN MEDIEVAL AND RENAISSANCE EUROPE
(CHAPTERS 3, 5, AND 8)

Aranda Doncel, Juan. "Estructura de la población morisca en tres parroquias sevillanas: San Julián, San Román, y Santa Lucía." *Boletín de la Real Academia de Córdoba de Ciencias, Bellas Artes y Nobles Artes* 45 (1976): 77–84.

Arnold, Ralph. *A Social History of England, 55 B.C. to A.D. 1215.* London and Toronto, 1967.

Ashtor, E. *A Social and Economic History of the Near East in the Middle Ages.* Berkeley and Los Angeles, 1976.

Aykroyd, Wallace K. *The Story of Sugar.* New York, 1967.

Baker, Anthony J. *African Link: British Attitudes to the Negro in the Era of the Atlantic Slave Trade.* London, 1978.

Balard, Michel. "Remarques sur les esclaves à Gênes dans la seconde moitié du XIIIe siècle." *Mélanges d'Archéologie et d'Histoire* 80 (1968): 627–80.

Balbi, Giovanna. "La schiavitù a Genova tra i sècoli XII e XIII." In *Mélanges offerts à René Crozet*, edited by Pierre Gallais and Yves-Jean Riou, 2:1025–29. 2 vols. Poitiers, 1966.

Bautier, R. H. *The Economic Development of Medieval Europe.* Translated by Heather Karolyi. London, 1971.

Benvenisti, Meron. *The Crusaders in the Holy Land.* New York, 1972.

Bloch, Marc. *Feudal Society.* Translated by L. A. Manyon. 2 vols. Chicago, 1964.

———. *French Rural History: An Essay on Its Basic Characteristics.* Translated by Janet Sondheimer. Berkeley and Los Angeles, 1966.

———. *Land and Work in Medieval Europe.* Translated by J. E. Anderson. New York, 1969.

———. *Slavery and Serfdom in the Middle Ages.* Translated by William R. Beer. Berkeley and Los Angeles, 1975.

Bolin, Stuve. "Mohammed, Charlemagne and Ruric." *Scandinavian Economic History Review* 1 (1953):5–39.

Boswell, John. *The Royal Treasure: Muslim Communities under the Crown of Aragon in the Fourteenth Century.* New Haven and London, 1977.

Bowsky, William M. ed. *The Black Death: A Turning Point in History?* New York, 1971.

Braudel, Fernand. *The Mediterranean and the Mediterranean World in the Age of Philip II.* Translated by Siân Reynolds. 2 vols. New York, 1972.

Brodman, James W. "Military Redemptionism and the Castilian Reconquest, 1180–1250." *Military Affairs* 44 (1980): 24–27.

Brooke, Christopher. *Europe in the Central Middle Ages, 962–1154.* New York, 1964.

The Burgundian Code: The Book of Constitutions or Law of Gundobad, Additional Enactments. Trans. Katherine Fischer Drew. Philadelphia, 1949, reprint, 1972.

Burns, Robert I., S. J. *The Crusader Kingdom of Valencia.* 2 vols. Cambridge, Mass., 1967.

———. *Islam under the Crusaders: Colonial Survival in the Thirteenth-Century Kingdom of Valencia.* Princeton, 1973.

Byrne, Eugene H. "Genoese Trade with Syria in the Twelfth Century." *American Historical Review* 25 (1920): 191–219.

Carrère, Claude. *Barcelone: Centre économique à l'époque des difficultés, 1380–1462.* 2 vols. Paris and The Hague, 1967.

Clissold, Stephen. *The Barbary Slaves.* Totowa, NJ, 1977.

Collantes de Terán Sánchez, Antonio. "Contribución al estudio de los esclavos en la Sevilla medieval." In *Homenaje al Profesor Carriazo*, edited by Luis Núñez Contreras, 2:109–121. Seville, 1972.

Collins, Roger. *Early Medieval Spain: Unity in Diversity, 400–1000.* New York, 1983.

Cortés Alonso, Vicenta. *La esclavitud en Valencia durante el reinado de los Reyes Católicos, 1479–1516.* Valencia, 1964.

———. "La población negra de Palos de la Frontera (1568–1579)." In *Actas y Memorias del XXXVI Congreso Internacional de Americanistas, Sevilla, 1964*, 3:609–18. Seville, 1966.

———. "Procedencia de los esclavos negros en Valencia (1482–1516)." *Revista española de Antropología Americana* 7 (1972): 125–51.

Deerr, Noël. *The History of Sugar.* 2 vols. London, 1949–50.

Dill, Samuel. *Roman Society in Gaul in the Merovingian Age.* London, 1926; reprint, New York, 1966.

Dockès, Pierre. *Medieval Slavery and Liberation.* Translated by Arthur Goldhammer. Chicago, 1982.

Doehardt, Renée. *Le haut Moyen Age occidental: Economies et sociétés.* Paris 1971.

Doering, J. A. "La situación de los esclavos a partir de las Siete Partidas." *Folia Humanistica* 4 (1966): 337–61.

Domínguez Ortiz, Antonio. "La esclavitud en Castilla durante la Edad Moderna." *Estudios de Historia Social de España* 2 (1952): 367–428.

Dopsch, Alfons. *The Economic and Social Foundations of European Civilization.* New York, 1969.

Duby, Georges. *The Early Growth of the European Economy: Warriors and Peasants from the Seventh to the Twelfth Century.* Translated by Howard B. Clarke. Ithaca, 1974.

———. "Medieval Agriculture, 500–1500." In *The Fontana Economic History of Europe*, edited by Carlo M. Cipolla, 1:175–220. London, 1972.

———. *Rural Economy and Country Life in the Medieval West.* Translated by Cynthia Postan. Columbia, S.C., 1968.

Dufourcq, Charles Emmanuel. *La Espagne catalane et le Maghrib aux XIIIe et XIVe siècles.* Paris, 1966.

Edwards, Paul, and James Walvin. "Africans in Britain, 1500–1800." In Kilson and Rotberg, eds., *The African Diaspora*, pp. 172–204.

Ehrenkreutz, Andrew S. "Strategic Implications of the Slave Trade between Genoa and Mamluk Egypt in the Second Half of the Thirteenth Century." In *The Islamic Middle East, 700–1900: Studies in Economic and Social History*, edited by A. L Udovitch, 335–45. Princeton, 1981.

Font Ruis, J. "La sociedad en Asturias, León y Castilla en los primeros siglos medievales." In *Historia social y económica de España y América*, edited by Jaime Vicens Vives, vol. 2. Barcelona, 1957.

Foote, Peter F., and David M. Wilson. *The Viking Achievement: A Survey of the Society and Culture of Early Medieval Scandinavia*. New York and Washington, 1970.

Fourquin, Guy. *Lordship and Feudalism in the Middle Ages*. Translated by Iris and A. L. Lytton Sells. New York, 1976.

———. *Le paysan d'Occident au Moyen Age*. Paris, 1972.

Franco Silva, Alfonso. *La esclavitud en Sevilla y su tierra a fines de la edad media*. Seville, 1979.

———. *Los esclavos de Sevilla*. Seville, 1980.

Friedman, Ellen G. "Christian Captives at 'Hard Labor' in Algiers, 16th–18th Centuries." *International Journal of African Historical Studies* 13/4 (1980): 616–32.

———. *Spanish Captives in Algiers in the Early Modern Age*. Madison, 1983.

Fulcher of Chartres. *A History of the Expedition to Jerusalem, 1095–1125*. Translated by Frances Rita Ryan. Edited by Harold S. Fink. Knoxville, 1969.

Galloway, J. H. "The Mediterranean Sugar Industry." *Geographical Review* 67/2 (1977): 177–94.

García Arenal, Mercedes. "Los moriscos de la región de Cuenca según los censos establecidos por la Inquisición en 1589 y 1594." *Hispania* 138 (1978): 151–99.

García de Valdeavellano, Luis. *Curso de historia de las instituciones españolas*. 2d ed. Madrid, 1970.

———. "Las instituciones feudales de España." Appendix to the Spanish translation of F. L. Ganshof, *El Feudalismo*, 229–305. Barcelona, 1963.

Gies, Joseph, and Frances Gies. *Merchants and Moneymen: The Commercial Revolution, 1000–1500*. New York, 1972.

Gioffrè, Domenico. *Il mercato degli schiavi a Genova nel sècolo XV*. Genoa, 1971.

Glick, Thomas F. *Islamic and Christian Spain in the Early Middle Ages*. Princeton, 1979.

Graullera Sanz, Vicente. *La esclavitud en Valencia en los siglos XVI y XVII*. Valencia, 1978.

Gregory of Tours. *History of the Franks*. Edited and translated by Ernest Brehant. New York, 1916; reprint 1973.

Gual Camarena, Miguel. "Una cofradía de negros libertos en el siglo XV." *Estudios de la Edad Media en la Corona de Aragón* 5 (1952): 457–66.

———. "Un seguro contra crímines de esclavos en el siglo XV." *Anuario de Historia de Derecho Española* 23 (1953): 247–58.

Guiral, Jacqueline. "Les relations commerciales du Royaume de Valence avec la Berberie au XVe siècle." *Mélanges de la Casa de Velázquez* 10 (1974): 99–131.

Hair, P. E. H. "Black African Slaves at Valencia, 1482–1516: An Onomastic Inquiry." *History in Africa: A Journal of Method* 7 (1980): 119–39.

———. "Protestants as Pirates, Slavers, and Proto-missionairies: Sierra Leone, 1568 and 1582." *Journal of Ecclesiastical History* 21 (1970): 203–24.

Heers, Jacques. *Esclaves et domestiques au Moyen Age dans le monde méditerranéen*. Paris, 1981.

———. *Gênes au XVe siècle: Activité économique et problèmes sociaux*. Paris, 1961.

Hellie, Richard. "Recent Soviet Historiography on Medieval and Early Modern Russian Slavery." *Russian Review* 35 (1976): 1–32.

———. *Slavery in Russia, 1450–1725*. Chicago, 1982.

Heyd, Wilhelm von. *Histoire du commerce du Levant au Moyen Age*. Translated by Furey Reynaud. 2 vols. Leipzig, 1885–86; reprint, Amsterdam, 1967.

Hilton, R. H. *Bond Men Made Free: Peasant Movements and the English Rising of 1361*. London, 1973.

———. *The English Peasants in the Late Middle Ages*. Oxford, 1975.

Hodgett, Gerald. A. J. *A Social and Economic History of Medieval Europe*. New York, 1974.

Imamuddin, S. M. *Some Aspects of the Socio-Economic and Cultural History of Muslim Spain, 711–1492 A.D.* Leiden, 1965.

Jacoby, David. "Citoyens, sujets et protégés en Chypre." *Byzantinische Forschungen* 5 (1977): 159–88.

Kilson, Martin L., and Robert I. Rotberg, eds. *The African Diaspora: Interpretive Essays*. Cambridge, Mass., and London, 1976.

King, P. D. *Law and Society in the Visigothic Kingdom*. Cambridge, Eng., 1972.

Ladero Quesada, Miguel Angel. "La esclavitud por guerra a fines del siglo XV: El caso de Málaga." *Hispania* 27 (1967): 63–88.

Lane, Frederick C. *Venice: A Maritime Republic*. Baltimore and London, 1973.

Lane Poole, Austin. *From Domesday Book to Magna Carta, 1087–1216*. 2d ed. Oxford, 1964.

Latouche, Robert. *The Birth of Western Economy: Economic Aspects of the Dark Ages*. Translated by E. M. Wilkinson. New York, 1961.

Laws of the Alamans and Bavarians. Translated by Theodore John Rivers. Philadelphia, 1977.

Leighton, Albert C. *Transport and Communication in Early Medieval Europe, A.D. 500–1100*. Newton Abbot, Eng., 1972.

Lewis, A. R. *Naval Power and Trade in the Mediterranean, A.D. 500–1100*. Princeton, 1951.

Lind, Joan Dist. "The Ending of Slavery in Sweden: Social Structure and Decision Making." *Scandinavian Studies* 50 (1978): 57–71.

Lippmann, Edmund O. von. *Geschichte des Zuckers, seiner Darstellung und Verwendung*. Leipzig, 1890.

Lombard, Maurice. *The Golden Age of Islam*. Translated by Joan Spenser. Amsterdam, 1975.

Loyn, Henry R. *Anglo-Saxon England and the Norman Conquest*. New York, 1963.

Loyn, Henry R., and John Percival, eds. *The Reign of Charlemagne: Documents on Carolingian Government and Administration*. London, 1975.

Luzzatto, Gino. *An Economic History of Italy from the Fall of the Roman Empire to the Sixteenth Century*. Translated by Philip Jones. London, 1961; reprint, 1968.

———. *Storia economica de Venezia dall'XI al XVI sècolo*. Venice, 1961.

———. *Studi di storia economica veneziana*. Padua, 1954.

Mack Smith, Dennis. *Medieval Sicily, 800–1713*. London, 1968.

McNeill, William H. *Plagues and Peoples*. Garden City, 1976.

Mallett, Michael E. *The Florentine Galleys in the Fifteenth Century, with the Diary of Luca di Maso degli Albrizzi, Captain of the Galleys, 1429–1430*. Oxford, 1967.

Marques, Antonio H. de Oliveira. *Daily Life in Portugal in the Late Middle Ages*. Translated by S. S. Wyatt. Madison, 1971.

———. *History of Portugal*. 2 vols. New York, 1972.

Marrero Rodríguez, Manuela. *La esclavitud en Tenerife a raíz de la conquista*. La Laguna de Tenerife, 1966.

Mayer, Hans Eberhard. *The Crusades*. New York and Oxford, 1972.

O'Callaghan, Joseph F. *A History of Medieval Spain*. Ithaca and London, 1975.

Origo, Iris. "The Domestic Enemy: The Eastern Slaves in Tuscany in the Fourteenth and Fifteenth Centuries." *Speculum* 30 (1955): 321–66.

———. *The Merchant of Prato: Francesco dó Marco Datini, 1335–1410*. New York, 1957.

Parreira, Henrique Gomes de Amorim. "História do açúcar em Portugal." *Anais: Estudos da História da Geografia da Expansão Portuguesa* 7 (1952): 1–15.

Patterson, Orlando. *Slavery and Social Death: A Comparative Study*. Cambridge, Mass., and London, 1982.

Pegalotti, Francesco Balducci. *La Practica della Mercatura*. Edited by Allan Evans. Cambridge, Mass., 1936.

Pereira, Moacyr Soares. *A origem dos cilindros na moagem da cana: Investigação em Palermo*. Rio de Janeiro, 1955.

Pérez Vidal, José. *La cultura de la caña de azúcar en el Levante español*. Madrid, 1973.

Pike, Ruth. *Aristocrats and Traders: Sevillian Society in the Sixteenth Century*. Ithaca, 1972.

———. *Enterprise and Adventure: The Geonese in Seville and the Opening of the New World*. Ithaca, 1966.

———. *Penal Servitude in Early Modern Spain*. Madison, 1983.

———. "Sevillian Society in the Sixteenth Century: Slaves and Freedmen." *Hispanic American Historical Review* 47 (1967): 344–59.

Piponnier, Françoise. *Coutume et vie sociale: La cour d'Anjou, XIVe et XVe siècles*. Paris and The Hague, 1970.

Pistarino, G. "Fra liberti e schiave a Genova nel Quattrocento." *Anuario de Estudios Medievales* 1 (1964): 353–74.

Prawer, Joshua. *The Crusaders' Kingdom: European Colonialism in the Middle Ages*. New York, 1972.

———. "Étude de quelques problèmes agraires et sociaux d'une seigneurie croisée au XIIIe siècle." *Byzantion* 22 (1952): 5–61.

Richard, Jean. *The Latin Kingdom of Jerusalem*. Translated by Janet Shirley. 2 vols. Amsterdam, 1979.

Riché, Pierre. *Daily Life in the World of Charlemagne*. Translated by Jo Ann McNamara. Philadelphia, 1978.

Riley-Smith, J. S. C. *The Feudal Nobility and the Kingdom of Jerusalem, 1117–1277*. Hamden, Conn., 1973.

———. *The Knights of St. John in Jerusalem and Cyprus, C. 1050–1310*. Vol. 1 in *A History of the Order of the Hospital of St. John of Jerusalem*, edited by Lionel Butler. London and New York, 1967.

Robasco Valdés, José Maria. "Dos aspectos de la esclavitud morisca: Málaga, 1569." In *Homenaje al Doctor Juan Reglà Campistol*, 1:293–302. Valencia, 1975.

Runciman, Stephen. *A History of the Crusades*. 3 vols. Cambridge, Eng., 1951–54.

Saunders, A. C. de C. M. *A Social History of Black Slaves and Freedman in Portugal, 1441–1555*. Cambridge, Eng., 1982.

Scobie, Edward. *Black Brittania: A History of Blacks in Britain*. Chicago, 1972.

Sellin, Johan Thorsten. *Slavery and the Penal System*. New York, 1976.

Setton, Kenneth M., ed. *A History of the Crusades*. 2d ed. 5 vols. Madison, 1969–.

Shyllon, F. O. *Black People in Britain, 1555–1833*. London, 1977.

———. *Black Slaves in Britain*. London, 1974.

Skrzinskaja, Elena C. "Storia della Tana." *Studi Veneziana* 10 (1968): 3–45.

Slicher van Bath, B. H. *The Agrarian History of Western Europe, 500–1850*. London, 1963.

Sobrequés Callicó, Jaime, ed. *Catálogo de la cancillería de Enrique IV de Castilla, Señor del Principado de Cataluña, Lugartenencia de Juan de Beaumont, 1462–1464*. Barcelona, 1975.

Stenton, Frank M. *Anglo-Saxon England*, Vol. 2, *The Oxford History of England*. 3d ed. Oxford, 1971.

Strong, L. A. G. *The Story of Sugar*. London, 1954.

Teixeira da Mota, A. "Entrée d'esclaves noirs à Valence (1445–1482): Le remplacement de la voie saharienne par la voie atlantique." *Revue française d'histoire d'outremer* 66/1–2 (1979): 195–210.

Thiriet, Freddy. *La Romanie véntienne au Moyen Age: Le développement et l'exploitation du domaine colonial vénitien (XIIe–XVe siècles)*. Paris, 1959.

Thompson, E. A. "Peasant Revolts in Late Roman Gaul and Spain." *Past and Present* 2 (1952): 11–23.

———. "Slavery in Early Germany." In *Slavery in Classical Antiquity: Views and Controversies*, edited by Moses I. Finley. Cambridge, Eng., 1960; reprint, 1969.

———. *The Visigoths in the Time of Ulfila*. Oxford, 1966.

Thompson, James Westfall. *Economic and Social History of the Middle Ages (300–1300)*. 2 vols. New York, 1928; reprint, 1959.

Torre y del Cerro, Antonio de la. "Los canarios de Gomera vendidos como esclavos en 1489." *Anuario de Estudios Americanos* 7 (1950): 47–72.

Trasselli, Carmelo. "Producción y comercio del azúcar en Sicilia del siglo XIII al XIX." *Revista Bimestre Cubana* 72 (1957): 138–41.

van Kleffens, E. N. *Hispanic Law until the End of the Middle Ages*. Edinburgh, 1968.

Vera Delgado, Ana Maria. "Revuelta mudéjar de 1500–1501: El destino de los vencidos." Actas del Congreso de Historia de Andalucía, 1976. Vol. 2, *Andalucía medieval*, pp. 387–93. Córdoba, 1978.

Verlinden, Charles. *The Beginnings of Modern Colonization: Eleven Essays with an Introduction.* Translated by Yvonne Freccero. Ithaca and London, 1970.

———. *L'esclavage dans l'Europe Médiévale.* Vol. 1, *Péninsule Ibérique—France.* Vol. 2, *Italie—Colonies italiennes du Levant—Levant latin—Empire byzantin.* Bruges, 1955, 1977.

———. "L'origin de Sclavus-Esclave." *Bulletin Ducagne: Archivum Latinitatis Medii Aevi* 17 (1942): 37–128.

Vicens Vives, Jaime, with Jorge Nadal. *An Economic History of Spain.* Translated by Frances M. López-Morillas. Princeton, 1969.

Vogt, John L. "The Lisbon Slave House and African Trade, 1486–1521." *Proceedings of the American Philosophical Society* 117 (1973): 1–16.

Vyronis, Speros, Jr. *Byzantium: Its Internal History and Relations with the Muslim World: Collected Studies.* London, 1971.

Wallace-Hadrill, J. M. *The Long-Haired Kings and Other Studies in Frankish History.* New York, 1962.

Walvin, James. *Black and White: The Negro in English Society, 1555–1945.* London, 1973.

———. *The Black Presence: A Documentary History of the Negro in England, 1555–1860.* London, 1971.

Weber, Max. *The Agrarian Sociology of Ancient Civilization.* Translated by R. I. Frank. Atlantic Highlands, N. J., 1976.

Weisser, Michael R. *Crime and Punishment in Early Modern Europe.* Sussex, 1979.

White, Lynn, Jr. *Medieval Technology and Social Change.* Oxford, 1962.

William of Tyre. *A History of Deeds Done beyond the Sea.* Translated and edited by Emily Atwater Babcock and A. C. Kery. 2 vols. New York, 1943.

Ziegler, Philip. *The Black Death.* New York, 1969.

SLAVERY IN THE WORLD OF ISLAM AND THE TRANS-SAHARAN TRADE (CHAPTER 4)

Ahsan, Muhammad Manazir. *Social Life under the Abbasids, 170–189 A.H.—786–902 A.D.* London and New York, 1979.

Anene, J. C. "Liaison and Competition between Land and Sea Routes in International Trade from the Fifteenth Century: The Central Sudan and North Africa." In *Les grandes voies maritimes dans le monde, XVe–XIXe siècles* (Colloque international d'histoire maritime, 7th, Vienna, 1965), edited by Michel Mollat, pp. 191–207. Paris, 1965.

Ashtor, E. *A Social and Economic History of the Near East in the Middle Ages.* Berkeley and Los Angeles, 1976.

Austen, Ralph A. "The Trans-Saharan Slave Trade: A Tentative Census." In *The Uncommon Market: Essays in the Economic History of the Atlantic Slave Trade,* edited by Henry A. Gemery and Jan S. Hogendorn, pp. 23–76. New York, 1979.

Ayalon, David. *L'esclavage du Mamelouk.* Jerusalem, 1951.

———. *The Mamluk Military Society.* London, 1979.

———. *Studies on the Mamluks of Eqypt (1250–1517).* London, 1977.

Aykroyd, Wallace K. *The Story of Sugar.* New York, 1967.

Bacharach, Jere L. "African Military Slaves in the Medieval Middle East: The Cases of Iraq (869–955) and Egypt (868–1171)." *International Journal of Middle East Studies* 13/4 (1981): 471–95.

Bertheir, Paul. *Les anciennes sucreries du Maroc et leurs réseaux hydraliques: Étude archélologique et d'histoire économique, un épisode de l'histoire de la canne à sucre.* Rabat, 1966.

Boahen, Abu. *Britain, the Sahara, and the Sudan, 1788–1861.* Oxford, 1964.

Braudel, Fernand. "De l'or du Soudan à l'argent d'Amérique." *Annales: E. S. C.* 1 (1946): 9–22.

Bovill, E. W. *The Golden Trade of the Moors.* 2d ed. London, 1970.

Brett, Michael. "Ifriqiya as a Market for Saharan Trade from the Tenth to the Twelfth Century A. D." *Journal of African History* 10 (1969): 347-64.

Brunschvig, R. "Abd." *Encyclopedia of Islam.* 2d ed., 1:24-40. Leiden, 1960.

Cahen, Claude. *Pre-Ottoman Turkey.* London, 1968.

Crone, Patricia. *Slaves on Horses: The Evolution of the Islamic Polity.* Cambridge, Eng., 1980.

Coulson, N. J. *A History of Islamic Law.* Edinburgh, 1964.

Curtin, Philip D. "The Lure of Bambuk Gold." *Journal of African History* 14 (1973): 623-31.

Deerr, Noël. *The History of Sugar.* 2 vols. London, 1949-50.

Derrick, Jonathan. *Africa's Slaves Today.* London, 1975.

Deschamps, Hubert. *Histoire de la traite des noirs de l'antiquité à nos jours.* Paris, 1971.

Dozy, Reinhart. *Spanish Islam: A History of the Moslems in Spain.* Translated by Francis Griffin Stokes. London, 1913; reprint, 1972.

Dufourcq, Charles Emmanuel. *La Espagne catalane et le Maghrib aux XIIIe et XIVe siècles.* Paris, 1966.

Farias, P. F. de Morães. "The Silent Trade: Myth and Historical Evidence," *History in Africa* 1 (1974): 9-24.

Fernandes, Valentim. *Description de la Côte d'Afrique de Ceuta au Sénégal.* Translated and edited by P. de Cernival and T. Monod. Paris, 1938.

———. *Description de la Côte occidentale d'Afrique (Sénégal au Cap de Monte, Archipels).* Edited by T. Monod, A. Teixeira da Mota, R. Mauny. Bissau, 1951.

Fisher, H. J. "The Eastern Maghrib and the Central Sudan." In *Cambridge History of Africa*, edited by Roland Oliver, 3:232-330. Cambridge, Eng., 1977.

Fomand, Paul G. "The Relations of the Slave and Client to the Master or Patron in Medieval Islam." *International Journal of Middle Eastern Studies* 2 (1971): 59-66.

Galloway, J. H. "The Mediterranean Sugar Industry." *Geographical Review* 67/2 (1977): 177-94.

Garrard, Timothy F. "Myth and Metrology: The Early Trans-Saharan Gold Trade." *Journal of African History* 23 (1982): 443-61.

Godinho, Vitorino de Magalhães. *L'économie de l'empire portugais au XVe et XVIe siècles.* Paris, 1969.

———. "I Mediterraneo saariano e as caravanas de ouro." *Revista de História* 11 (1955): 307-53.

Goitein, S. D. *Letters of Medieval Jewish Traders.* Princeton, 1973.

———. *A Mediterranean Society: The Jewish Communities of the Arab World as Portrayed in the Documents of the Cairo Geniza.* 3 vols. Berkeley and Los Angeles, 1967, 1971, 1978.

———. "Slaves and Slavegirls in the Cairo Geniza Records." *Arabica* 9 (1962): 1-20.

———. *Studies in Islamic History and Institutions.* Leiden, 1966.

Greenfield, Sidney M. "Plantations, Sugar Cane and Slavery." *Historical Reflections/Réflexions Historiques* 6/1 (1979): 85-119.

Grunebaum, Gustav E. von. *Classical Islam: A History, 600-1258.* Translated by Katherine Watson. Chicago, 1970.

Hamarneh, Saleh. "Sugarcane Cultivation and Refining under the Arab Muslims during the Middle Ages." *Annals of the Department of Antiquities, Hashemite Kingdom of Jordan* 22 (1977-78): 12-19.

Heyd, Wilhelm von. *Histoire du commerce du Levant au Moyen Age.* Translated by Furey Reynaud. 2 vols. Leipzig, 1885-86; reprint, Amsterdam, 1967.

Hodgson, Marshall G. S. *The Venture of Islam: Conscience and History in a World Civilization.* 3 vols. Chicago and London, 1974.

Hopkins, Anthony G. *An Economic History of West Africa.* New York, 1973.

Hrbek, Ivan. "Egypt, Nubia and the Eastern Sudan." In *Cambridge History of Africa*, edited by Roland Oliver, 10-97. Cambridge, Eng., 1977.

Hunwick, J. O. "Black Africans in the Islamic World: An Understudied Dimension of the Black Diaspora." *Tarikh* (1978): 20-40.

Ibn-Battuta. *Travels in Asia and Africa.* Translated and edited by H. A. R. Gibb. New York, 1927; London, 1929; reprint, New York, 1969.

Irwin, Graham W., ed. *Africans Abroad: A Documentary Survey of the Black Diaspora in Asia, Latin America, and the Caribbean during the Age of Slavery*. New York, 1977.

The Koran Interpreted. Translated by Arthur J. Arberry. 2 vols. in 1. New York, 1955.

Krueger, H. C. "Genoese Trade with North-West Africa in the Twelfth Century." *Speculum* 8 (1933): 377–95.

Law, R. C. C. "The Garamantes and Transsaharan Enterprise in Classical Times." *Journal of African History* 8 (1967): 181–200.

Levi-Provençal, Evariste. *Histoire de l'Espagne musulmane*. 3 vols. Paris, 1950.

Levtzion, Nehemia. *Ancient Ghana and Mali*. London, 1973.

——. "The Early States of the Western Sudan to 1500." In *History of West Africa*, edited by J. F. A. Ajayi and Michael Crowder, 1:114–51. London, 1976.

——. "The Western Maghrib and the Sudan." In *Cambridge History of Africa*, edited by Roland Oliver, 3:331–562. Cambridge, Eng., 1977.

Levy Reuben. *The Social Structure of Islam*. Cambridge, Eng., 1965.

Lewis, A. R. *Naval Power and Trade in the Mediterranean, A. D. 500–1100*. Princeton, 1951.

Lewis, Bernard. "The African Diaspora and the Civilization of Islam." In *The African Diaspora: Interpretive Essays*, edited by Martin L. Kilson and Robert I. Rotberg, pp. 37–56. Cambridge, Mass., and London, 1976.

——. *Race and Color in Islam*. New York, 1971.

Lippmann, Edmund O. von. *Geschichte des Zuckers, seiner Darstellung und Verwendung*. Leipzig, 1890.

Lombard, Maurice, *The Golden Age of Islam*. Translated by Joan Spenser. Amsterdam, 1975.

Lopez, Robert S. "Back to Gold, 1252." *Economic History Review* 9 (1956): 219–40.

Malowist, Marian, "Quelques observations sur le commerce de l'or dans le Soudan occidental au Moyen Age." *Annales: E. S. C.* 25/6 (1970): 1630–36.

Mantran, Robert. *L'expansion musulmane (VIIe–XIe siècles)*. Paris, 1969.

Martin, B. G. "Kanem, Bornu, and the Fazzan: Notes on the Political History of a Trade Route." *Journal of African History* 10 (1969): 15–27.

Mauny, Raymond. "Les deux Afriques." In *Les grandes voies maritimes dans le monde, XVe–XIXe siècles* (Colloque international d'histoire maritime, 7th, Vienna, 1965), edited by Michel Mollat, pp. 179–83. Paris, 1965.

——. *Les siècles obscurs de l'Afrique noire: Historie et archéologie*. Paris, 1971.

Meillassoux, Claude. "L'itineraire d'Ibn Battuta, de Walata à Malli." *Journal of African History* 13 (1972): 389–95.

Mez, A. *Die Renaissance des Islams*. Heidelberg, 1922.

Neumark, S. Daniel. "Trans-Saharan Trade in the Middle Ages." In *An Economic History of Tropical Africa*, edited by Z. A. Konczacki and J. M. Konczacki, 1:127–31. 2 vols. London, 1977.

Nöldeke, Theodore. "A Servile War in the East." *Sketches from Eastern History*. Translated by John Sutherland Black. London, 1892; reprint, Beirut, 1963.

O'Callaghan, Sean. *The Slave Trade Today*. New York, 1961.

Peters, F. E. *Allah's Commonwealth: A History of the Near East, 600–1100 A. D.* New York, 1973.

Pipes, Daniel. *Slave Soldiers and Islam: The Genesis of a Military System*. New Haven, 1981.

Popovic, Alexandre. *La revolte des esclaves en Iraq au IIe/IXe siècle*. Paris, 1976.

Rodison, Maxime. "Histoire économique des classes sociales dans le monde musulmane." In *Studies in the Economic History of the Middle East*, edited by M. A. Cook, pp. 139–43. New York and London, 1970.

Schacht, Joseph. *An Introduction to Islamic Law*. Oxford, 1964.

Shaban, M. A. *Islamic History: A New Interpretation*. 2 vols. Cambridge, Eng., 1971, 1976.

Swanson, John T. "The Myth of Trans-Saharan Trade during the Roman Era." *International Journal of African Historical Studies* 8/4 (1975): 582–600.

Talbi, Mohamed. "Law and Economy in Ifriqiya (Tunisia) in the Third Islamic Century: Agriculture and the Role of Slaves in the Country's Economy." In *The Islamic Middle East, 700–1900: Studies in Economic and Social History*, edited by A. L. Udovitch, pp. 209–49. Princeton, 1981.

Watson, Andrew M. "The Arab Agricultural Revolution and Its Diffusion, 700–1000." *Journal of Economic History* 34 (1974): 8–35.

———. "Back to Gold—And Silver." *Economic History Review* 20 (1967): 1–34.

Watt, William Montgomery. *A History of Islamic Spain*. Edinburgh, 1966.

SLAVERY IN AFRICA (CHAPTERS 6 AND 7)

Ajayi, J. F. A., and Michael Crowder, eds. *History of West Africa*. 2d ed. 2 vols. London, 1976.

Alagoa, E. J. "The Niger Delta States and their Neighbours to 1800." In Ajayi and Crowder, *History of West Africa*, 1:331–72.

Azurara, Gomes Eannes de. *The Chronicle of the Discovery and Conquest of Guinea*. Translated and edited by Charles Raymond Beazley and Edgar Prestage. 2 vols. London, 1896–1899.

Balandier, Georges. *Daily Life in the Kingdom of the Kongo from the Sixteenth to the Eighteenth Century*. Translated by Helen Weaver. New York, 1968.

Birmingham, David. *Trade and Conflict in Angola: The Mbundu and their Neighbours under the Influence of the Portuguese, 1483–1790*. Oxford, 1966.

Blake, John W. *West Africa: Quest for God and Gold*. Totowa, N.J., 1977.

———, ed. *Europeans in West Africa, 1450–1560*. 2 vols. London, 1942.

Boogart, Ernst van den, and Pieter C. Emmer. "The Dutch Participation in the Atlantic Slave Trade, 1596–1650." In *The Uncommon Market: Essays in the Economic History of the Atlantic Slave Trade*, edited by Henry A. Gemery and Jan S. Hogendorn, pp. 353–75. New York, 1979.

Boxer, Charles R. *The Portuguese Seaborne Empire, 1425–1825*. New York, 1969.

Brett, Michael. "Ifriqiya as a Market for Saharan Trade from the Tenth to the Twelfth Century A.D." *Journal of African History* 10 (1969): 347–64.

Cadamosto. *The Voyages of Cadamosto*. Translated and edited by G. R. Crone. London, 1937.

Camacho y Pérez-Galdos, Guillermo. "El cultivo de la caña de azúcar y la industria azucarera en Gran Canaria (1510–1535.)." *Anuario de Estudios Atlánticos* 7 (1961): 1–60.

Carreira, António. *Cabo Verde: Formação e extinção de uma sociedade escravocrata*. Lisbon and Bissau, 1972.

Chaunu, Pierre. "Le Maroc et l'Atlantique (1450–1550)." *Annales: E. S. C.* 11 (1956): 361–65.

Cipolla, Carlo M. *Guns, Sails, and Empires: Technological Innovation and the Early Phases of European Expansion, 1400–1700*. New York, 1965.

Cooper, Frederick. "The Problem of Slavery in African Studies." *Journal of African History* 20 (1979): 103–25.

Curtin, Philip D. *Economic Change in Precolonial Africa: Senegambia in the Era of the Slave Trade*. Madison, 1975.

Deerr, Noël. *The History of Sugar*. 2 vols. London, 1949–50.

Diffie, Bailey W., and George D. Winius. *Foundations of the Portuguese Empire*. Minneapolis, 1977.

Deschamps, Hubert. *Histoire de la traite des noirs de l'antiquité à nos jours*. Paris, 1971.

Duncan, T. Bentley. *The Atlantic Islands: Madeira, the Azores, and the Cape Verdes in Seventeenth-Century Commerce and Navigation*. Chicago, 1972.

Fage, J. D., *A History of West Africa*. 4th ed. Cambridge, Eng., 1969.

———. "Slavery and the Slave Trade in the Context of West African History." *Journal of African History* 10 (1969): 393–404.

———. "Slaves and Society in Western Africa, c. 1445–1700." *Journal of African History* 21 (1980): 289–310.

———. "Some Remarks on Beads and Trade in Lower Guinea in the Sixteenth and Seventeenth Centuries." *Journal of African History* 3 (1962): 343–47.

Fernandes, Valentim. *Description de la Côte d'Afrique de Ceuta au Sénégal.* Translated and edited by P. de Cernival and T. Monod. Paris, 1938.

―――. *Description de la Côte occidentale d'Afrique (Sénégal au Cap de Monte, Archipels).* Edited by T. Monod, A. Teixeira da Mota, R. Mauny. Bissau, 1951.

Fisher, Humphrey J. "The Eastern Maghrib and the Central Sudan." In *The Cambridge History of Africa,* edited by Roland Oliver, 3:232–330. Cambridge, Eng., 1977.

―――. " 'He Swalloweth the Ground with Fierceness and Rage': The Horse in the Central Sudan, I. Its Introduction." and "II. Its Use." *Journal of African History* 13 (1972): 369–88, and 14 (1973): 355–79.

Fisher, Humphrey J. and Allan G. B. Fisher. *Slavery and Muslim Society in Africa: The Institution in Saharan and Sudanic Africa and the Trans-Saharan Trade.* Garden City, 1971.

Garfield, Robert. "A History of São Tomé Island, 1470–1655." Ph.D. dissertation, Northwestern University, 1971.

Godinho, Vitorino de Magalhães. "A economia das Canarias nos seculos XIV e XV." *Revista de História* 4 (1952): 311–20.

―――. *A economia dos descobrimentos henriquinos.* Lisbon, 1962.

―――. *L'économie de l'empire portugais au XVe et XVIe siècles.* Paris, 1969.

Goody, Jack. *Technology, Tradition, and the State in Africa.* London, 1971.

Greenfield, Sidney M. "Madeira and the Beginnings of the New World Sugar Cane Cultivation and Plantations Slavery: A Study in Institution Building." In *Comparative Perspectives on Slavery in New World Plantation Societies,* edited by Vera D. Rubin and Arthur Tuden, pp. 536–52. Annals of the New York Academy of Sciences, vol. 292. New York, 1977.

―――. "Plantations, Sugar Cane and Slavery." *Historical Reflections/Réflexions Historiques* 6 (1979): 85–119.

Heers, Jacques. *Gênes au XVe siècle: Activité économique et problèmes sociaux.* Paris, 1961.

Herbert, Eugenia W. "Portuguese Adaptation to Trade Patterns: Guinea to Angola." *African Studies Review* 17 (1974): 411–23.

―――. *Red Gold of Africa: Copper in Precolonial History and Culture.* Madison, 1983.

―――. "The West African Copper Trade in the Fifteenth and Sixteenth Century." Unpublished paper presented at the Fourteenth International Congress of Historical Sciences, San Francisco, 1975.

Hopkins, Anthony G. *An Economic History of West Africa.* New York, 1973.

―――. "The Western Sudan in the Middle Ages: Underdevelopment in the Empires of the Western Sudan." *Past and Present* 37 (1967): 149–56.

Houtte, J. A. van. "The Rise and Decline of the Market of Bruges." *Economic History Review* 2d series, 19 (1966): 29–47.

Hrbek, Ivan. "Egypt, Nubia, and the Eastern Deserts." In *The Cambridge History of Africa,* edited by Roland Oliver, 3:10–97. Cambridge, Eng., 1977.

Hunwick, John. "Songhay, Borno, and Hausaland in the Sixteenth Century." In Ajayi and Crowder, *History of West Africa,* 1:264–301.

Inikori, J. E., ed. *Forced Migration: The Impact of the Export Slave Trade on African Societies.* New York, 1982.

Klein, Martin A. "The Study of Slavery in Africa." *Journal of African History* 19 (1978): 599–609.

Klein, Martin A. and Paul E. Lovejoy. "Slavery in West Africa." In *The Uncommon Market: Essays in the Economic History of the Atlantic Slave Trade,* edited by Henry A. Gemery and Jan S. Hogendorn, pp. 182–212. New York, 1979.

Lane, Frederick C. *Venice: A Maritime Republic.* Baltimore and London, 1973.

Lange, Dierk. "Progrès de l'Islam et changement politique au Kanem du XIe au XIIIe siècle." *Journal of African History* 19 (1978): 495–513.

Law, Robin. *The Horse in West African History: The Role of the Horse in the Societies of Precolonial West Africa.* Oxford, 1980.

Leo Africanus. *History and Description of Africa*. 3 vols. London, n.d.; reprint, New York, n.d.

Levtzion, Nehemia. *Ancient Ghana and Mali*. London, 1973.

———. "The Early States of the Western Sudan to 1500." In Ajayi and Crowder, *History of West Africa*, 1:114–51.

———. "The Western Maghrib and Sudan." In *The Cambridge History of Africa*, edited by Roland Oliver, 3:331–562. Cambridge, Eng., 1977.

Levtzion, Nehemia, and J. F. P. Hopkins, eds. *Corpus of Arabic Sources Relating to West Africa*. Cambridge, Eng., 1981.

Livermore, H. V. "On the Conquest of Ceuta." *Luso-Brazilian Review* 2 (1965): 3–13.

Lovejoy, Paul E. "Indigenous African Slavery." *Historical Reflections/Réflexions Historiques* 6 (1979): 19–61.

———. "Slavery in the Context of Ideology." In *The Ideology of Slavery in Africa*, edited by Paul E. Lovejoy, pp. 11–38. Beverly Hills and London, 1981.

———. *Transformations in Slavery: A History of Slavery in Africa*. Cambridge, Eng., 1983.

Lovejoy, Paul E. and Steven Baier. "The Desert-Side Economy of the Central Sudan." *International Journal of African Historical Studies* 8/4 (1975): 551–81.

Malowist, Marian. "Les débuts du système de plantations dans la période des grandes découverts," *Africana Bulletin* 10 (1969): 9–30.

———. "The Social and Economic Stability of the Western Sudan in the Middle Ages." *Past and Present* 33 (1966): 3–15.

Marques, Antonio H. de Oliveira. *History of Portugal*. 2 vols. New York, 1972.

Martin, B. G. "Kanem, Bornu, and the Fazzan: Notes on the Political History of a Trade Route." *Journal of African History* 10 (1969): 15–27.

Mauny, Raymond. *Les siècles obscurs de l'Afrique noire: Histoire et archéologie*. Paris, 1971.

Meillassoux, Claude. "The Role of Slavery in the Economic and Social History of Sahelo-Sudanic Africa." In *Forced Migration: The Impact of the Export Slave Trade on African Societies*, edited by J. E. Inikori, pp. 74–99. New York, 1982. This article originally appeared as "Role de l'esclavage dans l'histoire de l'Afrique occidentale." *Anthropologie et sociétés* 2 (1978):117–48.

———; ed. *L'esclavage en Afrique précoloniale*. Paris, 1975.

Mercer, John. *The Canary Islanders: Their Prehistory, Conquest and Survival*. London, 1980.

Miers, Suzanne, and Igor Kopytoff, eds. *Slavery in Africa: Historical and Anthropological Perspectives*. Madison, 1977.

Miller, Joseph C. *Kings and Kinsmen: Early Mbundu States in Angola*. Oxford, 1975.

———. "The Slave Trade in Congo and Angola." In *The African Diaspora: Interpretive Essays*, edited by Martin L. Kilson and Robert I. Rotberg, pp. 75–113. Cambridge Mass., and London, 1976.

Neumark, S. Daniel. "Trans-Saharan Trade in the Middle Ages." In *An Economic History of Tropical Africa*, edited by Z. A. Konczacki and J. M. Konczacki, 2 vols., 1:127–31. London, 1977.

Nicholson, Sharon E. "The Methodology of Historical Climate Reconstruction and Its Application to Africa." *Journal of African History* 20 (1979): 31–49.

Obayemi, Ade. "The Yoruba and Edo-Speaking Peoples and Their Neighbours before 1600." In Ajayi and Crowder, *History of West Africa*, 2:196–263.

Olivier de Sardan, Jean Pierre, "Captifs ruraux et esclaves impériaux du Songhay." In Meillassoux, ed., *L'esclavage en Afrique précoloniale*, pp. 99–134.

Palmer, Colin. *Human Cargoes: The British Slave Trade to Spanish America, 1700-1739*. Urbana, 1981.

Parry, J. H. *The Discovery of the Sea*. Berkeley and Los Angeles, 1981.

Pereira, Fernando Jasmins. *O açucar madeirense de 1500 a 1537: Produção et preços*. Lisbon, 1969.

Postma, Johannes. "The Dimension of the Dutch Slave Trade from Western Africa." *Journal of African History* 13 (1972): 237–48.

Rau, Virginia. "The Madeiran Sugar Cane Plantations." In *From Reconquest to Empire: The Iberian*

Background to Latin American History, edited by Harold B. Johnson, pp. 71–84. New York, 1970.

Rau, Virginia, and Jorge Borges de Macedo. *O açúcar da Madeira nos fins do século XV: Problemas de produção e comercio*. Funchal. 1962.

Rawley, James A. *The Trans-Atlantic Slave Trade: A History*. New York and London, 1981.

Ricard, Robert. "Le commerce de Berbérie et l'organisation économique de l'empire portugais aux XVe et XVIe siècles." *Annales de l'Institut d'Études Orientales* 2 (1936): 266–90.

———. *Études sur l'histoire des portugais au Maroc*. Coimbra, 1955.

Robertson, Claire C., and Martin A. Klein, eds. *Women and Slavery in Africa*. Madison, 1983.

Rodney, Walter. *A History of the Upper Guinea Coast, 1545–1800*. Oxford, 1970.

Rumeu de Armas, Antonio. *España en el Africa atlántica*. Madrid, 1956.

Ryder, Alan F. C. *Benin and the Europeans, 1485–1897*. London, 1969.

Saunders, A. C. de C. M. *A Social History of Black Slaves and Freedmen in Portugal, 1441–1555*. Cambridge, Eng., 1982.

Serrão, Joel. "Le blé des îles atlantiques: Madère et Açores aux XVe et XVIe siècles." *Annales: E. S. C.* 9 (1954): 337–41.

Siemens Hernández, Lothar, and Liliana Barreto de Siemens. "Los esclavos aborígenes canarios en la isla de Madera (1455–1505)." *Anuario de Estudios Atlánticos* 20 (1974): 111–43.

Smith, Abdullah. "The Early States of the Central Sudan." In Ajayi and Crowder, *History of West Africa*, 1:152–95.

Suret-Canale, J., and Boubacar Barry, "The Western Atlantic Coast to 1800." In Ajayi and Crowder, *History of West Africa*, 1:456–511.

Taylor, E. G. R. *The Haven-Finding Art*. London, 1965.

Terray, Emmanuel. "Long-Distance Trade and the Formation of the State: The Case of the Abron Kingdom of Gyaman." *Economy and Society* 3 (1974): 315–45.

Trimingham, John Spenser. *A History of Islam in West Africa*. London and New York, 1962.

Tymowski, M. "Les domaines des princes du Songhay (Soudan occidental)." *Annales: E. S. C.* 25/6 (1970): 1637–58.

Unger, Richard W. *The Ship in the Medieval Economy, 600–1600*. London and Montreal, 1980.

Vansina, Jan. *Kingdoms of the Savanna*. Madison, 1966; reprint, 1975.

———. "Long-Distance Trade Routes in Central Africa." *Journal of African History* 3 (1962): 375–90.

Verlinden, Charles, *The Beginning of Modern Colonization: Eleven Essays with an Introduction*. Translated by Yvonne Freccero. Ithaca and London, 1970.

Vogt, John L. "The Early São Tomé-Príncipe Trade with Mina, 1500–1540." *International Journal of African Historical Studies* 6/3 (1973): 453–67.

———. "Notes on the Portuguese Cloth Trade in West Africa, 1480–1540." *International Journal of African Historical Studies* 8/4 (1975): 623–51.

———. *Portuguese Rule on the Gold Coast, 1469–1682*. Athens, Ga., 1979.

Wilks, Ivor. "A Medieval Trade Route from the Niger to the Gulf of Guinea." *Journal of African History* 3 (1962): 337–41.

———. "The Mossi and Akan States to 1800." In Ajayi and Crowder, *History of West Africa*, 1:413–55.

THE TRANSATLATIC SLAVE TRADE
AND THE AMERICAS TO 1650 (CHAPTERS 9 AND 10)

Aguirre Beltrán, Gonzalo. "The Slave Trade in Mexico." *Hispanic American Historical Review* 24 (1944): 412–31.

Aimes, Hubert H. S. "Coartación: A Spanish Institution for the Advancement of Slaves into Freedmen." *Yale Review*, old series 17 (1909): 412–31.

Alden, Dauril. "Black Robes versus White Settlers: The Struggle for 'Freedom for the Indians' in Colonial Brazil." In *Attitudes of the Colonial Powers*, edited by Howard Peckham and Charles Gibson, pp. 19–45. Salt Lake City, 1969.

Andrews, Kenneth R. *Elizabethan Privateering: English Privateering during the Spanish War, 1585–1603*. Cambridge, Eng., 1964.

Ashburn, Percy M. *The Ranks of Death: A Medical History of the Conquest of America*. New York, 1947.

Bakewell, P. J. *Silver Mining and Society in Colonial Mexico: Zacatecas, 1546–1700*. Cambridge, Eng., 1971.

Barrett, Ward. *The Sugar Hacienda of the Marqueses del Valle*. Minneapolis, 1970.

Barrett, Ward, and Stuart B . Schwartz. "Comparación entre dos economías azucareras coloniales: Morelos, Mexico y Bahía, Brasil." In *Haciendas, latifundios y plantaciones en América latina*, edited by Enrique Florescano, pp. 532–72. Mexico City, 1975.

Berthe, Jean-Pierre. "Aspects de l'esclavage des Indiens en Nouvelle-Espagne pendant la première moitié du XVIe siècle." *Journal de la Société des Américanistes* 54/2 (1965): 189–209.

Borah, Woodrow W., and Sherburne F. Cook. *The Aboriginal Population of Central Mexico on the Eve of the Spanish Conquest*. Berkeley and Los Angeles, 1963.

Bowser, Frederick. "The African in Colonial Spanish America: Reflections on Research Achievements and Priorities." *Latin American Research Review* 7 (1972): 77–92.

———. *The African Slave in Colonial Peru, 1524–1650*. Stanford, 1974.

———. "The Free Person of Color in Mexico City and Lima: Manumission and Opportunity, 1580–1650." In *Race and Slavery in the Western Hemisphere: Quantitative Studies*, edited by Stanley L. Engerman and Eugene D. Genovese, pp. 331–68. Princeton, 1975.

Boxer, Charles Ralph. *The Portuguese Seaborne Empire, 1415–1825*. New York, 1969.

———. *Race Relations in the Portuguese Colonial Empire, 1415–1815*. Oxford, 1963.

———. *Salvador de Sá and the Struggle for Brazil and Angola, 1602–1686*. London, 1952.

Boyd-Bowman, Peter. "Negro Slaves in Early Colonial Mexico." *The Americas* 26 (1969): 134–51.

Brady, Robert L. "The Domestic Slave Trade in Sixteenth Century Mexico." *The Americas* 24 (1968): 281–89.

Breen, T. H., and Stephen Innes. *"Myne Own Ground:" Race and Freedom on Virginia's Eastern Shore, 1640–1676*. New York and Oxford, 1980.

Chandler, David L. "Health Conditions in the Slave Trade of Colonial New Granada." In *Slavery and Race Relations in Latin America*, edited by Robert Brent Toplin, pp. 51–88. Westport, Conn., 1974.

———. *Health and Slavery in Colonial Colombia*. New York, 1981.

Chapa, Jorge, "The Political Economy of Labor Relations in the Silver Mines of Colonial Mexico." Institute for the Study of Social Change, Working Papers Series, no. 105. Berkeley, 1978.

Chaunu, Pierre and Huguette. *Séville et l'Atlantique*. 8 vols. Paris, 1955–60.

Chevalier, François. *Land and Society in Colonial Mexico: The Great Hacienda*. Translated by Alvis Eustis. Berkeley and Los Angeles, 1970.

Conrad, Robert Edgar. *Children of God's Fire: A Documentary History of Black Slavery in Brazil*. Princeton, 1983.

Cook, Noble David. *Demographic Collapse: Indian Peru, 1520–1620*. Cambridge, Eng., 1981.

Cortés Alonso, Vicenta. "Los esclavos domésticos en América." *Anuario de Estudios Americanos* 24 (1967): 955–83.

Crosby, Alfred W., Jr. *The Columbian Exchange: Biological and Cultural Consequences of 1492*. Westport, Conn., 1972.

Curtin, Philip D. *The Atlantic Slave Trade: A Census*. Madison, 1969.

———. "Epidemiology and the Slave Trade." *Political Science Quarterly* 83 (1968): 190–216.

———. "Slavery and Empire." In *Comparative Perspectives on Slavery in New World Plantation Societies*, edited by Vera D. Rubin and Arthur Tuden, pp. 3–11. Annals of the New York Academy of Sciences, vol. 292. New York, 1977.

Cushner, Nicholas P. *Lords of the Land: Sugar, Wine and Jesuit Estates of Coastal Peru, 1600–1767*. Albany, 1980.

Davidson, Basil. *The African Slave Trade: Precolonial History, 1450–1850*. Boston and Toronto, 1961. (Also published as *Black Mother*. London, 1961.)

Davidson, D. M. "Negro Slave Control and Resistance in Colonial Mexico, 1519–1650." *Hispanic American Historical Review* 46 (1966): 235–53.

Deerr, Noël. *The History of Sugar*. 2 vols. London, 1949–50.

Degler, Carl N. *Neither Black nor White: Slavery and Race Relations in Brazil and the United States*. New York, 1971.

———. "Slavery and the Genesis of the Southern Labor System." *Comparative Studies in History and Society* 2 (1959): 49–66, 488–95.

Denevan, William M., ed. *The Native Population of the Americas in 1492*. Madison, 1976.

Dunn, R. S. *Sugar and Slaves: The Rise of the Planter Class in the English West Indies, 1624–1713*. Williamsburg, 1972.

Eder, Donald Gray. "Time under the Southern Cross: The Tannenbaum Thesis Reconsidered." *Agricultural History* 50/4 (1976): 600–614.

Elkins, Stanley M. *Slavery: A Problem in American Institutional and Intellectual Life*. Chicago, 1959.

Ferry, Robert J. "Encomienda, African Slavery and Agriculture in Seventeenth Century Caracas." *Hispanic American Historical Review* 61/4 (1981): 609–36.

Flecknoe, Richard. *A Relation of Ten Years Travels in Europe, Asia, Affrique, and America*. London, 1656.

Floyd, Troy S. *The Columbus Dynasty in the Caribbean, 1492–1526*. Albuquerque, 1973.

Foner, Laura, and Eugene D. Genovese, eds. *Slavery in the New World: A Reader in Comparative History*. Englewood Cliffs, N.J., 1969.

Fox, John S. "The Beginning of Spanish Mining in America: The West Indies and Castilla de Oro." Ph.D. dissertation, University of California, Berkeley, 1940.

Freyre, Gilberto. *The Mansions and the Shanties*. Translated and edited by Harriet de Onis. New York, 1963.

———. *The Masters and the Slaves: A Study in the Development of Brazilian Civilization*. Translated by Samuel Putnam. New York, 1946.

———. *New World in the Tropics: The Culture of Modern Brazil*. New York, 1959.

Furtado, Celso. *The Economic Growth of Brazil: A Survey from Colonial to Modern Times*. Translated by Ricardo W. de Aguiar and Eric Charles Drysdale. Berkeley and Los Angeles, 1963.

Fyfe, Christopher. "The Dynamics of African Dispersal: The Translatlatic Slave Trade." In *The African Diaspora: Interpretive Essays*, edited by Martin L. Kilson and Robert I. Rotberg, pp. 57–74. Cambridge, Mass., and London, 1976.

Galenson, David W. *White Servitude in Colonial America: An Economic Analysis*. Cambridge, Eng., and New York, 1981.

Gemery, Henry A., and Jan S. Hogendorn, eds. *The Uncommon Market: Essays in the Economic History of the Atlantic Slave Trade*. New York, 1979.

Gerhard, Peter. "A Black Conquistador in Mexico." *Hispanic American Historical Review* 58/3 (1978): 451–59.

Gibson, Charles. *The Aztecs under Spanish Rule*. Stanford, 1964.

Handlin, Oscar and Mary. "Origins of the Southern Labor System." *William and Mary Quarterley*, 3d series, 7 (1950): 199–222.

Hanke, Lewis. *All Mankind Is One: A Study of the Disputation between Bartolomé de las Casas and Juan Ginés de Sepúlveda in 1550 on the Intellectual and Religious Capacity of the American Indians*. De Kalb, Ill., 1974.

———. *Aristotle and the American Indians: A Study in Race Prejudice in the Modern World*. Rev. ed. Bloomington, 1975.

———. *The Imperial City of Potosí: An Unwritten Chapter in the History of Spanish America*. The Hague, 1956.

———. *The Spanish Struggle for Justice in the Conquest of America*. Philadelphia, 1949; reprint, Boston, 1965.

Haskett, Robert S. "Santiago de Paz: Anatomy of a Sixteenth-Century Caribbean Sugar Estate." *UCLA Historical Journal* 1 (1980): 51–79.

Helmer, Marie. "Note sur les esclaves indiens au Pérou (XVIe siècle)." *Bulletin de la Faculté des Lettres de Strasbourg* 43/7 (1965): 683–90.

Hemming, John. *Red Gold: The Conquest of the Brazilian Indians*. London, 1978.

Inikori, J. E. "The Origin of the Diaspora: The Slave Trade from Africa." *Tarikh* 5, 6 (1978): 1–19.

———, ed. *Forced Migration: The Impact of the Export Slave Trade of African Societies*. New York, 1982.

Israel, Johanthan, I. *Race, Class and Politics in Colonial Mexico, 1610–1670*. London, 1975.

Jacobs, Wilbur R. "British-Colonial Attitudes and Policies toward the Indian in the American Colonies." *Attitudes of Colonial Powers toward the American Indian*, edited by Howard Peckham and Charles Gibson, pp. 81–106. Salt Lake City, 1969.

Jane, Cecil, trans. and ed. *Select Documents Illustrating the Four Voyages of Columbus*. Vol. 1, *The First and Second Voyages*. Hakluyt Society Publications, 2d series, vol 65. London, 1930.

Jordan, Winthrop D. *White over Black: American Attitudes Toward the Negro, 1550–1812*. Chapel Hill, 1968.

Kent, R. K. "Palmares: An African State in Brazil." *Journal of African History* 6 (1965): 161–75.

Kiemen, Mathias C. *The Indian Policy of Portugal in the Amazon Region, 1614–1693*. Washington, D.C., 1954.

Kiple, Kenneth, F., and Virginia Himmelsteib King. *Another Dimension to the African Diaspora: Diet, Disease, and Racism*. Cambridge, Eng., 1981.

Klein, Herbert S. *The Middle Passage: Comparative Studies in the Atlantic Slave Trade*. Princeton, 1978.

———. *Slavery in the Americas: A Comparative Study of Virginia and Cuba*. Chicago, 1967.

Lafaye, Jacques. "L'église et l'esclavage des Indiens de 1537 à 1708." *Bulletin de la Faculté des Lettres de Strasbourg* 43/7 (1965): 191–203.

Lapeyre, Henri. "La trata de negros con destino a la América española durante los últimos años del reinado de Carlos V., 1544–1555." *Cuadernos de Investigación Histórica* 2 (1978): 335–39.

Liss, Peggy K. *Mexico under Spain, 1521–1556: Society and the Origins of Nationality*. Chicago and London, 1975.

Lockhart, James. *Spanish Peru: A Colonial Society*. Madison, 1968.

Lovejoy, Paul E. "The Volume of the Atlantic Slave Trade: A Synthesis." *Journal of African History* 23 (1982): 473–501.

MacLeod, Murdo J. *Spanish Central America: A Socioeconomic History, 1520–70*. Berkeley and Los Angeles, 1973.

McNeill, William H. *Plagues and Peoples*. Garden City, 1976.

Marchant, Alexander. *From Barter to Slavery: The Economic Relations of Portuguese and Indians in the Settlement of Brazil, 1500–1580*. Baltimore, 1942.

Markham, C. R. ed. *The Journal of Christopher Columbus (during his First Voyage, 1492–93) and Documents Relating to the Voyages of John Cabot and Gaspar Corte Real*. Hakluyt Society Publications, 1st series, vol. 86. London, 1893; reprint, n.d.

Marzhal, Peter. *Town in the Empire: Government, Politics, and Society in Seventeenth-Century Popoyán*. Austin, 1978.

Mattoso, Katia M. de Queiros. *Être esclave au Brésil, XVIe–XIXe*. Paris, 1979.

Mayer, Vincent, Jr. "The Black on New Spain's Northern Frontier: San José de Parral, 1631 to 1641." *Occasional Papers of the Center for Southwest Studies*, no. 2. Durango, Col., 1974.

Mellafe, Rolando. *Negro Slavery in Latin America*. Translated by J. W. S. Judge. Berkeley and Los Angeles, 1975.

Miller, Joseph C. "Mortality in the Atlantic Slave Trade: Statistical Evidence on Causality." *Journal of Interdisciplinary History* 11/3 (1981): 385–423.

Mintz, Sidney W. *Caribbean Transformations*. Chicago, 1974.

Morgan, E. S. "Slavery and Freedom: The American Paradox." *Journal of American History* 59 (1972): 5–29.

Mörner, Magnus. *Race Mixture in the History of Latin America*. Boston, 1967.

Otte, Enrique, and Conchita Ruiz-Burruecos. "Los Portugueses en la trata de esclavos negros de las postrimerías del siglo XVI." *Moneda y Crédito* 85 (1963): 3–40.

Palmer, Colin A. *Human Cargoes: The British Slave Trade to Spanish America, 1700–1739*. Urbana, 1981.

———. *Slaves of the White God: Blacks in Mexico, 1570–1650*. Cambridge, Mass., 1976.

Parry, John H. *The Discovery of the Sea*. Berkeley and Los Angeles, 1981.

———. *The Spanish Seaborne Empire*. New York, 1966.

Pike, Ruth. *Enterprise and Adventure: The Genoese in Seville and the Opening of the New World*. Ithaca, 1966.

Pi-Sunyer, Oriol. "Historical Background to the Negro in Mexico." *Journal of Negro History* 42 (1957): 237–46.

Pinto, Françoise Latour de Veiga, with A. Carreira. "Portuguese Participation in the Slave Trade: Opposing Forces, Trends of Opinion within Portuguese Society, Effects on Portugal's Socio-economic Development." In UNESCO, *The African Slave Trade from the Fifteenth to the Nineteenth Century*, pp. 119–47. Paris, 1979.

Pollak-Eltz, Angelina. "Slave Revolts in Venezuela." In *Comparative Perspectives on Slavery in New World Plantation Societies*, edited by Vera D. Rubin and Arthur Tuden, pp. 439–45. Annals of the New York Academy of Sciences, vol. 292. New York, 1977.

Powell, P. W. *Soldiers, Indians and Silver: The Northward Advance of New Spain, 1550–1600*. Berkeley and Los Angeles, 1952.

Price, Richard, ed. *Maroon Societies: Rebel Slave Communities in the Americas*. Garden City, 1973.

Radell, David L. "The Indian Slave Trade and Population of Nicaragua during the Sixteenth Century." In Devenan, *Native Population*, pp. 67–76.

Ratekin, Mervyn. "The Early Sugar Industry in Española." *Hispanic American Historical Review* 34 (1954): 1–19.

Rawley, James. A. *Trans-Atlantic Slave Trade: A History*. New York and London, 1981.

Rice, C. Duncan. *The Rise and Fall of Black Slavery*. New York, 1975.

Riley, G. Michael. *Fernando Cortés and the Marquesado in Morelos, 1522–1547: A Case Study in the Socioeconomic Development of Sixteenth-Century Mexico*. Albuquerque, 1973.

Rose, Willie Lee, ed. *A Documentary History of Slavery in North America*. New York, 1976.

Rout, Leslie B., Jr. *The African Experience in Spanish America: 1502 to the Present Day*. New York, 1976.

———. "The African in Colonial Brazil." In *The African Diaspora: Interpretive Essays*, edited by Martin L. Kilson and Robert I. Rotberg, pp. 132–71. Cambridge, Mass., and London, 1976.

Russell-Wood, A. J. R. *The Black Man in Slavery and Freedom in Colonial Brazil*. New York, 1982.

———. "Iberian Expansion and the Issue of Black Slavery: Changing Portuguese Attitudes, 1440–1770." *American Historical Review* 83/1 (1978): 16–42.

Saco, J. A. *Historia de la esclavitud de la raza africana en el Nuevo Mundo, y en especial en los países Américo-Hispanos*. 2d ed. 3 vols. Havana, 1937–43.

Sánchez-Albornoz, Nicolás. *The Population of Latin America*. Translated by W. A. R. Richardson. Berkeley and Los Angeles, 1974.

Sanders, William T. "The Population of the Central Mexican Symbiotic Region, the Basin of Mexico, and the Teotihuacan Valley in the Sixteenth Century." In Devenan, *Native Population*, pp. 85–150.

Sandoval, Alonso de. *De Instauranda Aethopum Salute*. (Originally published in Seville, 1627). Edited by Angel Valtierra. Bogotá, 1956.

Sandoval, Fernando B. *La industria del azúcar en Nueva España.* Mexico City, 1951.

Sater, William F. "The Black Experience in Chile." In *Slavery and Race Relations in Latin America,* edited by Robert Brent Toplin, pp. 13–50. Westport, Conn., 1974.

Sauer, Carl Ortwin. *The Early Spanish Main.* Berkeley and Los Angeles, 1966.

Scelle, George. *La traite négriere aux Indes de Castille: Contrats et traites d'assiento.* 2 vols. Paris, 1905–06.

Schwartz, Stuart B. "Free Farmers in a Slave Economy: The *Lavradores de Cana* of Colonial Bahia." In *Colonial Roots of Modern Brazil: Papers of the Newberry Library Conference,* edited by Dauril Alden, pp. 147–97. Berkeley and Los Angeles, 1973.

———. "Indian Labor and New World Plantations: European Demands and Indian Responses in Northeastern Brazil." *American Historical Review* 83/1 (1978): 43–79.

———. *Sugar Plantations and the Formation of a Brazilian Society.* Forthcoming.

———. "The Manumission of Slaves in Colonial Brazil: Bahia, 1684–1745." *Hispanic American Historical Review* 54/4 (1974): 603–35.

———. "The *Mocambo*: Slave Resistance in Colonial Bahia." *Journal of Social History* 3 (1970): 313–33.

———. *Sovereignty and Society in Colonial Brazil: The High Court of Bahia and Its Judges, 1609–1751.* Berkeley and Los Angeles, 1973.

Sempat Assadourian, Carlos. *El tráfico de esclavos de Córdoba de Angola a Potosí, siglos XVI–XVII.* Córdoba, Argentina, 1966.

Sherman, William L. *Forced Native Labor in Sixteenth-Century Central America.* Lincoln, 1979.

Simpson, Leslie Byrd. *The Encomienda in New Spain: The Beginnings of Spanish Mexico.* Rev. ed. Berkeley and Los Angeles, 1966.

Starr, Raymond, and Robert Detweiler, eds. *Race, Prejudice and the Origins of Slavery in America.* Cambridge, Mass., 1975.

Tannenbaum, Frank. *Slave and Citizen: The Negro in the Americas.* New York, 1947.

Teixeira da Mota, A., F. Mauro, and J. Borges de Macedo. "Les routes portugaises de l'Atlantique." *Anuario de Estudios Atlánticos* 25 (1968): 129–46.

UNESCO. *The African Slave Trade from the Fifteenth to the Nineteenth Century.* Paris, 1979.

Verger, Pierre. *Flux et reflux de la traite des nègres entre le Golfe de Benin et Bahia de Todos os Santos du XVIIe au XIXe siècle.* Paris and the Hague, 1968.

Vigil, Ralph H. "Negro Slaves and Rebels in the Spanish Possessions, 1503–1558." *The Historian* 33 (1971): 637–55.

Vila Villar, Enriqueta. *Hispanoamérica y el comercio de esclavos.* Seville, 1977.

———. *Historia de Puerto Rico (1600–1650).* Seville, 1974.

———. "The Large-Scale Introduction of Africans into Veracruz and Cartagena." In *Comparative Perspectives on Slavery in New World Plantation Societies,* edited by Vera Rubin and Arthur Tuden, pp. 267–80. New York, 1977.

Vogt, John. *Portuguese Rule on the Gold Coast, 1469–1682.* Athens, Ga., 1979.

Wallerstein, Immanuel. *The Modern World-System: Capitalist Agriculture and the Origins of the European World-Economy in the Sixteenth Century.* New York, 1974.

West, Robert C. *The Mining Community in Northern New Spain: The Parral Mining District.* Ibero-Americana, vol. 30. Berkeley and Los Angeles, 1949.

Wolf, Eric. *Sons of the Shaking Earth.* Chicago, 1959.

Zavala, Silvio. "Los esclavos indios en Guatemala." *Historia Mexicana* 19/4 (1970): 459–65.

———. *Los esclavos indios en Nueva España.* Mexico City, 1967.

INDEX

INDEX

Abbasid dynasty, caliphs of, 74
Abd ar-Rahman I (ruler of Islamic Spain), 111
Abd ar-Rahman III (caliph of Córdoba, Spain), 71
Aburrazach, Thahir, 111
Afonso, João, 136
Afonso, (king of the Kongo), 145–46
Afonso V (king of Portugal), 142
Africa, 4, 6, 8, 12, 15; geography of, 116, 136; cavalry warfare in, 119–20; slave raids in, 120–21, 139; methods of augmenting population in, 122; uses of slaves in, 122–26; assimilation of slaves in, 123
Africanus, Leo: and African slavery, 114; on Borno slave raids, 121; on agricultural prosperity of Kano, 124
Ager publicus, 18
Agriculture: in Rome, 19; in medieval Europe, 45, 51, 56; technological revolution of, in Europe, 64; development of, in Atlantic islands, 150–51. *See also* Sugar
Al-Bakri, 114
Alcaçovas, treaty of, 142
Alcaldí del rey, 165
Alexander the Great, 67, 79
Alfonso V (king of Aragon), 96
Alfonso VIII (king of Castile), 108
Alfonso X (king of Castile), 110–11
Alfred (king of Wessex), 48–49
Algarve, 112
Al-Hamdani: on Ghana gold mine, 85

Al-Idrisi: on Gharbil slave raids, 121
Allods, 58
Almagro, Diego de, 208
Al-Malik al-Afdal (viceroy of Fatimid dynasty), 74
Al-Mamun, 77–78
Al-Maqrizi: on Mansa Musa's pilgrimage to Mecca, 126
Almoxarife dos escravos, 155–56
Alooma (king of Borno), 121
Al-Sharishi: on Ghana slave women, 123
Al-Umari: on slavery as state power, 125
Al-Zuhri: on Ghana slave raids, 120–21
American South, 5, 6–7, 11
Americas, 3; influence of Spanish Indies on, 8; studies of slavery in, 14–15
Amherst, Sir Jeffrey, 178
Ancillae, 51
Anglo-Saxon kingdom, 46–47
Angola, 187
Anjou, duke of, 155
Anushirwan, Chosroes I., 79
Arabian Peninsula, 67–68
Aragon, Crown of, 109, 110, 163
Arguin Island, 139–40
Aristotle: on slavery, 17
Asiento system, 187–88, 191–92; *Asentistas* of, 187–88, 189. *See also* Licensing
Ashtor, E.: on sugar industry in Egypt and Syria, 80
Athenion, 20
Atienza, Pedro de, 196

Augustus (emperor of Rome), 21, 27, 31
Austen, Ralph A.: on trans-Saharan slave trade, 86
Azambuja, Diogo de, 142
Azeneque Berbers, 139
Azurara, 138, 151

Bahia, 191
Balard, Michel: on slaves in Genoa, 100
Balbi, Giovanni: on concubinage in Genoa, 98–99; on slave sales in Genoa, 103
Baldwin III (king of Jerusalem), 94
Ballester, Miguel, 196
Barberà, Guillem de, 167
Barrett, Ward: on Mexican sugar plantations, 199
Barros, João de: on sugar cane in Madeira, 150
Batle, Juan, 167
Bautier, R.-H.: on blockade of Christian-Muslim trade, 103
Bayle general, 165–66
Benin, 144
Benjamin of Tudela: on port of Barcelona, 108
Black Death, 88, 105–6, 136. See also Disease
Bloch, Marc: on serfdom in France, 57
Bône, 65
Borah, Woodrow W.: on population of Mexico, 177–78
Bos, Francisca, 167
Bowser, Frederick: on slaves in Peru, 203; on manumission in Mexico City and Peru, 209
Boxer, C. R.: on Portuguese slave system, 205
Bozales, 185, 186, 206
Braudel, Fernand, 97
Brazil, 11, 175; labor supply problems in, 180–82; capitanias of, 180–81; black slavery in, 182, 199–200; slave trade to, 191, 192–94; uses of slaves in, 194, 195, 200–201; land grants in, 199–200. See also Portugal; Sugar
"Bridewealth," 122
British Isles, 63
Burgos, laws of, 179
Burgundian Code, 47–48
Burns, Robert I.: on slaveholders in kingdom of Valencia, 109

Burone, Guglielmo, 98
Byzantine Empire: church and state in, 37–38; slavery in, 37, 38

Cacao: black slaves in industry of, 201
Cadamosto: on Azeneque Berbers in Portugal, 139; on indigenous African slavery, 147; on population of Madeira, 151
Caffaraino, Guglielmo, 100
Cairo Geniza: records of, 72–73
Canaries, the: Guanches in, 152, 168–69
Cape Verde Islands, 140, 141, 187
Capitãos do campo, 214
Captaincies (capitanias), 180–81
Carabela redonda. See Ships
Caravel. See Ships
Cardona, Hugo de. See Ravensburger Handelsgesellschaft
Cargadores, 188
Carolingian period: estates of, 53
Carta de alforria, 159–60, 208. See also Manumission; Portugal
Carta de libertad, 208, 209. See also Manumission; Spain
Casa de Contratación, 186, 187, 188. See also Asiento system; Licensing
Castellanos, Juan de, 204
Castile, 108, 133, 168–69
Castration: centers of, 74–75
Cato the Elder: on rural slavery, 22
Charlemagne (Frankish king), 43, 53, 62
Charles V (king of Spain), 179, 185, 197, 198
Chevage, 57
Chile, 201–2
Christianity: effects of, in Rome, 33–35, 92, 206; black slaves and, in Seville, 162–63; Spanish campaign for, 184–85
Christians, 6, 12; slavery in states of, 107; as captives, 108
Chromatius, 35
Cicero, Marcus Tullius: on treatment of slaves, 35
Cimarrons, 212–15
Cleon, 19–20
Closed system, of slavery, 14
Coartación, 209
Cofradía, of Nuestra Señora de Gracia, 168
Collantes de Terán, Antonio: on slaves in Seville, 162
Colombia, 201

Coloni, 36, 50, 51–52, 53
Columbus, Christopher, 173–74, 175, 184
Columbus, Diego (son of Christopher Columbus), 212
Columella, 21, 22, 23
Comnenus, Alexius (emperor of Byzantium), 90
Concubinage, 14; in Byzantine Empire, 37; in Islamic world, 73–74; in Italy, 98–100; in the Sudan, 123; in Seville, 162; in colonial Latin America, 207
Constantine (emperor of Rome), 27, 29, 35
Consulado, 186. *See also Asiento* system; Licensing; Seville
Cook, Noble David: on population decline in Peru, 178
Cook, Sherburne F.: on population decline in Mexico, 177–78
Córdoba, 71
Corredores, 165
Corsairs, 132
Cortés, Hernando, 179, 198
Costa da Mina, 142, 143, 144–45
Crassus, 20
Criollo, Joseph, 211
Criollo negro, 185
Crusades, 65, 67, 88, 90–95
Cuneo, Michele: on death of captives of Spain, 174–75
Curtin, Philip D.: on origins of slavery in Africa, 118; on New World slavery, 173; on Atlantic slave trade, 192, 194; on slave trade to Brazil, 194
Cyprus, 152

Dar-al-Islam, 66. *See also* Islamic world
Datini, Francesco, 102
d'Aveiro, João Afonso, 144
Davidson, D. M.: on Spain's Christianization and Hispanization of slaves, 206
Davis, David Brion: on slaveowners' control, 7
Debt bondage, 24
Degler, Carl N.: on slavery in Brazil and North America, 205
Demesne, 51, 52, 56
Dhimmi, 68
Dibalami, Duanama, 121–22
Diffie, Bailey W.: on Valencian sugar, 150
Diniz (king of Portugal), 107–8
Diocletian (emperor of Rome), 36

Disease: effects of on New World, 176–78; on ships in Atlantic crossing, 189–90. *See also* Black Death
Dockès, Pierre: on slavery, 5, 9
Domar, Evsey D.: on the state and serfdom, 10
Domnole (bishop of Le Mans), 51
Donatary (donatário), 180
Duarte (king of Portugal), 150
Duby, Georges: on slavery, 46, 51
Dutch West India Company, 191

Eannes, Gil, 133
Egypt, 3, 80
Ehinger, Heinrich, 186
Elkins, Stanley M., 205
Encomendero, 202
Encomienda system, 179, 201
England: blacks in, 155; indentured servants in colonies of, 171, 183; black slaves in colonies of, 183
Ergastulum, 22
Escobar, Pero, 142
Eunous (Antiochus), 19–20
Eunuchs, 24, 38, 61, 63–64, 69, 74–75
Europe, 4, 6, 8, 11, 12, 53–54; varieties of slavery in, 15, 169–70; domestic slavery in, 56–57; slaving network in eastern steppes of, 63–64; fifteenth-century slavery in, 131, 132; trade of, 154

Fage, John: on African slave trade, 147–48
Falcandus, Hugh, 96
Familia: in Carolingian empire, 53
Familia Caesaris, "the family of the emperor," 26, 50, 78
Fauconnier, Renaud, 94
Ferdinand II (king of Aragon), 163, 166, 174, 185
Fernandes, Valentim, 86, 139, 145, 150
Feudalism: governmental system of in Europe, 54
Figueroa, Rodrigo de, 197
Finley, Moses I., 5, 23; on slave societies, 9, 17–18; on origins of slavery in ancient world, 10–11; on slavery in Rome, 25, 36; on Timotheus, Aulus Kapreilius, 33; on slavery in Islamic world, 67, 86
Florentius, 17
Florin, Jean, 197
Fourquin, Guy, 55

France: blacks as slaves in, 155
Franci. See Coloni
Frankish kingdom: effects of church on slavery in, 61
Frederick II (king of Sicily), 94, 96
Freeholders: in western medieval Europe, 58
Freitas, Lanzarote de (*almoxarife* of Lagos), 138
Freyre, Gilberto, 205
Frisians, 60
Fugitive slaves: in colonial Latin America, 14, 209–12; in Rome, 29; in Visigothic kingdom, 49; in Italy, 101; in Africa, 127; in Portugal, 159; in Seville, 163; in Valencia, 167
Fulcher of Chartres, 93

Gang slavery, 9; in Rome, 21–22, 24; in Middle Ages, 51; decline of in Carolingian period, 53; in Islamic world, 77, 86–87; in Brazil and Spanish colonies, 195; in North American English colonies, 216; in New World, 217
Garrido, Juan, 196
Genoa, 102, 103, 104, 106, 132–33, 197
Genovese, Eugene, 13
Germanic kingdoms, 36; slavery in, 45–46, 47, 50; Roman code in, 46; "thirding" in, 46; ruralization of, 50
Gioffrè, Domenico: on black slaves in Genoa, 106
Goitein, S. D.: on the Geniza papers, 73
Gomes, Fernão, 142
Gonçalves, Antao, 138
Goody, Jack: on slavery, 10
Gouvenot, Laurent de, 185
Gracchus, Tiberius, 21
Greece, 4, 16–17
Gregory of Tours, 48
Gregory the Great (pope), 60

Habib b. Ali Ubaida, 81
Hadrian I (pope), 62
Harems, 74. *See also* Concubinage
Haskett, Robert S.: on Mexican sugar plantation, 199
Hawkins, John, 148, 155, 200
Henry (prince), "the Navigator," 138–39, 150, 151
Henry the Fowler (German emperor), 62
Herbert, Eugenia W., 148

Herrera, Pedro Gonzalo de, 213
Hieronymite friars, 185
Hopkins, A. G.: on European trade with West Africa, 135–36
Hopkins, Keith: on Roman manumissions, 35
Horse trade, 120, 140
Hospitalers (Knights of St. John), 93–94
House of Muhammad: freedmen of, 75
Hummay (ruler of Kanem), 121
Huns, 45

Iberian kingdoms: slavery in, 12, 69, 107, 154, 171, 205–6; Atlantic expeditions of, 173
Iberian Peninsula: Muslim conquest of, 59, 68–69
Ibn-Battuta: on origins of eunuchs, 75; records of Saharan caravan trade by, 83–84; and fourteenth-century African slavery, 114; on domestic slavery in Africa, 123–24; on education of women slaves in Africa, 124; on pilgrimages and slave trade, 126
Ibn-Hauqal: on Sicilian sugar production, 96
Idonei, 50, 51
Inikori, J. E.: on Atlantic slave trade, 192
Irnerius, 110
Isabella I (queen of Castile), 163, 174, 179, 184, 185
Islamic Spain, 69–71, 73, 78
Islamic world, 4, 6, 9, 12, 15; internal strife in, and Europe, 64–65; ethnicity in, 66; urban civilization in, 66–67; caravan traffic of, 67; uses of slaves in, 68, 72–73, 75–76, 86–87; sources of slaves in, 69–71; commercial system of, 71; treatment of slaves in, 71–73; freed people in, 75–76; sugar cane agriculture in, 79; blacks as slaves in, 81, 84–85, 86
Italy, 18; medieval urban life in, 59; Christian-Muslim trade and, 62–63, 103; ethnicity of slaves in, 98, 106, 155; uses of slaves in, 98, 100–101, 104; integration of slaves into families in, 101–2; indentured servants in, 106

Janissaries, 9, 78. *See also* Military
Jesuits, 181
John I (king of Portugal), 136, 150
John II (king of Portugal), 142, 144, 155, 180–81

John III (king of Portugal), 180–81
Jones, A. H. M.: on Roman domestic slaveowners, 24
Julius Caesar, 18
Junian Latin, 30
Justinian, code of, 38–39, 110
Justinian (emperor of Byzantium), 16, 38
Jahiz: on eunuchs in Islamic world, 75
James I (king of Aragon), 109
James II (king of Aragon), 111, 167

Kanem, 121–22
Karmatian state: labor force of, 76
Klein, Herbert S., 205
Kongo, the, 145–46
Koran, the, 68, 71, 72, 74, 75, 121
Kublai Khan, 80

Ladeiras. See Palenques
Ladinos, 185
Lançados, 156
Lane, F. C., 100
Las Casas, Bartolomé de, 180
Latifundia, 18, 28
Latin America, colonial: uses of slaves in, 198–204; racial mixing in, 207–8; punishment of slaves in, 209–10
Latouche, Robert, 49, 55
Law, Robin: on horse and slave trades in Africa, 120
Leo V (emperor of Byzantium), 62
Lewis, Bernard: on Muslims' attitudes toward blacks, 81
Licensing: Spanish system of, 185–86; Portuguese and *asiento* system of, 186–88
Lisbon, 155–57, 181
Lisbon House of Slaves (Casa dos Escravos de Lisboa), 155–56, 157
Livy: on Roman captives, 18
Lockhard, James: on sale of skilled slaves in Peru, 203
Lovejoy, Paul E.: on Islam's influence on African slavery, 119; on Atlantic slave trade, 192, 194
Lovell, John, 200

MacMullen, Ramsey: on slaves vs. free poor in Rome, 28
Madeira, 151–52
Magyars, 53, 64
Malaguetta, 140

Mali, 125
Mallett, Michael E.: on origins of slaves in Florence, 105
Malocello, Lanzarotto, 133
Mamluks, 9, 14, 77–78. *See also* Military
Mancipia, 51
Manioc, agriculture of, 181
Manor, 51, 54–55. *See also* Villa
Manse, 51, 55–56
Manse lidile, 55
Manses ingénuiles, 55
Manses serviles, 55
Manuel I (king of Portugal), 157
Manumission, 14; in Rome, 28, 29–31, 35; in Germanic states, 50; in Islamic world, 75; in Italy, 101–2; in Portugal, 159–61; in Seville, 163; in kingdom of Valencia, 167; in Canary Islands, 168–69; and the *peculium*, 169; of blacks in English colonies, 183; in colonial Latin America, 208–9
Maqqari brothers, 82–83
March, Ausias, 112
Marchione, Bartolomeo, 156
Marius the consul, 20
Marriage: of slaves in Byzantine Empire, 38; between slaves and free in Merovingian France, 48; between slaves and free in Spain, 48; between slaves and *coloni*, 52; of *servi* in Carolingian period, 53; and serfdom, 57; of slaves in Islamic world, 73–74; and freedom for women slaves in Italy, 102; between Europeans and Africans, 143–44; in Seville, 162; between Guanches and Europeans, 169; of slaves in Spanish colonies, 206–7
Marseilles, 60
Martel, Charles, 69
Marxism, scholars of: on slavery, 9
Mary (2d wife of James II of Aragon), 111
Mattoso, Katia: on slave trade to Brazil, 191
Mauny, Raymond: on African trade, 84
Mayer, H. E.: on Castle Safed, 92
Mayoral, 163
Medici, Cosimo de', 98
Medici, Ferdinand de', 97
Medina, 72
Mellafe, Rolando, 186, 209–10
Mendoza, Antonio de (viceroy of Mexico), 212
Mesopotamia, 3, 16, 68

Mestizos, 207, 215–16
Mexico, 197, 199, 201, 202. *See also* Spain; Sugar
Middle Passage, 196
Military, slaves in: in Rome, 26–27; in German states, 49; in Islamic world, 68, 77–78, 86–87; in Africa, 125; in Spanish conquests, 196; in New World, 216. *See also* Janissaries; Mamluks; Muhammad (king of Songhay)
Ministeriales (*also Chevaliers-serfs*), 53
Mita, system of labor, 179–80, 198
Mocambos. See Palenques
Moors. *See* Muslims
Mozarabes, 69
Muhammad, 67, 68, 71–72
Muhammad, Ali b., 76–77
Muhammad (king of Songhay), 125
Mulatos, 207
Musa, Mansa (ruler of Mali), 126
Muslims, 3, 8, 12, 37, 64, 69–70, 108, 109–10, 134, 154, 162, 164

Navigation, instruments of, 135
New World, 3, 4, 178, 184, 209, 215, 216. *See also* Americas; Brazil; Latin America, colonial; Mexico; Peru
Nieboer, H. J.: on slavery in agricultural societies, 9–10
Nolasco, St. Peter, 110
Nomads, 116–17
Norman Conquest, 58–59
Normans, 96, 97

Old Cairo (Fustat), 12
Olivier de Sardan, Jean-Pierre: on Islamic and pagan slavery practices, 126–27
Open system, of slavery, 14
Origo Iris: on Italian slavery, 98, 99, 100, 101, 105
Ovando, Nicolás de (Spanish governor in Caribbean), 196

Palenques, 213–15
Paleologus, Michael, 104
Palmares, 214–15
Palmer, Colin: on free persons in Mexico City, 209
Pardos (*also Zambos*), 207
"Party kingdoms" (*reinos de taifas*), 64–65, 78

Pasha, Judar, 125
Pater familias, 27
Patterson, Orlando: on slavery, 5, 6, 7, 10
"Pawning," 122
Pax Romana, 21
Peculium, 28, 48, 50
Pegolotti, Francesco di Balduccio: on varieties of sugar, 113
Pereira, Duarte Pacheco: on origin of Madeiran sugar, 150
Perestrello, Bartolomeo, 150
Peru, 197, 198, 201, 202
Pesagno, Manuel, 107–8, 133
Peter of Aragon, 109
Petronius: on Roman slave life, 31–33
Philip II (king of Spain and Philip I of Portugal), 181, 187, 191
Philip III (king of Spain and Philip II of Portugal), 182
Piezas de Indias, 192
Pike, Ruth: on ethnic diversity in Seville, 163
Pilgrimages: and the Islamic slave trade, 126
Pirates, 18, 190
Pizarro, Francisco, 208
Plato: on slavery, 17
Plutarch: on slavery, 22
Pompey, 19, 26
Pontiac's rebellion, 178
Portugal, 4, 8; trade of, 107–8, 136, 137, 139, 141, 142, 146–47, 155, 157–58, 160, 186–87; expansion of, 132–33, 135, 137–38, 139–40, 141, 144, 149–50, 181; and Christianity in the Kongo, 145, 146; uses of African slaves by, 148, 158–59, 171; treatment of African and Muslim slaves by, 159; rebellion against Spain by, 187. *See also* Brazil; Sugar
Portugal, Jorge de, 185
Portuguese Order of Christ, 138–39
Potosí, 202
Prescott, William H.: on Spanish conquests, 176
Príncipe Island, 144–45
Pringar, 210
Privateers, 200
Prostitution: of slaves in Rome, 24–25
Publius Licinius Nerva (governor of Sicily), 20
Pueri regales (*also pueri aulici*), 50–51

Quilombos. See Palenques

Ravensburger Handelsgesellschaft, 112, 152
Rawley, James: on Atlantic slave trade, 192
Rayises, 91-92
Razzias, 69
Recife, 191
Reinel, Pedro Gomez, 187
Rendeiros, 187
Repartimiento system, 179-80, 199, 201
Revolts, of slaves, 14, 19-20, 46, 156, 160, 163, 211-12
Rice, C. Duncan: on African slavery in English colonies, 183-84
Rio de Janeiro, 191
Rodney, Walter, 141, 147
Roman law, 3-4, 16, 88, 110-11, 208, 216
Rome, 3, 4, 6, 8, 11, 12, 13, 15; empire of, 9, 14, 45, 67; expansion of, 17-18; as slave society, 17-19; uses of slaves in, 19, 24-26; rural land use in, 21; conditions for slaves in, 22, 27-28; enslavement of children in, 23-24; technological progress in, 25; religion and slaves in, 28; decline of slavery in, 35-36
Russell-Wood, A. J. R.: on Portuguese justifications for slavery, 205

Sahel, the, 117
Sakaliba, 69
Salvius (also Tryphon), 20
San Bernardo, parish of, 162-63
San Ildefonso, parish of, 163
San Lorenzo de los Negros, 214
Sandoval, Alonso de: on conditions on slave ships, 190-91
Santa Hermandad, 212-13
Santafé, maestre, 112
Santafé, Nicolau de, 111, 112
Santarém, João de, 142
São Jorge da Mina, 143
São Paulo de Luanda, 189
São Tomé, 144-45, 187, 189
Sassanid Persian empire, 67-68
Saunders, A. C. de C. M.: on slaves brought to Lisbon, 157; on Portugal, 158
Scandinavia, 4, 58
Schwarz, Stuart B.: on black stereotypes, 205
Sebastian III (king of Portugal), 181
Seignorialism, 54
Seiler, Hieronymous, 186
Seljuk Turks, 90
Serfdom, 3, 43, 57-58, 59, 107

Servi, 51, 53
Servi casati, 51
Seville, 160-62, 166-67, 185-88
Shells: as currency, 146-47
Sherley, Sir Anthony, 188
Ships, 133-34; used by Portugal and Spain, 134-35, 156, 188-89; conditions for slaves on, 189-91
Sierra Leone, 140-41
Siete Partidas, 110-11
Sijilmasa, 81-82
"Silent trade," 86
Siurrana, Francisco, 111
Slave markets: in Byzantine Empire, 59-60; in Islamic world, 59-60; and Italian traders, 97; in Genoa, 103
Slave trade: routes of, in Middle Ages, 60-61; Verdun's role in, 61; Muslims in, 61-62; and Islamic world, 67; and Italy, 103-4; in Africa, 148; in Caribbean, 179
Slavs, 57
Smith, Adam: on slave labor, 23
Smallpox, 176-77
Sobrer, Guillem, 167
Songhay, 124
Spain, 4, 8, 93, 107-13, 155, 160-68; slavery in colonies of, 171, 179, 180, 185-86, 194-95, 203-4; expansion of, 175-76; assimilation of slaves in colonies of, 206. See also Mexico; Sugar
Spanish Indies, 8
Spartacus, 19, 20
St. Augustine, 34
St. Melania, 35
Stoicism, 35
Sudan, the: states of, 117-18, 119
Sugar: in New World, 12, 175-76, 196, 198-99; in Islamic world, 67, 79-81; in Crusader states, 88, 93-95; in Sicily, 95-97; three-roller mill for, 96; in European colonies, 106; in Valencia, 111-12; methods of growing and refining, 112-13; Portuguese agricultural expansion of, 136; on São Tomé, 145; in Madeira, 149; as currency, 152; in Atlantic islands, 152-53; in Brazil, 182, 199-200; in Caribbean islands, 197; in Peru, 198. See also Agriculture
Suqi-er-raqiq, 71

Tacitus, 70

Tai Tsung (emperor of China), 79
Taillage, 58
Tangomaos, 156
Tannenbaum, Frank: on Latin and North American slave systems, 205
Teive, Diogo de, 151
Teixeira, Tristão Vaz, 150
Timotheus, Aulus Kapreilius, 33
Torres, Antonio do, 174
Transatlantic slave trade: estimated numbers in, 193
Trans-Saharan trade: routes of, 81–82; commodities of, 84; black slaves in, 86–87; estimated number of slaves in, 87
Tristão, Nuño, 138
Turks: Janissaries of, 71; trade of, 78

Urban II (pope), 90–91

Valencia: uses of slaves in, 109; slavery in city of, 163–67; blacks in, 167–68. *See also* Sugar
Valiente, Juan, 196
Valladolid, Juan de, "the Negro count," 163
Vandals, 46
Varro: on Roman slavery, 21–22
Velasco, Luis de (viceroy of Mexico), 212
Vellosa, Gonzalo de, 196–97
Venetian census (of 1563), 106
Verdun. *See* Slave trade
Vergara, Pedro de, 168–69

Vicens Vives, Jaime: on Barcelona gold and slave trade, 108–9
Vich, Don Galceran de, 112
Vici, 52
Vikings, 53, 64
Vila Villar, Enriqueta: on transatlantic slave trade, 188, 189, 192, 194
Villa, 21, 36, 51. *See also* Manor
Visigoths, 45–46; kingdom of 47, 48, 49–50
Vivaldi brothers, 132–33, 134
Vogt, Joseph; on slavery in the New Testament, 34

Wallerstein, Immanuel: his term *world-economy* applied to Islam, 67
Weber, Max: on slave labor, 23
Welsers: sugar plantations of, 152
Wergeld, 47
West Africa, 3, 131, 132
Westermann, William L.: on the church and slavery, 35
William of Tyre, 93
Wolf, Eric: on decline of Indian population in Spanish colonies, 178
World-economy. See Wallerstein, Immanuel

Yanga, 213–14
Yanguicos: *palenque* of, 213

Zanj (*also* Zindj) revolt, 76–77
Zarco, João Gonçalves, 150

William D. Phillips, Jr., is professor of history at San Diego State University, where he has taught since 1970. He is the author of *Enrique IV and the Crisis of Fifteenth-Century Castile, 1425–1480*, published by the Medieval Academy of America, and has written articles on the social and economic history of medieval and early modern Spain. He is currently at work on a major study of the Castilian wool trade.